The Counselor and the LAW

A Guide to Legal and Ethical Practice

Anne Marie "Nancy" Wheeler, JD
and Burt Bertram, EdD

AMERICAN COUNSELING
ASSOCIATION

6101 Stevenson Avenue, Suite 600 | Alexandria, VA 22304 | www.counseling.org

Seventh Edition

The Counselor and the LAW

and the

A Guide to Legal and
Ethical Practice

10   9   8   7   6   5   4   3   2

American Counseling Association

6101 Stevenson Avenue, Suite 600 | Alexandria, VA 22304

Associate Publisher   Carolyn C. Baker

Digital and Print Development Editor   Nancy Driver

Production Manager   Bonny E. Gaston

Copy Editor   Kimberly W. Kinne

Cover and text design by Bonny E. Gaston.

Library of Congress Cataloging-in-Publication Data

Wheeler, Anne Marie, 1954– author.
    The counselor and the law : a guide to legal and ethical practice/Anne
Marie "Nancy" Wheeler, JD and Burt Bertram, EdD.—Seventh edition.
    pages cm
    Includes bibliographical references and index.
    ISBN 978-1-55620-350-3 (pbk.: alk. paper)
    1. Counseling—Law and legislation—United States.   2. Counselors—
Legal status, laws, etc.—United States.   3. Counselors—Malpractice—
United States.   I. Bertram, Burt, author.   II. Title.
    KF2910.P75W44 2015
    344.7303'106—dc23   2014046508

To our readers—

Whether you are reading this book voluntarily (e.g., a practicing counselor thirsty for new knowledge) or involuntarily (e.g., a graduate student taking the required ethics and legal issues course), may you incorporate some new ideas into your professional practices that will benefit both you and the many clients you will serve.

 Contents

 Preface

As we send this 7th edition to press, the world of the professional counselor continues to evolve. However, the imperative to serve our clients' best interests never changes even though the complexities of modern life continue to create new legal and ethical dilemmas. Underscoring this point, the 2014 *ACA Code of Ethics* (American Counseling Association, 2014a) added an entire new section (Section H) specifically devoted to technology. The widespread use of technology by practicing counselors continues to create new opportunities and new challenges. In this edition of *The Counselor and the Law*, we have updated every chapter to reflect changes brought by the 2014 *ACA Code of Ethics*, recent court cases, and new legislation. We remain committed to identifying and thoughtfully addressing the timeless legal and ethical challenges associated with the practice of counseling, as well as peeking behind the curtain to anticipate future legal and ethical implications of such changes. To that end, we anticipate that by the time we are ready to begin work on the 8th edition, it is quite likely we will need to address new legal and ethical issues arising from the implementation of the Patient Protection and Affordable Care Act (2012) or other sweeping health care policies. Remaining current requires mindful awareness of the evolution of legal and ethical practices. We are honored to assist our readers in meeting this worthy professional standard.

This book has an interesting collaborative heritage. Originally written by attorneys Thomas Burgum and Scott Anderson and published in 1975, *The Counselor and the Law* reflected the counseling profession before state licensure—and before the proliferation of state and federal laws that have shaped the conduct of the practice of counseling. Since the first publication there have been six updates. In 1985, attorneys Bruce Hopkins and Barbara S. Anderson collaborated to update the original manuscript; then in 1990, Hopkins and Anderson released the 3rd edition; and in 1996, Barbara Anderson (without Hopkins) completed the 4th edition. In 2007 we were asked to take over the authorship and charged with the responsibility of completing a major update of the book.

The 5th and 6th editions—published in 2008 and 2012, respectively—marked the first time that the authorship reflected a collaborative perspective of an attorney and a practicing counselor. We believe that our perspectives provided a unique understanding of the law as it relates to the day-to-day practice of counseling. As you read this book, you are likely to hear two distinct voices and perspectives. Nancy Wheeler will offer the lawyer's perspective: She will tell you about the law and how it affects counseling practice. Burt Bertram's voice will reflect an insider's perspective: He will talk about the gray areas of practice that don't always fit neatly in a black-and-white world. Together we offer advice and suggestions designed to help practicing counselors and students understand and navigate the complexities of real-world practice.

In this, the 7th edition of *The Counselor and the Law*, we continue our commitment to connect the realities of the practice of counseling with state and federal laws and with the *ACA Code of Ethics*. It is our hope that this book will serve to provide real answers to practicing counselors who are challenged daily to act in the best interests of their clients and at the same time to be mindful of the legal and ethical duties and responsibilities that govern the profession of counseling. We also hope this book will be a window of understanding for students as they attempt to imagine and prepare for professional practice. Of course, we did not, nor could we, address every situation. Laws vary from state to state, and the specifics of any particular situation can influence how state or federal laws or the *ACA Code of Ethics* will apply. In addition, this book is not intended as a substitute for the considered opinion and advice of your personal lawyer concerning the particular circumstances of a case in the context of local laws and customs.

We are grateful to all the past authors for providing a solid foundation upon which we have built our collaborative effort. We thank our colleagues in the ACA Ethics and Professional Standards Department for their helpful collaboration. Finally, we want to express our heartfelt appreciation to Carolyn Baker, associate publisher.

—Anne Marie "Nancy" Wheeler and Burt Bertram

 About the Authors

Anne Marie "Nancy" Wheeler, JD, is an attorney licensed in Maryland and the District of Columbia; she has extensive experience with counselors and the broader field of mental health. For over 25 years, she has managed the American Counseling Association Sponsored Insurance Program's Risk Management Helpline. On a daily basis, she helps practicing counselors think through and understand challenging legal and ethical issues. For more than 30 years, she has worked with psychiatrists, facilities, and physician associations. This background gives her a unique window of understanding about the multifaceted issues that often confront practicing counselors. She is also an affiliate faculty member of the Graduate Pastoral Counseling Program of Loyola University Maryland, which is accredited by the Council for Accreditation of Counseling and Related Educational Programs (CACREP). Since the early 1990s, she and coauthor Bertram have jointly developed and copresented more than 150 seminars and workshops nationwide on legal and ethical issues. They have also produced several tapes, CDs, and podcasts on risk management strategies and legal and ethical issues.

Burt Bertram, EdD, is a Florida licensed mental health counselor and licensed marriage and family therapist. He has been in private practice in the Orlando area for more than 35 years. He practices from an interpersonal perspective; his professional counseling is primarily focused on the resolution of sensitive and complex relationship issues in every aspect of life—personal, workplace, and community. In addition to his private practice, Dr. Bertram provides personal development, coaching, and counseling to practicing physicians associated with the Florida Hospital System in Orlando, Florida. He is also an adjunct faculty member in the CACREP-accredited Graduate Studies in Counseling Program at Rollins College in Winter Park, Florida, where he teaches ethics as well as practicum; internship; and family, couples, and group counseling. Since the early 1990s, he and coauthor Wheeler have together developed and copresented more than 150 seminars and workshops on legal and ethical issues across the country. They have also produced several tapes, CDs, and podcasts on risk management strategies and legal and ethical issues.

Chapter 1

The Counseling Profession

The practice of counseling and the profession of counseling have evolved into maturity. In this chapter we provide an introduction to some of the legal responsibilities and accountabilities that have come with the maturing of the profession. Most notably we focus on the influence of state counselor licensing laws that have dramatically affected the activities of both licensed and unlicensed professional counselors.

Our Perspective

We understand that, for many practicing mental health professionals and most graduate students, the legal system is a foreign and sometimes frightening place. It is filled with adversarial relationships and governed by rules that are unfamiliar and unfriendly. We want to begin with a word of encouragement. No one knows how often counselors actually engage in unprofessional, unethical, or illegal practice-related behaviors. According to U.S. government data (U.S. Department of Labor, Bureau of Labor Statistics, 2014), nearly 1.5 million counselors (a number that includes licensed and unlicensed educational, vocational, school, rehabilitation, mental health, substance abuse, and marriage and family counselors) were working in America in 2012. Data compiled by the American Counseling Association (ACA; 2014b) indicate that there are 140,000 licensed counselors. The relative infrequency of licensing board discipline, lawsuits, criminal arrest, or censure by ethics committees compared with the number of counselors suggests that formal accusations of questionable behaviors are rare. In our experience, even when there is an accusation against a mental health professional, the resolution often favors the professional.

We would be remiss, however, in not stating the obvious: Counselors and other mental health professionals sometimes do engage in behaviors that result in harm to the very people we are in practice to serve: our clients.

> Counselors who are mindful and respectful of ethics and the law can develop practices that are creative, thoughtful, passionate, and always in the best interests of the client.

Many of these harmful behaviors come down to the counselor's failure to know, understand, or abide by the various state and federal laws that govern the practice of counseling. In this book, we are not recommending a rule-bound defensive practice wherein practitioners are fearful and innovation and creativity are stifled. On the contrary, the core message of this book is simple: We believe that counselors who are mindful and respectful of ethics and the law can develop practices that are creative, thoughtful, passionate, and always in the best interest of the client.

For nearly 30 years, we have worked with or followed legal cases in which the behavior of a counselor has resulted in harm to a client, and we have concluded that offending practitioners seem to fall into one of three broad categories:

- *Intentional disregard*: A small percentage of offending practitioners are intentionally opportunistic, abusive, exploitive, and self-serving in their dealings with their clients. These individuals are not interested in knowing, understanding, or abiding by the law. The best interest of the client is not their primary concern. Such harmful practitioners are not likely to read this book unless it is required in a graduate course or perhaps as part of a licensing board disciplinary process. We can only hope that all such practitioners either withdraw from the profession or have a life-altering transformational experience that induces them to abandon their abusive, self-serving values and behaviors.
- *Careless disregard*: There are offending practitioners who operate along a continuum ranging from innocently unaware to lazy or careless. In their hearts, these practitioners may want to

do what is best for their clients. However, because they have not taken the time to study and understand the law and our evolving ethics, their interactions with their clients might easily cross legal and ethical boundaries that would have sounded an alarm to a more knowledgeable and mindful practitioner. For these practitioners, the harm done to a client is unintentional but real. Reading this book can be an important step toward becoming actively mindful (no longer innocently unaware, lazy, or careless) of the implications to clients of the laws and the ethics that govern our profession.

- *Wrong place, wrong time*: Some offending practitioners know and understand legal and ethical mandates and are actively committed to abiding by them, yet they still become involved in situations in which a client is harmed (or alleges harm). As mental health professionals, we sometimes tell our clients that bad things can happen to good people. The same is true for good counselors. Sometimes bad things happen to good counselors—harmful things that simply could not have been foreseen or prevented. It is our hope that this book can help fortify the vast majority of practicing counselors so that if, in the unlikely event you are in the wrong place at the wrong time, you will have a depth of knowledge and understanding about the law that will empower you to get help for your client and for yourself before things spin out of control.

It is our hope that this book will serve as a guide to practitioners who are committed to the development of counseling practices that are ethical, legal, and always in the best interest of the client.

The title of this book, *The Counselor and the Law: A Guide to Legal and Ethical Practice*, seems straightforward, but actually the definitions of *counselor* and *law* can be fraught with confusion. Before we move into the specifics, we define these essential terms so that we all know who and what we are talking about.

The Counselor

It seems obvious: Counselors provide counseling. And although that's true, it's not that simple. The label *counselor* in our culture is so generic that it almost defies an objective definition in terms of identifying a specific professional endeavor. There are insurance counselors, camp counselors, funeral counselors, and numerous other roles that are created simply by placing a descriptive noun in front of the word *counselor*. As used in this book, the term *counselor* denotes a practitioner, educated and trained at the graduate level, who is a member of the counseling profession.

History and Highlights of the Profession

What is the profession of counseling? Counseling as a profession, separate and distinct from its sibling and first-cousin professions, is relatively new. The genealogy of counseling is well documented. Gladding (2013), Kottler (2011), Neukrug (2012), and others have ably documented the story of how counseling as a profession has struggled during the past six decades to emerge separate and distinct from psychiatry, psychology, social work, philosophy, education, and career guidance. Today the counseling field has developed all the characteristics necessary to qualify as a full and mature profession. More than 60 years ago, the American Personnel and Guidance Association (the original name of ACA) was established. During the past 60+ years, ACA has provided the leadership and the energy to create the profession of counseling. It has made notable accomplishments in the following areas:

- *ethics*—creating the *ACA Code of Ethics* (most recently revised in 2014), a process for obtaining opinions on ethical issues and a process for filing a complaint against a professional member alleging ethical misconduct;
- *interest divisions*—creating and supporting specialized interest areas (divisions) within ACA in which professional members can affiliate, learn, and share ideas with others of similar professional interest;
- *professional development*—convening an annual national professional development conference as well as a host of other regional and state professional development meetings, conferences, publications, and activities;
- *training standards*—sponsoring efforts that resulted in the establishment of the Council for Accreditation of Counseling and Related Educational Programs (CACREP), the organization that defines the standards for training of graduate-level counselors and monitors the implementation of these standards;
- *national certification*—initially sponsoring and advocating the National Board of Certified Counselors (NBCC), the organization that has established a nationally recognized certification credential that attests to a baseline of general counselor knowl-

edge as well as to specialty credentials in school counseling, mental health counseling, and addictions counseling; and

- *state licensing*—working together with other professional associations and groups to lead the state-by-state struggle to license professional counselors.

Professional Counselors

The efforts and activities outlined in the preceding section form the basis of what we now know as the professional counselor. State licensing is required for independent private practice. Professional counselor positions in agencies, schools, government, and nonprofit organizations may or may not require state licensure. Some professional counselors, such as school counselors or addictions counselors, may require specialty certification. Most of the information in this book is relevant to all professional counselors (licensed, certified, and unlicensed), including mental health, school, child, couple and family, substance abuse, and rehabilitation counselors; to graduate students in master's- and doctoral-level counseling and related programs; and to the broader field of counseling-related professionals, including counseling psychologists, psychologists, social workers, pastoral counselors, career counselors, and psychiatrists. All of these professionals share a common activity: They all engage in the practice of counseling.

Licensed Professional Counselors

In 1976, Virginia became the first state to license and regulate professional counselors. Thirty-four years later, in 2010, California became the last state to enact state licensing of professional counselors. Today all 50 states plus the District of Columbia and Puerto Rico have licensed the title or practice activities (or both) of professional counselors.

The Law

The purpose of this book is to empower professional counselors (licensed and unlicensed) to understand and thereby respond in a thoughtful and ethical manner to the laws that affect the day-in and day-out practice of counseling. To do this, two things are necessary. First, we want to be clear about what we mean by law; second, we want to provide some detail regarding how state laws and statutes have influenced the legal definition of the practice of professional counseling, regardless of the practice setting.

The word *law*, like the word *counselor*, is also confusing, especially to nonlawyers (and who could be less lawyerlike than many counselors?). For the purposes of this book, we define *law* as a set of rules, enacted by a legislative body, that governs a particular activity within society. Laws are everywhere, governing nearly everything. Laws, also called *statutes*, derive from elected officials who are members of federal or state (lawmaking) bodies. Municipal (city, town, and county) councils and commissions also promulgate ordinances.

As professional counselors and as citizens or residents of the United States, we are all affected by laws that address every aspect of our lives, from whom we can marry, to how we drive our cars, to the proper treatment of children, to the taxes we pay. It's probably safe to say that no one really knows all the laws that affect our every waking moment. However, for counselors, some laws are critical to our functioning. The following list identifies some of those that directly affect the practice of counseling:

- federal laws that have a direct bearing on counselors and the practice of counseling, such as the Health Insurance Portability and Accountability Act of 1996 (HIPAA), the Health Information Technology for Economic and Clinical Health (HITECH) Act, the Americans With Disabilities Act of 1990 (ADA), and the Family Educational Rights and Privacy Act of 1974 (FERPA, or the Buckley Amendment);
- state laws and statutes, such as counselor licensure laws, the rules developed by state licensing boards to implement the law and regulate the day-to-day practice activities of licensed and nonlicensed professional counselors, and state abuse reporting laws (child and vulnerable adult); and
- local laws, including municipal laws that affect when and where counseling can occur, such as zoning and occupational licensing laws.

In addition, there is a body of law that derives from the common law that began in England and has developed over hundreds of years. Common law emphasizes precedent set by cases in which judges make decisions. Common law is distinct from statutory law, which is created by a legislature, not a judge (see Chapter 3 for a complete discussion). The *Tarasoff* case (*Tarasoff v. Regents of the University of California*, 1976, discussed in Chapter 6) is an example of how common law changed clinical counseling and mental health practices across the country to permit or require the therapist to breach confidentiality when a client poses a serious risk of harm to a third party.

Licensing Standards for Counselors

In many ways, for all the laudable efforts by academics and members of the various professional associations to define and legitimize the practice of counseling, nothing has moved the profession of counseling along faster than the emergence of state licensure of professional counselors. To be fair, it's extremely doubtful that any state would have passed licensing statutes were it not for the relentless efforts of leaders within the professional associations. Yet, only legislative bodies can create laws, and many leaders in the field of counseling would argue that we needed licensing laws to finish the task of defining ourselves and differentiating the work we do from similar services provided by other counseling-related professions.

The practice of counseling has been defined and redefined for decades. However, as the licensing of professional counselors has spread across the country, the struggle to define the practice of counseling has moved from an academic discussion to a legislative and statutory reality. State legislatures have enacted "practice act" counselor licensing statutes that include specific definitions of the practice of counseling. State statutory definitions have become the driving force determining, from a legal perspective, what professional counseling is and what professional counselors can do (scope of practice) as defined by the law.

As important as state licensing of counseling has been to the legitimizing of professional counseling, it came with a heavy price. There was never a national model of licensing. Like most state statutes, counselor licensing was a product of vigorous negotiation among many perspectives and interest groups within each state. Therefore, every state created a unique professional counselor licensing law, resulting in significant variability across the country. The state-by-state differences are particularly relevant in four important areas: (a) license title; (b) definition of counseling, including the scope of practice (activities professional counselors are permitted to undertake); (c) required graduate education requirements; and (d) postdegree supervision prior to independent licensure. Over time, the differences between two of these categories (graduate education requirements and postdegree supervision) seem to be coalescing toward some consensus. Licensure title and definition/scope of practice remain diverse. The discussion below provides an overview of some of these differences.

License Title

State statutes establish licensure titles for professional counselors. Currently six titles are used to designate independent practice:

- Licensed Professional Counselor (LPC),
- Licensed Mental Health Counselor (LMHC),
- Licensed Clinical Professional Counselor (LCPC),
- Licensed Professional Clinical Counselor of Mental Health (LPCC),
- Licensed Clinical Mental Health Counselor (LCMHC), and
- Licensed Mental Health Practitioner (LMHP).

The most frequently used license title is LPC, which is used in more than half of the states; LMHC and LCPC are each used by seven states (ACA, 2014b). To make matters even more complicated, states have established licensure tiers to reflect the degree of independence allowed by the practitioner.

- Nine states and the District of Columbia have one tier of licensure.
- Thirty-four states and Puerto Rico have two tiers of licensure.
- Six states have three tiers of licensure.
- One state, Maine, has four tiers of licensure. (ACA, 2014b)

Differences in license title combined with title differences in one-, two-, three-, and four-tiered licensing has created further confusion. The same license title in one state can mean something else in another state. This situation leads to misunderstanding among the public and is counterproductive to the establishment of a clear identity for licensed counselors, particularly for the title that designates independent practice. For example, Illinois has a two-tiered license structure. Licensed Clinical Professional Counselor (LCPC) is the title designation for independent practice, whereas the Licensed Professional Counselor (LPC) title in Illinois requires practitioners to be supervised. Consider the five states that surround Illinois: Iowa, Missouri, Kentucky, Indiana, and Wisconsin. Licensed Professional Counselor is the title for independent practice in two of the surrounding states, Missouri and Wisconsin. In Indiana and Iowa, the title Licensed Mental Health Counselor (LMHC) designates independent practice. In the fifth state, Kentucky, Licensed Professional Clinical Counselor (LPCC) is required for independent practice.

Definition of Counseling and Scope of Practice

The definition of professional counseling and the scope of practice descriptions are essential elements associated with every licensure law. Many state counselor licensing laws embed the scope of practice within the definition of counseling, whereas other states include a separate scope of practice definition or have enumerated specific practice limitations in other sections of the licensing statute. Presented below are five examples of the definition of counseling and the scope of practice from five states (Virginia, Florida, Oregon, California, and New York). Virginia, Florida, and Oregon are examples in which the scope of practice is embedded within the definition of counseling. Conversely, California has embedded the definition of counseling within the scope of practice, and New York has placed the definition of counseling in one section and the scope of practice in another. Carefully review each definition of counseling and scope of practice description. Note the similarities among the five examples as well as the differences. What is legal in one state but not acceptable in another? How do these examples compare with the definition of counseling and scope of practice in the state in which you practice or intend to practice?

Virginia—LPC

In 1976, Virginia became the first state to enact a law governing the licensure and activities of professional counselors. The scope of practice is embedded in the definition of counseling:

> "Counseling" means the application of principles, standards, and methods of the counseling profession in (i) conducting assessments and diagnoses for the purpose of establishing treatment goals and objectives and (ii) planning, implementing, and evaluating treatment plans using treatment interventions to facilitate human development and to identify and remediate mental, emotional, or behavioral disorders and associated distresses that interfere with mental health.

> "Practice of counseling" means rendering or offering to render to individuals, groups, organizations, or the general public any service involving the application of principles, standards, and methods of the counseling profession, which shall include appraisal, counseling, and referral activities. (Va. Code Ann. § 54.1–3500, 2013)

Florida—LMHC

Florida passed its first counselor licensure law in 1981. The Florida Board of Clinical Social Work, Mental Health Counseling, and Marriage & Family Therapy licenses and regulates clinical social workers, mental health counselors, and marriage and family therapists. The statute includes a detailed definition of the practice of mental health counseling that incorporates a description of the scope of practice.

> The "practice of mental health counseling" is defined as the use of scientific and applied behavioral science theories, methods, and techniques for the purpose of describing, preventing, and treating undesired behavior and enhancing mental health and human development and is based on the person-in-situation perspectives derived from research and theory in personality, family, group, and organizational dynamics and development, career planning, cultural diversity, human growth and development, human sexuality, normal and abnormal behavior, psychopathology, psychotherapy, and rehabilitation. The practice of mental health counseling includes methods of a psychological nature used to evaluate, assess, diagnose, and treat emotional and mental dysfunctions or disorders (whether cognitive, affective, or behavioral), behavioral disorders, interpersonal relationships, sexual dysfunction, alcoholism, and substance abuse. The practice of mental health counseling includes, but is not limited to, psychotherapy, hypnotherapy, and sex therapy. The practice of mental health counseling also includes counseling, behavior modification, consultation, client-centered advocacy, crisis intervention, and the provision of needed information and education to clients, when using methods of a psychological nature to evaluate, assess, diagnose, treat, and prevent emotional and mental disorders and dysfunctions (whether cognitive, affective, or behavioral), behavioral disorders, sexual dysfunction, alcoholism, or substance abuse. The practice of mental health counseling may also include clinical research into more effective psychotherapeutic modalities for the treatment and prevention of such conditions. (Fla. Stat. § 491.003(9), 2013)

Oregon—LPC

Enacted in 1989, the Oregon Board of Licensed Professional Counselors and Therapists is responsible for the licensing and regulation of professional counseling. The definition of counseling includes a description of the scope of services LPCs in Oregon may provide. Note the specific language that authorizes assessment, diagnosis, or treatment.

> 7(a) "Professional counseling" means the assessment, diagnosis or treatment of mental, emotional or behavioral disorders involving the application of mental health counseling or other psychotherapeutic principles and methods in the delivery of services to individuals, couples, children, families, groups or organizations.
>
> (b) "Professional counseling" may include, but is not limited to:
>
> (A) Application of intervention methods based on cognitive, affective, behavioral, systemic or human development principles;

(B) Provision of counseling services to address personal growth or wellness;

(C) Definition of goals and the planning of action reflecting interests, abilities, aptitudes or needs as they relate to problems, disabilities or concerns in personal, social, educational, rehabilitation or career adjustments;

(D) Research activities, including reporting, designing or conducting research in counseling with human subjects;

(E) Referral activities, including the referral to other specialists when indicated to provide ethical treatment;

(F) Consulting activities that apply counseling procedures and inter-personal skills to provide assistance in solving problems relating to an individual, group or organization; and

(G) Record keeping activities, including documentation of counseling treatment, therapeutic services or clinical supervision. (Or. Rev. Stat. § 675.715(7), 2013)

California–LPCC

In 2009, California was the last state to enact a statute licensing and regulating professional counselors. The California Board of Behavioral Sciences regulates professional clinical counselors, marriage and family therapists, educational psychologists, and clinical social workers. The California statute combines the definition of counseling and the scope of practice description under the heading Scope of Practice.

(a) (1) "Professional clinical counseling" means the application of counseling interventions and psychotherapeutic techniques to identify and remediate cognitive, mental, and emotional issues, including personal growth, adjust-ment to disability, crisis intervention, and psychosocial and environmental problems, and the use, application, and integration of the coursework and training required by Sections 4999.32 and 4999.33. "Professional clinical counseling" includes conducting assessments for the purpose of establishing counseling goals and objectives to empower individuals to deal adequately with life situations, reduce stress, experience growth, change behavior, and make well-informed, rational decisions.

(2) "Professional clinical counseling" is focused exclusively on the applica-tion of counseling interventions and psychotherapeutic techniques for the purposes of improving mental health, and is not intended to capture other, nonclinical forms of counseling for the purposes of licensure. For purposes of this paragraph, "nonclinical" means nonmental health.

(3) "Professional clinical counseling" does not include the assessment or treatment of couples or families unless the professional clinical counselor has completed all of the following training and education:

[The statute delineates graduate coursework, supervised experience and continuing education requirements necessary for a professional clinical counselor to provide services to couples and families.] (Cal. Bus. & Prof. Code § 4999.20, 2014)

New York—LMHC

New York's first counselor licensure law was enacted in 2002. The regulatory body is the State Board for Mental Health Practitioners, which licenses and regulates Creative Arts Therapists, Marriage & Family Therapists, Mental Health Counselors, and Psychoanalysts. The New York statute is an example of a scope of practice limitation imposed separately from the definition of counseling. In New York, LMHCs are required to obtain a medical evaluation by a physician when a patient/client presents with a serious mental illness.

Definition of Mental Health Counseling

The practice of the profession of mental health counseling is defined as follows:

a. the evaluation, assessment, amelioration, treatment, modification, or adjustment to a disability, problem, or disorder of behavior, character, development, emotion, personality or relationships by the use of verbal or behavioral methods with individuals, couples, families or groups in private practice, group, or organized settings; and

b. the use of assessment instruments and mental health counseling and psychotherapy to identify, evaluate and treat dysfunctions and disorders for purposes of providing appropriate mental health counseling services. (N.Y. Educ. Law §8402, 2013)

Boundaries of Professional Competency

It shall be deemed practicing outside the boundaries of his or her professional competence for a person licensed pursuant to this article, in the case of treatment of any serious mental illness, to provide any mental health service for such illness on a continuous and sustained basis without a medical evaluation of the illness by, and consultation with, a physician regarding such illness. Such medical evaluation and consultation shall be to determine and advise whether any medical care is indicated for such illness. For purposes of this section, "serious mental illness" means schizophrenia, schizoaffective disorder, bipolar disorder, major depressive disorder, panic disorder, obsessive-compulsive disorder, attention-deficit hyperactivity disorder and autism ... (N.Y. Educ. Law §8407, 2013)

Graduate Education

Over the past 10–15 years, there has been a growing consensus regarding the required coursework and overall number of graduate semester hours necessary for the awarding of a master's degree in clinical mental health counseling. By raising accreditation standards for all clinical counseling programs from a 48- to 60-semester hour requirement, CACREP has influenced counselor education programs across the nation. An increasing number of graduate counselor education programs are moving to adopt these national standards.

Postdegree/Prelicense Supervised Experience

Supervised postdegree/prelicense experience requirements are completely controlled by state statutes and regulations promulgated by the counseling licensing board. Accreditation entities or professional associations do not seem to have much influence on the postdegree/ prelicense experience requirements. Table 1 provides an overview sample of eight states concerning requirements for postdegree/prelicense supervised experience. Among the eight states, there is a range of 2–4 years of required post-master's experience, 1,200–3,600 hours of which must be direct client contact. (Some master's practicum/ internship experience may count). All the examples have supervision requirements; however, the range and specificity of the requirement varies state by state. In most states, 100–120 hours is the typical requirement. The differences occur around the modality of the supervision. In Michigan, supervision must occur in the physical presence of the supervisor (the supervisor has to be in the room), whereas in Colorado, 70 hours of the required 100 hours must be face to face. In comparison, Texas permits live Internet webcam supervision between the supervisor and supervisee. In recent years, states have moved to create standards for clinical supervisors. Most states now have an approved course of training for licensed counselors who want to provide prelicense supervision. All states require license applicants to pass a recognized exam, whereas some states within our sample (e.g., Colorado, Maryland, and Texas) require applicants to pass a separate state jurisprudence exam.

License title, definition of counseling/scope of practice, education requirements, and prelicense supervised experience capture only some of the important differences among the counseling licensing laws. Other areas to remain mindful of include confidentiality and privileged communication responsibilities, record keeping, duties to report unprofessional conduct to the licensing board, and prescriptive (*must* or *shall*) versus permissive (*may* or *can*) words that define the extent of the counselor's *legal duty* to take certain action. An example of prescriptive versus permissive language relates to the *ethical duty* to take action to warn or protect a potential victim when a client has made a credible threat. In most states the language in the law is prescriptive (the counselor shall or must take action);

Table 1

Sampling of Required Postdegree/Prelicense Supervised Experience

State and Statute[a]	Post-Master's Supervised Experience[b]	Requirement Supervision	Requirement Supervisor	Exam
Arizona (LPC) Ariz. Rev. Stat. § 32-3301 (2013); Ariz. Admin. Code §§ R4-6-501 to 505 (2004)	• 2 years/3,200 hours of full-time work; 1,600 hours of which is direct client contact	100 hours—must receive minimum of 10 hours of direct observation or review of audio/videotape	As defined by rule, 12 hours of board approved training plus 6 hours of training for each license renewal	NCE, NCMHCE, or CRCE
Colorado (LPC) Mental Health Practice Act (2011)	• 2 years experience • 2,000 hours of direct client contact	100 hours—70 hours must be face-to-face individual supervision Audio and video electronic supervision permitted—requires initial 2-hour face-to-face meeting between supervisor and supervisee followed by direct face-to-face meeting every 6 months thereafter	Licensed as a professional counselor, marriage and family therapist, clinical social worker, psychologist, medical doctor, or doctor of osteopathy who completed a residency in psychiatry, all licensed in jurisdiction at time of supervision OR person who at time of supervision possesses the same education, experience, and training as that necessary to adequately supervise an LPC	NCE and Colorado Jurisprudence Exam
Georgia (LPC) Professional Counselors, Social Workers, and Marriage and Family Therapists Licensing Law (2010)	• 4 years experience (1 year can count from practicum/ internship) • 2,400 hours of direct client contact	120 hours supervision	LPC and 3 years of experience Expansion of required credentials in process	NCE
Maryland (LCPC) Maryland Professional Counselors and Therapists Act (2014)	• 2 years/2,000 hours post-master's • 1,500 hours face-to-face	100 hours face-to-face supervision	Board approved completion of board approved training	NCE and Maryland Professional Counselors and Therapists Law Exam

(Continued)

Table 1 (*Continued*)
Sampling of Required Postdegree/Prelicense Supervised Experience

| State and Statute[a] | Post-Master's Supervised Experience[b] | Requirement | | |
		Supervision	Supervisor	Exam
Michigan (LPC) Mich. Pub. Acts 421 (1988)	• 2 years experience • 3,000 hours of direct client contact	100 hours of supervision in the immediate physical presence of the supervisor	LPC with approved training in supervision	NCE or CRCE
Pennsylvania (LPC) 49 Pa. Code §§ 49.11–49.18 (2002)	• 3 years experience • 3,600 hours—direct client contact • 3,000 hours experience	Two hours of supervision for every 40 client contact hours	LPC and 5 years experience (1,800 hours) Remainder can be provided by non-LPC	Any one of the following: NCE, CRCE, ATCB, CBMT, PEPK, AAODA, EMAC
Texas (LPC) Licensed Professional Counselor Act (1999)	• 1,500 hours direct client contact	4 hours per month of face-to-face or live Internet webcam/no more than 50% can be group supervision	Board approved LPC (24 months experience)	NCE and Texas Jurisprudence Exam
Washington (LMHC) Wash. Rev. Code § 18.225 (2005)	• 3 years/3,000 hours experience • 1,200 hours of direct client contact	100 hours (minimum)	Board approved supervisor	NCE or NCMHCE

Note. NCE = National Counselor Exam; NCMHCE = National Clinical Mental Health Counseling Examination; CRCE = Certified Rehabilitation Counselor Examination; ATCB = Art Therapy Credentialing Board; CBMT = Certified Board for Music Therapists; PEPK = Practice Examination of Psychological Knowledge; AAODA = Advanced Alcohol and Other Drug Abuse Counselor (examination); EMAC = Examination for Master Addictions Counselors; LPC = Licensed Professional Counselor; LCPC = Licensed Clinical Professional Counselor; LMHC = Licensed Mental Health Counselor.
[a]Independent practice license. [b]Overall experience and direct client contact.

in Texas the language is permissive (the counselor may take action). The Texas counselor licensing law code of ethics states:

> (n) A licensee may take reasonable action to inform medical or law enforcement personnel if the licensee determines that there is a probability of imminent physical injury by the client to the client or others or there is a probability of immediate mental or emotional injury to the client. (22 Tex. Admin. Code § 681.41(o), 2013)

For a more complete discussion of a counselor's ethical and legal duty to take action when a client threatens harm to another person, see Chapter 6.

National consensus, supported by law, regarding the activities associated with professional counseling remains elusive. Therefore, when we talk about the counselor and the law, it is critical for you to keep in mind that definitions vary state by state. We make general statements and give examples, but we always caution you to consult the most recent counselor licensing law and supporting rules in your state.

Efforts Toward National Standards and Definitions

Currently there are no legally recognized or accepted national licensing standards for counselors and counseling. There are, however, national practitioner certifications, national accreditation standards for graduate programs in counselor education, and momentum toward the creation of a process that will facilitate licensure portability (the ability, once licensed by one state, to have that license recognized in another state).

Nationally Recognized Accreditation

The process of establishing national standards for the accreditation of counselor education programs has been greatly enhanced by CACREP. The mission of CACREP is to promote the professional competence of counseling and related practitioners through (a) the development of preparation standards, (b) the encouragement of excellence in program development, and (c) the accreditation of professional preparation programs (CACREP, 2014b). Currently there are 607 accredited graduate counselor education programs (master's or doctoral level) at 262 institutions encompassing seven different programs of study (C. Bobby, personal communication,

May 6, 2014). In addition, the Council for Rehabilitation Education (CORE) currently accredits 89 graduate programs in rehabilitation counseling in 89 different universities (F. Lane, personal communication, March 15, 2014). Accreditation of graduate counselor education programs has been a significant step toward establishing recognized national standards of scholarship, coursework, practicum, and internship experience for the training of master's- and doctoral-level counselors. Creation of national standards for counselor education preparation is a prerequisite for counselor licensing portability. The program accreditation efforts of CACREP and CORE are helping the counseling profession build a foundation on which licensure portability can be achieved (see the following sections). Many counselor education programs are not yet accredited by CORE or CACREP; others are somewhere in the accreditation process.

In another step toward building a unified identity within the field of counseling, CORE and CACREP recently announced a historic agreement. CORE has agreed to become a corporate affiliate of CACREP. Among other aspects of the agreement, counseling programs can now apply under CACREP's newly developed and adopted Clinical Rehabilitation Program standards and undergo a review process conducted jointly by CACREP and CORE (CACREP, 2014a).

Nationally Recognized Counselor Certification

The NBCC developed the National Counselor Exam (NCE) for the following purpose:

> [to] assess knowledge, skills, and abilities viewed as important for providing effective counseling services. The NCE is designed to be general in nature. It is intended to assess cognitive knowledge which should be known by all counselors regardless of their individual professional specialties. Satisfactory performance on the NCE is one of the criteria used by NBCC to identify professionals who may be eligible to become a National Certified Counselor. (NBCC, 2014)

Currently there are more than 55,796 NBCC- credentialed counselors (K. McCaskill, personal communication, May 6, 2014). NBCC also has developed three specialty credentials:

- National Certified School Counselor (NCSC),
- Nationally Certified Clinical Mental Health Counselor (NCCMHC), and
- Master Addictions Counselor (MAC).

National Consensus and License Portability

What is counselor license portability? Portability is best understood by posing two questions. If you completed your master's or doctoral degree in counselor education in state X, how important would it be to you to know that you had met all the academic requirements for licensure in any state in America? Of, if you were licensed in state Y and decided to move to state Z, how important would it be to you to know that the requirements for licensing in state Z were comparable to state Y so you could immediately be licensed? If your answer to these two questions was "very important," then license portability is imperative. To that end, in 2005, an organized and comprehensive effort was launched to address a variety of issues related to portability, including agreed upon national definitions and standards. A small group of leaders in the field of counseling representing the ACA and the American Association of State Counseling Boards decided it was time to create a process that could lead toward the realization of these agreed upon definitions and standards. This small group came to be known as the Oversight Committee.

> The Oversight Committee identified 30 major organizational stakeholders in the profession of counseling and issued invitations to participate in 20/20: A Vision for the Future of Counseling. These groups reflected the membership, accrediting, certifying, and honorary organizations within professional counseling. (Kaplan & Gladding, 2011, p. 369)

All of the 30 organizations accepted the invitation; each named a delegate to represent the organization. This initiative was active from 2006 to 2014. The delegates agreed upon a consensus decision-making model. "Consensus was defined as a minimum of 90% of the delegates giving their approval to a concept" (Kaplan & Gladding, 2011, p. 368).

The initiative yielded several major outcomes. All 30 organizations formally adopted the "Principles for Unifying and Strengthening the Profession," which consists of the following seven principles:

1. Sharing a common professional identity is critical for counselors.
2. Presenting ourselves as a unified profession has multiple benefits.
3. Working together to improve the public perception of counseling and to advocate for professional issues will strengthen the profession.
4. Creating a portability system for licensure will benefit counselors and strengthen the counseling profession.
5. Expanding and promoting our research base is essential to the efficacy of professional counselors and to the public perception of the profession.

6. Focusing on students and prospective students is necessary to ensure the ongoing health of the counseling profession.
7. Promoting client welfare and advocating for populations we serve is a primary focus of the counseling profession. (Kaplan & Gladding, 2011, p. 372)

In March 2010, the delegates met and approved a definition of counseling. Twenty-nine of 30 organizations approved this definition. The delegates made it clear that the definition should be viewed as a basic framework and that each participating organization could add a statement that further reflects each group's particular specialty or area of concern. The consensus definition of counseling is as follows:

> Counseling is a professional relationship that empowers diverse individuals, families, and groups to accomplish mental health, wellness, education, and career goals. (ACA, 2014c)

Once there was consensus on the definition of counseling, the delegates focused their attention on the issue of license portability. Embedded in portability are three critically important issues; agreement on these three issues would be a significant step along the path toward national definitions and standards. Those issues are as follows:

- licensure title,
- licensure scope of practice, and
- licensure education requirements.

The 20/20 initiative concluded work in early 2014, having reached consensus at the final meeting on licensure title and licensure scope of practice. The process is now in the hands of the 30 participating organizations to formerly endorse licensure title and licensure scope of practice. Consensus was not achieved on licensure education requirements.

Licensure Title

In reviewing input from all delegates, the licensure title work group "found that the delegates had generated 14 possible licensure titles … the most common licensure title in the United States, Licensed Professional Counselor, was the highest rated title by far." The work group recommended the LPC title. The title was then approved by 92% of the delegates in attendance. According to the facilitator of the 20/20 initiative (K. Kraus, personal communication, December

4, 2013), "The vote was 22 yes, 2 no, and 0 abstentions." The recommended title was submitted to all participating organizations; 28 of 29 (96%) voting organizations voted to endorse the title Licensed Professional Counselor. The only organization that declined to endorse the title was the American Mental Health Counselors Association (Kraus, 2014).

Licensure Scope of Practice

The scope of practice work group dealt with more complicated issues and therefore required a more sophisticated analysis of the data. Initially the work group reported identifying 154 discrete items for possible inclusion in the scope of practice. No clear list of highest rank items emerged, resulting in a decision to submit all the data to a content/frequency analysis. Six broad descriptive categories evolved from the discussion. The 20/20 delegates in attendance approved these descriptive categories. The vote was 27 yes (96%), 1 no (4%), and 0 abstentions (K. Kraus, personal communication, December 4, 2013). To facilitate the eventual adoption by states and other licensing jurisdictions, the delegates requested the assistance of an attorney to create the specific narrative.

> The independent practice of counseling encompasses the provision of professional counseling services to individuals, groups, families, couples and organizations through the application of accepted and established mental health counseling principles, methods, procedures and ethics.
>
> Counseling promotes mental health wellness, which includes the achievement of social, career, and emotional development across the lifespan, as well as preventing and treating mental disorders and providing crisis intervention.
>
> Counseling includes, but is not limited to, psychotherapy; diagnosis; evaluation; administration of assessments, tests and appraisals; referral; and the establishment of counseling plans for the treatment of individuals, couples, groups and families with emotional, mental, addiction, and physical disorders.
>
> Counseling encompasses consultation and program evaluation, program administration within and to schools and organizations, and training and supervision of interns, trainees, and pre-licensed professional counselors through accepted and established principles, methods, procedures, and ethics of counselor supervision.
>
> The practice of counseling does not include functions or practices that are not within the professional's training or education. (K. Kraus, personal communication, December 4, 2013)

This definition was submitted to all participating organizations; 27 of 28 (93%) voted to endorse the recommended scope of practice. The American Rehabilitation Counseling Association and the National Rehabilitation Counseling Association declined to endorse the scope of practice (Kraus, 2014).

We ask that you recall the five different definitions of counseling and scope of practice definitions presented earlier in this chapter. Please take a moment to determine for yourself, did the 20/20 delegates get it right? In your opinion, are the 20/20 definition of *counseling* and the scope of practice description compatible with the five state definitions presented earlier in this chapter? Moreover, is it possible that one day down the road, the 20/20 product might serve as a national model for states as amendments and changes are made to each state counselor licensing law?

Licensure Examination Requirements

Although the delegate organizations were not able to come to a consensus on licensure education requirements, the potential of realizing that goal may have increased as a result of an agreement between CORE and CACREP in which CORE has agreed to become a corporate affiliate of CACREP (CACREP, 2014a).

Consensus among the 30 participating groups on these three issues (licensure title, licensure scope of practice, and licensure education requirements) will not automatically result in portability, but it will provide a compelling outline that state counseling licensing boards can use as they encourage state legislatures to consider amending counseling laws to make states more portability friendly. Similar to the 34-year process that ultimately resulted in the licensing of counselors in all 50 states, the goal of portability will take time and will require the steadfast dedication of a generation of leaders within the counseling profession.

Summary

The good news is that we have come a long way in the past 60 years. We have fought the good fight and have legitimized and codified (by law) our professional activities. We are no longer just well-intentioned people who set out to be helpful. Embedded in the good news of our professional status is the fact that we are now legally held to defined duties as well as standards of practice. In the pages that follow, we address the laws and statutes that define the practice of counseling and discuss the relationship of these laws to the evolving ethics and standards of practice of our profession.

Chapter 2
The Counseling Relationship

Who is a client? What standard of care and legal duties do we owe to clients? What should be included in a well-crafted informed consent, and how do we handle the important legal and ethical considerations associated with fees? In this chapter, we address these questions as well as the ethical concerns and complications associated with termination of the counseling relationship and referral of clients. In our discussion, we refer to the standards defined in the 2014 *ACA Code of Ethics* (see Appendix A).

It's all about the relationship! For counseling practitioners, nothing is more important than the counseling relationship. Regardless of your preferred theory of counseling, the common denominator that cuts across all perspectives is the primacy of the counseling relationship. The same can be said when we think about the legal implications of the practice of counseling: The counseling relationship remains the central concept. We encourage you to combine a legal perspective of the counseling relationship with your existing clinical understanding. Together they form the foundation of competent professional practice. The legal perspective need not be a burden, nor should it invite you to practice defensively or to view the counseling relationship as having an adversarial element. In fact, we hope that you will see how knowledge, understanding, and adherence to the law will serve only to support and strengthen the counseling relationship.

Who Is a Client?

A person (or a couple or a family) becomes a client when the professional relationship is initiated. At that moment, counselors incur a "duty" to act in the best interests of the client. If counselors fail to meet the standards of practice as defined by applicable professional association codes of ethics and federal and state statutes including licensing laws, abuse reporting mandates, and requirements to prevent harm to self or others, they may incur both legal and ethical consequences. Counselors must carefully consider the conditions that must be met before legal and ethical duties are established. However, it is prudent, whenever you are in your professional role, to meet the standards whenever you are interacting with a person who may become a client.

Typically, it would not be reasonable for a court, licensure board, or ethics body to conclude that a counselor–client duty begins when a casual conversation takes place in a grocery story checkout lane. But it could! It is not so much the location or even the modality of the interaction that a counselor has with a person that defines whether a professional relationship has been established; rather, it is the substance of the interaction and the ground rules that the counselor communicates to the person that define the necessary conditions to establish a counseling relationship.

From the other person's perspective, it's likely that once the person begins interacting with a mental health professional (face to face or in some cases on the phone or electronically over the Internet), that person may assume that a professional relationship has been established. Thoughtful experts often advise practitioners to institute a screening or assessment session before establishing a treatment relationship, if possible. We agree. In a perfect world counselors should have the opportunity to determine, through a review of intake information and an initial interview, whether they have the requisite competence (education, training, experience, or supervision) and legal authority to properly render treatment and, therefore, incur a duty. However, in the real world, unless we clearly inform clients otherwise, they are likely to assume the counseling relationship has begun as soon as there is interaction.

After the initial contact with the person (or couple or family), you may determine that you do not have the competence or legal authority to provide treatment and therefore want to decline care. During the initial phone contact, you might decide you cannot provide treatment because of other variables (e.g., you lack adequate time in your schedule, the presenting problem is outside your scope of practice or expertise, the potential client cannot afford to pay for services and your pro bono schedule is full, or a conflict of interest exists so it is not in the person's best interests for you to provide treatment). It is possible that there may be still other, more idiosyncratic variables that discourage you from accepting a person as a client. For instance, counselors are not immune from unresolved emotional issues. We can imagine how an unresolved event (e.g., the death of a parent) might temporarily discourage the counselor from working with a person who presents with complicated grief. However, we caution you to be mindful of the power of bias and prejudice; be sure that your decision to decline service is not based on characteristics or identities of an entire class of people. Just remember, the person you are speaking with may believe that a counselor–client relationship has been established; it is up to you to clearly communicate that you are declining a counseling relationship. If you decline to accept the person into your care, whenever possible, provide the person with sound information regarding alternatives.

> Access the *ACA Code of Ethics* online at http://www.counseling.org/knowledge-center/ethics or refer to Appendix A in this book.

Duty and Standard of Care

A legal perspective on the counseling relationship begins with the concept of *duty*. Duty means that there is a legal obligation to act in the best interests of the client, to use a *standard of care* that is consistent with the degree of learning, skill, and ethics ordinarily possessed and expected by reputable counselors practicing under similar circumstances. The concept of duty is based on the recognition that as professional counselors, we have a fiduciary relationship with our clients. A *fiduciary relationship* is one in which a person claims to act in the best interests of another, and the other accepts that trust. As counselors, we promise our clients that we will act in their best interests; we ask for their trust, and in so doing we intentionally create the professional relationship that is core to our work. We then have an ethical and legal duty to fulfill that trust. The standard of care is the yardstick against which your professional behavior will be evaluated. So you might ask, what exactly is this standard of care, and how can I be sure I am fulfilling my duty?

> *Duty* is a legal obligation to act in the best interests of the client.

Standard of care is a level of care that is consistent with the degree of learning, skill, and ethics ordinarily possessed and expected by reputable counselors practicing under similar circumstances.

The standard of care is an ever-evolving and ever-rising concept that is formed through a combination of influences:

- *Real-world practice:* Actions and behaviors of practicing professionals engaged in the day-to-day practice of counseling in the real world influence the standard of practice.
- *Education:* Graduate-level coursework common to all practicing counselors grounds practitioners in theory and basic skills.
- *Ethics:* Ethics codes from the primary professional associations help practitioners determine behaviors and practices that are in the best interests of the client as well as those that are deemed harmful.
- *State and federal laws:* Laws define the practice of counseling (or other mental health disciplines) and further describe specific professional activities that are sanctioned.
- *Credentials:* Specialty credentials provide specific guidance regarding best practices and advanced skills for certain issues.
- *Research:* Clinical research identifies best practices for presenting issues or concerns.
- *Policies:* Institutional, agency, or organizational policies and procedures shape all types of professional conduct.
- *Case law:* Opinions from courts interpret or expand the concept of duty (see Chapter 4).
- *Third-party payers:* Third-party payers (insurance, managed care, etc.) have a growing influence on the standard of care by determining clinical activities that will and will not be reimbursed.

As professional counselors, we also have contractual duties arising from our relationship with clients. A *contract* is a legal relationship, written or oral, created by an agreement between the parties. In a counseling relationship, this contractual relationship is generally expressly stated; however, the relationship may be implied. Typically, the client completes the informed consent process and documentation and agrees to a fee for the professional service (fee-for-service private practice, insurance or managed care copayment, or agency sliding scale fee). The client then regularly attends sessions in the counselor's office and pays the agreed-upon fee. It is also possible for a contract to be implied on the basis of the circumstances of the relationship between the parties, even though no fees may be charged, as is often the case in some school, agency, or residential settings.

We need to be mindful of the difference between well-intended helpful and supportive behaviors with another person (acquaintance, friend, or colleague) and behaviors that cross a boundary and can be misunderstood as providing a professional service. The difficulty arises when the other person believes that there is an implied contractual professional relationship (even though the other person may not express it this way), and therefore the other person comes to expect your behavior to reflect your professional duty. Practitioners are understandably anxious regarding this type of scenario and sometimes overreact and try to avoid any situation in which their caring could be mistaken for a professional relationship.

We are *not* recommending that you stop being a friend or caring for others. Our guidance in this regard is to encourage you to recognize the limits of being helpful and supportive, to be willing to make a referral, and to encourage the other person to act on the referral rather than rely on you. It is important to know at what point the fiduciary and contractual obligations come into existence—simply stated, when does an individual become a client?

Informed Consent for Treatment

The informed consent for treatment has ethical (ACA, 2014a, Standard A.2.a.), legal, and clinical implications. The intent underlying an informed consent document is to define the basic counseling relationship between counselor and client. Misunderstanding and disappointment, which are often the genesis of a liability claim and/or licensure board complaint, can be reduced when clients are made knowledgeable of the ground rules of the counseling relationship. The therapeutic relationship is enhanced when clients understand what is expected or required to have a successful counseling relationship. Toward that end, the informed consent for treatment is a powerful clinical and legal tool. Typically, the consent for treatment is both verbal and written (Standard A.2.a.), but the underlying assumption is that consent is informed—meaning that the client fully understands the rules of the counseling relationship. The quality of the client's understanding can be significantly compromised by many factors, including age, education, and physical or developmental capabilities. Cultural differences can also affect the client's understanding. Therefore, although we assume counselors will provide this information in writing, it is important to remain open to alternative means of communication (whether verbal or through an interpreter, translator, or some combination thereof). The critical variable is to do everything that is reasonable to ensure that clients really understand what they are consenting to (for themselves or for minors in their care).

Obtaining informed consent from a minor, in addition to consent from a parent or guardian, is legally required in some but not all states; nevertheless, it is both ethically and clinically in the best interests of the client. We recommend that you fully engage minors, to the extent that they are developmentally capable, in the informed consent for treatment process. As we said in the beginning of this chapter, it's all about the relationship—which is especially true when working with a child or adolescent.

The content of the informed consent form is influenced by agency or institutional policies, state licensing laws and rules, HIPAA requirements, and other binding directives. When developing an informed consent for agency or private practice, the following checklist may be helpful. It is important to keep in mind that not all categories are appropriate for every practice setting.

- *Voluntary or involuntary client participation:* What is the motivation for the treatment relationship? Are clients voluntarily participating? If so, they can terminate without external consequences (courts, schools, employers, etc.). As an alternative, is the treatment required such that failure to participate in or complete the treatment could result in negative consequences for the client? These variables should be fully disclosed in the informed consent.
- *Client and counselor involvement:* What level of involvement and what type of involvement will be expected from the client? What will the counselor provide? How will this be provided? This information helps clients understand what is expected of them.
- *Emergencies:* What are the procedures for emergencies? (This includes how the counselor can be reached in the event of an emergency.)

- *No guarantees:* The counselor (agency or organization) cannot guarantee results (e.g., that clients will become happier, less tense, or less depressed or that they will be able to save their relationships, stop drug use, or obtain good jobs). Only promise what you can deliver. Generally, such promises (if there are any at all) revolve around the counseling process, not the outcome of the process.
- *Risks associated with counseling:* Define what, if any, risks are associated with the counselor's particular approach to counseling. We are not talking about physical risks (unless, of course such risks are involved in a given approach); rather, we are talking about the risks associated with change and growth. The client's perspective can change, and as a result, important relationships may be affected and essential life priorities may shift.
- *Confidentiality, privilege, and privacy:* Be specific about how you will handle confidential information and how confidentiality will be addressed in couples counseling, family counseling, child or adolescent counseling, and group counseling situations. How may confidential and privileged information be released? (For a complete discussion of these topics, including HIPAA, see Chapter 5.)
- *Exceptions to confidentiality, privilege, and privacy:* Define specific circumstances in which confidentiality and privilege cannot be maintained (e.g., mandatory abuse reporting) and the range of actions the counselor may consider. (For a complete discussion of these topics, see Chapter 5.)
- *Counseling approach or theory:* What is the counseling orientation or theoretical belief system of the counselor or the agency or organization? How will that affect treatment? It is particularly important to address this aspect of counseling if the counselor or agency subscribes to a particular therapeutic modality or is involved in a best practices clinical trial that will require the client to work within that model.
- *Ethics guidelines:* What ethics codes define the counselor's practice? How might a client obtain a copy of these guidelines?
- *Licensing regulations:* What license does the counselor hold? How may a client check on the status of a licensee?
- *Credentials:* Beyond licensing, what special or advanced credentials, education, training, or experience does the counselor or the agency or organization possess?
- *Counseling and financial records:* What will they include? How long will they be maintained? How will they be destroyed? State law often affects the answers to these questions.

- *Fees and charges:* What are the specific fees and charges? How will fees be collected? How are financial records maintained? Do you charge for appearance as a witness in court or at a deposition? Remember that state laws and rules of court may dictate whether you can charge for acting as a "witness of fact" (one with direct knowledge, usually gleaned from what you learned from the client) as opposed to an "expert witness" (one who testifies on the basis of his or her education, skill, training, and experience).
- *Insurance and managed care:* How do you handle managed care and other third-party payers? Are you a provider? What responsibility will you (or your office) take for filing insurance forms? How will copayments be handled?
- *Responsibility for payment:* Who is responsible for payment of counseling charges? How will delinquent accounts be handled? What charges will be assessed for delinquent accounts?
- *Disputes and complaints:* How will fee or other disputes be resolved? Provide the address and phone number of the state licensing board for complaints if required by the applicable state licensing statute.
- *Appointment cancellation policy:* How much notice for cancellation of a scheduled appointment is required? What fees, if any, will be charged for late cancellation?
- *Affiliation relationship:* Describe independent contractor, partnership, or other relationships with any other practitioners in the office suite (see Chapter 11).
- *Supervisory relationship:* Describe any required supervisory relationship along with the reason for the supervision. Provide the supervisor's name, contact information, and credentials.
- *Colleague consultation:* Indicate that, in keeping with generally accepted standards of practice, you frequently consult (on a confidential basis) with other mental health professionals regarding the management of cases. The purpose of the consultation is to assure quality care. Every effort is made to protect the identity of the client.
- *Social media requests:* Indicate that while you are pleased that the client may value your relationship, you have found that there can be unforeseen and uncomfortable implications associated with mixing a professional counseling relationship with a personal relationship and for that reason declining social media requests is now the recommended ethical course of action (see Chapter 7).

- *Electronic communication (texting, e-mail, etc.)*: Expectations surrounding electronic communication are rapidly changing. It is important to inform clients of your texting and e-mail policy—specifically, to what extent, if at all, do you communicate via e-mail or text, for what purpose(s) do you use e-mail or texting (appointment setting/confirmation vs. confidential/clinical communication), and what boundaries in terms of timeliness of response can the client expect? Finally, if texting and e-mail are acceptable forms of communication, it will be important to inform the client if and how electronic communication should be used in the event of an emergency.

An important part of the informed consent process includes an honest discussion with your client about the possible implications and consequences of receiving a mental health diagnosis. (Of course, not every counseling relationship involves the rendering of a diagnosis.) This discussion is particularly important in circumstances in which a mental health diagnosis will be made and communicated to a third party (managed care or insurance company, employer, school, etc.). Mental health professionals can never say with certainty how a mental health diagnosis may affect the client in the future. There have been situations in which clients have experienced problems securing life or disability insurance; other clients have encountered problems obtaining a security clearance necessary to qualify for certain types of employment. It is sad, but there are people within our culture who make negative judgments about other people who have mental health diagnoses. We understand that this situation can create a catch-22 situation for both the practitioner and the client. Payment to the practitioner/agency or reimbursement to the client for counseling services is frequently dependent on the submission of a claim with an appropriate mental health diagnosis; if there is no mental health diagnosis, there will be no payment. However, in the spirit of informed consent, counselors have a responsibility to talk with clients about the possible future implications and consequences of mental health diagnoses. We also have both a legal and ethical responsibility to render accurate diagnoses—neither to underdiagnose (to state a diagnosis that is less severe or more general than the available clinical evidence supports) nor overdiagnose (to state a diagnosis that is more severe or complicated than the clinical evidence supports that might result in more easily obtaining approval for mental health benefits). This is an area filled with potential tension and can be a significant test for the counseling relationship. It is also a prime example of the need to ground the counseling relationship on a firm ethical, legal, and clinical foundation.

Counselors have an obligation to monitor the ongoing counseling relationship with each client to determine when or if changes in treatment are warranted and then, if necessary, to obtain an updated informed consent (ACA, 2014a, Standard A.6.d.). Examples of this include (a) a client moving from one modality of treatment (individual, couple, family, or group) to another modality, especially when the new modality involves other people; (b) changing roles (e.g., changing from a mediator to counselor role); (c) involving a new counselor in the treatment (e.g., inclusion of a cotherapist); and (d) changing the treatment relationship to include a research affiliation. These and other such eventualities affect the client–counselor relationship and the expectations around confidentiality, privilege, and privacy. It is essential that clients are apprised of and consent to these changes.

We close this section with a suggestion: Think of informed consent as an ongoing process rather than a single event. It is essential that consent be secured at the outset of counseling, but don't expect that clients will remember everything they read and agreed to many weeks or months earlier. Be prepared to revisit key aspects of the consent. Remember, it's your responsibility to secure and maintain the client's active informed consent for treatment throughout the clinical relationship.

Fees

Private practitioners can reasonably expect to be fairly compensated for providing a competent service. Counselors should not believe or feel, or be encouraged to believe or feel, that there is something wrong about being appropriately compensated for the important work we perform. However, the issue of fees has both ethical (ACA, 2014a, Standard A.10.) and legal implications that can make the provision of quality counseling services more complicated than some other marketplace exchanges.

Under most circumstances, private practitioners are legally entitled to establish a fee for their time and expertise. An exception includes counselors who enter into contractual agreements with third-party payers in which there is an agreed-upon fee for counseling services. In addition, there is a tradition of service and altruism within the counseling profession that can create tension for some practitioners.

Balancing real-world financial needs against this tradition can be challenging. In establishing fees, you are encouraged to be aware of the financial status of clients and the locality in which you practice. Fees vary greatly across the country. Establishing a stated "usual and customary" fee communicates an important message about the value of the counseling service. Counselors are advised to consider the financial ability of clients, and if the cost of services "create[s] undue hardship for the client, the counselor may adjust fees, when legally permissible, or assist the client in locating comparable, affordable services" (Standard A.10.c.). As the code suggests, nothing prevents practitioners who have set a usual and customary fee from making an adjustment to that fee on a case-by-case basis.

An area of potential ethical jeopardy occurs when practitioners accept clients in their private practices when clients qualify for services at the agencies in which the practitioners are employed (Standard A.10.a.). In essence, this amounts to making a referral to the practitioner's own private practice when that counselor or someone else within the agency or organization could have provided the services to the client, likely at a significantly lower cost. Often agencies or organizations have policies that prohibit employees from such activities. However, clients are always free to make a choice about who, or under what circumstances, they want to see as a counselor. The counselor's obligation is to ensure that clients have been provided full and unbiased information upon which to make an informed choice. To that end, counselors should advise potential clients of the availability of the same or similar services offered by the client's employer. In the event the client elects to remain in the private practice (and that is not against agency policy), the counselor is encouraged to fully document the discussion in the client's chart.

Regardless of the amount of fees charged, counselors should have clear written fee arrangements with clients. These fee arrangements should specify the fees and costs to the client so there is no misunderstanding. We remind you that a solid and trusted counseling relationship is the cornerstone of good clinical practice. Misunderstandings about fees and charges create immediate tension and can quickly undermine the quality of the counseling relationship and can even set into motion an adversarial situation that can lead to accusations of unethical behavior and complaints to the licensing board. Therefore, we strongly encourage you to be very clear about fees and charges during the informed consent process. Consider the following when discussing fees with your client:

- *fees for services*—fees and charges for all counseling services (individual, couple, family, or group);
- *additional time*—fees and charges for additional time if the session runs late;
- *telephone/video conferencing/e-mail/texting consultation*—fees and charges for substantive electronic consultation (other than administrative or counselor-initiated check-in);
- *other services*—fees and charges for other services (letters, reports, testing, evaluations, phone calls on behalf of the client, coordination of services with other providers, research, etc.);
- *judicial involvement*—fees and charges for consultation with attorneys, depositions, and court appearances (this may be affected by local laws, rules, or practice);
- *billing and interest*—the billing–invoicing process and interest charged on overdue accounts; and
- *cancellations and missed appointments*—fees and charges, if any, if a client does not provide 24-hour notice of session cancellation or fails to show for a scheduled appointment.

Counselors put themselves and the counseling relationship at risk when they allow a client to amass a substantial outstanding balance without a clear and honest discussion that results in a plan for payment—a plan that genuinely meets the needs and abilities of both the counselor and the client. In the absence of this discussion, the counselor can be distracted by the outstanding balance. It can become the elephant in the room between the counselor and the client. As we all know, when there is an unspoken meta-issue, it influences or dominates the interaction within a relationship. Have a direct and honest conversation with your client about fees, charges, and payments at the beginning of the relationship and during treatment before it becomes an obstacle to the delivery of quality care. It is the respectful thing to do.

In the case of nonpayment of fees, counselors can pursue legal action against clients in small claims or other courts but should be cautioned that attempting to collect overdue fees can push clients to file counterclaims against the counselor. Probably the best course of action is to meet with the client and openly and honestly discuss the outstanding debt, with a view toward encouraging responsibility and prompt payment. Counselors are not obligated to continue services to a nonpaying client indefinitely but should take steps, absent a crisis, to refer the client to another therapist or counseling service. As with all difficult situations, be sure to thoroughly document information about the past-due account, your attempts to invite payment, and your chosen course of action.

Terminating the Counseling Relationship

In a perfect counseling practice, clients reach an appropriate stopping point at which a debriefing of the experience leads client and counselor to a natural point of closure. During this debriefing, you talk with your client about how and when (or if) the client can return for additional treatment. In the real world of practice, however, debriefing and closure conversations do not generally occur.

Client-Initiated Termination

More often than not, clients terminate the counseling relationship. In many cases, the final session occurs without the counselor realizing it is the final session. This situation happens in a number of ways. Sometimes clients seem to lose interest in the counseling process, as evidenced by the client's failure to complete homework assignments or by the client presenting for counseling with low energy and minimal investment in the discussion. Other times, clients chronically cancel appointments or fail to return phone calls. There are also times when clients terminate counseling by either leaving a message to that effect or simply not showing up for a scheduled appointment.

The ethical and legal tension associated with these no-closure terminations is that, from your point of view, the counseling relationship has ended; however, you don't know how the client views it. Things can get complicated when, months later, you receive a call in the middle of the night from law enforcement or from the hospital advising you that the client has an immediate need and you have been identified as his or her counselor. At that moment you are being asked (sometimes pressured) to immediately accept this client back into your practice. You may or may not want the client back, but there was never a discussion of how or when (or even whether) the client could return to treatment. There is a lack of clarity. If you don't accept the client, you could risk inviting the client to feel abandoned. If you do accept the client, you have done so without the opportunity to really explore the client's commitment to the counseling relationship. There are some actions you can and should take when clients appear to have initiated termination without explicitly communicating their decision. Clinical documentation is essential. (Of course, the counselor should be documenting the clinical process all along the way.) Therefore, if the client begins to demonstrate a reduced commitment to treatment or exhibits ambivalence toward engaging in the counseling relationship, there should be evidence of that in the clinical record. When a client exhibits a pattern of chronic cancellations, doesn't keep appointments, or simply drops out of treatment without explanation (and does this when there is no reason to believe there is a crisis), we suggest that you write a letter to the client indicating that you accept his or her apparent decision to terminate treatment. Furthermore, if that was not the client's intention, you expect to be contacted within a reasonable time frame. Otherwise, you will close the file and terminate the professional relationship. In the letter, you can indicate how the client can reinitiate a treatment relationship in the future (should that be something you are willing to consider). If you have taken this action and you receive a call in the middle of the night, you are in a much stronger position to either accept or decline a treatment relationship.

Many practitioners, especially those in independent private practice, may want to leave the door open to their clients. Many private practitioners in their statement of office practices or informed consent may choose to communicate to their clients the expectation that the counselor and the client are creating an as-needed relationship, very similar to a primary care physician. Under those circumstances, the counselor and the client understand that in the absence of a formal termination, the counselor–client relationship is permanent. The ethical and legal ramification of this office practice is that the counselor retains a duty to the client and may, at any time, be called upon to fulfill that duty.

Counselor-Initiated Termination and Referral

The counselor may also terminate the counselor–client relationship. In the course of treatment, you have an ethical duty to appropriately terminate the counseling relationship and make a referral if you determine that you no longer can be of assistance to the client (e.g., the client has needs beyond your skills and competence). It is also appropriate to terminate if it is apparent that the client no longer needs or can benefit from your services (in order to avoid creating or maintaining a dependency). Finally, you have a responsibility to terminate treatment if the client is being harmed in some way through the counseling process (ACA, 2014a, Standard A.11.c.).

Terminating the counseling relationship with a client and making a referral is generally a straightforward activity, assuming the termination is handled appropriately and assuming the motivation for termination is consistent with ethical and legal practice. For example, counselors can legally and ethically terminate the counseling relationship if the client fails to pay the agreed upon fees for service. However, serious problems can occur when counselors terminate the counseling relationship during a client emergency or crisis. Ethically, abandonment of the client is prohibited: "Counselors do not abandon or neglect clients in counseling. Counselors assist in making appropriate arrangements for the continuation of treatment . . ." (Standard A.12.). The core issue is to do all that is reasonable so the client does not feel abandoned. Client abandonment (real or perceived) often leads to the client initiating an ethics or licensure board complaint or a malpractice lawsuit.

Counselors often struggle with decisions concerning whether to terminate and refer a client when the client poses issues that are beyond the counselor's competence or when the counselor holds values that are at odds with the client's values. If issues of discrimination are involved, the ethical dilemma can quickly become a legal problem. Several court cases have emerged in the twenty-first century that are instructive on the topic of appropriate termination and referral.

Bruff v. North Mississippi Health Services, Inc. (2001)

Bruff provides case precedent (legally binding only on courts under the federal jurisdiction of the Fifth Circuit Court of Appeals but persuasive authority in other jurisdictions) that may help counselors sort through the difficulties in making such decisions. In *Bruff*, a hospital-based employee assistance program (EAP) counselor refused to counsel a homosexual client on relationship issues. The counselor was terminated after the hospital offered "reasonable accommodations" and she did not pursue all available job options. The counselor sued the hospital's parent company on the theory that the hospital discriminated against her on the basis of her religious beliefs and thereby violated Title VII of the Civil Rights Act of 1964, as amended by the Civil Rights Act of 1991. Following a substantial jury award against the employer, the appellate court reversed the decision and held that the hospital was not required under Title VII to accommodate the counselor by excusing her from counseling on subjects that conflicted with her religious beliefs. The court indicated that the burden would have fallen on the other two available EAP counselors and would have involved more than *de minimis* cost to the medical center.

On the basis of the evidence produced by both sides about professional standards and ethics codes, the court declined to take a position. In fact, the court specifically stated that its inquiry was strictly limited "to what extent Title VII requires the Medical Center to accommodate Bruff's religious beliefs" (*Bruff v. North Mississippi Health Services, Inc.*, 2001, p. 497, n.4). However, the *Bruff* case and a similar case where a federal appellate court ruled in favor of an employer and against a counselor in a Title VII religious accommodation case (*Walden v. Centers for Disease Control and Prevention*, 2012) have garnered considerable attention regarding the legal and ethical ramifications of a counselor's refusal to counsel clients on issues pertaining to sexual orientation. Hermann and Herlihy (2006) cautioned counselors that they must respect clients' values, even if they are different from their own and that refusal to counsel clients on the basis of age, culture, ethnicity, or sexual orientation may lead to ethical sanctions, licensure board complaints, and malpractice lawsuits.

Ward v. Wilbanks (2010, 2012)

The *Ward* case involves a suit brought by a student who was dismissed from the master's degree program in counseling at Eastern Michigan University. In a Summary Judgment Opinion and Order (see further discussion in Chapter 12), the court found in favor of the university. The essence of the issue was that, as part of a program accredited by CACREP, students understood their obligation to abide by the *ACA Code of Ethics*, the contents of which were infused throughout the curriculum. As a normal part of the university's practicum experience, the student was assigned to meet with a new client. Prior to meeting with the client, she read the case notes (work done by a previous counselor) and determined that she could not work with this client because she could not "affirm" the client's homosexual lifestyle. The Opinion and Order Denying Plaintiff's Motion for Summary Judgment (Doc. #79) and Granting Defendant's Motion for Summary Judgment (Doc. #82) stated the following:

> The controversy arose when plaintiff encountered a client who sought counseling regarding depression, but who had previously been counseled about his homosexual relationship. After plaintiff reviewed the file approximately two hours before the scheduled appointment, she asked her supervisor, Dr. Callaway, under whose license she was practicing, whether she should refer the client to another counselor because she could not affirm the client's homosexual behavior. Time constraints precluded a full discussion of the conflict, but given her desire not to

harm the client, Dr. Callaway opted to cancel the appointment and reschedule it for a later date with a different counselor.

Dr. Callaway later informed plaintiff that she would not be assigned any more clients, and that she, Callaway, would be requesting an informal review before herself and plaintiff's advisor, Professor Dugger, as to whether she had violated University and ACA policies prohibiting "unethical, threatening, or unprofessional conduct," an "inability to tolerate different points of view," "imposing values that are inconsistent with counseling goals," and "discrimination based on . . . sexual orientation" (p. 3).

The outcome of the informal review was that the student needed to make some changes and was therefore given three choices: (a) to complete a "remediation program" to help her learn not to impose her values on her clients, (b) to leave the counseling program voluntarily, or (c) to request a formal hearing. She refused to participate in the remediation program, choosing instead to have a formal hearing.

At the formal hearing, she again refused to participate in a remediation program and maintained her position that she could not work with clients whose behaviors were contrary to dictates of the Bible. The student further indicated that she was not amenable to learning how to separate client lifestyle or behaviors from her personal values. Once again, this was not a situation in which the counselor took issue with the values of one client but rather with an "entire class of people" (Summary Judgment Order). She stated that she could not counsel clients who failed to comport with her religious teaching (e.g., persons who engaged in fornication; ACA, 2011, p. 8). The importance of the ethical issues in this case prompted the ACA to become an active agent, including submitting an amicus curiae (friend of the court) brief in support of the actions taken by the faculty of Eastern Michigan University.

The plaintiff in this case essentially argued that her First Amendment right to free speech was violated by requiring her to change her beliefs regarding homosexuality and by requiring her to express a particular viewpoint. The plaintiff further argued that this was a First Amendment Retaliation claim and that it was a violation of the Free Exercise Clause in which "Congress shall make no laws respecting an established religion, or prohibiting the free exercise thereof." These defenses, among others, were found to be irrelevant or insufficient. The court gave primary emphasis to the right and responsibility of a CACREP-accredited training program at Eastern Michigan University to adopt academic standards that include a code of ethics from a recognized professional organization that requires students and practicing professionals to engage in professional behavior as defined by the standard (*Ward v. Wilbanks,* 2010).

The plaintiff in the *Ward* case then appealed the decision to the Sixth Circuit Court of Appeals. That court decided that there were issues of fact still in dispute, so it remanded the case (sent it back) to the federal district court for a trial. In its decision, the appellate court indicated that the university was unable to identify any written policy that would prevent Ward from seeking a referral for the client. However, the court also stated that Ward should not prevail as a matter of law regarding her claims of free speech and free exercise of religion. Eastern Michigan University agreed to settle the case out of court for $75,000, a rather nominal amount, in order to avoid costly and protracted litigation. As part of the settlement, the university was able to retain its curriculum, practices, and policies.

Counseling is unpredictable at best; counselors can never know or predict the background events and dynamics that constitute the client's story. Counselors are clearly at odds with the *ACA Code of Ethics* when they take the position (a) that they will not accept into treatment clients who hold values or engage in behaviors that are personally offensive to the counselor or (b) that they will terminate treatment and refer the client elsewhere should these offending values or behaviors surface during the course of treatment. The primary responsibility of a counselor as stated in the *ACA Code of Ethics* is "to respect the dignity and promote the welfare of clients" (Standard A.1.a.). The *Code* also states that

> Counselors are aware of—and avoid imposing—their own values, attitudes, beliefs, and behaviors. Counselors respect the diversity of clients, trainees, and research participants and seek training in areas in which they are at risk of imposing their values onto clients, especially when the counselor's values are inconsistent with the client's goals or are discriminatory in nature. (Standard A.4.b.)

Finally, the *Code* takes a strong nondiscrimination stance:

> Counselors do not condone or engage in discrimination against prospective or current clients, students, employees, supervisees, or research participants based on age, culture, disability, ethnicity, race, religion/spirituality, gender, gender identity, sexual orientation, marital/partnership status, language preference, socioeconomic status, immigration status, or any basis proscribed by law. (Standard C.5.)

---

[1]Another relevant case, *Keeton v. Anderson-Wiley* (2010, 2011, 2012), is discussed in Chapter 12 in the context of counselor educator gatekeeping.

Even though the *Bruff*, *Walden*, and *Ward*[1] cases were narrowly construed to apply to specific settings (agency, EAP, and counselor-in-training settings, respectively), there are lessons to be learned for all counselors. The best way to handle counselor-initiated termination of counseling or a decision to refer a client before counseling begins is to have solid documentation in the client record that provides evidence of sound clinical decision making. Such documentation will include awareness of a growing problem (specifying what that is), the steps you took to address the problem, and, after careful thought (and possibly consultation with a colleague or clinical supervision), your conclusion that termination and referral was the appropriate course of action. Providing the client with a referral to another qualified provider or to supportive resources is typically an ethical course of action (Standard A.11.). What is not ethically appropriate is a practice of broad-brushed referrals based solely on clients' race, religion, national origin, or sexual orientation.

In the writers' experience, some counselors in training who are grappling with issues of personal or religious values become hung up on the words "affirm" and "validate" when it comes to counseling clients with different values. Although one could argue that this is purely an issue of semantics, perhaps it would help some to conceptualize the issue more as "respecting" the client and his or her values. The counselor or counselor-in-training is not expected to "adopt" or "approve of" the client's viewpoints and values but should respect them and not rush to refer a client solely because of differences in values.

From a legal perspective, future case law may provide counselors and counselors-in-training with greater clarity on these complex issues. Counselors should also be aware of recent attempts to address such issues through state legislation (often called "freedom of conscience" or "convictions of conscience" clauses) and proposed constitutional amendments that would allow counselors and other mental health professionals to refuse services to certain clients based on their religious beliefs. Arizona is one state that has passed such legislation. Ariz. Rev. Stat. § 15-1862 (2014).

Summary

As we said in the introduction of this chapter, it's all about the relationship. Protecting and respecting the counseling relationship during every phase (beginning, middle, and end) of the counseling relationship is essential. The counseling relationship is best served by use of a well-conceived informed consent process that is crafted to address the expectations and realities that the client will likely experience. Financial aspects, well managed or poorly handled, can have a dramatic affect on the quality of the counseling relationship. Finally, the legal and ethical considerations associated with terminating the counseling relationship and referring the client must also be carefully considered. We hope that you appreciate how important the legal, ethical, and business dimensions of the counseling relationship are to the overall quality of the counseling relationship. When these dimensions are responsibly managed, the counseling relationship is unencumbered, that is, free of unnecessary tension and less likely to lead to ethical or legal problems for the counselor.

Chapter 3
Overview of Law and Ethics

Virtually every aspect of American society is affected by the law. Counselors and other health professionals are subject to a variety of legal and ethical considerations governing their professional practices. It is important that counselors understand the basic concepts of the legal system, the general body of law affecting professional practice, and the impact of professional conduct and ethics standards so that they are prepared to address problems that may arise in practice.

Legal mandates should be distinguished from ethics codes, which are developed by the profession to guide professional practice. This chapter is designed to help counselors understand and appreciate the differences, similarities, and relationships between the law and ethics.

The American Legal Structure

The American legal system as we know it today evolved from the common law system of England. Rather than codified written laws, the common law was derived from court decisions, which reflected the customs and values of the time. Americans also are governed by the U.S. Constitution, which established our tripartite form of government (legislative, executive, and judicial branches) to initiate, administer, and enforce laws passed by the U.S. Congress (federal laws). Individual states also have legal systems with legislative, executive, and judicial branches similar to those of the federal government.

Within this structure, laws governing our society originate from two sources: laws (sometimes called *statutes*) passed by governmental bodies, such as the Congress or state legislatures; and *rules of law* made by the courts in interpreting the Constitution, federal and state law, and the existing common law. Law made by courts, sometimes called *judge-made law*, takes into account the relevant facts of each particular case, the applicable statutes and administrative regulations governing the situation, and decisions from other court cases (called *precedents*) that might bear on the facts of the case before the court. This all-inclusive approach to interpreting individual cases results in an ever-evolving body of law—within the overall framework of the Constitution—which reflects the changing character of our society.

In appropriate cases, courts also consider standards of conduct relevant to a particular profession. Taking the customary conduct of similarly situated professionals into account when interpreting the particular facts of a case has been an important safeguard for both the public and the affected professionals in many cases. The practice of counseling as well as other mental health professions has been shaped by this activity. Throughout this book, we highlight several important cases that have served to shape the counseling profession.

All of this information boils down to a simple but powerful fact: Our body of laws is dynamic and ever-changing. It is not possible to predict accurately the result of any particular case that might be presented in the future, but rules of law guide the analysis of situations that may develop. It is those rules of law that we attempt to present in the remaining chapters, along with practical suggestions for incorporating the law into one's counseling practice.

Criminal, Civil, and Administrative Law

There are two major types of law: *criminal law* and *civil law*. Criminal (penal) law includes acts that are prosecuted by the government, not by private individuals. Crimes are punishable by fine, imprisonment, or death and include offenses such as murder, rape, burglary, robbery, and assault with a deadly weapon. Individuals can also be prosecuted for aiding and abetting someone who has committed such crimes or for failing to notify proper authorities in some situations (e.g., child abuse) when they have knowledge of such crimes.

Civil law generally includes everything that is not criminal in nature concerning the civil rights of individuals or other bodies. Some of these civil wrongs are called *torts*, which are wrongful actions taken by one private person against another (other than breach of contract). Intentional torts include battery, defamation, and invasion of privacy. Unintentional torts include negligence, which is the basis of most malpractice suits against professionals, including counselors. Other types of action that are governed by civil law include contract and property disputes. Civil laws are enforced by private persons bringing suit against the violators in a court of law. The sanctions awarded to successful plaintiffs are usually in the form of monetary damages to compensate the plaintiff for his or her loss.

Beyond civil and criminal law, *administrative law* has assumed new prominence for counselors and other mental health professionals in recent years. Administrative law is created (usually by a process of *rulemaking*) by government administrative agencies charged with the task of developing regulations to help define the laws, or statutes, that are passed by Congress or a state legislative body. For example, pursuant to the federal Health Insurance Portability and Accountability Act of 1996 (usually referred to as HIPAA), the HIPAA Privacy Rule (2013) was promulgated by the U.S. Department of Health and Human Services. Subsequent rule-making activity has continued to hone HIPAA almost two decades after the initial enactment of the statute and regulations, making the law relevant to an increasingly electronic world.

The Court System

Our court system is composed of both federal and state courts. Trial courts are the original venues for resolving disputes; the facts of particular cases are explored at this level and appropriate law is applied. Many cases are settled before or during the trial stage. As explained in the following section, few cases are appealed to a higher court.

Federal Courts

Federal courts were created by Article III, Section 2, of the Constitution of the United States and have the power to hear cases "arising under this Constitution" and the laws of the United States. Federal law provides for several situations in which cases may be brought in federal courts. One is when the case arises under the laws of the United States or presents a question of federal law (federal question jurisdiction; 28 U.S.C. § 1331, 2013). Another is when the case involves citizens of different states and the amount in controversy exceeds $75,000 (diversity jurisdiction; 28 U.S.C. § 1332, 2013). Potential litigants may have the option to bring their claims in either state or federal court if the jurisdictional requirements of the federal system can be met.

State Courts

Most state courts are patterned after the federal system, with trial courts, a middle-level appellate court, and a top-level appellate court (often called a supreme court) as the final arbiter of decisions involving state and federal laws that affect the residents of the state. The names of these courts may vary from state to state, but their function is essentially the same. They can hear both civil and criminal cases arising under either state or federal laws, and their decisions are binding on the residents of the state unless overturned by a higher court within the state or by a federal court.

Appellate Process

In both the state and federal court systems, cases originate in the trial court (called the *Federal District Court* in the federal system). Both parties put on ("try") their case at this level, witnesses are heard, evidence is taken, the relevant law is applied to the facts, and a decision is rendered either by a judge or by a jury. The judge then assigns the appropriate remedies to the parties.

Parties may have the right to appeal decisions of the trial or district court to the intermediate-level appeals court. In the federal system, these 13 courts are called the *U.S. Circuit Courts of Appeals*. Their function is to review how the law has been applied to the facts of each particular case and to determine whether the trial court made any errors in its decision; if so, the case should be overturned, reversed, or sent back to the trial court for additional findings of fact. The state appeals courts generally operate in a similar manner.

The losing party can request that his or her case be heard at the third and final level: either the highest court in the state system or, in the federal system, the U.S. Supreme Court. In addition, parties who have had cases decided by the highest court of a state may move to the U.S. Supreme Court through the process known as a *petition for certiorari*, or asking the Court to hear the case. The nine justices of the Supreme Court then vote to decide whether to hear the case, and, if at least four justices agree, the Court will issue a *writ of certiorari* asking that the case be forwarded to the Supreme Court. Cases accepted by the Supreme Court generally involve issues of federal law in which decisions of circuit courts on similar issues conflict with one another. Very few cases actually end up in the U.S. Supreme Court.

Ethics Standards

At some level nearly every human being has developed his or her own set of beliefs about what is good and what is bad, resulting in the adoption of our morals and values, which may be viewed as our personal code of conduct. Our personal morals and values are influenced by our family-of-origin values, religious moral education, formal civics instruction, and informal observation of the behavior and interaction of important individuals and groups as well as the personal conclusions reached from the lessons of life.

Ethical behavior is not just something nice to have—it is critical to our survival as a society. Think of the impact on individuals and our society of the recent economic turbulence caused at least in part by actions of financial professionals who, one by one, engaged in behavior that placed personal short-term financial gain ahead of the overall well-being of the nation's economy. Our culture is awash in recent examples of financial moral and ethics travesties, including the intentional bilking of investors by Jordan Belfort, known as the "Wolf of Wall Street," as well as Bernard Madoff's Ponzi scheme in which thousands of individual and institutional investors were deceived and financially destroyed. There are also very public breaches of moral and ethical standards that involve high-profile individuals who demonstrated serious lapses in moral and ethical behavior, each of which serves as a cautionary tale in our culture.

There are many more private and personal examples of ethical failure that never garner media attention. As we step away from looking at the public examples, we invite you to reflect on your own experience with moral or ethical dilemmas—the times you adhered to your standards and the times you failed. Most ethical decisions are in-the-moment and very private. This fact leads to an inescapable conclusion: No matter how many laws we pass or codes of ethical conduct we develop, everything comes down to a private decision. There are no ethics police patrolling our thoughts and monitoring our personal or professional behavior. Ethicist Rushmore Kidder (1995) suggested that *ethics* can be defined as the "obedience to the unenforceable" (p. 66). Certainly there are often negative and painful consequences that follow unethical behavior, but in the moment that a decision is made, it is just you and your integrity.

Making an ethical decision that involves a choice between a purely right and purely wrong action is generally not difficult for most of us. However, human beings are quite adept at engaging in mental gymnastics that permit us to conclude that under the very specific circumstances in which we find ourselves, the wrong action is not really all that wrong or maybe not wrong at all. We will return to that discussion, but first we will address what Kidder (1995, p. 17) described as "right versus right" choices. Under right versus right circumstances, we can easily make an argument for all the available options, yet only one option can be chosen. Life is filled with such choices. Examples of right versus right choices often involve the following:

- Truth versus Loyalty: honesty or integrity versus commitment, responsibility, or promise-keeping;
- Individual versus Community: involves the tension around us versus them, self versus others, or smaller versus larger group;
- Short-term versus Long-term: difficulties arise when immediate needs or desires run counter to future goals or prospects;
- Justice versus Mercy: fairness, equity, and even-handed application of the law often conflicts with compassion, empathy, and love. (Kidder, 1995, pp. 112–113)

We can very easily become ensnared in a right versus right choice. Only careful and mindful deliberation of implications, nuances, and consequences within each position can help us arrive at a choice that is in alignment with our personal morals and values. We will see how right versus right dilemmas often occur when counselors are faced with an ethical challenge.

Professional Ethics

Ethics standards defining professional behavior are not unique to counselors or mental health professionals. Long before the first iteration of the *ACA Code of Ethics*, other professions were wrestling to develop and promulgate behaviors considered acceptable in the performance of a specific professional service. Professional counselors are guided in their professional conduct by the ethics codes promulgated by professional associations, such as the 2014 *ACA Code of Ethics* (see Appendix A). The 2014 version of the *Code*, immediately following its Preamble, specifies that it serves six main purposes:

1. The *Code* sets forth the ethical obligations of ACA members and provides guidance intended to inform the ethical practice of professional counselors.
2. The *Code* identifies ethical considerations relevant to professional counselors and counselors-in-training.
3. The *Code* enables the association to clarify for current and prospective members, and for those served by members, the nature of the ethical responsibilities held in common by its members.
4. The *Code* serves as an ethical guide designed to assist members in constructing a course of action that best serves those utilizing counseling services and establishes expectations of conduct with a primary emphasis on the role of the professional counselor.
5. The *Code* helps to support the mission of ACA.
6. The standards contained in this *Code* serve as the basis for processing inquiries and ethics complaints concerning ACA members.

In furtherance of the sixth purpose, a complaint procedure has been established and penalties for violations of the standards have been set. These penalties may include a variety of remedial requirements, probation, suspension, or permanent expulsion from the association (ACA, 2005).

Ethical decisions generally complement the legal parameters but also cover issues that tend to fall into the gray areas (i.e., not expressly prohibited, yet not specifically allowed by the law). They take into account the subtle fact variations in each situation and the reasonable approach to addressing it. The concept of what is ethical also changes with the maturity and perspective of the counseling profession and society at large. For example, as information technology has begun to play a larger role in practice over the past decade, questions regarding its impact on client confidentiality and informed consent have arisen. The most recent version of the *Code* has incorporated new requirements for counselors in this area (ACA, 2014a, Standard H). As technological advances become even more widespread in counseling, and as counselors are affected by new laws, such as HIPAA and HITECH (see Chapter 5), future editions of the *Code* are likely to contain even more standards for practicing counselors.

On occasion, ethics standards and responsibilities conflict with legal standards and requirements. For example, a counselor may wish to preserve a minor's ethical right to confidentiality but may be faced with a parent's demand for information that a particular state law allows. If a conflict between ethics and the law occurs, the *Code* directs that counselors make known their commitment to the *ACA Code of Ethics* and take steps to resolve the conflict. If the conflict cannot be resolved, "counselors, acting in the best interests of the client, may adhere to the requirements of the law, regulations, and/or other governing legal authority" (Standard I.1.c.). We encourage counselors also to refer to two other ACA publications, *ACA Ethical Standards Casebook* (Herlihy & Corey, 2015) and *Ethics Desk Reference for Counselors* (Barnett & Johnson, 2015), for specific examples that illustrate and clarify the meaning and intent of each major section of the *Code*. These books present typical situations faced by counselors in practice and analyze the ethical considerations involved in each situation. Counselors are well advised to study the implications of these analyses carefully and to apply the results to their professional practices.

Ethical Decision Making

Ethical decision making is often not as simple or as easy as we might imagine or desire. In every walk of life, including the counseling profession, otherwise good people engage in unethical behaviors. What explains this? What if there are psychological forces—aspects about our human nature—that complicate our ethical decision-making ability?

The purpose of this discussion is not to provide an excuse for failure to engage in competent ethical behavior but rather to place the discussion into a larger context, a context that appreciates the complex cognitive and environmental forces that affect ethical decision making. Harvard Business School professor Max H. Bazerman and Notre Dame College of Business professor Ann Tenbrunsel, both prominent ethicists, are authors of *Blind Spots* (2011). The authors introduced several important concepts for consideration. They suggested that there are psychological and cognitive forces that invite times "when we unwittingly behave unethically" (Bazerman & Tenbrunsel, 2011, p. 27). One of these forces is what the authors referred to as *bounded ethicality*—cognitive limitations that can make us unaware of the moral implications of our decisions. The authors argued that it is common for decision makers to err by limiting their analysis to the data in the room, rather than asking what data would best answer the question being asked. In addition, groups can fall victim to "group think—the tendency for cohesive groups to avoid a realistic appraisal of alternative courses of action in favor of unanimity." Group think "can prevent groups from challenging questionable decisions" (Bazerman & Tenbrunsel, 2011, p. 22).

The second cognitive limitation, originally identified by Ann Tenbrunsel (Tenbrunsel & Messick, 2004), is called *ethical fading*, defined as a process by which ethical dimensions are eliminated from a decision. Ethical fading can occur when common everyday features of an organization blind us to the ethical implications of a decision. Under such circumstances, we may reclassify an ethical decision by thinking of it as a business decision. As an example, counselors may come to approach the rendering of a mental health diagnosis as a necessary administrative hoop that must be satisfied in order for the client to receive services. As a result, the ethical implications of the diagnostic decision can "fade" from view.

Bazerman and Tenbrunsel pointed out that human minds use two distinct modes of decision making. Ethical decision making tends to be most compromised when our minds are overloaded. These two modes are called System 1 and System 2 thinking.

- System 1 thinking is our intuitive system of processing information: fast, automatic, effortless, implicit, and emotional. System 1 is the most efficient, and thus serves as an appropriate tool for the vast majority of decisions we make on a daily basis.
- System 2 thinking is slower, conscious, effortful, explicit, and more logical. When you weigh the costs and benefits of alternative courses of action in a systematic and organized manner, you are engaging in System 2 thinking. (Bazerman & Tenbrunsel, 2011, pp. 37–38)

The authors pointed out that it is quite common to have emotional System 1 responses to ethical problems, even though such a response might yield a decision different from the decision we would reach if we engaged in System 2 thinking. Why? Because it takes time and energy to shift from the automatic System 1 mode to the more timely and deliberate System 2.

Legal and Ethical Decision-Making Model

Bazerman and Tenbrunsel's theory makes a compelling case for why the *ACA Code of Ethics* (ACA, 2014a) instructs counselors to use "a credible model of decision making that can bear public scrutiny of its application" (p. 3; see also Standard I.1.b.). An ethical decision-making model uses a System 2 approach—one that is deliberate, explicit, and logical and more likely to yield defensible results when counselors are faced with explaining their decision-making process. Of course, not every ethical decision requires a System 2 approach; frequently the System 1 response is perfectly acceptable. However, we encourage counselors to take some time to revisit routine ethical decisions to ensure that they are operating from current legal and ethical standards and that their decision making has not become "bounded."

Several authors have proposed ethical decision-making models, including Corey, Corey, Corey, and Callanan (2015); Welfel (2013); Remley and Herlihy (2010); and Forester-Miller and Davis (1996). The legal and ethical decision-making model we developed (see Exhibit 1) includes dimensions that we believe are essential to a System 2 legal and ethical decision-making process. All the models offer benefits, and we encourage counselors to choose one that best fits their practice.

Exhibit 1
Legal and Ethical Decision-Making Model

1. *Define the problem, dilemma, and subissues.*
   - What are the core concerns (legal, ethical, clinical, or a combination)?
2. *Identify the relevant variables.*
   - Who are the people, and how might they influence the outcome of the particular dilemma at issue?
   - What are the issues, dynamics, and multicultural considerations?
3. *Review/consult the law, ethics codes, and institutional policy.*
   - What federal and state laws, ethics codes (especially *ACA Code of Ethics*), and applicable institutional policy apply to the facts?
4. *Be alert to personal influences.*
   - What personal values, bias/prejudice, or countertransference may be affecting perception?
5. *Obtain outside perspective.*
   - Whenever possible, engage in colleague consultation and/or supervision and/or obtain legal advice.
6. *Enumerate options and consequences.*
   - What are the possible courses of action and intended consequences?
   - Also consider the unintended consequences. Remember to involve the client in the decision making, unless clinically inappropriate (e.g., where client involvement would likely trigger violence against a third party).
7. *Decide and take action.*
   - Implement the decision and be prepared to reconsider options.
8. *Document decision-making and follow-up actions.*
   - Provide written evidence of clinical and ethical decision making and results of implementation.

Define the Problem, Dilemma, and Subissues

Careful decision making should never be a "Ready—Fire—Aim" activity. Yet, in our experience, counselors who are faced with a legal or ethical situation too often leap to a decision, firing before they aim (too reflexively applying a System 1 approach). Ethical decision making begins by defining the legal or ethical problem. Most clinical issues do not become legal or ethical problems without some aspect of a "dilemma." By definition a dilemma has competing alternatives, all of which have both positive and negative aspects. The dilemma embedded in the problem may be between what is legal and what is ethical or what is legal and ethical and also in the best interests of the client. An example of a frequent dilemma involves the tension surrounding how to respond when a client confides that he is considering suicide. Under some circumstances a counselor might feel caught between conflicting forces: the client's autonomy and self-determination versus the counselor's duty to take action to protect the client from harm. Involuntary hospitalization infringes on the client's freedom, but failure to take action might result in the client's death. Naming the competing tensions embedded within most difficult legal or ethical issues is the first step in the decision-making process.

Identify the Relevant Variables

Relevant variables include people other than the client (individual, couple, or family) who are important characters involved in the story and should be considered. The existence and influence on the client of these other people must be taken into consideration. In addition, there are nearly always idiosyncratic variables unique to every client situation that should be considered. What clinical dynamics and multicultural considerations are influencing this situation? Dynamics can include the age or stage of the client as well as the interpersonal dynamics between the client and her family members and social network. Contextual and environmental factors, including culture, race, class, socioeconomics, and issues of privilege and opportunity, must also be considered. It is through these contextual and environmental influences that clients create their worldviews. Keeping the client's worldview in mind is a demonstration of respect as counselors work their way through the legal and ethical decision-making process.

Know the Law, Ethics Codes, and Institutional Policy

State and federal statutes, ethics codes, and institutional policies can guide or dictate actions that counselors must take when faced with difficult or sensitive client situations. It is our experience that counselors have only a general impression of the ethics code. We certainly do not believe that counselors can or should commit the ethics code to memory, but we strongly urge counselors to have easy access to a copy of the relevant ethics code so that their decision making can be informed by a careful review of the pertinent sections. In a similar manner, counselors should have easy access to relevant state and federal statutes, including state counselor licensing laws, abuse reporting (child, elder, and other) statutes, confidentiality and privileged communication statutes, and federal HIPAA/HITECH laws (see Chapter 5 for a more complete listing). For counselors who work within institutions (schools, agencies, hospitals, and corporations), other considerations are also relevant. Most institutions have promulgated policies that define actions counselors must take when legal or ethical situations present; these policies must be understood and incorporated into the decision-making process.

Be Alert to Personal Influences

We have included personal influences in our legal and ethical decision-making model because we have found that unless counselors remain ever mindful, these subtle but powerful personal influences can sabotage the best of intentions. In this context we define *personal influences* as values, biases, prejudices, and countertransference. Veteran counselors might think that students or newer practitioners are most vulnerable to being hooked by personal influences. That is not our experience. We have found that counselors at every stage of their careers are equally vulnerable to being human. Good intentions notwithstanding, counselors can never escape their humanity. As time goes by, counselors age, have different experiences, and move through different stages of life. Counselors might not be aware that they are being influenced in their clinical decisions and legal and ethical decision making by new values, biases, and prejudices. The point here is not that counselors shouldn't have values, biases, prejudices, or moments of countertransference; no human being can be free of such influences. However, when counselors are engaged in a legal or ethical decision-making process, we urge them to take a reflective moment to ask themselves, "Could my own stuff be influencing my thinking regarding this situation?"

Obtain Outside Perspective

Consult—Consult—Consult! Having conducted hundreds of classes and workshops on legal and ethical issues for counselors in which participants have been given legal and/or ethical case studies to evaluate, we have reached one overwhelming conclusion. Two heads are better than one, and three heads are even better! When confronted with a legal or ethical dilemma, seek formal supervision and consult a colleague or, where indicated, a knowledgeable health care attorney. The treating counselor is embroiled in the case and can easily lose perspective. Although the dilemma might not trigger personal influences of the counselor, an outside perspective can still be extremely useful. When working your way through a legal or ethical dilemma, it is important to have at your fingertips a list of competent colleagues who can be called upon when an outside perspective is necessary.

Enumerate Options and Consequences

What are the possible courses of action? What are the intended consequences? What unintended consequences can you imagine? In a busy clinical practice, there is a tendency to grab onto the first course of action that comes to mind. Resist the quick solution. Give it some time. Have you identified the dilemma within the problem? Have you considered the relevant laws, ethics codes, and institutional policies? Have you taken a moment to identify any personal influences that may be affecting your thinking? Have you obtained an outside perspective? If the answer is "yes" to all of these questions, then you are ready to make a list of options. For each option, enumerate the intended consequence (i.e., what you think is likely to happen if you were to implement each option). Finally, try to imagine any unintended consequence that could occur (i.e., how your option could go wrong). Depending on the complexity of the situation, you may want to write down the various options and consequences. Whenever possible, involve the client in your decision making. There are situations in which involving the client might not be possible (e.g., the client is not available). In addition, there are situations in which involving the client is not appropriate, such as where the client might trigger violence against a third party.

Decide and Take Action

Take action! Implement the decision and be prepared to make adjustments and consider other options as events unfold. As the situation evolves, a new round of legal and ethical decision making and action may be necessary, in which case the decision-making model can be reengaged.

Document Decision-Making and Follow-Up Actions

The entire decision-making process should be documented in the client's chart, including options considered and ruled out. Documentation should also include what happened next. Provide follow-up information in the chart, including any additional actions taken to resolve the problem.

In the final analysis, the decision you made may not work out; in fact, you may be criticized for it. However, the standard of care requires that you engage in careful clinical decision making and use a decision-making model—not that you must always be right. When an outcome is adverse, a licensing board or civil complaint may be filed against you. By using a legal and ethical decision-making model and documenting the conclusions you reached, you make it easier for an attorney to defend your professional judgment.

Ethics and the Law

The ethics standards of a profession are usually enforced through the internal procedures of the professional association, not specifically by courts of law. However, in the absence of any clear statutory authority or case law precedent to guide a court in a case involving the conduct of an individual counselor, courts may apply the standard of care developed by other similarly situated professionals (in this case, other counselors). Courts may also look to the self-imposed standards of the profession to determine liability. Therefore, counselors should act in accordance with the standards of counselors in their local communities and thoroughly study and follow the *ACA Code of Ethics* as a means of avoiding potential liability. Just as courts have used the ethics guidelines and standards of care developed by the legal, accounting, and medical professions, a court could find that a counselor has breached his or her professional duty to a client on the basis of the counseling profession's own internal ethics standards.

Summary

Managing the legal and ethical complexities embedded into the fabric of most counseling cases can seem daunting. It is the rare counselor who never finds himself involved in the court and justice system. Clients often come to counseling because of their involvement with police and courts, and in some circumstances counselors must become involved either on behalf of their clients or because of their own actions. For all these reasons it is important that counselors understand the basic concepts of the legal system, the general body of law affecting professional practice, and the impact of professional conduct. In this chapter we stress that the foundation of ethical practice rests on the competent use of a decision-making model. When confronted with complex legal or ethical dilemmas, counselors serve the best interests of their clients and their own best interests when they use a legal and ethical decision-making model that can help them sort through the complexities and contradictions of legal and ethical dilemmas.

Chapter 4

Civil Malpractice Liability, Licensure Board Complaints, and Criminal Actions

Chapter 2 focused on the professional relationships between counselors and their clients and the fiduciary and contractual duties that arise from those relationships. For example, one of those duties, subject to a variety of limitations, is to protect client confidences (see Chapter 5). Counselors face a myriad of other professional obligations and must take steps to comply with those duties. This chapter explores these other obligations and the types of legal actions, including civil malpractice lawsuits and licensure board complaints, that follow when counselors do not fulfill their duties.

Competence and Preparation

One of the fundamental goals of professional preparation and competence is to protect clients from harm, just as the fundamental goal of law is to protect society from harm. Exactly what level of professional preparation and competence is required of a counselor obviously depends on the type of counseling practice as well as the state in which the counselor practices. Corey et al. (2015, p. 304) aptly stated that "striving for competence is a lifelong endeavor." Competence and preparation include such issues as meeting the required levels of education, training, and skill; knowing when to refer to other professionals or seek consultation or supervision; acquiring expertise in specific practice areas; appropriately representing professional credentials; and enhancing professional growth through continuing education. These areas, among others, may be investigated by state and professional regulatory boards and are supported by the 2014 *ACA Code of Ethics.*

For example, the *ACA Code of Ethics* specifies that

> Counselors practice only within the boundaries of their competence, based on their education, training, supervised experience, state and national professional credentials, and appropriate professional experience. Whereas multicultural counseling competency is required across all counseling specialties, counselors gain knowledge, personal awareness, sensitivity, disposition, and skills pertinent to being a culturally competent counselor in working with a diverse client population. (Standard C.2.a.)

Counselors are also admonished to complete "appropriate education, training, and supervised experience" before practicing in a new specialty area to ensure their own competence and to protect others in the process (Standard C.2.b.). They are also required to "accept employment only for positions for which they are qualified" and to hire only counselors "who are qualified and competent" (Standard C.2.c.). For example, to become adept at the skill of diagnosing mental health disorders, counselors cannot simply attend a weekend seminar and think that they have mastered the art of diagnosis. Counselors are also expected to engage in continuing education to maintain their skills and are expected to keep current with issues presented by diverse populations (Standard C.2.f.).

In addition, counselors may claim or imply that they have only those professional credentials that they actually possess; they are responsible for correcting "any known misrepresentations of their qualifications by others" (Standard C.4.a.). For example, if a client calls a counselor *doctor* and the counselor does not possess a doctoral degree in a mental health discipline, the counselor is ethically obliged to bring the error to the client's attention. The majority of states now have licensing statutes that recognize specific credentials for counselors.

Restricting one's counseling practice to fit within the limits of one's professional training is more than just an ethical standard—it is also important from a legal standpoint. Because of a counselor's legal duty to a client, the analysis of a claim of negligence or malpractice is greatly affected by professional identity. How counselors hold themselves out to the public will determine the expected practice standards by which they may be judged. Counselors who hold themselves out or advertise themselves as specializing in a given area will be judged according to the level of skill required of a specialist.

One last area to note in discussing competence is that counselors must "monitor themselves for signs of impairment from their own physical, mental, or emotional problems" and must "refrain from offering or providing professional services when impaired" (Standard C.2.g.). This same section of the *Code* also requires counselors to assist colleagues and supervisors when they show signs of impairment (Standard C.2.g.). The caveat regarding the duty to avoid impaired practice applies to counselors whether the impairment is based on mental or physical health, substance abuse, or adverse prescription medication reactions. It is also important to recognize that impairment can be generated by subtle and nonpathological stressors and life events. The list of stressors and distractions that can impair professional judgment and competence includes every imaginable life event, from lack of sleep (caused by caring for a newborn or tending to the needs of an ill family member), to the anticipation of a wedding or vacation, to the mental and emotional preoccupation associated with marital or family problems. Over the course of their careers, counselors will frequently be challenged with a myriad of nonpathological invitations to impairment. Self-monitoring in the form of recognition and appropriate response to impairment of competence is both ethically and legally essential. This does not mean that a counselor who has one difficult night's sleep must cancel all client appointments for the following day. However, that counselor should be mindful of her reactions and attentiveness and make adjustments as necessary. During times of impairment that could adversely affect client care, it may be necessary to limit, suspend, or terminate professional responsibilities altogether.

Duty of Care and Potential Malpractice Liability

Professional counselors must exercise due care in their counseling relationships or face potential liability in a civil suit for failing to perform their duties as required by law. Counselors can be sued in a court of law for acting wrongly toward a client or for failing to act when there was a recognized duty to do so, when action or inaction results in injury to another. The end result, or *judicial relief*, is usually in the form of monetary damages awarded to the injured party to compensate for the injuries inflicted.

Negligence

For counselors, the primary area in which civil liability is found rests in the law of torts (see Chapter 3). A *tort* is basically a private injury against the person, property, or reputation of another individual that legal action is designed to set right. Torts can take various forms and fall into two categories. The first, called *negligence*, is the unintentional violation of an obligation one person owes to another, such as a counselor's obligation to use his or her care and skill in dealing with a client, but it may also include failing to follow all the requirements of a protective statute.

There are four elements to be proven in a negligence action:

1. Duty: There must be a legal duty arising from a special relationship between the parties that will be determined by the facts of the situation. Engaging in a casual conversation at a dinner party or giving a lecture at a local civic gathering might not easily be characterized as constituting a special relationship, but counselors should be circumspect about giving specific advice in these and other settings. A court will then look to the professional identity of counselors (legally and ethically defined) to determine what skills and experience they should be expected to have and by what standards of practice they should be bound. In many cases, state licensing statutes will determine the outcome.

2. Breach: The legal duty arising from that relationship must have been breached. That is, the mental health professional failed to uphold the standard of care or practice expected of a counselor in that position or violated some law (e.g., failed to report suspected child abuse or neglect).

3. Causation: The plaintiff must prove causation. This means that the injuries received would not have occurred but for the counselor's breach of duty. Even when other contributing causes are present, the counselor may be held liable for damages if the injury to the client was foreseeable and resulted from the counselor's conduct.

4. Damages: There must have been an actual injury to the plaintiff, such as physical harm, emotional distress, or depression, that is evidenced by specific symptoms, worsening of problems, changes in life circumstances, or the like. Typically, some evidence of financial loss also is presented.

This is a very simplified explanation of a complicated analysis that captivates lawyers and law students, but it should raise a variety of questions about the entire picture of professional practice for mental health practitioners, therapists, and counselors.

Malpractice

Malpractice is the term that pertains to most civil suits against professional counselors. As applied to counselors, a malpractice lawsuit is based on negligence in carrying out professional responsibilities or duties. Professional malpractice is regulated by state law and usually applies only where the professional person is licensed or certified according to state statute. However, other counseling professionals can still be held liable for their actions on the basis of a negligence theory (see the preceding section), intentional infliction of emotional distress, or other torts even if the term *malpractice* does not technically apply. Another somewhat broader term that is widely used, especially in conjunction with insurance policies, is *professional liability*. Malpractice is typically found in the following types of situations:

- The procedure used by the counselor was not within the realm of accepted professional practice.
- The technique used was one the counselor was not trained to use (lack of professional competence).
- The counselor failed to follow standard counseling procedures, resulting in harm to the client.
- The counselor failed to warn and/or protect others from a violent client.
- Informed consent to treatment was not obtained.
- The counselor failed to explain the possible consequences of the treatment.

As in charges of negligence, the establishment of a professional malpractice case requires that the plaintiff prove the elements of duty, breach, causation, and damages.

The duty owed by the counselor is premised on the existence of a fiduciary relationship between the counselor and the client (see Chapter 2), one that fosters both trust and confidence. The client has the right to expect due care from the counselor, and the counselor is obligated to provide the standard of care.

The primary problem in a malpractice suit is to determine which standard of care applies to ascertain whether a counselor has breached his or her duty to a client. Professional action or inaction is typically judged by whether a reasonably prudent counselor in the same or similar circumstance would have acted in the same manner as the counselor did. If the answer is "yes," liability usually will not be found. However, when the counselor holds himself or herself out as an expert in a particular discipline, he or she must then meet the standard of care required of an expert in that area. The courts also look to licensing statutes, as well as professional standards of practice and codes of ethics, to determine the standard of care to apply in each situation. Courts also borrow from case precedents involving other related professions, such as psychiatry, psychology, and medicine, to measure counselor performance.

Malpractice claims may arise from a variety of issues in the counseling relationship, although all share the common elements of professional duty of care, breach of that duty, causation, and resulting injury. Watch for these elements in the examples discussed in this book.

Intentional Torts

The second category of tort occurs where there has been a direct, intentional abrogation of some person's legal rights, such as the invasion of privacy through an illegal search. Other intentional torts include defamation of character, assault, battery, infliction of emotional distress, or any intentional violation of a protected interest.

A counselor might be held liable for one of the intentional torts, even though the conduct was unintentional, if the resulting injury was substantially certain to occur from the counselor's act. This situation might be more likely in counseling relationships than elsewhere because of the intimate nature of counseling. Counselors should be more aware of the particular vulnerabilities of their clients and may be judged on that basis. An injured client frequently will allege two or more separate causes of action at the same time; for example, the client may claim that an alleged inappropriate touching was an assault that caused emotional distress. The same alleged injury could also form the basis for a claimed breach of fiduciary and contractual duties as well as negligence by mishandling the transference/countertransference phenomenon.

Criminal Action

Certainly few counselors ever anticipate that they might become defendants in a criminal action simply by practicing their profession. But counselors should be aware of certain occupational hazards that could lead to criminal liability. The ideal goal for professional counselors is to maintain appropriate boundaries between themselves and their clients (see Chapter 9) so they may interact with clients in a professional, or clinical, manner. On occasion, however, situations arise that might lead counselors to go much further in protecting their clients or providing emotional support and comfort than the law literally allows. In such cases, a counselor may intentionally or unwittingly risk criminal liability as an accessory to a crime for failing to report child abuse, contributing to the delinquency of a minor, or committing insurance fraud or sexual misconduct.

In addition to the possibility of administrative sanctions and civil or criminal liability, the costs of defending even a baseless allegation can be significant. Professionals cannot totally insulate themselves from frivolous claims, but they can limit their exposure by paying careful attention to the duties arising from the counseling relationship. Counselors must have a clear understanding of their professional identity, the nature of the professional relationship, the level of professional preparation and competence necessary, the duty of care expected of a counseling professional, and the standards of practice or codes of ethics that establish the permissible boundaries of conduct for the profession.

Common Complaints Against Counselors

Complaints against counselors take a number of forms and are filed in a variety of forums. It's often helpful to look at statistics regarding actual complaints to see what the most frequent claims are and what types of claims garner the greatest severity of loss (the highest damage amounts). Table 2 presents the closed claims experience for participants in the ACA-sponsored professional liability insurance program as reported by Healthcare Providers Service Organization (HPSO) and underwriter CNA in the 10 years between January 1, 2003, and December 31, 2013, in *Understanding Counselor Liability Risk* (CNA & HPSO, 2014). One significant point worth noting is that approximately 40% of professional liability claims during that decade concerned counselors who were involved in inappropriate sexual/romantic relationships with current clients, clients' partners, or clients' family members (CNA & HPSO, 2014, p. 26). (See Chapter 9 for more information on boundary violations.)

Licensure Board Complaints

Counselors are often concerned about malpractice suits but do not always realize that many more complaints are filed at the state li-

Table 2

Severity by Primary Allegation

Allegation	ACA Code of Ethics Section	Percentage of Closed Claims	Total Paid Indemnity	Average Paid Indemnity
Improper counseling relationship with current student	F	1.6%	$1,000,000	$1,000,000
Multiple relationships with client despite potential for client harm	A	1.6%	$500,000	$500,000
Failure to monitor services provided by other counselors / counselors-in-training	F	1.6%	$275,000	$275,000
Counseling plan failed to provide reasonable likelihood of success	A	1.6%	$275,000	$275,000
Failure to practice within boundaries of competence	C	15.8%	$2,649,681	$264,968
Failure to obtain consultation for questions of ethics or professional practice	C	1.6%	$250,000	$250,000
Failure to clarify, adjust or withdraw from potentially conflicting roles among multiple clients	A	1.6%	$142,500	$142,500
Sexual/romantic interactions/relationships with current clients, client's partners or client's family members	A	39.7%	$2,229,435	$89,177
Failure to identify and resolve adverse consequences of treatment	A	3.2%	$140,000	$70,000
Failure to clarify the relationship of counselor with couples or family clients	A	1.6%	$70,000	$70,000
Failure to consult with other professionals if unclear regarding reporting responsibility	B	1.6%	$50,000	$50,000
Improper acceptance/requesting of fees from clients	A	4.6%	$127,500	$42,500
Improper sharing of confidential information without client consent and/or without legal justification	B	12.7%	$303,500	$37,938
Failure to provide client with pre-termination counseling referral recommendations	A	3.2%	$31,500	$15,750
Use of inaccurate, lapsed or deceptive licenses or certifications	C	1.6%	$15,000	$15,000
Sexual relationships with former clients, their partners or family members prior to end of five-year waiting period	A	1.6%	$9,500	$9,500
Defamation/slander/libel	C	1.6%	$7,500	$7,500
Failure to initially and continually inform client regarding limitations of confidentiality	B	1.6%	$1,125	$1,125
Failure to explain confidential nature and parameters of all group work to all members	B	1.6%	$600	$600
Overall		100%	$8,077,841	$128,220

Note. This information is based on analysis by the Healthcare Providers Service Organization and American Casualty Company, CNA. See *Understanding Counselor Liability Risk* (CNA & HPSO, 2014). Published with permission.

censure board level. Although such complaints often are dismissed, this is usually done after considerable time, effort, and expense. An adverse result at the licensure board level is not the same as an expensive monetary award in a civil lawsuit, but it is not negligible; the consequences can range from required continuing education or a reprimand to probation, suspension, or actual revocation of the counselor's license. Attorneys representing disgruntled clients often will use the licensure board complaint process as a springboard for subsequent civil malpractice suits, so it is extremely important that you take board complaints seriously.

If you become the target of a licensure board complaint, it is important to notify your professional liability insurance carrier promptly. A good professional liability policy will provide some payment of attorney's fees so you may receive legal assistance in responding to the complaint. If you are a member of ACA, staff responsible for Ethics and Practice Standards may be able to assist with issues involving ethics. If appropriate, they may also provide you with access to the ACA-sponsored Risk Management Service for further guidance and suggestions for obtaining local counsel to represent you in a board investigation. If you are a member of another professional organization or maintain your professional liability insurance through another carrier, check with those entities to see what resources are available to you.

If you are tempted to respond to a licensure board complaint without legal counsel, consider the following scenario. You are treating a client who is going through a bitterly contested divorce and custody matter. The client's estranged spouse files a licensure board complaint against you. The board requests your statement and subpoenas your treatment records. Can you provide a statement or the records if the client, who is not the complainant, refuses to waive counselor–client privilege? The following case from the state of Maryland demonstrates how difficult this issue can become in real life.

The facts underlying *Maryland State Bd. of Physicians v. Eist* (2011) are as follows: An experienced psychiatrist, Dr. Eist, was notified by the Maryland Board of Physicians that a patient's estranged husband had filed a complaint, alleging that the psychiatrist had overmedicated his ex-wife and children. (Although the ex-wife was the primary patient, the psychiatrist had also occasionally treated two of the couple's children.) Prior to the board complaint, the complainant and his spouse were embroiled in a bitter divorce and custody dispute. The board subpoenaed the psychiatrist's treatment records; the psychiatrist then notified his patient and asked whether she or the children's attorney planned to contest the board's subpoena. Both the patient and the children's attorney responded that they would not consent to the release of records on the grounds that the information was privileged. As a precautionary measure, the psychiatrist's attorney even sent a letter to the board, raising the issue of privilege but stating that the psychiatrist would comply with any court order if the board decided to seek one. Although the original complaint against the psychiatrist was eventually dismissed, the board continued in its pursuit of sanctions (a reprimand and $5,000 fine). The board viewed Dr. Eist's failure to respond in a timely manner to the board's subpoena as an unlawful failure to cooperate with a board investigation. Basically, the board insisted that it had subpoena power under the applicable state statute and that it should not have to institute legal action to enforce a subpoena whenever staff believed records were necessary to proceed with an investigation. An administrative law judge and intermediate appellate court sided with the psychiatrist. However, the Maryland Court of Appeals (the highest court in the state) subsequently ruled that the psychiatrist or the patient(s) should have initiated a legal action in court and filed a motion to quash the subpoena or motion for protective order. The U.S. Supreme Court denied a writ of certiorari in the case, which resulted in the Court of Appeal's decision as the final ruling.

What does this case mean for counselors? Although this state case precedent is binding only in the state of Maryland, it does offer some valuable lessons for any counselor. First, any time you are served with a subpoena, obtain legal advice. Especially in a case such as this where the complainant is not the client, counselors should speak with their legal counsel about whether to file appropriate motions to bring about a court order (from a judge). In addition, do not ignore a subpoena (see Chapter 5 for an in-depth discussion of subpoenas). Second, do not assume that any licensure board complaint is frivolous or that you can easily get it dismissed without legal representation. The complaint, investigation, and administrative hearing process may differ from state to state.

What are the typical issues that lead to licensure board complaints against counselors and other mental health providers? The following claims are among the most often investigated by state boards for counselors, physicians, and other health care providers across the country:

- engaging in behavior in which boundary violations occur (this includes sexual misconduct; see Chapter 9);
- failing to check credentials of employed therapists;
- failing to make fees and charges clear to clients (including failure to give advance notice of the counselor's practice of charging for missed sessions);
- misrepresenting credentials (e.g., holding oneself out as a doctor when no doctoral degree has been obtained);
- altering records;
- making child custody recommendations when appropriate evaluation of all parties has not been conducted;
- violating confidentiality;
- using false advertising;
- practicing outside the scope of one's experience, education, training, and licensure;
- submitting insurance claims in the name of a psychologist or psychiatrist without mentioning that the counselor actually performed the work; and
- practicing while impaired, including substance abuse impairment.

We offer some steps that you can take in your practice to help avoid complaints:

1. Obtain current copies of your licensure board statutes and regulations, as well as the *ACA Code of Ethics* or other ethics codes pertinent to your practice or adopted by your state, and read them carefully. Check these documents regularly (perhaps on an annual basis); many are available on the Internet.
2. Always represent your credentials and professional identity accurately and correctly. (For example, make sure to correct your clients if they erroneously apply to you a title that you don't have.) Supervisors should ensure that supervisees accurately portray their own credentials and those of the supervisor.
3. Carefully draft informed consent or professional disclosure statements that may be required by your state. Specify your fees and charges in writing.
4. Obtain continuing education on a regular basis or as required by your state licensure board.
5. Be especially careful to avoid harmful dual relationships, be mindful of any boundary crossings, and keep current on changes in the various ethics codes on the topic of boundary violations (see Chapter 9).

6. Develop a resource network of trusted colleagues and an attorney with whom you may consult when difficult situations arise.

7. Carefully document actions taken or rejected and your reasons for your decisions (see Chapter 10).

8. Obtain legal advice when faced with a licensure board complaint; check your malpractice policy to see whether defense costs are covered. Address clients' grievances before they turn into formal complaints.

9. Because monetary disputes often result in complaints, think twice and obtain legal advice before submitting bills to a collection agency.

10. Obtain information about licensure board issues and complaints from your state board's website.

These steps will not only help protect you from a licensure board action; many of them will also help you avoid the slippery slope into a malpractice lawsuit.

Despite the counselor's best intentions, it is not always possible to avoid licensure board complaints. Because clients do not need attorneys to file a board complaint, sometimes there is no rational basis for, or screening of, a complaint before it arrives at the board. Nonetheless, the board may have a legal obligation to investigate the charges. On occasion, the client's mental health diagnosis (e.g., paranoid personality disorder) actually can fuel a complaint; the client may believe the counselor is going to harm him. In addition, to promote the client's best interests, a counselor may give the client the name and address of the board as part of the informed consent process. This practice is actually required by the counselor licensure laws in some states. Although we concur with this practice, we also suggest that you encourage clients to contact you first to try to resolve any disputes.

One example of a board complaint that was successfully defended is the following. A client suffering from major depression had a history of acting out aggressively when things didn't go his way. He was involved in fights, threatened suicide, engaged in binge drinking, and was accused of arson and property theft. The client filed a licensure board complaint that was rambling and disorganized. Among the allegations in the complaint were the claims that the counselor failed to diagnose his symptoms, attributed his symptoms to his character, and presented herself as knowing everything. The client further alleged that the counselor told him that he wouldn't need medication if he received counseling from her. The counselor had a very different account of their interaction. Several items helped in the counselor's defense: (a) The counselor cooperated with the board; (b) the counselor's records were organized and provided good documentation of care and recommendations; (c) referrals were made; and (d) the counselor maintained an accurate accounting of appointments, including the times that the client failed to show (which refuted his version of treatment dates). Even though the complaint was eventually dismissed, the insurance company expended significant funds in providing legal assistance (P. L. Nelson, executive director, ACA Insurance Trust, personal communication, January 9, 2006).

Diagnosis and Scope of Treatment

The education, training, experience, and other qualifications required for a licensed counselor to render specific mental health diagnoses are typically set forth in state licensing laws. Thus, if counselors render mental health diagnoses, they have a duty to do so with the care and skill expected of other counselors who hold similar qualifying licenses. Obviously, giving a diagnosis you are not qualified or licensed to render could leave you vulnerable to subsequent liability for malpractice. Your determination that a client has a condition requiring medical psychotherapeutic treatment generally also will define the appropriate treatment regimen that is considered the standard of care for that diagnosis. The treatment you provide the client must be consistent with the accepted standard of care for that treatment to avoid potential liability.

The decision to use the *Diagnostic and Statistical Manual of Mental Disorders* (5th ed.; *DSM-5*; American Psychiatric Association, 2013) to diagnose mental health disorders and submit diagnoses to insurance companies is complicated by a wide range of legal and ethical issues. These issues include professional licensing, competence, training, economic realities, and reimbursement policies of third-party payers as well as practitioners' sociopolitical and cultural perspectives and values. The legal authority to render a mental health diagnosis has long been a major battleground between licensed professional counselors and other mental health providers (e.g., psychologists, social workers, and psychiatrists). Legal authority to render an independent mental health diagnosis must be provided by statute—specifically the state counselor licensing law. Many counselors across the country now have the authority, granted by law, to diagnose mental disorders. Be sure to verify the limits of authority defined in your counselor licensing law.

Having the legal authority, however, is not synonymous with having the requisite knowledge and skill to render a "proper diagnosis" (ACA, 2014a, Standard E.5.a.). As a counselor, you are ethically charged and legally admonished to practice within the boundaries of your competence. Therefore, establishing competence through education, training, and supervised practice in diagnosing mental disorders is critical. Lacking the ability to demonstrate diagnostic competence can make you vulnerable to an allegation of *misdiagnosis* (rendering an incorrect diagnosis) or *missed diagnosis* (failure to recognize and act on clinically relevant client symptoms of a mental health condition that requires attention). Both of these failures could lead to malpractice allegations. Counselors who are well trained in making diagnoses can provide thoughtful and appropriate diagnoses and can more proficiently respond to an allegation of misdiagnosis or missed diagnosis should the situation arise.

In many ways, diagnosis has become entangled with economic realities driven by the reimbursement policies of third-party payers. Third-party payers (HMO, PPO, Medicaid, and other insurance programs) generally will not provide coverage without a mental health diagnosis. Therefore, for private practitioners as well as for agencies, organizations, and treatment facilities that are economically dependent on third-party payers, the rendering of a diagnosis has become the doorway to financial survival. As a result, there can be a temptation, even in the absence of clinical justification, to render a diagnosis for every client who presents for counseling. Too often, economic pressures and agency funding realities have resulted in a skewing of the purpose of diagnosis. Under these conditions, diagnosis, originally conceptualized to be a clinical classification system designed to support treatment and research, has now shifted to become a mandatory box on the claim form that must be completed with an acceptable code in order to receive payment for services. Practitioners engage in all types of rationalization and justification; but when these mental gymnastics are carried too far, practitioners can easily cross the line and open themselves to charges of insurance fraud. Here are some examples of crossing the line:

- *up-coding*—rendering a more serious diagnosis than symptoms warrant to gain authorization for an increased number of counseling sessions;
- *down-coding*—allowing concerns about possible future implications of a serious mental health diagnosis for the client to convince the practitioner to render a less serious diagnosis; and
- *treatment misrepresentation*—providing a modality of treatment that is not authorized by the third-party payer (e.g., couples counseling) while coding the service with an acceptable treatment modality (e.g., individual psychotherapy).

These and other examples can place you at risk of an allegation of insurance fraud. In addition, if you up-code or down-code a diagnosis and the client experiences a crisis that raises questions about the level of care you provided, you might find it difficult to explain why the level of care did not match the diagnosis.

Another area of ethical and legal complexity surrounding diagnosis is driven by the sociopolitical and cultural perspectives and values held by individual practitioners. These perspectives and values are best understood by describing two polar-opposite viewpoints. At one end of a continuum are practitioners who subscribe to the medical model. They believe mental health conditions exist in a form that can be objectively assessed and accurately diagnosed. These practitioners believe it is necessary and desirable to conceptualize, diagnose, and treat mental health problems with the precision that other health care professionals apply to the conceptualization, diagnosis, and treatment of physical health concerns. They believe that client progress can be behaviorally assessed, resulting in an objective determination of when treatment goals have been met. At the other end of the continuum are practitioners who raise serious questions about using a medical model to diagnose and treat mental health problems. These practitioners believe that human beings are far too complex and too culturally and contextually influenced to be conceptualized by a list of behaviors and symptoms as defined in the *DSM-5* (American Psychiatric Association, 2013). Furthermore, they contend that documenting progress is not something that necessarily has behavioral dimensions that can be objectively measured. Many practitioners point to the cultural insensitivity of many aspects of mental health diagnosis, and they provide historical examples in which mental health diagnoses were used by members of the dominant culture to oppress and "pathologize" individuals and groups.

In recognition of these differences of opinion, the 2014 *ACA Code of Ethics* has attempted to find a point of compromise on the issue of diagnosis. Counselors are instructed to "take special care to provide proper diagnosis" (ACA, 2014a, Standard E.5.a.); they are cautioned to "recognize that culture affects the manner in which clients' problems are defined and experienced" (Standard E.5.b.) and that there have been "historical and social prejudices in the misdiagnosis and pathologizing of certain individuals and groups" (Standard E.5.c.). The *Code* concludes by providing counselors with support in refraining "from making and/or reporting a diagnosis if they believe that it would cause harm to the client or others" (Standard E.5.d.).

Where does this leave the practicing counselor? We maintain that, for most counselors, there is a legal and ethical path through these conflicting perspectives. For practitioners who are highly offended by mental health diagnoses, we encourage you to work in settings that do not require the rendering and submission of mental health diagnoses. Diagnosis is one thing; client assessment is quite another. On one hand, practitioners who are offended by the *DSM-5* conceptualizations and classifications still have both an ethical and legal duty to engage in a careful and ongoing assessment of the client in order to provide treatment that addresses the client's needs. On the other hand, for practitioners who are comfortable with the medical model, the big challenge is to resist manipulating the diagnosis in a manner that will place your clients and you at risk. It has been our experience that most counselors find themselves somewhere in the middle. As with many in-the-middle situations, you probably can see truth and wisdom as well as caution and concern in all the positions. As a result, inevitably you will experience some level of cognitive dissonance and discomfort at some time about some circumstances. We encourage you to clarify the limits of your discomfort so that you can become very clear about what you will and won't do when rendering and submitting a mental health diagnosis.

Failure to Treat or Refer

The counselor's primary ethical responsibility is to respect the dignity and promote the welfare of clients. Coupled with the legal duty to render competent diagnoses and provide proper treatment on the basis of one's training, skill, and experience, these criteria establish the standards of practice each counselor is expected to meet with each client. This process may sound fairly simple, but in day-to-day practice myriad issues arise that complicate the counseling relationship and the responsibilities of the counselor.

Generally speaking, courts will not find counselors negligent merely because the client fails to improve during the counseling relationship or the approach the counselor chooses in treatment proves to be erroneous. Courts have ruled that no presumption of negligence arises from a mere mistake in judgment if that mistake is the type that could be made by a careful and skilled practitioner of that specialty. Again, however, the counselor will be judged according to standards applicable to the counseling profession.

It is important to remember that, at the outset of counseling, you should initiate with your client a discussion of the limits of the proposed course of treatment as well as the potential risks and benefits. Problems may arise when a counselor determines, or should have determined, that a course of therapy or treatment is not effective for the client, or if the client is being harmed by continuing counseling. As long as the counselor is not discontinuing treatment and referring clients solely on the basis of the counselor's own values, attitudes, beliefs, and behaviors, appropriate termination and referral may be indicated (ACA, 2014a, Standards A.11. and A.12.). From a legal standpoint, a court could also find that there is a legal duty to consult or refer when the counselor is not competent to meet the client's needs.

Two legal decisions reflect some confusion in this area about when a counselor or other mental health professional should determine that referral or consultation is necessary. One (*Grote v. J. S. Mayer & Co.*, 1990) involves an industrial psychologist who administered a series of vocational skills tests to a client and met with him four times in the following year. There was only limited telephone contact with the client after that time, the most recent occurring 7 years after the initial contact. Eight years after the last contact, the psychologist was called to court to defend claims that he had failed to refer the client to a clinical psychologist for treatment of his mental illness, prevented him from seeking appropriate treatment, and aggravated his condition. As it turned out, the court dismissed the client's claim because he did not bring an expert to testify about the psychologist's breach of duty. However, in similar circumstances, it is quite possible that a court could find that a referral should have been made during the initial testing and evaluation.

The other case (*Nally v. Grace Community Church*, 1984, 1987, 1988, 1989) involved a young man who committed suicide after counseling by a minister in California. Among the issues was whether the client should have been referred to someone more competent to handle his problems. The California Supreme Court refused to hold the pastoral counselor liable for failing either to refer the young man to another professional or to warn the client's parents that their son was on the verge of suicide. We do not advise interpreting this case to mean that professional counselors do not have a duty to refer. It's important to recognize that the *Nally* case involved a nonlicensed person doing pastoral work.

In addition, state licensure boards could interpret their state laws to require that licensed therapists refer clients to other professionals for services in certain circumstances. For example, state boards could require counselors to refer clients for needed services, such as medication management, that counselors may not legally perform. This duty could be invoked in situations where counselors fail to refer appropriate clients for medication management by a psychiatrist or other physician.

Group Counseling

Group treatment, in all its typical forms (counseling and therapy groups, psychoeducational groups, and support groups), are widely used in most agency and school counseling settings. The counselor's duty to each member of a group is the same as in individual counseling sessions: Professional services must be rendered according to the recognized standard of care expected of a competent counselor. Should counselors fail to practice to the recognized standard, they may be liable for breach of professional duty to clients. Counselors leading groups must be well trained and skillful in the use of group-work techniques and must be careful to follow accepted standards of practice with groups. For instance, as discussed earlier, the concept of privileged communication may not always apply in groups unless it is expressly granted by state statute. Consequently, the counselor must inform all group participants of the limits of confidentiality within the group setting, including the participant's responsibilities to other group members and, if applicable, the absence of the legal privilege concerning group discussions.

The Best Practices Guidelines in Group Work, originally developed in 1998 by the Association for Specialists in Group Work and revised in 2007, defined group workers' responsibilities in planning, performing, and processing groups (Thomas & Pender, 2008). The best practices document stresses the need to screen members before they are admitted to a group, prepare clients adequately before they enter the group so that they are fully informed, set a norm of confidentiality among group members, protect group clients from undue pressure or coercion, treat each member of a group individually and equally, and ensure proper follow-up for group members who choose to leave the group prematurely. The guidelines also emphasize the need for adequate professional preparation before practicing group therapy as well as for ongoing assessment of the group experience. Because a court may take such professional standards into account when judging whether the actions of a group counselor have been negligent, counselors should become familiar with these guidelines and make every effort to provide services accordingly.

Legal and ethical complications can arise when the structure of the treatment program or other administrative decisions require counselors to engage in group work that is not consistent with best practices. For example, Section A.7.a. of the Association for Specialists in Group Work Best Practices Guidelines states, "Group workers screen prospective group members if appropriate to the type of group being offered" (Thomas & Pender, 2008). Problems arise when agency or treatment program protocols automatically place new clients in a group without a thoughtful screening of the client's readiness.

Competent group leadership requires ongoing attention. Counselors must constantly evaluate the quality of the interaction within the group, its appropriateness for each particular member, whether to refer individual members of the group for special help, and whether to bring in an additional counseling professional to assist in the group sessions. Counselors must also be alert to unanticipated encounters within a group and be prepared to handle potentially explosive situations with a high degree of professional skill to protect each member of the group. Because of these many variables, counselors are strongly encouraged to "process" the group experience with a knowledgeable colleague or supervisor. The opportunity to reflect on the unfolding dynamics within the group is an invaluable learning opportunity and an important risk management activity. Experienced and responsible group leaders understand these and many other best practices; inexperienced or disinterested counselors who are assigned to lead a group often lack the requisite knowledge and skill. What too often follows is a group experience that can range from "not helpful" to "harmful."

One additional note of caution is in order. As in all counseling situations, the group counselor has the obligation to remain objective and to use good professional judgment with all group members. From time to time, it may be difficult to abide by this dictate with some group members. We are aware of a situation in which one experienced group leader found himself so angry with a group member's repeated personal and physical attacks that he felt compelled to return the attack physically. Recognizing that these feelings violated his professional responsibility both to the group and to the disruptive client, and catching himself before he acted, the counselor immediately sought the help of a professional colleague to deal with his own anger and frustration. A less experienced counselor might not have acted so responsibly, and a malpractice action (or even criminal liability) could have resulted.

Crisis Intervention

For the purposes of this discussion, crisis intervention comes in two forms: (a) crisis intervention that involves an existing client or a new client who specifically presents for counseling because of a recent crisis and (b) crisis intervention in which there is no preexisting client relationship or an expectation of a continued treatment relationship. These two forms of crisis intervention involve somewhat different ethical and legal challenges.

Almost everything written in our book on this topic addresses the first type of crisis—situations in which the counselor has an established treatment relationship with the client or where there is the expectation of a continued professional relationship. In this context, crisis intervention is an integral part of the treatment process. Many clients begin a counseling relationship because of a crisis. Client crises often flare up during the course of treatment: Clients threaten suicide or homicide, they become the victims of crimes or are involved in violent accidents, they are arrested or overdose on drugs, they experience trauma or reexperience the memory of traumas, they suffer traumatic losses (breakup of a marriage, death of a loved one, loss of employment, etc.), and they experience psychotic breaks or other deeply troubling mental health situations. Counselors respond to these types of crises every day. Most legal and ethical dilemmas revolve around how the counselor responds to crises.

The second type of crisis intervention, in which there is no preexisting treatment relationship and no expectation of a treatment relationship with the individual, presents different legal and ethical challenges. In its purest form, this type of crisis intervention is not counseling or psychotherapy. The single purpose of crisis intervention in this context is to address the immediate need of a person in such a way that the person can become stabilized and self-directing. In this context, crisis intervention might involve giving a person a bottle of water or directing him or her to a facility that offers food, clothing, or shelter. It might also involve sitting on a pile of rubble and listening as the person tells the story of how he or she escaped the ravages of the tornado that leveled his or her neighborhood. In a completely different way, crisis intervention might include holding the hand of a victim of sexual assault while she sobs away the terror that has engulfed her. Counselors are more frequently being asked to volunteer as crisis intervention workers. The American Red Cross and other disaster response organizations provide extensive training to mental health professionals who want to volunteer for crisis duty. Tragic events, both natural disasters (hurricanes, tornadoes, floods, fires, and earthquakes) as well as man-made traumas (school and workplace shootings, hostage situations, and terrorism), have placed mental health professionals in the forefront of crisis intervention activities.

Counselors in these types of crisis situations typically have no relationship with the person prior to the crisis and likely will have no future contact with the person once the victim has stabilized. Although there is some state law variation, the general legal principle that applies to people in a rescue mode is this: *A person is responsible for harm to another only if the failure to exercise reasonable care increases the risk of harm to another.* The counselor offers to listen to the distressed person, provides words of encouragement or suggestions, and has a duty to use his or her training and skill to assist the distressed individual until therapy or medical treatment can be provided. In this setting, the counselor is not responsible for knowing the history or problems of the person being counseled that are not revealed during the crisis intervention. Consequently, the counselor ordinarily will be subject to a negligence suit *only if* the counselor fails to use reasonable care in counseling *and* that failure increases the risk of harm to the person. Even if the counselor did not use reasonable care, he or she usually will not be held liable for negligence unless that failure *also* increased the risk of harm or left the person in a worse position than before the intervention.

It should be noted that the term *client* has not been used to describe the person being counseled in crisis intervention because that term denotes the existence of a special professional relationship between the crisis intervention counselor and the individual in need of assistance. If such a relationship exists, however, the counselor may be held to the same standard of care described previously for the counselor–client relationship. For example, if a Louisiana-based counselor volunteered to do crisis management after Hurricane Katrina, his or her liability risk would be quite small. If the person requiring services had been an active client of the counselor's before the hurricane, the counselor might have a greater duty because the preexisting professional relationship would be presumed to have provided the counselor with the knowledge required to render a higher level of assistance.

Repressed or False Memory

In the mid-1990s, the practice of reviving repressed memories of child sexual abuse led to a number of lawsuits against mental health professionals. The concern was that therapists were using hypnosis, guided imagery, or drugs (e.g., sodium amytal) to induce or recover memories of abuse for which there was no corroborating evidence. One jury in Minnesota reportedly awarded more than $2.6 million to a woman who claimed she was injured by false memories of abuse induced after her psychiatrist told her she suffered from multiple personality disorder, probably as the result of repeated sexual abuse by relatives (ACA, 1995). Another jury in California awarded almost $500,000 in damages to a successful winery executive who sued his daughter's therapist and psychiatrist for inducing false memories of abuse in the young woman through suggestion and sodium amytal injections (*Ramona v. Ramona*, 1994). Prior to this lawsuit, Ramona had been sued by his daughter for abuse that she claimed she had repressed for many years.

Concerns about repressed memories stemmed from the increased numbers of child sexual abuse reports that could not be documented or otherwise corroborated as well as the increased number of cases that can be verified and the techniques used to reveal these memories. What is known today is that child sexual abuse is a risk factor in a variety of psychiatric disorders. Children who have been abused may try to cope with the trauma in a variety of ways, some of which may lead to a lack of conscious awareness of the abuse for some time. The memories and feelings resulting from the abuse may emerge at a later time. Questioning can influence memories, particularly in young children, and repeated questioning can lead an individual to believe in a "memory" of an event that did not occur. Furthermore, even without an initial recollection of abuse, a trusted person who suggests past abuse as a possible explanation for problems or symptoms can have significant influence (American Psychiatric Association, 1993, 2002).

Debate over repressed memory was quite lively in the 1990s. The False Memory Syndrome Foundation was established in Philadelphia and served as a resource and catalyst for litigation. Mental health provider associations responded by trying to help guide their members to navigate the complex practice issues presented by this problem. The Psychiatrists' Purchasing Group released an article in April 1994 with suggestions for managing risks when dealing with cases of recovered memories of abuse. Some of the recommendations that follow are drawn from this article:

- Be mindful of the kinds of questions you ask (e.g., if the client raises a past history of anorexia, you should avoid a barrage of questions that might suggest that you believe the client was abused as a child).
- Remain empathetic and nonjudgmental in your responses and in conversations with the client about possible memories of abuse. If the client has always remembered the abuse, document that. The real problem arises with uncovering repressed memories of abuse.
- Avoid prejudging the truth of the client's reports and statements.
- If a client raises the issue of abuse, talk frankly about the clinical uncertainty of repressed memories at the present time.
- Follow established assessment and treatment techniques.
- Do not pressure the client to believe events that may not have occurred.
- Caution the client not to break off close relationships precipitously unless there is evidence of current danger.
- If you are not specifically trained and competent in this area, consult with a supervisor or more qualified colleague, or refer the client to an experienced therapist.

In addition, you should avoid accepting, without question, the judgment or diagnosis of a prior therapist (e.g., that the client has dissociative identity disorder). Keep in mind that you may have a duty under state law to report the alleged child sexual abuse if you have a reasonable suspicion that it actually occurred. Finally, carefully document, in the client's files, the allegations, the circumstances under which the memory was revealed, the techniques you used to evaluate and assess the veracity of the memory, and the various treatment options you considered, including consultation or referral to other colleagues.

Although much of the attention given to cases involving repressed memories of abuse occurred in the 1990s, the issue still exists. The CNA and HPSO report (2014) mentioned above included a case study of a counselor claim in which a husband and wife sought treatment for marital problems; the counselor also engaged in individual treatment. The counselor used eye movement desensitization and reprocessing (EMDR, which when used correctly, is an acceptable form of treatment for trauma recovery) with the wife to assist her in recalling prior trauma. To be specific, the counselor encouraged the client to "recall" past incidents of sexual abuse and rape, despite the client's belief that such abuse had never occurred. The therapy turned into an ongoing period of sexual relations between counselor and client before turning into a lawsuit alleging multiple boundary violations, misdiagnosis, sexual misconduct, mishandling of the transference phenomenon, and abandonment. The counselor also lost his license as a result of his actions.

The issue of recovering repressed memories of abuse is also instructional for counselors in a general sense. Before jumping on the next bandwagon that comes along in the counseling field, make sure there is adequate support in the literature for the techniques you adopt. Be mindful of possible countertransference issues and your own unfinished business that may be affecting your response to the client's presenting concerns. Also, consult with colleagues; consultation is an invaluable tool in double-checking your own competence and providing evidence, if needed in a subsequent lawsuit, that you took the time to confirm acceptable practice parameters.

Supervision

Supervisors are important resources for handling issues that may arise with a counseling client. However, legal exposure can sometimes result from the supervisory relationship itself. *Supervision* is a formal process whereby a standard of practice is communicated to the counselor being supervised, and the supervising counselor has an obligation to ensure that the supervisee is providing that standard of care to his or her clients. It should not be confused with *consultation*, a process whereby one counselor seeks advice from another, but the person seeking consultation is usually free to accept or reject the consultant's advice.

In the context of supervision, a supervisor may be held legally liable for injuries to clients caused by the negligence of a supervisee if those acts occurred in the course and scope of the supervisory relationship. Courts will look to a number of factors to determine whether the supervisor should be held accountable, including the supervisor's control over the supervisee, the location and time at which the act occurred, the supervisee's motivation, and details about the negligent act (such as whether it was within the supervisee's scope of duty and whether it was foreseeable). Depending on the facts, the supervisor may well be found to be vicariously liable for the acts of the supervisee.

Most counselors agree that the process of supervision is critical to the profession's ability to deliver counseling services that meet acceptable standards of care. Nonetheless, supervising counselors should minimize their exposure to liability as they perform this service to the profession. Recognizing that supervisors can be drawn into malpractice cases because of the acts of their supervisees is the first step. Some of the steps that supervisors and supervisees must take to protect themselves and their clients include the following:

- establishing ground rules for the supervisory relationship;
- planning sufficient time for contact and discussion of cases;
- reviewing every case, not just the cases the supervisee presents;
- having access, where possible, to firsthand evidence of the supervisee's work (e.g., audio- or videotapes or live supervision);
- agreeing upon procedures for record keeping; and
- documenting any specific instructions and directives provided.

Supervisors should have some mechanism in place for determining that advice is being followed.

There are also ethical requirements regarding supervision. Supervisors must have training in supervisory methods; they must monitor and hold regular meetings with their supervisees, educate them about their clients' rights, and ensure that clients are aware of the supervisee's credentials (ACA, 2014a, Standards F.1.a., F.1.b., F.1.c., F.2.a.). The 2014 *ACA Code of Ethics* also specifies that counseling supervisors must be aware of and address the role of multicultural-ism and diversity in the supervisory relationship (Standard F.2.b.). In addition, the *Code* has greatly expanded upon the analysis of establishing boundaries between supervisors and supervisees and permitting certain potentially beneficial nonprofessional relationships with supervisees (Standard F.3.a.). Responsibilities (e.g., dealing with emergencies and termination of the supervisory relationship) are addressed (Standard F.4.), along with evaluation, remediation, and endorsement (Standard F.6.). New language in the 2014 *Code* makes it clear that students and supervisees have the same obligations to clients and have the same responsibilities to follow the *ACA Code of Ethics* as counselors (Standard F.5.a.). Because an increasing number of state licensure boards are also beginning to address the roles and responsibilities of supervisors in their regulations, counselors are advised to review their licensing regulations if they contemplate entering into supervisory relationships.

One last note relates to supervising participants in a school peer-counseling program. As in other direct supervisory programs, a supervising counselor may be held responsible for the acts of peer counselors. Be certain that all students understand the limits and scope of the program they are working within, including issues relating to confidentiality. If situations arise that are beyond their expertise, be sure that they know to report back to the supervisor immediately.

Birth Control and Abortion Counseling

At some point in their careers, most counselors who work with minors will be confronted with requests for information and ad-vice concerning birth control and abortion. Counselors employed by state welfare and family planning agencies certainly deal with such requests on a daily basis. In fact, many state welfare systems include funds for dissemination of family planning information to their clients. Sex and family life education classes are now mandated in many state school systems. Many local jurisdictions have estab-lished adolescent health clinics that are empowered to dispense birth control and family planning information to minors who seek their services. Furthermore, because of the widespread nature of sexu-ally transmitted diseases as well as AIDS and HIV infection, public service announcements on radio, on television, online, and in print media openly discuss the use of condoms and advocate safe sex. Minor children are confronted with these messages on a daily basis.

Counselors are generally free to inform clients of the availability of birth control methods without fear of legal liability and to refer clients to family planning or health clinics for more information. In a few states, however, counselors might be held accountable for providing such information to minors without the consent of their parents. The provision of birth control for adolescents remains a highly emotional issue in many communities, and parental consent may be the preferred avenue in some jurisdictions. Referral to a health clinic or physician is typically appropriate when minors request contraceptive information or advice. If the counselor decides to provide birth control information, it must be both accurate and complete, and it is important that the client fully understand the information given. Some school boards prescribe that information concerning abstinence also be provided, so it is important that counselors be informed of statutes, local regulations, and school policies in this area.

Advising clients, whether minors or adults, concerning birth control is to be distinguished from counseling such clients about abortion, particularly when the client is already pregnant. Counselors must be cautious not to impose their own views on clients in this highly emotional area and may in fact be restricted from advancing specific options if they work in certain federally funded clinics. Thus, it is critical that counselors become aware of the limits of information that may be provided.

Sexual Misconduct

Despite public condemnation by all the major mental health organizations and considerable publicity about sexual misconduct lawsuits in recent years, a large percentage of all negligence suits brought against psychiatrists, psychologists, and counselors continues to include claims of sexual misconduct (see Chapter 9). Clients who have been victims of such relationships may file ethics, administrative (licensure board), or legal complaints against their former counselors. Sometimes they file complaints in multiple venues. Insurance companies now routinely exclude coverage for sexual misconduct, limit the damages that will be paid, or pay only for the legal defense of the counselor and not for any damages that may be awarded (*St. Paul Fire & Marine Insurance Co. v. Love*, 1990; *Scottsdale Insurance Co. v. Flowers*, 2008).

Standard A.5.a. of the 2014 *ACA Code of Ethics* specifically forbids any type of sexual or romantic relationships or interactions with current clients, their romantic partners, or their family members. Furthermore, the *Code* restricts counselors from becoming involved sexually or romantically with a former client within a minimum of 5 years following termination of counseling (Standard A.5.c.). (The former minimum period was 2 years.) Even after that time, the counselor still has the obligation to put the best interests of the client first and must ensure that the relationship is not exploitative. (See Chapter 9 for a more comprehensive discussion of this issue.)

Other Civil Actions

Dissatisfied clients may also pursue legal remedies against counselors for a variety of actions outside the traditional negligence or malpractice analysis. Frequently these claims will be coupled with a cause of action for malpractice or negligence, so it is important to understand the elements of each type of action.

Illegal Search and Seizure

The potential for civil liability on the basis of illegal search and seizure usually arises in a school, hospital, or custodial setting and is thus more likely to affect counselors who practice in those types of institutions. Counselors are likely to be involved with disciplinary matters in a school or institutional setting and may be asked to search either a student or resident or that individual's room or locker storage areas. In so doing, counselors risk invading the individual's constitutionally protected rights to privacy and to freedom from unreasonable search and seizure as set forth in the Fourth Amendment.

The Fourteenth Amendment extends this constitutional guarantee to searches and seizures by federal and state government officials and is enforced by means of the exclusionary rule, whereby evidence obtained as the result of an illegal search may not be used as evidence in a court of law (*Mapp v. Ohio*, 1961). If a counselor is asked to assist the police in conducting a search, the counselor may request to see a search warrant. A search warrant may not always be required, so it is advisable for counselors to consult with legal counsel and their school administration before acting.

Individuals' privacy rights also are guaranteed by the Constitution, and any

> illegal search by a private individual is a trespass in violation of the right of privacy. . . . Any intentional invasion of, or interference with property, property rights, personal rights, or personal liberties causing injury without just cause or excuse is an actionable tort. (*Sutherland v. Kroger Co.*, 1959, pp. 723–724)

As a general rule, teachers and counselors have always been considered private persons in the jargon of search and seizure. The only professional recognized under the law was the law enforcement officer. Counselors were not liable for an alleged illegal search of a pupil or resident so long as they were motivated by reasonable cause and acted with reasonable judgment, without malice, and with the best interests of the student or resident in mind. Consequently, Fourth Amendment proscriptions generally did not apply to counselors, but they could be sued in tort for invasion of privacy unless these criteria were met.

In *New Jersey v. T.L.O.* (1985), however, the Supreme Court ruled that public school officials, including counselors, are instrumentalities of the state and are subject to the Fourth Amendment commands:

> In carrying out searches and other disciplinary functions pursuant to such policies, school officials act as representatives of the State, not merely as surrogates for the parents, and they cannot claim the parents' immunity from the strictures of the Fourth Amendment. (pp. 336–337)

Despite the fact that counselors and other public school and institutional administrators are "representatives of the State" and are therefore bound by the parameters of the Fourth Amendment, this does not mean that all searches are improper. Courts use a balancing of interests test to determine whether a search is reasonable according to the facts presented. As one court concluded, although a student "has a constitutional interest in freedom from governmental intrusion into his privacy . . . the State has an interest in educating children, and to do so, it is necessary to maintain order in and around the classroom" (*Interest of L. L.*, 1979, pp. 348–349). See also *In re Juvenile 2006-406* (2007).

The Supreme Court gave school officials broad powers to search students suspected of carrying weapons, dealing drugs, or violating other laws or school rules in the *New Jersey v. T.L.O.* case. Although the opinion adopts the position that the Fourth Amendment's prohibition on unreasonable searches and seizures applies to public school officials and that students have legitimate expectations of privacy, the Court also recognized that schools have an equally legitimate need to maintain a learning environment for all students. In order to meet this latter need, the Court ruled that the legality of a student search "should depend simply on the reasonableness, under all the circumstances, of the search" (*New Jersey v. T.L.O.*, 1985, p. 326). Whether a search is reasonable will depend on whether

> there are reasonable grounds for suspecting that the search will turn up evidence that the student has violated or is violating either the law or the rules of the school. Such a search will be permissible in its scope when the measures adopted are reasonably related to the objectives of the search and not excessively intrusive in light of the age and sex of the student and the nature of the infraction. (*New Jersey v. T.L.O.*, 1985, p. 326)

School authorities, including counselors, stand in a unique position when it comes to searching school premises. Search warrants are unnecessary to access a student's locker or dormitory room so long as the official has "reasonable grounds for suspecting" that illegal substances or items capable of undermining the order and good health of the school environment may be concealed there. Counselors are advised to avoid searches of students to the extent possible (including drug testing), but where this is not possible, counselors must be guided by a standard of reasonableness, as determined by all the facts of the case. The Washington Supreme Court ruled unconstitutional a public high school policy requiring all members of the band to submit to a search of their luggage prior to embarking on a concert trip. Although the court recognized a statistical probability that some contraband would be found, it ruled that the search was impermissible because school officials lacked any reasonable information or belief that drugs or alcohol were hidden in the students' luggage (*Kuehn v. Renton School Dist. No. 403*, 1985).

In June 1995, the U.S. Supreme Court applied a balancing-of-interests test to uphold a local school board policy involving student searches in *Vernonia School Dist. 47J v. Acton* (1995). This case involved testing all student athletes' urine samples for illegal drugs at the beginning of each sport season and randomly throughout the season. Justice Scalia wrote for the majority:

> Fourth Amendment rights, no less than First and Fourteenth Amendment rights, are different in public schools than elsewhere; the "reasonableness" inquiry cannot disregard the schools' custodial and tutelary responsibility for children. For their own good and that of their

classmates, public school children are routinely required to submit to various physical examinations, and to be vaccinated against various diseases. . . . Particularly with regard to medical examinations and procedures, therefore, "students within the school environment have a lesser expectation of privacy than members of the population generally." (*Vernonia School Dist. 47J v. Acton*, 1995, p. 357, quoting *New Jersey v. T.L.O*, 1985, p. 348)

Justice Scalia went on to explain that privacy expectations of student athletes are even less than those of other students because of the communal showering, dressing, and changing in locker rooms that is required in sports participation. Furthermore, student athletes voluntarily choose to play on a sports team, thus subjecting "themselves to a degree of regulation even higher than that imposed on students generally" (p. 648). Student athletes agree to comply with, for example, rules of conduct, dress, training hours, and minimum grade point averages, so they "have reason to expect intrusions upon normal rights and privileges, including privacy" (p. 650). The Court concluded that the drug testing was reasonable, especially in light of these facts: The tests were used to screen only for drugs and not other health conditions; the tests were reliable; results were disclosed only to a limited number of school personnel and parents; and test conditions were similar to those people typically encounter in public restrooms.

The Court further explained that the school board had an important—perhaps compelling—concern for deterring drug use among students of its schools "for whom it has undertaken a special responsibility of care and direction." In view of these circumstances, the policy of the Vernonia, Oregon, school board is reasonable and constitutional, according to the Court. However, Justice Scalia cautioned that not all suspicionless drug testing would be considered appropriate. Each case must meet the test: Is the search one that a reasonable guardian and tutor might undertake?

Counselors working in school settings should be aware that some court cases have not followed the Vernonia School District case on state constitutional grounds. For example, an Indiana appellate court refused to uphold suspicionless drug testing on the basis of its reading of the Indiana constitution (*Linke v. Northwestern School Corp.*, 2000). However in light of school violence across the country (highlighted by the 1999 Littleton, Colorado; 2007 Virginia Tech; and 2012 Newtown, Connecticut school shootings, among dozens of others in recent years), courts may be more willing to give schools latitude in conducting searches in order to preserve student safety. Whereas locker searches are generally upheld when there is reasonable suspicion of harmful contraband, strip searches are usually considered highly invasive and may not pass legal scrutiny (Darden, 2006). School counselors should consult local legal counsel if they are asked to participate in any search, seizure, or drug testing activity.

Defamation

A counselor spreads false rumors about the unprofessional conduct of another therapist in the community. A second counselor hears from a third party that her client is abusing drugs, and she calls the client's employer to discuss the situation without first speaking with the client. Both counselors are inviting lawsuits that are based on charges of defamation.

The tort action called *defamation* embodies the public policy that each person should be free to enjoy his or her reputation unimpaired by false attacks, except in certain cases where a paramount public interest dictates that individuals be free to write or speak without fear of civil liability. Violations of this right form the basis for the action, which turns on whether the communication or publication tends, or is reasonably calculated, to cause harm to the reputation of another. In early common law this action was broken down into two separate actions: *slander*, a spoken or uttered word that defames a person, and *libel*, a defamatory writing. For most purposes today, the two forms are treated as one action.

The key elements of a defamation suit brought by a private person are as follows:

1. A false statement is presented as fact concerning another person or entity (typically, such statement exposes the defamed person to hatred, ridicule, contempt, or pecuniary loss).
2. The information must have been published or communicated to someone other than the defamed person.
3. The person making the statement must have intended harm, or at least have been negligent.
4. The defamed person must have suffered some harm, loss, or injury as a result of the defamatory communication. (http://www.law.cornell.edu/wex/defamation)

In addition to obvious injuries, such as loss of a job, honor, or award, damages for defamation may also be based on mental suffering and loss of reputation. Some states continue to recognize the common law action for slander in which a communication may be actionable if it

- imputes to another the commission of a serious crime;
- imputes that someone has a loathsome disease;
- imputes that a woman is unchaste; or
- adversely affects someone's business, trade, or profession.

Counselors may be exposed to liability for defamation in the publication of records, in letters of reference or recommendation, or in loose talk that may be untrue or damaging to the client as revealed to a third party. To avoid this, limits must be placed on written or verbal statements about clients. The same is true of any online comments or postings (see Chapter 7). If the client can be identified from information provided in a conversation or in writing, even though the name is carefully withheld, the counselor may become the subject of a lawsuit as a result of that indiscretion.

The major defense to a defamation action is the truth of the statement or information communicated to the third party. In many states this is an absolute defense, just as in common law, although some states also require the statement to have been made in good faith and for a legitimate purpose. Absent some legitimate professional purpose, counselors who make even truthful statements about clients in those states could find themselves subjected to a defamation suit, just as for any other rumors or gossip.

The law also recognizes that in some situations the interests of the immediate participants or of society at large are so great that important, bona fide communications should be permitted freely without fear of resulting lawsuits. Such privileges are granted by statute in almost all states for the proper discharge of official duties and are to be distinguished from the privileged communications discussed in Chapter 5 concerning confidentiality. In that discussion, privilege is analyzed as a protection from revealing client confidences should a counselor be called to testify in court. This is a right that belongs to the client and binds the counselor to silence. When the term *privilege* is used in connection with defamation actions, it describes a privilege *to communicate*, which protects the counselor against money-damage defamation suits. The two privileges are not analogous.

Two types of communications are protected from defamation actions: those that are absolutely privileged and those that are qualifiedly privileged. *Absolute privilege* is based on the concept that the public interest in unimpeded communication in certain cases completely outweighs society's concern for an individual's reputation. Thus, members of the legislature, judges, jurors, lawyers, and witnesses may speak freely in the exercise of their official functions without fear of civil suit.

Qualified privilege exists in situations where society's interest in unhampered communication is conditionally limited by the general mores as to what is fair and reasonable. Stated another way, on the basis of their positions, certain individuals have a right to receive confidential reports or information that is not appropriate for publication to society at large. Generally, any statement made in a reasonable manner by one who is carrying out duties for a legitimate purpose will be protected by the qualified privilege. Counselors are frequently called upon in the course of their professional duties to make statements concerning clients to other people who have a corresponding legal duty or interest in receiving that information. For example, a prospective employer may request information about the client in the course of conducting a security background investigation. Counselors may need to notify a social service agency of problems in a family to ensure the safety of a client. So long as such communications are made in good faith, with appropriate permissions or releases from the clients where needed; express only facts as known to the counselor; and are made only to persons having a proper interest in receiving the information, they will usually be protected.

Counselors must be cautious whenever they disclose client information to others. If false information is ever transmitted to a third party, corrections should be made as quickly as possible. Counselors who act in a professional manner and are cautious about client information communicated to third parties will generally be protected from defamation actions by the qualified privilege. Here again, it is important to follow the ethics guidelines and obtain clear instructions and releases from clients, preferably in writing, detailing the information to be released. In addition, this discussion is applicable to defamatory statements made by counselors about their colleagues.

Invasion of Privacy

Despite the truthfulness of a defamatory statement and the qualified immunity granted in the counseling situation, a counselor may still be held liable in an action for invasion of privacy if derogatory information is communicated to a third party who has no need or privilege to receive it. The action is based upon undue interference in the affairs of an individual through exposure or communication of his or her private affairs. The injury may result from truthful, but damaging, publications, and the person bringing the suit need not prove that he or she has suffered any special injuries. In recent years, concern about dissemination of computer records containing personal and financial information has grown because of the potential for serious harm resulting from erroneous material. The problem is no less severe in the context of educational records and testing or in client records maintained in clinical practice. Counselors working in educational institutions should be thoroughly familiar with the requirements of FERPA (1974, or the Buckley Amendment), discussed in Chapter 5 and should take care to protect the student and family rights as set forth in the law.

Counselors employed in all fields are subject to potential liability for invasion of privacy (a) if they administer educational or psychological tests without first fully informing the client of the criteria to be used, what skills or factors the test is designed to measure, and the possible uses of the test results; or (b) if they fail to explain test results. Some state laws now require testing agencies to provide various notices to test subjects and to disclose fully the factors outlined. The 2014 *ACA Code of Ethics* also admonishes counselors to obtain informed consent from clients prior to any assessment and further holds counselors responsible for using and interpreting competently any tests administered and for releasing information only upon consent of the client, and then only to professionals who can competently interpret the results (Standards E.2., E.3., E.4.). Counselors should keep these criteria in mind when conducting testing and protect the written records of that testing accordingly.

The confidentiality of records also poses a problem for counselors because of concerns about invasion of privacy. The questions as to what should be included in a client or student record, and who might have access to that record, can generally be answered by the rules concerning defamation. First, reasonable care must be taken to ensure that the contents of records are accurate. A counselor who makes an entry designed to injure the client would run a serious risk of liability, even if the information were true. As noted, the reckless disregard of the rights of another can be sufficient to destroy the qualified privilege counselors enjoy in this area. Entering misleading or false information, or failing to make adequate corrections of such information, could meet this lower threshold definition of malice.

Second, the contents of records should be made known only to those who have a legitimate interest in them (e.g., parents, professional colleagues, prospective employers) as defined by statute or regulation, or as established by a written authorization to release of information signed by the client or a parent of a minor client. These general rules are, of course, subject to more specific regulations or laws that may govern records in a particular state institution, agency, or school system. Counselors generally will not be held liable in a suit for invasion of privacy if required by law to disclose information or if the disclosure was not malicious and was made to serve certain overriding competing public interests, such as following health regulations, reporting cases of abuse, or protecting a potential victim.

Breach of Contract

Counselors have certain duties arising from either express or implied contracts with clients. Express contracts usually are in writing and are signed by the parties, and they spell out the rights and responsibilities of each. Express contracts may be made orally and are just as binding on the parties, although proving the specific terms of the agreement may be difficult at some later time.

Implied contracts arise either through the relationship of the parties or as a result of actions of the parties that cause them to respond in a certain way or rely on each other. If a client comes to the counselor's office for a session each week at the same time and is charged a fee for services, which is paid, the parties may be held to have agreed to a contract that includes those terms. All these aspects of the relationship form the basis of the contract with the client, even though it is not expressly written. Should the counselor, absent some justification, fail to uphold his or her end of the bargain under the contract, the client can hold the counselor responsible for breaching the contract. Likewise, if a counselor breaches confidentiality, this may be viewed as breaching an implied contract that is based on the counselor's professional disclosure statement and ethics code.

Courts also may view professional advertising as terms of an express or implied contract with clients. For example, a firm or practice that advertises in a directory that its owners or employees are *certified*, *licensed*, *bonded*, or the like will be held to fulfill those terms or be found in breach of contract. In a similar manner, holding oneself out in advertising or client information brochures as an expert in any area also will bring increased responsibilities. Many states regulate the content of professional advertising in their licensing statutes, restricting the use of counseling titles such as *professional counselor*. Along this line, deceptive or misleading advertising may simultaneously give rise to an action for violation of state deceptive or fraudulent advertising statutes.

Counselors should exercise care in all aspects of a client relationship, but it is especially important to examine critically the whole spectrum of items that may form the basis of any contract with clients, whether express or implied. Written agreements detailing such items as the number and timing of sessions, fees, and payment terms will help to protect counselors (see the discussion of informed consent in Chapter 2). A counselor should never contract with a client concerning specific results or outcome of treatment, which may prove impossible to achieve.

Copyright Infringement

Original works that are published as articles, books, lectures, curricula, and the like are considered the intellectual property of their creators and are subject to the protection of federal and international copyright laws. This protection gives the copyright holder the exclusive right to print, publish, or otherwise reproduce the work as well as to display and distribute copies, whether for free or for sale. Using protected material without permission is considered an infringement of the author's or publisher's rights and carries civil and criminal penalties.

Writers other than the original author may use copyrighted material properly in their own work as long as the fair use provisions of the Copyright Act of 1976 are followed, or if permission is secured from the copyright holder. The act sets out four factors to consider in determining *fair use*: (a) whether the material is used for commercial benefit or for nonprofit educational purposes, (b) the medium of the work created, (c) how much of the work is used, and (d) the effect of using the work on the market and salability of the new work. With this in mind, quoting 5 or 10 lines from a research report in support of your findings in a clinical study, with proper attribution to the author, probably falls within the parameters of fair use. Even in that case it is prudent to request permission in advance. However, duplicating copies of an entire course syllabus, research study, or article for distribution to clients or students would infringe on the copyright protection and should not be done.

The widespread use of computers has proved of immeasurable benefit to counselors and administrators worldwide in recent years. Many agencies and institutions now commonly preserve counseling records and data on computer databases and use computers to facilitate client assessment and research. With the efficiency of this wonderful tool, however, a host of concerns have developed of which counselors should be aware. Many of these have been addressed in the 2014 *ACA Code of Ethics* and other professional ethics codes and relate, in large part, to the misuse of information or assessment tools. Other concerns relate to client misconceptions about computer assessment, counselor competence and training, accuracy of computer-based assessment programs, and the validity of test results.

Another important consideration for counselors who use computers for record keeping and testing is the application of federal copyright laws and licensing agreements. Most adults are aware of the general proscriptions against plagiarism and the protection for written and creative works offered by copyright laws. Such protections also extend to computer operating programs and applications software in word processing, databases, assessment tools, and reporting. Applications software includes testing materials, scoring keys, normative tables, and report forms, according to the Eighth Circuit Court of Appeals. In *Applied Innovations, Inc. v. Regents of the University of Minnesota* (1989), the court ruled that the development, reproduction, marketing, and distribution of software for scoring the Minnesota Multiphasic Personality Inventory infringed upon the University of Minnesota's copyright of the test because it included copyrighted portions of the instrument. Obviously not all counselors are engaged in developing such scoring software, but this proscription applies to users of such programs as well.

It should be pointed out that borrowing computer programs and using bootlegged computer programs are infringements on the rights of copyright holders and compromise the integrity of testing instruments. Such actions also deprive test and software creators of revenue to which they are legally entitled, and perhaps more important they could lead to the promulgation of defective products that could adversely affect client treatment. Counselors are urged to comply with copyright laws and licensing agreements when they purchase computer software, just as they exercise care to comply with copyright laws in written or other materials.

Insurance Fraud

Insurance fraud is a broad term that involves obtaining money from an insurance company by lying, cheating, or deceit. Although insurance companies may bring civil suits against service providers who misrepresent or misstate services in order to receive insurance reimbursement, insurance fraud may also be pursued by state licensing agencies and through criminal prosecution. There are a variety of federal and state laws designed to address fraud and abuse by medical and mental health providers who see clients in programs such as Medicaid. All mental health service providers need to understand the specific provisions of insurance programs through which they seek payments and should exercise care in complying with those provisions. Although this is a complex area, there are some specific practice recommendations to minimize the risk of liability for counselors.

First, as a counselor, you must render mental health diagnoses only if you are qualified and competent to render them under state licensing statutes. Report diagnosis codes accurately, and do not be persuaded to use an improper code to gain coverage. Be sure your client understands the full implications of any diagnosis you make and that once it is submitted to an insurance company it will become a part of the client's permanent health record.

Some insurance policies cover only individual psychotherapy sessions or cover individual sessions at a higher copayment rate than conjoint, marital, or family counseling. Be sure to investigate the terms of the particular policy your client is covered under and to use the appropriate codes for third-party billing, even though reimbursement may be limited or denied.

In submitting insurance claims, be careful to state the number of and length of client visits accurately. Do not assume that an insurance company will view two half-hour appointments in 1 week as equivalent to a single 1-hour appointment, particularly where the insurance company's responsibility for coverage is limited to one visit per week. Keep complete and accurate records of visits, and bill only for those you document.

The person who provides treatment must usually be the one to sign the insurance claim, even though consultants or supervisors may have been involved with the case. It is appropriate to note the names of supervisors or consultants along with the name of the provider, but these should be clearly identified. This identification is especially important where an insurance policy covers therapy only when provided by a licensed psychiatrist, psychologist, or mental health counselor. Such services may not be reimbursed if provided by an intern or an unlicensed counselor, even though they may be working under the supervision of a licensed practitioner. Furthermore, charging insurance companies for missed appointments, or routinely setting lower fees or waiving copayments for clients without insurance coverage may be viewed as insurance fraud.

Counselors who engage in arrangements in which one therapist pays another a certain percentage of fees may be subject to a number of complex federal and state "fraud and abuse" laws that prohibit arrangements that may be viewed as "kickbacks"; also, they may run afoul of laws and ethics codes prohibiting fee splitting. (See Chapter 11 for a more comprehensive discussion of this topic as well as false claims liability.) As counselors see more clients insured through Medicaid and Tricare (and possibly Medicare in the future), the consequences of failing to properly draft employment, independent contractor, and space rental agreements become real. Consequences include civil fines, criminal penalties, and possible loss or restriction of licensure. Yet one more reason to seek specific legal advice is that many states have enacted laws that mirror, or even go beyond, the scope of the federal laws prohibiting fraud and abuse.

Other Criminal Actions

In addition to criminal insurance fraud, counselors may be vulnerable to other criminal charges. Sometimes such charges arise when counselors try to protect clients who are involved in criminal activity; unfortunately, such counselors may end up being considered accessories to the clients' crimes. At other times, when counselors cross boundaries with minor clients, they may be prosecuted for contributing to the delinquency of minors.

Accessory to a Crime

Although counselors are honor bound to protect the integrity and promote the welfare of their clients, they also have an obligation to society at large that may override their duty to an individual client. The law makes it clear that any person who advises or encourages the commission of a crime may be charged as an accessory to the crime, even though the person took no active part in its commission.

This is called *accessory before the fact*, and an individual convicted of such activity faces criminal penalties. The elements of the offense in many states include the following: (a) evidence exists that the defendant in some way contributed to the crime by aiding or advising the alleged perpetrator, (b) the defendant was not present when the crime was committed, and (c) the alleged perpetrator is convicted of the crime or admits to it (*State v. Woods*, 1982). (Some states have somewhat different definitions of the crime. See, e.g., *Marshall v. Commonwealth*, 2012.)

However, merely concealing knowledge that a felony (i.e., a serious crime, such as murder, rape, or burglary) is to be committed does not make the party concealing it an accessory before the fact. Thus, a counselor who learns from a client during counseling that a crime is to be committed may not always be obligated to reveal that knowledge to authorities, but counselors must be cautious in this gray area. Particularly in view of the *Tarasoff* decision (see Chapter 6), counselors must reach a balance between protecting the confidential communications of a client and the need to preserve the safety and well-being of society. Although there is no one hard-and-fast rule to follow across the country, you may have a duty to act if you believe a client is about to commit a crime that would threaten the safety, health, or well-being of others. This is an active duty that may extend from attempting to discourage your client to contacting local law enforcement authorities, depending on the circumstances of the case and the law in your state.

A person who assists or aids a felon after a crime has been committed, knowing that the crime has been committed, may be similarly charged as an *accessory after the fact*. Such a person is generally defined as "one who, knowing that a felony has been committed by another, receives, relieves, comforts, or assists the felon, or in any manner aids him [or her] to escape arrest or punishment" (*Criminal Law*, 21 Am. Jur. 2d §174). Three elements must be met:

1. A felony must have already been committed.
2. The person charged as an accessory must have knowledge that the person he or she is assisting committed the felony.
3. The accessory must harbor or assist the felon, intending to shield the felon from the law.

Evidence that a person helped to hide a felon, loaned the felon money, gave advice to the felon, provided goods to the felon, offered transportation to the felon, blocked the path of pursuers, or gave false information tending to mislead authorities has been held sufficient to sustain a conviction as an accessory after the fact. It is inaccurate, however, to say that *any* affirmative assistance or relief automatically results in charges that one has been an accessory. Even those acts just enumerated have not always been sufficient to justify conviction when there is no evidence that assistance was provided with the intention of harboring or assisting the felon.

Contributing to the Delinquency of a Minor

Although contributing to the delinquency of a minor is of primary concern to school counselors and those who work with families and children, others should be aware of the variety of acts that can trigger the offense. The majority of prosecutions for contributing to the delinquency of minors pertain to people who patently attempt to subvert the morals of a juvenile. Even where such acts are unintentional, however, a counselor may not escape liability.

Contributing to the delinquency of a minor is not a common law offense. Unfortunately, not all state legislatures have defined the specific conduct that constitutes the crime, and many jurisdictions leave it to the jury to determine whether a defendant's conduct was criminal.[1] A broad definition of the offense might include any actions that tend to injure the health, morals, or welfare of juveniles or that encourage juveniles to participate in such actions. There is no certainty as to what constitutes this conduct from state to state.

State courts also are divided on the question of intent. The traditional view is that a guilty intent, or mens rea, is a necessary element of the offense, but some states do not require mens rea. In these latter states, the danger of a counselor inadvertently crossing the boundary of acceptable conduct is greatest. Most counselors would never deliberately do or encourage any act that would harm a minor. It is the inadvertent act—committed in the mistaken belief that it is legal and, more important, that it is in the best interest of the client—that causes concern. It is not possible in this book to analyze the laws of each state, so to avoid such liability counselors must research the law in the state or states in which they practice, seek advice from local counsel, and keep abreast of any changes in the statutes or cases that may occur.

---

[1]See "Contributing to Delinquency" (1970) for an in-depth study of the offense.

Summary

Counselors are not expected to "play lawyer." However, it is important that every counselor take active steps to become his or her own risk manager. In short, risk management is a method for identifying potential areas of risk and taking steps to address those areas of vulnerability. In Appendix B, we offer strategies applicable to most counseling practice settings. These strategies are designed to help reduce the risk of a lawsuit, licensure complaint, or ethics investigation or to allow you to respond appropriately in the event of an adverse action.

Chapter 5

Confidentiality, Privilege, and HIPAA Privacy

The effectiveness of the counselor–client relationship depends upon the level of trust between the parties. Therapeutic trust can be established only if clients believe that their communications with the counselor will be protected under the principles of confidentiality, privilege, and privacy. Although these terms are often used interchangeably, it is helpful to highlight the different nuances of these three terms in order to come to a full understanding of the counselor's obligations to protect client information. This chapter begins with a description of these terms and then discusses the myriad of issues that arise in counseling practices related to confidentiality and privilege. It also addresses some of the new HITECH (2009, as amended by 2013 Omnibus Rule) provisions that expand many counselors' potential obligations under HIPAA.

Confidentiality

Confidentiality refers to the ethical duty of counselors to protect the private communications of their clients. (For details, see ACA, 2014a, Section B.) The term also has legal implications that flow from the counselor's legal duty. A counselor may be sued for failure to protect a client's confidences unless the counselor is acting pursuant to an exception recognized by law (e.g., written authorization by the client, threat of imminent harm by the client against self or others, release of information required by child or elder abuse reporting laws, or as otherwise compelled by law).

> *Confidentiality* is the counselor's ethical duty to protect private client communication.

As part of the informed consent process, both at the initiation of counseling and throughout the relationship, counselors should inform clients of their right to expect confidentiality and the limits of confidentiality (ACA, 2014a, Standards B.1.b. and B.1.d.). Counselors can explain to clients that they are bound by the *ACA Code of Ethics*, which states that "counselors respect the privacy of prospective and current clients" (Standard B.1.b.) and "disclose information only with appropriate consent or with sound legal or ethical justification" (Standard B.1.c.). Clients should understand how the counselor will share information with treatment team members, subordinates, supervisors, and other professionals (Standards B.3.a., B.3.b., D.1.e., F.1.c.).

Counselors also have an obligation to maintain an awareness and sensitivity regarding different cultural meanings of confidentiality and views on disclosure that may be different from those of the counselor (Standard B.1.a.). This does not mean that counselors should disregard ethical or legal considerations of confidentiality but that they should, in the spirit of collaborative relationships, have ongoing dialogue with their clients about how, when, and with whom information will be shared.

Privileged Communication

Privilege is a legal term and refers to the protection of confidential communications between two parties. In most states, counselor–client communications are protected from disclosure in the context of certain legal and administrative proceedings, similar to the way in which attorney–client and doctor–patient communications are protected. In other words, the privilege applies when the counselor is called as a witness in a court of law or administrative agency hearing. It is important to note that the privilege usually belongs to the client (who is the holder of the privilege), yet the counselor may be charged with the responsibility of upholding the privilege. The concept of privilege has its roots in English common law. Today, privilege laws protecting counselor–client communications are typically found in evidence codes or counselor licensure laws.

For the privilege to apply, the communication must have been made in confidence, with the indicated desire that it remain so. This desire need not be explicitly stated; a simple action such as closing the office door so that a conversation can remain private indicates the desire for privacy. The communication generally must not be made in the presence or hearing of third persons; if it is, the privilege may be considered waived. In some jurisdictions, the presence of certain third parties does not cause the privilege to be waived. For example, the presence of a spouse in marital therapy or the presence of a parent, interpreter, or another therapist involved with the client does not always invalidate the privilege.

> *Privilege* is the protection of confidential communications between two parties in the context of a judicial setting.

There are exceptions to the privilege in many states because lawmakers sometimes find that the interests of justice are better served by allowing access to private health information in order to correctly resolve the issues in litigation. For instance, the privilege may be waived when the client puts his or her emotional condition into issue in a lawsuit or when civil commitment proceedings are commenced against a person who is mentally ill and presents a danger to self or others. Privilege is considered waived when the client initiates a malpractice action or licensure board proceeding against the counselor. In a similar manner, a defendant who claims insanity as a defense in a criminal case cannot also claim the physician–patient or counselor–client privilege and withhold evidence of his or her condition, because it is relevant to the defense of insanity. In addition, some courts have interpreted their states' privilege laws to permit otherwise privileged information to be revealed in the context of child custody or abuse litigation. This use of privileged information is permissible because the public policy of protecting children may be deemed greater than the policy reasons for protecting counselor–client communications. Some state courts do not recognize the concept of privilege at all in criminal cases. It is important for practicing counselors to become knowledgeable of the privilege laws in the states in which they practice.

Judges are usually reluctant to expand the privilege in the absence of state legislation. Thus, in states where the counselor–client relationship is not expressly recognized by statute as privileged, a counselor could be required to testify concerning information received from a client. However, the counselor's own thoughts and impressions, or the contents of conversation in a counseling session, may still be protected if they meet the definition of *psychotherapy notes* under HIPAA or *personal notes* under the laws of some states. (See the discussion of HIPAA in the next section.) Federal courts have more flexibility in recognizing privileged communications within the scope of the Federal Rules of Evidence and Criminal Procedure.

The case of *Jaffee v. Redmond* (1996) was the first U.S. Supreme Court case to definitively uphold the concept of a psychotherapist–patient privilege in the federal court system. In this case, a policewoman sought counseling from a licensed clinical social worker after she fatally shot a suspect during a stabbing incident at an apartment complex. The family of the deceased suspect sued the police officer, the police department, and the village, alleging use of deadly force in violation of the suspect's civil rights. In the course of discovery before the trial, the plaintiffs (family of the deceased suspect) learned that the policewoman had been in counseling and sought to compel the social worker to testify at the trial and to turn over her notes and records on her sessions with the policewoman.

The trial court ruled that there is no privilege between a social worker and client, but the policewoman refused to grant a waiver of her rights and the social worker refused to reveal the substance of the counseling sessions. As a result, the judge told jurors that they could assume the information withheld would have been unfavorable to the policewoman, and the jury awarded $545,000 to the suspect's family.

The case ultimately was presented before the U.S. Supreme Court, which carefully looked at the common law principles underlying testimonial privileges and specifically delved into the policy behind Rule 501 of the Federal Rules of Evidence. The Court addressed the question of "whether a privilege protecting confidential communications between a psychotherapist and her patient 'promotes sufficiently important interests to outweigh the need for probative evidence'" (p. 9). The Supreme Court answered this affirmatively on the basis of both "reason and experience" (p. 10). The resulting decision thus confirmed the existence of a psychotherapist–client privilege in federal court proceedings.

However, the privilege in federal courts is not absolute; for example, some federal courts following *Jaffee* have held that the privilege is waived when the patient puts his emotional condition into issue. For instance, see *Schoffstall v. Henderson* (2000) and *Wetzel v. Brown* (2014); also see Speaker ex rel. *Speaker v. County of San Bernardino*

(2000). However, at least one federal court has found allegations of "garden variety emotional distress" will not serve to waive privilege (*Dochniak v. Dominium Management Servs., Inc.*, 2006).

Does *Jaffee* apply to counselors as well as social workers and other mental health professionals? This question was answered by the federal Court of Appeals for the Ninth Circuit in the case of *Oleszko v. State Compensation Insurance Fund* (2001). This court ruled that communications between an unlicensed EAP counselor and a client are protected from compelled disclosure, following the federal psychotherapist–patient privilege established in *Jaffee*.

It is important for counselors to realize that the *Jaffee* and *Oleszko* decisions apply to federal court cases. Most legal disputes are heard in state courts, so the state counselor–client or psychotherapist–patient privilege would apply. As a counselor, what should you do if you are called to testify in court in a state that does not expressly recognize the counselor–client privilege? You should apprise the court of whether you are a licensed professional counselor (or other licensed professional). You should also explain that you are bound by a code of ethics that requires respect for the client's right to privacy and that testifying would violate professional obligations, if you have not been given a release by your client to testify. Although the decisions in *Jaffee* and *Oleszko* would not necessarily apply in state court, the judge may be willing to look at the policy underpinnings of those cases. You might suggest that your client's attorney attempt to obtain a ruling from the court on the applicability of the privilege; this is usually done in advance by a motion or at trial by a direct request to the judge.

Privacy and HIPAA

Privacy refers to the basic right of a person to be left alone and to control his or her personal information. The term *privacy* is the new buzzword in the health care arena in recent years as a result of the enactment of HIPAA, which called for a variety of standards addressing transactions and code sets, unique identifiers, privacy, and security. The term *privacy* is now often used interchangeably with the word *confidentiality*. The HIPAA Privacy Rule (2013, as amended), which is most pertinent to this chapter, was promulgated on the federal level to provide a uniform level of protection that was previously nonexistent because of a patchwork of state laws. This Rule came about as a result of concern that transmission of health care information through the Internet and other electronic means could lead to widespread gaps in protection of patient and client confidentiality. The HIPAA Privacy Rule, in its final form, applies to both paper and electronic transmissions of protected health information (PHI) by *covered entities* (which are explained in this section). The HIPAA Security Rule (2013, as amended) dovetails with the HIPAA Privacy Rule and requires technical, administrative, and physical safeguards to protect security of PHI in electronic form.

> *Privacy* is the basic right of a person to be left alone and to control his or her personal information.

As a counselor or other mental health provider, the first thing that you must determine is whether you are considered a covered entity under HIPAA. The test is whether you transmit any PHI in electronic form in connection with any transactions for which the Secretary of Health and Human Services has adopted a standard. These transactions include such things as health care claims, health plan enrollment and eligibility, and coordination of benefits. For example, if you submit a claim electronically (even if you do so only one time) or use a billing service to do this on your behalf, you are likely to be considered a covered entity who must then comply with all applicable HIPAA regulations. If you do not file for any insurance reimbursement or conduct any electronic transactions, you are probably not a covered entity. However, even if you do not technically fall under HIPAA, you should realize that the privacy standards for maintaining and releasing records and allowing client access to records are likely to be influenced over the next several decades by HIPAA requirements, which are mandatory for most health care providers. In fact, a post-HIPAA decision from a North Carolina appellate court upheld the concept that HIPAA may influence the standard of care in a mental health breach of confidentiality suit, even though HIPAA does not, by itself, create a legal private cause of action against the defendant health care provider (*Acosta v. Byrum*, 2006).

Furthermore, if you are not technically a HIPAA "covered entity," it is crucial that you follow any confidentiality and privacy laws that may apply to you at the state level. If you are a school counselor, you may be obligated to comply with FERPA (1974, also known as the Buckley Amendment; see "Counseling Minors"), implementing regulations under FERPA and applicable school policy.

If you determine that you are a covered entity under HIPAA, what are some of the things you must do? First, you should familiarize yourself with the various HIPAA resources that may be available to help you navigate the HIPAA rules. Next, you must familiarize yourself with the standards and compliance deadlines. The compliance deadline for the HIPAA Privacy Standard was April 14, 2003. If you discover that you are a covered entity but are not yet compliant, you must appoint a privacy officer. This may be you (if you are a solo practitioner) or your office manager (if you are part of a small-group practice).

> For help in assessing whether you are a covered entity under HIPAA, visit the website for the Centers for Medicare and Medicaid Services (2013) at http://www.cms. gov/Regulations-and-Guidance/HIPAA-Administrative-Simplification/HIPAAGenInfo/AreYouaCoveredEntity.html

Next, you should gather all policies and documents and evaluate them to see if they are HIPAA compliant. Policies regarding client access to records, amendment of records, and accounting of disclosures are mandatory. Authorization forms and informed consent forms may need to be revised. Why is it so important that counselors take the time to truly reflect on what their privacy policies should be? Take the example of four Massachusetts hospitals that transferred confidential patient records to physicians, who, in turn, turned them over to a billing company; these records were found by a *Boston Globe* reporter in the local dump (Kowalczyk, 2010). Proper destruction of records would have involved shredding or incineration. Because the parties involved did not follow policies dictating responsibility for, method of, and training of the work force effectuating the destruction of the records, the public had access to what were, in fact, confidential records.

In addition to creating thoughtful policies and procedures and training the office staff on your established privacy practices, you also must develop a Notice of Privacy Practices and disseminate it to clients. Furthermore, you will need to enter into contracts with your "business associates" (e.g., billing service, attorney, or accountant with whom you share PHI; see U.S. Department of Health and Human Services, Office for Civil Rights [OCR], 2013). Business associate contracts are designed to protect sensitive information that must be shared with people other than counselors or their own HIPAA-trained employees. In the preceding example, if the hospitals and physicians had used appropriate training and business associate contracts with the billing company, perhaps a breach of privacy could have been averted.

Even if you are not technically a covered entity, some of HIPAA's requirements may be good practices for you to adopt for risk management purposes. For example, all counselors should train their office staff, if any, on the rules of confidentiality and should have policies on the release of records and clients' rights to access records. It's not advisable to adopt another counselor's Notice of Privacy Practices verbatim if you are not a covered entity. It is better to develop such a notice as part of your informed consent and explain why you are not a covered entity. You should also describe what practices you follow to preserve client confidentiality and what limits of confidentiality the client can expect.

Another issue that requires careful thought is whether to keep separate psychotherapy notes, which are defined by the HIPAA Privacy Rule as follows:

> notes recorded (in any medium) by a health care provider who is a mental health professional documenting or analyzing the contents of conversation during a private counseling session or a group, joint, or family counseling session and that are separated from the rest of the individual's medical record. (45 C.F.R. § 164.501, 2014)

The definition excludes items such as counseling start and stop times, diagnosis, functional status, treatment plan, symptoms, prognosis, and progress to date. The HIPAA Privacy Rule mandates obtaining a specific authorization to release psychotherapy notes. Although it may take extra work to separate these psychotherapy notes from the official record, counselors should carefully consider whether it might help protect the privacy of their clients. Maintenance of separate psychotherapy notes is not required by the HIPAA Privacy Rule, but some clients may develop an expectation that their records and private communications will be protected to the fullest extent allowed by law. (See Chapter 10 for more information.) In addition, counselors who keep separate psychotherapy notes on children may be able to further protect some of the most private information disclosed by the child during therapy sessions. For further information, see the federal government's mental health guidance document on sharing mental health information (U.S. Department of Health and Human Services, OCR, 2014e).

The issue of whether to maintain separate psychotherapy notes is further complicated by mental health laws in some jurisdictions (e.g., Maryland, the District of Columbia, New York, and Illinois) that specifically protect personal notes. These laws have definitions that differ slightly from the HIPAA definition of psychotherapy notes. Furthermore, whether state or federal law will apply depends on which law is more stringent or provides greater protection of the client's rights. HIPAA provides what is called a *floor level of privacy* but does not preempt, or supersede, state laws that provide a greater level of privacy protection to clients. The bottom line is that the decision of whether to keep separate psychotherapy notes or personal notes should be made after carefully consulting with colleagues and local legal counsel.

HITECH Changes to HIPAA

Post-HIPAA regulatory activity hit new heights in 2009 with passage of the HITECH Act, passed as part of the American Recovery and Reinvestment Act of 2009 (ARRA). HITECH set forth new privacy and security compliance requirements, funding, and incentives for adoption of electronic health records and increased penalties for violation of the law by "covered entities" (including counselors, psychologists, and other mental health professionals who come under HIPAA) and "business associates" of the covered entities.

As evidence that the federal government is ramping up enforcement of HIPAA and HITECH, the first civil monetary penalty was imposed in February 2011 against Cignet Health of Prince George's County, Maryland. The action started with a simple failure to provide patients with access to their health records; subsequently, after failing to respond to both informal government requests and then a subpoena to produce the records, the health care entity was cited for both access violations as well as a failure to cooperate with an investigation and ordered to pay more than $4.3 million in penalties (U.S. Department of Health and Human Services, OCR, 2011a). Within days of imposition of the first HIPAA civil monetary penalty, the Department of Health and Human Services announced a $1 million settlement with the General Hospital Corporation and Massachusetts General Physicians Organization, Inc. (Mass General) because of a breach resulting from an employee leaving confidential records (including HIV/AIDS information) on a subway train (U.S. Department of Health and Human Services, OCR, 2011b).

There are other notable enforcement actions in which health care entities have been sanctioned or agreed to significant settlements. In July 2011, UCLA Health System agreed to a settlement in the amount of $865,500 because employees had improper access over several years to the records of Hollywood celebrities (American Health Lawyers Association, 2011; Hennessy-Fiske, 2011). In addition to the penalty, UCLA Health System agreed to a corrective action plan, which called for ongoing and robust employee training, sanctions for offending employees, and oversight by an independent monitor for 3 years. Counselors who hire employees or "independent contractors" (see Chapter 11) are especially vulnerable if these workers are starstruck when a national or local celebrity client comes into the counseling office for professional services.

The following examples of medical and mental health violations were reported to the U.S. Department of Health and Human Services under the HITECH mandates and were posted on the department's website:

- An unencrypted laptop computer was stolen from the covered entity's unlocked testing office. The laptop computer contained the PHI of approximately 689 individuals.
- An employee left an external portable hard drive containing electronic PHI in a vehicle that was stolen . . . Following the breach, the responsible employee was terminated for violating [the employer's] policies.
- PHI was released from the covered entity when . . . imposter[s], posing as representatives of the legitimate recycling service used by the covered entity, removed [PHI of approximately 1,300 individuals].
- A laptop computer was stolen from a hospital employee's vehicle. The computer contained the PHI of 943 individuals. The PHI involved in the breach included names, contact information, dates of birth, social security numbers, medical record numbers, and health insurance information, including diagnosis code in numeric form and billing code description.
- A shared desktop computer that was used for backup was stolen from the reception desk area, behind a locked desk area, probably while a cleaning crew had left the main door to the building open and the door to the suite was unlocked and perhaps ajar.

- An employee's car was broken into, and a tote bag, which had a spreadsheet containing [PHI], was stolen from the car.
- The covered entity failed to adhere to its own policy to shred PHI, and a third party found patient PHI in a paper recycling container behind the covered entity's building.
- An unencrypted laptop computer [containing PHI] was stolen from a personal vehicle.
- A business associate employee sent an e-mail to multiple patients without concealing patient e-mail addresses.
- The covered entity inadvertently sent 23 boxes containing PHI to a recycling center.
- An employee's laptop was stolen out of a locked office; evidence shows that the laptop was password protected but not encrypted. (U. S. Department of Health and Human Services, OCR, 2014b)

Our concern is that many counselors have become complacent with HIPAA at a time when HITECH imposes new legal requirements that have extended obligations and penalties under HIPAA. For example, if a counselor has a laptop, tablet, thumb drive, or smart phone that contains confidential client information and the unencrypted device is lost or stolen, the counselor may be legally required to report the breach to affected clients, the federal government, and in some cases the media. The problems may be compounded if the counselor does not have written policies and procedures in place. This is not a theoretical problem for health care providers. The U.S. Department of Health and Human Services reported in an April 2014 press release that it had levied a combined $1,975,000 penalty against two healthcare organizations after laptops were stolen. The government made clear that unencrypted laptops and other mobile electronic devices represent a significant risk to the security of patient information (U.S. Department of Health and Human Services, 2014).

Counselors, psychologists, and other mental health service providers are among those now listed by name on what is commonly called the "Wall of Shame" (U.S. Department of Health and Human Services, OCR, 2014b). As required by the HITECH Act, the U.S. Department of Health and Human Services, OCR, must post a list of breaches of unsecured PHI affecting 500 or more persons. As of 2014, these breaches are posted in a format that allows users to search and sort the posted breaches. In addition, this new format includes brief summaries of the breach cases that OCR has investigated and closed as well as the names of private practice providers who have reported breaches of unsecured PHI. Perusing this list gives counselors and other mental health providers a chilling reminder that loss and theft of laptops, other portable electronic devices, and paper records; hacking incidents; and myriad other breaches may lead to fines and other penalties. Civil monetary penalties for noncompliance now range as high as $1.5 million per violation, depending on the level of neglect and other factors. Willful privacy breaches, in certain cases, may also lead to criminal prosecution. Therefore, policies and procedures to prevent privacy and security breaches are an absolute necessity for all providers who are HIPAA covered entities.

Turning specifically to the new breach notification requirements under HITECH, the Omnibus Final Rule defines *breach* as the "acquisition, access, use or disclosure of protected health information in a manner not permitted [by the rule] which compromises the security or privacy of the protected health information" (45 C.F.R § 160.164, 2014). The rule specifically excludes certain unintentional or inadvertent disclosures or acquisitions from the definition of a breach, such as where the information was disclosed in good faith and within a particular work force, but the rule should be consulted for details.

The first thing that must be determined is whether there was an actual breach of unsecured PHI. Notification is required only when there is a breach of *unsecured* PHI. For example, if the information were encrypted[1] as described by the rule (consistent with guidelines promulgated by the National Institute of Standards and Technology), it would be considered secure. The only other method of securing PHI in a fail-safe manner is complete destruction of the information, which obviously can occur only after treatment has ended and the mandatory or required period for record retention has passed (see Chapter 10). Privacy breaches of paper records may also trigger the breach notification requirements. For instance, paper records that are purged as part of a document retention and destruction policy should not just be dumped in a trashcan or recycling bin. They should be shredded to avoid the possibility of an unsecured breach.

Furthermore, the 2013 final rule clarifies that there is a *presumption* of a breach under the above definition unless a risk assessment by a provider or business associate demonstrates a low probability

---

[1]Encryption of messages sent by cell phones and other electronic devices is becoming easier to accomplish. See Wood (2014).

that PHI has been compromised. Four factors must be considered in making a risk assessment to determine whether notice is required:

1. What was the nature and extent of PHI, including types of identifiers and likelihood of re-identification (e.g., improper acquisition or loss of social security numbers and sensitive clinical information likely would call for notice)?
2. Who was the unauthorized person who used or received PHI?
3. Was the PHI actually acquired or viewed?
4. To what extent has the risk been mitigated?

If the risk assessment findings indicate anything beyond a low probability that unsecured PHI has been compromised, clients must be notified in writing via first-class mail sent to the last known address. As an alternative, the notice may be sent by e-mail if the client has agreed to accept such notices electronically. If the covered entity has incomplete or outdated contact information for 10 or more individuals, the entity must provide substitute individual notice by either posting the notice on its website home page or providing notice through broadcast media or major print in the area where the affected clients are likely to reside. If the covered entity has incomplete or outdated contact information for fewer than 10 individuals, the rule is relaxed somewhat to permit substitute notice by an alternative means of written, telephone, or other communication. The notice must be sent without unreasonable delay, but in no event later than 60 days from the date of discovery of the breach. Notice from the covered entity counselor must contain the following information:

- a brief description of what happened, including the date of the breach and the date of discovery of the breach, if known;
- a description of the types of unsecured PHI involved in the breach;
- steps the clients should take to protect themselves from potential harm resulting from the breach;
- a brief description of the counselor's actions to investigate the breach, mitigate harm to clients, and protect against further breaches; and
- contact procedures for clients to ask questions or obtain additional information. For substitute notice through Internet posting, broadcast media, or major print, the notice must include a toll-free number for individuals to contact the covered entity to determine whether their PHI was breached.

There are many more details laid out in the rule, including the need to notify the U.S. Department of Health and Human Services immediately if there is a breach of unsecured PHI involving 500 or more individuals. As mentioned above, these large-scale breaches are published on the department's website and also require notification to the media. After maintaining client records for several years, it's quite possible that even counselors in solo practices may have 500 or more client records stored on a computer or other electronic device. However, even one breach of PHI requires entry on a form that must be submitted to the U.S. Department of Health and Human Services no later than 60 days after the end of the calendar year. Detailed instructions may be found on the website of the U.S. Department of Health and Human Services, OCR (2014a). Furthermore, counselors should check state law because some states are enacting breach notification laws.

The 2013 Omnibus Rule also specifically permits patients to receive copies of their records in electronic form and/or have the records sent in electronic form to third parties, assuming that electronic health records are the medium used to track their health data. Note that "psychotherapy notes" as defined by HIPAA do not always have to be released directly to clients at their request. However, state law must also be consulted to address this issue because if state law is more protective of patient rights, it controls. Also note that if a client requests that psychotherapy notes be sent to a third party, specific authorization must be obtained.

Counselors are advised to keep abreast of future HIPAA and HITECH rulemaking that may affect their obligations to clients and currently existing HIPAA procedures. The Department of Health and Human Services maintains an index of up-to-date guidance and information on its website (U.S. Department of Health and Human Services, OCR, 2014c). Both HIPAA "covered entities" and "business associates" (such as outside billing services) must now comply with the new breach notification requirements for any discovered breaches of unsecured PHI, and both may be penalized for failure to follow the law. Business associate contracts may need to be revised to reflect the new breach notification requirements. In addition, if you developed HIPAA policies and procedures before HITECH went into effect, you will want to review them for compliance with breach notification and other new provisions.

Specific Concerns Regarding Confidentiality, Privilege, and Privacy

Approximately 17.5% of closed claims against counselors insured by HPSO in the 10-year period ranging from 2003 through 2012 involved confidentiality, privilege, and privacy allegations (CNA & HPSO, 2014). These issues cause a great deal of confusion and concern for many counselors. The ACA-sponsored professional liability insurance program's Risk Management Helpline reported that in 2010 and 2011, there were 205 inquiries about confidentiality, privilege, and privacy issues, including requests for advice on subpoenas (P. L. Nelson, executive director, ACA Insurance Trust, personal communication, May 16, 2011). These 205 questions represented 31% of the total number of inquiries received by the Risk Management Helpline. The specific confidentiality, privilege, and privacy concerns that counselors frequently encounter across the country include subpoenas, counseling minors, couples and family counseling, group counseling, confidentiality of substance abuse records, counseling public offenders and responding to requests from law enforcement, confidentiality after a client's death, and confidentiality and technology. (The latter is addressed in Chapter 7.)

Subpoenas

A *subpoena* is an official court document that requires the recipient to appear in court to be questioned as a witness, or to be deposed at another location, about facts underlying a lawsuit. A subpoena may also require the production of documents. Subpoenas may come from attorneys representing your client or someone who is proceeding against your client, and you must respond carefully unless the subpoena is withdrawn or overruled by a judge. Although rules vary among states regarding service of subpoenas, you should never ignore a subpoena. Subpoenas are generally drafted broadly to elicit as much information as possible, even though that information may not be relevant or may be protected by a privileged communication statute. Counselors must be careful to protect their clients' privileged communications to the fullest extent permitted by law. The following steps are designed to help a counselor respond to a subpoena for confidential client information:

1. Consult an experienced health care attorney (see Appendix C). State law and HIPAA may apply, depending upon the circumstances. Remember that state law may outweigh HIPAA if it is

more protective of the client's privacy rights. If your attorney agrees, go on to Steps 2, 3, and 4.

2. Ascertain whether the client, after consulting his or her attorney, will provide you with written authorization to release information or to testify. If you maintain psychotherapy notes as defined by HIPAA, you must have a specific authorization form in order to release these notes. (If your state has specific protection for personal notes, you might not be required to release them, even with client authorization.)

3. If the client's attorney declines to provide you with signed authorization from the client, request that the client's attorney file a motion to quash the subpoena or a motion for a protective order. Typically, a hearing on the motion will be held. The motion should eventually lead to a court order from the judge regarding whether you must testify or turn over information. (In some jurisdictions, receipt of "satisfactory assurances" from the person sending the subpoena that the client and his or her attorney have received notice and had an opportunity to file an appropriate motion may suffice. It's best to obtain legal consultation on the process.)

4. If the preceding steps do not produce either your client's informed authorization or a court order, send a written notice to the attorney who issued the subpoena or had the court clerk issue it. This notice should be customized to the particular facts and may include language similar to the following:

> In order to testify or release records or other protected health information pursuant to the subpoena that was served on me in [name of case] on [date], I must receive one of the following: (a) written, informed authorization from [client's name] to release the information requested [and specific authorization to release psychotherapy notes, if applicable]; or (b) a court order [from the judge and qualified to comply with HIPAA, if necessary] to release the information or testify, as commanded by the subpoena.

Remember that if you are a HIPAA-covered entity, any protective order you receive must meet all the requirements of 45 C.F.R. § 164.512(e) (2013).

5. If you are subpoenaed to court or a deposition and the time is inconvenient or you will not be available, call the attorney who had it issued. Assuming you've appropriately handled the privilege issue (see above), it's often possible for the attorney to schedule you at a set date and time or put you "on

call" in case you're not needed. If you're subpoenaed with very little notice, perhaps there's a defect with the "service" of the subpoena according to applicable court rules. Ask your local attorney whether you must comply on short notice.

Counseling Minors

Virtually all the standards for protecting client confidences that apply to adults are equally applicable to minors. (In most states, minors are people under the age of 18.) Certainly some information revealed in counseling sessions would be detrimental to family relationships if divulged to parents or guardians and would destroy the trust between the client and counselor. Nonetheless, parents or guardians who are legally and financially responsible for the upbringing of their children usually have some right to know what is learned in the counseling process. In addition, counselors may feel that sharing certain information with parents or guardians could further the progress of counseling.

The 2014 *ACA Code of Ethics* urges counselors to be sensitive to the cultural diversity of families and to respect the inherent rights and responsibilities of parents or guardians over the welfare of their children or charges according to the applicable law and custodial arrangements (Standard B.5.b.). The *Code* also recognizes the need for counselors to balance the ethical rights of minor or incompetent clients with the parental and familial rights and responsibilities to protect these clients (Standard A.2.d.). The relevant inquiry often boils down to this: Is the minor client's right to confidentiality outweighed by the need to inform a parent, guardian, or other appropriate adult of information received in the course of counseling? Many factors should be considered in the analysis, including the age, maturity, and educational level of the client; the relationship with parents or guardians; whether disclosure can reasonably be expected to help the situation or could cause harm; and the severity of potential harm or injury that could come if the information is not disclosed (e.g., if the client is using crack cocaine). Counselors should also take into account whether the minor client has been consulted about the disclosure and the position or relationship of the adult who has requested the information. State law differs regarding whether the parent controls the ability to access or release information about a minor child. (See Appendix C for information about accessing state laws.)

Requests for information about a minor client from nonparents are frequent in school settings. Sharing student information with teachers and administrators is common in schools and is usually considered necessary to the progress of the student but should be limited to those who have an educational need to know. Applicable laws may require permission from a parent or guardian before sensitive confidential information is divulged to a third person.

Counselors in schools that receive federal funding are generally bound by the provisions of FERPA (the Buckley Amendment), implementing regulations, and state or local school board policies concerning the disclosure of students' educational records. Although many school counselors have interpreted FERPA to allow them to keep their counseling records as sole possession notes and therefore to keep such records from parents, the U.S. Department of Education has stated its opinion that a school counselor's notes are generally part of the educational record. According to the Family Policy Compliance Office of the U.S. Department of Education, certain portions may be excepted from the educational record if they are memory joggers used only by the counselor (R. Norment, program analyst, Family Policy Compliance Office, U.S. Department of Education, personal communication, May 19, 2006). This may be an issue that will ultimately be clarified by future court decisions. Also, questions have arisen concerning requests for information from noncustodial parents. FERPA makes it clear that noncustodial parents have the same rights to educational records as custodial parents in the absence of a court order to the contrary. Because of the different interpretations of FERPA, school counselors should seek advice from their school system's attorney or their own attorney when subpoenaed or otherwise requested to reveal confidential information to parents or others.

Couples and Family Counseling

Couples and family counseling presents unique challenges with respect to managing the complexities of confidentiality, privilege, and privacy. If, during the course of treatment, all members were present in every session, that would make things easier. However, in the real world of clinical practice, that is usually not what happens. Ultimately, there will be times when meeting with an individual or a subsystem of the family will be clinically appropriate. In addition, there will be times when someone is missing from a session—because of illness, travel schedules, or prior commitments.

Given this reality, it is best that all parties agree upon some ground rules for how information is discussed during sessions in which not all members are present. The 2014 *ACA Code of Ethics* states that, in the context of couples and family counseling, counselors "clearly define who is considered 'the client' and discuss expectations and limitations of confidentiality" (Standard B.4.b.). This section of the *Code* further requires counselors to seek agreement and to document the understanding among all parties having capacity to give consent regarding confidentiality. We suggest that counselors include this topic in the informed consent document and also have a ground rules discussion with members of the client system (family or couple) during the initial orientation. In the informed consent document and during the initial conversation with the clients, a decision should be made about how privately disclosed information will be handled. In family counseling this is particularly important if there are adolescent members of the family. When you meet privately with the adolescent, it is essential that everyone understands and agrees that you will not be disclosing the content of the private session with the parent. Of course, there are the normal exceptions to this rule when there is legitimate concern for the safety of the adolescent or someone else. The same is true for couples counseling. There may be times when it is appropriate to meet privately with one partner. The ground rules of such meetings need to be clearly defined in advance and, if possible, reiterated prior to the private meeting.

While we are on the topic of confidential private communication in the context of family or couples counseling, we want to draw a distinction between disclosures that are private as compared with disclosures that involve a secret. Individual family members should have a right to some level of personal privacy. To the extent possible, at every developmental stage children should be allowed to decide if, when, or how they want to disclose personal information. Also, there are occasions when a family member needs a safe place to talk through an issue and consider how to disclose the information to the family. Secrecy is different. When a family member or subsystem discloses a family secret (e.g., history of abuse, illegal or dangerous activity), the counselor should not promise to conspire with the family members to permanently keep that information a secret. In couples counseling such disclosures often occur when one partner privately discloses infidelity. In family counseling it could be a family secret of physical or sexual abuse or a family member's involvement in some illegal or dangerous activity. If ground rules are not in place regarding how such disclosures will be handled, there may be risks for clients and the counselor. Most counselors would likely agree that conspiring with a client to hide these types of disclosures from other family members is not in anyone's best interest. At the same time, it is not the counselor's responsibility to speak for family members but rather to facilitate a meaningful dialogue among the affected parties. These situations must be patiently and thoughtfully worked through; the facts of each unique client situation must be considered. This is a perfect example of a time to use the legal and ethical decision-making model presented in Chapter 3.

There are also important legal considerations that involve disclosures made in the context of family or couples counseling. As a rule of thumb, counselors must not release any information (in any form) without obtaining written authorization from everyone involved. In a couples counseling context, both parties must authorize the release of information. In a family context, a parent or legal guardian usually has the legal authority to release information, but that depends on state law. We strongly encourage counselors to seek permission from adolescent members of the family when disclosing information gained from family counseling in which the adolescent was a participant. Giving the adolescent the opportunity to grant permission makes a strong statement of respect that can help maintain a working clinical relationship. However, the counselor should be mindful of the specific state laws.

Disclosures made in the context of family or couples counseling often become legally complicated when there is a change in the purpose of the professional relationship, such as shifting from marriage or couples counseling to divorce counseling; ending couples counseling and beginning individual counseling with one party (often, but not always, while a divorce process is unfolding); or, in a family counseling context, shifting from family to individual or individual to family counseling. In most family or couples counseling circumstances, there is no court involvement and therefore issues of privilege do not arise to a point of contention. However, when issues of separation, divorce, child custody, or visitation become the focus, confidentiality, privilege, and privacy concerns require careful consideration. When, during couples counseling, one party decides to end the relationship, that partner (or his or her attorney) may seek to obtain access to the joint counseling records. Although clients are usually entitled to access their own records, release of joint records typically requires written authorization of both parties or a court order in accordance with Standard B.2.d.

Custody Issues

There is probably no more contentious issue for counselors to address than child custody conflicts. Although many custody concerns technically go beyond the scope of the confidentiality, privilege, and privacy issues covered in this chapter, we address them here because counselors must often consider all custody-related issues at the same time they are served with subpoenas and faced with other requests for information. When counselors have had a prior treatment relationship with any member of the family (individual counseling, couples counseling, or family counseling), the counselor should not opine on which parent should receive custody or offer suggestions regarding visitation. Custody recommendations typically should be made by an independent mental health professional trained to evaluate parenting circumstances and make child custody or visitation recommendations. The treating counselor might be subpoenaed as a fact witness to provide the court with information gained through the counseling relationship. Under such circumstances the counselor should first obtain written authorization from the clients or attempt to secure a court order. If authorization is obtained from all involved parties, the counselor who is deposed or goes to court can provide only information learned through the counseling, and this does not include the counselor's opinion about custody or visitation issues. State counselor licensing laws sometimes specifically underscore this point, but in the absence of state law, Standard E.13.c. of the *ACA Code of Ethics* (ACA, 2014a) is clear: "Counselors do not evaluate current or former clients, clients' romantic partners, or clients' family members for forensic purposes. Counselors do not counsel individuals they are evaluating."

Custody issues are complex and sometimes can emerge unexpectedly. Parents have been known to request counseling for minor children without fully disclosing to the counselor the specifics of existing court orders or decrees. There have been situations in which well-meaning counselors have run afoul of state counseling board regulations as a result of being squeezed between parents (or guardians). For example, a counselor may enter into a treatment relationship with a child on the basis of an assumption that the adult who brings the child has the authority to consent to treatment.

Never-married parents can present an additional layer of complexity. Questions can arise about the legal relationship between the child and a person who asserts to be the child's parent (often a male, but it could be a female from a current or former same-sex union). In many cases the woman was living with the father of the child or living with a same-sex partner. In other cases the procreating relationship had ended and the biological father may or may not have been aware of the existence of the child and may or may not have been involved in the child's life. It's also possible the mother of the child was not certain as to the identity of the father.

The legal rights of both mothers and fathers are complex and governed by state law. It is essential that counselors be informed about the legal rights of unmarried parents so they know how to respond when an unmarried parent attempts to assert his or her rights. The assertion of rights might come in the form of authorization or refusal of authorization to provide treatment to the child or a request to the counselor for information about the child; in addition, it may be that a parent has initiated action to gain custody or primary residency of the child. The legal issues surrounding married and divorcing parents, divorced parents, and never-married parents can be a minefield if the counselor does not inquire into the legal status of the parents or guardians. In fact, the "Code of Ethics" for professional counselors in the Texas counselor licensure regulations includes a *requirement* that counselors obtain copies of the relevant legal documents and follow the law:

> Prior to the commencement of counseling services to a minor client who is named in a custody agreement or court order, a licensee shall obtain and review a current copy of the custody agreement or court order, as well as any applicable part of the divorce decree. A licensee shall maintain these documents in the client's records. When federal or state statutes provide an exemption to secure consent of a parent or guardian prior to providing services to a minor, a licensee shall follow the protocol set forth in such federal or state statutes. (22 Tex. Admin. Code § 681.41(t)(6) (2013)

Even counselors who do not practice in Texas may see the merit in inquiring about custody issues and requesting copies of any orders or decrees that may provide guidance in determining who has the legal right to consent to treatment for the minor. Counselors are advised to consult a local attorney when such issues arise.

Child custody issues clearly generate intense emotions in clients; counselors can easily become collateral damage during the course of a bitter divorce and custody battle. For counselors to remain helpful to clients and not be drawn into the fight, they must fully understand their ethical and legal requirements. Consultation with a lawyer and colleague is important in handling requests for information or subpoenas, deciding whether or not to counsel minors, and responding to requests to testify in court.

Group Counseling

Successful counseling groups are built on a foundation of confidentiality—what is discussed in the group stays in the group. Competent group counselors discuss the importance of confidentiality while screening potential group members. Confidentiality is also introduced as an essential ground rule during the initial meeting of the group; members are asked (orally or in writing) to commit to honoring confidentiality. (In the District of Columbia, counselors are required to provide group clients with a written statement describing the prohibition against unauthorized disclosure of mental health information and penalties for such disclosure; see D.C. Mental Health Information Act, 2013.) It is good practice for counselors to clearly communicate to all members of the group that even though they will not reveal client information, they cannot guarantee that group members will refrain from doing so. Therefore, more than just imposing a ground rule, group counselors should help educate group members about how easy it is to inadvertently violate confidentiality.

Just as important, group counselors should help clients understand how they can talk to a loved one or friend outside the group about what they are learning about themselves in group without identifying other group members or providing identifying information. Finally, throughout the life of the group, group counselors should remind other group members of the importance of confidentiality and that breaches of confidentiality are the business of the group, to be discussed and worked through (Bertram, 2011). These ethical considerations can become compromised when state law or the interpretation of a judge does not recognize disclosures made by group counseling clients as privileged communications. Counselors need to know whether their state protects privileged communication in groups. If not, counselors should fully explain this special circumstance to group members. However, the absence of privileged communication does not remove the ethical responsibility to preserve confidentiality. It does mean that under some circumstances, the group leader and conceivably group members could be subpoenaed to testify about disclosures made by a member of the group. Certainly if a counselor were to receive a subpoena to provide confidential information about a client gained by participating in a group, the counselor would immediately seek legal and colleague consultation to determine how best to proceed.

Confidentiality of Substance Abuse Records

Counselors should be aware of the strict confidentiality rules that apply to records of alcohol and drug abuse treatment if the treatment is part of a federally assisted program. The law (Public Health Service Act, 2014) and its implementing regulations (Confidentiality of Alcohol and Drug Abuse Patient Records, 2014) are broadly construed to include providers who receive Medicare or Medicaid funding. Counselors should obtain consultation when they receive third-party requests or subpoenas for records of substance abuse treatment to ensure that both federal and state law requirements are met.

Counseling Public Offenders and Responding to Requests From Law Enforcement

Probably the greatest problem facing counselors in prisons, other adult custodial penal institutions, and juvenile justice facilities and programs is the persistent tension between the ethics guidelines stressing confidentiality and the requirements of sharing information among agencies involved in the correctional process. Clients may wish to discuss particular problems, such as drug use in prison, but counselors may be required to reveal that information or risk losing their jobs. Clients also know that counselors may be required to report to courts and correctional officials on the progress of their clients, so they might be inclined to present themselves in a more positive light.

Some state statutes may permit access to prison records, beyond the correctional institution, by local parole boards, probation departments, and even community service boards for planning and coordinating postrelease mental health services for offenders. Other than those records restricted by federal law, such as those relating to AIDS or HIV status and substance abuse, counseling records may not be fully protected.

Despite potentially conflicting job requirements and state laws, counselors working with public offender clients still are bound by the ethical duty to maintain client confidences. Client confidences must be protected when possible, but clients should be advised at the outset that certain information must be included in periodic court reports (if such reports are required by the state). Clients must also understand that counselors may need to report certain criminal activities, including threats of violence that are disclosed in counseling. Counselors should take extra care in maintaining and documenting prison and other public offender setting counseling records, and information included in periodic reports should be limited to that which is requested.

How should a counselor manage a request from law enforcement personnel for confidential information to identify or locate a client who is a suspect, fugitive, or missing person? Under HIPAA, counselors and other health care providers who are "covered entities" are permitted to respond to law enforcement for such purposes but must limit the disclosure to name and address, date and place of birth, social security number, blood type, type of injury, date and time of treatment (or death), and a description of distinguishing physical characteristics (45 C.F.R. § 164.512(f)(2), 2013). However, it is important to recognize that release of this limited information is "permitted," not required, without a court order or warrant issued by the court. Some law enforcement officers may mistakenly tell the counselor that HIPAA requires release of information to law enforcement in all such situations. In fact, release of this information pertaining to a client might violate state laws protecting mental health information in certain circumstances, both for HIPAA covered entities and those counselors who are not covered entities. For example, if a police officer calls a counselor and asks for information to track down a client who is suspected of having burglarized houses, the counselor should tell the officer that a court order would be required in order to reveal any information, including whether the person in question is a client.

Even given HIPAA's constraints, release of relevant information may sometimes be warranted where it is necessary to help save the client's life or the life of another person. For example, if a police officer tells a counselor that the client left a suicide note at home that morning and the counselor knows that the client planned a trip that day to a certain location, release of the particulars of that location may be appropriate to save the client's life. In a similar manner, if the officer tells the counselor that the client took his former wife hostage under gunpoint and threatened to murder her at their mountain cabin, the counselor may be justified in releasing the address of the cabin and the client's cell phone number. The HIPAA Privacy Rule does permit a counselor to release information, when consistent with law and ethics standards, to "prevent or lessen a serious and imminent threat to the health or safety of an individual or the public" (45 C.F.R. § 164.512(j) (1)(i), 2013). The HIPAA standard in this area is consistent with most state laws, which allow release of mental health information in order to protect the safety of the patient or others. (See Chapters 6 and 8 for further discussion of threats of harm to others and self.)

If the counselor is presented with a search warrant for a particular client's records, the counselor should respectfully request to speak with his or her attorney before turning over any information. However, if the police or other law enforcement official with the warrant threatens to look through all of the counselor's records to find the one in question, the counselor will usually want to comply with the request for the individual record requested. There is a reasonable basis for complying with the search warrant because it is issued by a judge after a finding of probable cause. This type of situation occurs rarely, but counselors should have a preexisting relationship with a local attorney so that advice can be obtained for the particular situation given applicable state laws.

Must a counselor release information at the request of the medical examiner's office? The counselor should tactfully ask the medical examiner (or coroner) what authority that official has to require release of mental health information and whether the medical examiner could furnish the counselor with a copy of the applicable statute. Whereas a court order may be required for release of mental health information in some states, failure to respond to a medical examiner's request or subpoena may, in other states, cause a problem for the counselor. For example, in Florida, any person who refuses to make available prior medical or other information pertinent to a death investigation may be guilty of a misdemeanor (Fla. Stat. Ann. § 406.12, 2014).

In general, when faced with requests or demands for information from law enforcement, counselors should first try to obtain legal consultation and colleague consultation. Both HIPAA (if a counselor is a HIPAA-covered entity) and state law should be researched. Furthermore, if a counselor conducts substance abuse treatment for which federal funds are received, the federal substance abuse confidentiality regulations (Confidentiality of Alcohol and Drug Abuse Patient Records, 2014) may apply. In the end, good professional judgment is imperative.

Confidentiality After a Client's Death

One of the most difficult issues a counselor may face is how to handle requests for information after a client's death. Confidentiality does not automatically end upon a client's death. The 2014 *ACA Code of Ethics* states the following: "Counselors protect the confidentiality of deceased clients, consistent with legal requirements and the documented preferences of the client" (Standard B.3.f.). From a legal perspective, the issue is often very murky. Some state statutes permit the administrator or executor of the deceased person to access records. Often, that administrator is a spouse or close relative of the client. Would the client want his spouse or significant other to access his private counseling records? Counselors should obtain advice from legal counsel and consult with a trusted colleague when faced with such requests for access to a deceased client's records.

Confidentiality and Technology

Counselors who are HIPAA-covered entities have obligations to guard the privacy and security of PHI. However, it's important for all counselors to recognize that their obligations go well beyond protection of the traditional paper record. The 2014 *ACA Code of Ethics* states the following: "Counselors take precautions to ensure the confidentiality of all information transmitted through the use of any medium" (ACA, 2014a, Standard B.3.e.). As Medicare, Medicaid, and private health insurance carriers are pushing toward greater use of electronic health records (EHRs), counselors who engage in electronic record keeping must ensure that their electronic records remain private. Some counselors may have software installed on their computers to maintain their records. Others may prefer the relative convenience and perceived security of cloud-based records storage.[2]

Counselors who choose cloud-based EHR maintenance should remember that a valid HIPAA Business Associate contract with the EHR vendor might be required. If the vendor refuses, it may be advisable to investigate another EHR vendor. Counselors should also have procedures regarding who may access such records—and how—in the event of their disability, serious illness, or death (Wheeler & Reinhardt, 2014).

---

[2]The authors do not have the capacity to evaluate specific software programs, cloud-based EHR vendors, or other EHR vendors. However, in the wake of the widely publicized Target data breach and other breaches involving national security, new devices and software are emerging constantly. The makers of one new cell phone, the Blackphone, are advertising a private operating system that will work only with privacy-enabled applications (Censer, 2014).

In the past decade or so, counselors and other mental health professionals have had complaints brought against them because of e-mail messages being sent to the wrong person, voice mail being inappropriately overheard, and computerized records landing in the hands of the wrong party. It's essential to develop procedures to minimize the risk of such technology-related privacy breaches. It's also important to keep up with the latest developments in device security. See Chapter 7 for further information about online technology and social media concerns for counselors.

Summary

Understanding the reach and limits of confidentiality, privilege, and privacy is key to a successful counselor–client relationship. Breaches can cause serious harm to clients and can lead to legal and administrative headaches for the counselor. However, it is also important to remember that one of the primary ethical and legal duties of a professional counselor is to protect the client and others from harm. As a result of that duty, and the competing societal interests in safety and security, there are several counseling situations in which the ethical and legal confidentiality requirements must bend to accommodate public safety interests. In some cases, the counselor has an affirmative obligation to report information learned through the counseling relationship to appropriate authorities. These duties to report or otherwise protect the client are discussed in the next chapter.

Chapter 6

Duties to Report, Warn, and/or Protect

As discussed in Chapter 5, the general rule is that counselor–client communications are confidential and should be protected. However, there are important exceptions to this rule. This chapter addresses when confidentiality must be broken to report behavior of clients or others to government agencies, law enforcement, or affected individuals. School and workplace violence are also discussed.

Duty to Report

Over the past several decades, state legislatures have enacted statutes to protect certain populations susceptible to physical or emotional injury by others. For example, mandated reporters (including counselors and other health care providers) must report child abuse as well as elder or vulnerable adult abuse to the applicable social service agency or police. Some states have passed laws requiring reporting of domestic violence. Ethics codes and state licensure board regulations frequently mandate reporting of unprofessional conduct of their licensees. Because details of the reporting requirements and procedures vary among states, counselors are encouraged to learn the reporting requirements in their states.

Abuse of Children and Elderly or Vulnerable Adults

In all states, child abuse must be reported when known, and all states either permit or require the reporting of abuse of adults who are elderly, disabled, or mentally ill.[1] In these cases, the counselor–client privilege does not apply, and there may be significant penalties if the counselor fails to report the abuse or neglect. In *Searcy v. Auerbach* (1992), the Ninth Circuit Court of Appeals ruled that a psychologist who did not follow statutory procedures for reporting child abuse was not immune from civil liability; in other words, he could be successfully sued for neglecting to make the required report. (In this case, the psychologist disclosed his opinion about abuse to the child's father but failed to make the mandated report to the appropriate agency.)

These reporting laws came about because the public policy supporting protection of a vulnerable population (e.g., children, people with disabilities, elderly people) was viewed as more important than a client's or patient's right to keep the information confidential. Reporting past incidents of abuse may be required in some states. For example, the Maryland Attorney General's Office issued an opinion stating that past child abuse must be reported even in cases where the victim has long passed the age of majority[2] (78 Md. Op. Att'y Gen. 189, 12/3/1993). (A Maryland court could reach a different conclusion, but an opinion of the attorney general is likely to be given considerable weight in the court's consideration of the issue.)

How should you handle a situation when you are not sure whether the specific circumstance meets the definition of abuse or neglect? You should consider calling the applicable protective services agency—perhaps requesting to speak to a supervisor—and state the relevant facts without giving names or other identifying information. If the agency representative confirms that it is indeed a reportable incident, then you can relay the names and contact information as required by law. We suggest this step because it helps establish a good-faith report, which is typically required in order to receive immunity from suit as a result of the report. You should also seek the advice of an attorney in your state if the reporting duty is not clear. In addition, you may wish to obtain a copy of your state's child abuse law, which is often available online through your state government's website.[3]

---

[1] For more information about each state's adult protective services programs, call the Eldercare Locator of the U.S. Administration on Aging at 800-677-1116 or view specific state resources provided by the National Center on Elder Abuse at http://www.ncea.aoa.gov/Stop_Abuse/Get_Help/State/index.aspx

[2] The age of majority is the legal age at which a person is considered an adult for purposes of making certain decisions or entering into contracts. In most states, the age of majority is 18.

[3] More information on child abuse reporting laws may be found at the Child Welfare Information Gateway at https://www.childwelfare.gov. This website consolidates information from what was formerly known as the National Clearinghouse on Child Abuse and Neglect Information and the National Adoption Information Clearinghouse.

Domestic Violence

Most states do not require health professionals to report domestic violence unless it comes under another reporting requirement, such as child abuse laws or elder or vulnerable adult abuse laws. However, California, Colorado, Kentucky, and New Hampshire are examples of states with specific reporting statutes for suspected cases of domestic violence, also frequently called *intimate partner violence*. In Colorado, the reporting duty applies only to physicians (Colo. Rev. Stat. § 12-36-135, 2013). In Kentucky, domestic violence reporting is a subset of the adult abuse reporting laws, and the reporting duty runs to any person having reasonable cause to suspect that an adult has suffered abuse, neglect, or exploitation (Ky. Rev. Stat. § 209A.010 *et seq.*, 2013). In New York, there is no mandatory duty to report, but health care staff in hospitals that provide maternity and newborn services must give information regarding family violence to all parents of newborns (N.Y. Pub. Health Law § 2803-P, 2013).

In addition, almost all states have some type of reporting requirement for physicians (and other providers, depending on the state) who treat patient injuries caused by guns, knives, or other weapons. Sometimes these reporting laws also includes burn injuries. This type of reporting duty does not usually involve counselors, especially in the outpatient setting.

How can you decide whether you have a mandatory duty to report in your state? There are useful online resources for accessing state domestic violence reporting requirements.[4] The National Domestic Violence Hotline may also be a helpful tool to have on hand when you are counseling victims of domestic violence.[5] Furthermore, the ACA-sponsored Risk Management Helpline, accessible by calling ACA Ethics staff, may be able to provide assistance or resources to counselors who are ACA members.[6]

Past Crimes of Clients

There is usually no duty to report past crimes of clients, unless the crime falls under a reporting statute (e.g., child abuse) or the client is also threatening future harm against a third party (see the section titled "Duty to Warn and/or Protect"). When in doubt, check with your supervisor, consult with a colleague, or seek legal advice.

---

[4]See the Domestic Violence and Sexual Assault Data Resource Center at http://www.jrsa.org/dvsa-drc/index.html

[5]The National Domestic Violence Hotline number is 800-799-SAFE.

[6]The ACA Ethics Consultation Line may be accessed at 1-800-347-6647, ext 314. The toll-free number for the Risk Management Helpline is available to ACA members who first contact ACA Ethics and receive a referral number, if appropriate.

Unprofessional Conduct of Colleagues

At some point in your counseling career, you are likely to be faced with a colleague's unprofessional conduct or impairment. According to the 2014 *ACA Code of Ethics*, you should first attempt to resolve the issue informally, provided your action does not violate the client's confidentiality rights (ACA, 2014a, Standard I.2.b.). For example, if you are having lunch in a busy restaurant with some professional colleagues and one of them discusses a client within earshot of other restaurant patrons, your obligation is to remind your colleague that any consultations should be handled in a private environment. If informal resolution is not appropriate, other possible action may include referral to state or national ethics committees, the state licensure board, or other institutional authority. Again, the *ACA Code of Ethics* suggests that action should take into consideration a client's confidentiality rights (Standard I.2.b.). You should check with your state licensure board to determine whether there is a mandatory duty to report and whether it trumps the duty to preserve confidentiality if you learn of a colleague's unprofessional conduct through a client. Comprehensive information about the various state licensure boards, licensing requirements, and the boards' contact data is available from ACA's *Licensure Requirements for Professional Counselors* (2014b).

Duty to Warn and/or Protect

The California Supreme Court shocked practicing mental health professionals across the country when it ruled in 1976 that a therapist who knows or should have known that a patient poses a "serious danger of violence to others" and does not exercise reasonable care to protect the intended victim or notify the police can be held liable (*Tarasoff v. Regents of the University of California*, 1976, p. 345). The case involved a graduate student at the University of California–Berkeley, Prosenjit Poddar, who revealed in counseling that he intended to kill a young woman, Tatiana Tarasoff, because she had refused to continue to date him. The psychologist considered the threat to be serious and called the campus police. The campus police detained the student briefly but released him because he seemed to be rational. They neither notified the city police nor warned Ms. Tarasoff. The psychologist also reported his concerns to his supervisor, a psychiatrist, who directed that no further action be taken because Poddar did not meet the civil commitment criteria in effect at the time. Shortly thereafter, Poddar murdered Tarasoff, whose parents sued the psychologist, the psychiatrist, the outpatient treatment center affiliated with the university, the campus police, and the university's board of regents.

The court found that certain duties and obligations arise on the part of a therapist from the special relationship with the client and that this relationship may create affirmative duties for the benefit of third parties. The court specifically stated the following ruling:

> Once a therapist does in fact determine, or under applicable professional standards reasonably should have determined, that a patient poses a serious danger of violence to others, he bears a duty to exercise reasonable care to protect the foreseeable victim of that danger. (p. 345)

However, the court also recognized that the confidential character of the therapeutic relationship is critical to its success and ought to be preserved:

> We realize that the open and confidential character of psychotherapeutic dialogue encourages patients to express threats of violence, few of which are ever executed. Certainly a therapist should not be encouraged routinely to reveal such threats; such disclosures could seriously disrupt the patient's relationship with his therapist and with the persons threatened. To the contrary, the therapist's obligations to his patient require that he not disclose a confidence unless such disclosure is necessary to avert danger to others, and even then that he do so discreetly, and in a fashion that would preserve the privacy of his patient to the fullest extent compatible with the prevention of the threatened danger. (p. 347)

Consequently, the court concluded that the psychotherapist–patient privilege ought to be preserved when possible but not when it conflicts with protection of life. Of course, this poses a difficult call for the counselor, who may not be able to truly ascertain whether a client's threats are credible. The counselor might be sued by the client for invasion of privacy or breach of confidentiality. Many states have enacted statutes limiting the liability of the counselor and other mental health professionals when they breach a client's confidentiality in order to protect a third party. To avoid potential liability, it is important to understand the limits of the *Tarasoff* court's opinion and of any subsequent decisions or legislation in the state where you practice.

Court Decisions After *Tarasoff*

Tarasoff and a number of subsequent cases (e.g., *McIntosh v. Milano,* 1979) held that liability applies when the psychotherapist reasonably believed, or should have believed, that the client posed a serious danger to an identifiable potential victim. In the first instance, the counselor must make the judgment that the client poses a serious danger. In the second, there must be an identifiable potential victim. According to these precedents, a mental health professional should consider the following factors when deciding whether a client might act upon a threat to a third person: the clinical diagnosis of the patient, the context and manner in which the threat is made, the patient's opportunity to act on the threat, the patient's history of violence, actions that provoked the threat, whether the threats are likely to continue, the patient's response to treatment, and the patient's relationship with the potential victim.

> The *Tarasoff* case in California ruled that a therapist who knows or should have known that a patient poses a "serious danger of violence to others" and does not exercise reasonable care to protect the intended victim or notify the police can be held liable.

In several cases, courts have declined to impose liability in the absence of a readily identifiable victim. Other courts have held that the duty to warn is broad and extends to foreseeable victims of the client who may not be specifically identifiable but nonetheless would be likely targets if the client were to become violent or carry through on threats (*Hedlund v. Superior Court*, 1983; *Jablonski v. United States*, 1983, overruled on other grounds; Matter of McLinn, 1984). The Arizona Supreme Court also used this standard and found a psychiatrist liable for failing to protect a foreseeable victim within the "zone of danger," that is, probably at risk of harm from the patient's violent conduct (*Hamman v. County of Maricopa*, 1989).

Another court rejected the foreseeable-victim analysis altogether, holding that there is a duty to exercise due care in determining whether a patient poses an unreasonable risk of serious bodily harm to others (*Perreira v. Colorado*, 1989). It is interesting that a Florida appeals court declined to follow *Tarasoff* in 1991, ruling that imposing a duty to warn third parties would require a psychiatrist to foresee a patient's dangerousness, which is virtually impossible, and would undermine psychiatrist–patient confidentiality and trust. The court realized the difficulty of predicting dangerousness, comparing it with a therapist using a crystal ball (*Boynton v. Burglass*, 1991). Florida has a statute permitting psychiatrists to warn third parties, but reporting is not mandatory according to case law (*Boynton v. Burglass*, 1991; Fla. Stat. § 491.0147, 2013). The *Boynton* court specified that the ruling also applied to psychologists, psychotherapists, and other mental health professionals. Therefore, in Florida, counselors may breach confidentiality to prevent clear and imminent physical harm to a person, but there is no mandatory duty as exists in California under *Tarasoff*. However, counselors in Florida should be mindful of any new case law that may further define the duty to warn/protect; they should also be aware of any duty imposed by their licensure laws.

Texas is also among the few states that have expressly decided not to adopt the *Tarasoff* ruling. In 1999, the Texas Supreme Court held that mental health professionals have no common law duty to warn readily identifiable third persons of a patient's threats against them (*Thapar v. Zezulka*, 1999). However, by statute in Texas, counselors are permitted to make certain disclosures to law enforcement or medical personnel in situations in which there is a risk of imminent physical injury to a third party. There is no specific grant of immunity built into the statute, which could create a decision-making challenge for the therapist (Tex. Health & Safety Code § 611.004, 2013).

Two related cases from California, where *Tarasoff* was decided, appear to expand the meaning and intent of the California immunity statute: *Ewing v. Goldstein* (2004) and *Ewing v. Northridge Hosp. Med. Ctr.* (2004). In those cases, a California appeals court decided that psychotherapists who predicted or actually believed that a patient posed a threat of serious bodily injury or death to a third person have a duty to warn, even though the threat was relayed to the therapist by a family member of the patient, not the actual patient. This ruling could raise serious questions for counselors and other mental health professionals if courts interpret the immunity laws in such a broad fashion. For example, who should be considered a family member for purposes of deciding whether there is a duty to warn/protect?

Most cases impose liability on a therapist for failing to warn/protect only when there is resulting personal injury. However, the Vermont Supreme Court ruled that the duty to warn and/or protect applied in a property damage case. In *Peck v. Counseling Service of Addison County, Inc.* (1985), a client told his counselor that he wanted to burn down his father's barn. He then promised his therapist that he would not carry out that threat, but in fact he did. The court was quite concerned that arson posed a grave danger to human life and was unwilling to limit the duty owed by the therapist.

Evolution of the Law

The cases described in the preceding section demonstrate that courts around the country continue to grapple with the issues of confidentiality and the competing duty to warn and/or protect potential victims of violent patients or clients. In the 1980s and 1990s, a majority of state legislatures passed laws providing immunity for mental health professionals who take action to protect potential third-party victims from the dangerous behavior and threats of patients and clients. However, there are many differences among these state laws as to what actions trigger a duty, what actions of the mental health professional will fulfill that duty, and whether counselors are among those covered by the statutory protection.

In Virginia, there is an immunity law that clearly applies to professional counselors as well as other mental health professionals. It specifies that mental health service providers have a duty to take precautions to protect identified or readily identifiable third parties from violent behavior or serious harm when the client has communicated to the counselor, orally, in writing, or by sign language, a specific and immediate threat to cause serious bodily injury or death. The counselor may seek the client's involuntary admission to the hospital (civil commitment), make reasonable attempts to warn the potential victim, notify the appropriate law enforcement authority, or provide counseling in the session in which the threat was communicated until the provider reasonably believes the client no longer has the intent or ability to carry out the threat (Va. Code Ann., §54.1-2400.1, 2013). The law also makes health care providers immune from civil suit for breaching confidentiality in communicating such threats, failing to predict harm in the absence of a threat, or failing to take precautions other than those specified in the law.

As the law concerning this issue continues to evolve, it is important to keep informed of judicial and legislative actions in your state that affect your practice area. You may wish to subscribe to one of the many mental health law bulletins available through commercial publishers as well as publications of the ACA. These tools can help keep you apprised of legal developments that you might otherwise miss.

Clients With AIDS/HIV Positive Status

Another dilemma that arises for counselors is whether to warn partners of HIV-positive clients or those with AIDS and/or to report to a public health agency when the clients are not practicing safe sex.

Knowing the potential for transmission of HIV and the potentially deadly nature of the resulting AIDS infection, society certainly has an interest in protecting unsuspecting partners of clients who may be HIV positive. However, there is a strong reason to protect the confidentiality of clients who are HIV positive. Virtually all states now have statutes governing the reporting of HIV and AIDS cases to public health authorities and corresponding confidentiality duties, but many of the laws that either permit or require reporting apply only to physicians.

The 2014 *ACA Code of Ethics* provides an ethical perspective in Standard B.2.c.:

> When clients disclose that they have a disease commonly known to be both communicable and life threatening, counselors may be justified in disclosing information to identifiable third parties, if the parties are known to be at serious and foreseeable risk of contracting the disease. Prior to making a disclosure, counselors assess the intent of clients to inform the third parties about their disease or to engage in any behaviors that may be harmful to an identifiable third party. Counselors adhere to relevant state laws concerning disclosure about disease status.

Consistent with current ethics standards, you should follow the statutory mandate if you practice in a jurisdiction where statutes clearly define the actions you must take regarding reporting of AIDS and HIV. Your state public health department may be able to help you ascertain your obligations under state law. What should you do if you practice in a state in which the obligations are not clear for counselors or in which you're not certain whether the law is consistent with your ethics code? First, make sure that you remain current about appropriate ways to protect against transmission of AIDS and HIV. Next, consider speaking with your client and educating him or her about safe sex practices and seeing then if the client is willing to make responsible decisions. If the client refuses to inform his or her partner(s), you might call the appropriate public health agency without giving a name and find out what it is able to do without compromising the client's confidentiality. Another possibility is to refer the client for a medical evaluation by a physician, who may be able to make a report to the appropriate public health authorities without facing liability for breach of confidentiality. The health agency may be able to do contact tracing or take other action to protect third parties at risk. Another option is to see whether the client is willing to speak directly to the public health agency in your presence. In any event, if your duty is unclear, you should consider obtaining consultation from the public health agency, an attorney, and a colleague well-versed in ethical decision making. These suggestions may be applicable to other public health and infectious disease issues, such as Ebola.

Workplace Violence

In the last several decades, violence has escalated against people in the workplace. The U.S. Department of Labor, Occupational Safety and Health Administration (OSHA) has established a website with information on prevention of workplace violence: https://www.osha.gov/SLTC/workplaceviolence/index.html. A useful resource for counselors is the document entitled "Guidelines for Preventing Workplace Violence for Healthcare and Social Service Workers" (U.S. Department of Labor and Occupational Safety and Health Administration, 2004). This document may be of particular interest to counselors working in large health care institutions and agencies as well as those counselors who own or operate counseling agencies. It addresses the importance of management commitment and staff involvement, analysis of the particular worksite, hazard prevention and control, training, and recordkeeping and evaluation.

What happens when an employee under the care of a mental health therapist makes explicit threats against his coworkers in the context of a counseling session? First, the situation should be analyzed under the statutes and case law of the particular jurisdiction that deal with potential duty to warn and/or protect, discussed above. In addition, one might question whether there may be a "duty to commit" under the involuntary civil commitment scheme of the state in question. The court in one case involving psychiatric care of a veteran with posttraumatic stress disorder (PTSD), *Currie v. United States* (1987), declined to impose liability on treating psychiatrists for failing to commit the patient.

The facts in *Currie* were as follows: An IBM employee was under the care of mental health professionals at a Veterans Administration (VA) Medical Center in North Carolina. He threatened to blow up IBM, after which one of his psychiatrists asked him to commit himself voluntarily. The employee agreed but never carried through on this plan. (He also threatened to kill his psychiatrists.) The employee was dismissed from his employment at IBM. VA doctors warned IBM and several law enforcement agencies. They also discussed whether the employee/patient could be involuntarily committed but concluded that North Carolina law would not support the commitment because they believed his dangerousness was not attributable to his mental illness but, rather, to his anger at IBM for his discharge and at his psychiatrists for refusing to give him excuses for failing to attend work.

The employee/patient shot and killed a coworker at IBM. Currie, the administratrix of the deceased coworker's estate, sued the federal government, alleging that government psychiatrists breached a duty to civilly commit the employee/patient. The federal district court declined to impose liability, opting to hold the therapists to a standard of good faith. The U.S. Court of Appeals for the Fourth Circuit also refused to impose a duty to commit.

Counselors should not construe this case to mean that civil commitment is not an option in deciding how to handle a potentially violent client. State law will often influence the decisions that mental health professionals must make. However, it is encouraging that a federal appellate court recognized that mental health professionals do not have complete control over their patients' or clients' decisions.

Potential workplace violence puts counselors in a difficult position. For example, if an employee expresses a desire to "kill the boss," is he just blowing off steam or does he have a plan to carry out a real threat? If the counselor, in a knee-jerk fashion, just makes a warning without exploring the factors and intent, the employee could be fired and the risk of violence might actually be exacerbated. On the other hand, failing to take steps to warn and protect could lead to serious injury or death as well as a lawsuit against the counselor. These situations truly call for careful assessment that is based on the guidelines at the end of the chapter and on consultation with colleagues and local counsel.

School Violence and New Legislative Initiatives That Affect All Mental Health Professionals

Although violence has increased in school settings in recent years, the *perception* of school violence and media attention has perhaps contributed most to the fear of school violence. In fact, only between 1% and 2% of homicides among school-aged children actually occur on school premises or on the way to or from school (CDC, 2013). Nonetheless, counselors must be vigilant when their clients threaten harm, verbally or by their actions, and this vigilance must be heightened for counselors who work in schools and universities. Counselors must also consider the problem of bullying in the school setting (see Chapter 8) when making decisions involving potentially violent clients. Furthermore, following the Columbine and Virginia Tech tragedies, among others, counselors should realize that their actions may be judged with the benefit of hindsight. The report of the Virginia Tech Review Panel (2007) to the Virginia governor following the Virginia Tech massacre took aim at various components of the university, specifically opining that the counseling center failed to provide needed support and services to Seung Hui Cho, the shooter.

In addition, counselors should be aware that, after the Sandy Hook Elementary School shooting in December 2012, several states rushed to implement new gun laws to reduce the risk of violence. New York was one state that quickly passed a broad statute intended to reduce gun violence, including a provision requiring mental health professionals to report certain patients for purposes of revoking gun permits. It is interesting that the text of the New York law passed on January 15, 2013, does not explicitly mention counselors. For purposes of the law, the term "mental health professional" was defined to include physicians, psychologists, registered nurses, and licensed clinical social workers. Under this 2013 law,

> When a mental health professional currently providing treatment services to a person determines, in the exercise of reasonable professional judgment, that such person is likely to engage in conduct that would result in serious harm to self or others, he or she shall be required to report, as soon as practicable to the director of community services. (New York Secure Ammunitions and Firearms Enforcement [SAFE] Act of 2013)

That agency is, in turn, required to report the identity of the mental health patient to the division of criminal justice services if it supports the mental health professional's opinion. The information may be used to ascertain whether a firearms license should be revoked or suspended. Law enforcement would also be authorized to confiscate firearms owned by an allegedly dangerous patient.

Following passage of this New York law, a number of critics (including some prominent mental health professionals) suggested that such laws could erode important confidentiality protections. The concern was that some mental health patients with homicidal or suicidal ideation would interpret the mere possibility of being reported to local authorities as a deterrent from seeking treatment. Another concern is that the law could prevent patients from honestly sharing their thoughts and fears with their therapists. Although numerous legal challenges were made to the New York SAFE Act, most portions of the law have been upheld, including the provision on mental health reporting.

The New York law does not require a mental health therapist, using reasonable professional judgment, to take action that would endanger himself or herself or increase potential danger to the victim(s). Furthermore, criminal and civil immunity applies to the reporting therapist for his or her decision whether or not to disclose, if done reasonably and in good faith. The new law extends beyond some existing state laws that provide immunity from suit to mental health professionals who warn a potential victim or notify law enforcement in instances where a patient/client has made specific threats against a specific identifiable victim. Ascertaining a specific threat is quite different from making a generalized determination of what constitutes a "dangerous" client. The New York statute, while drafted with good intentions to prevent gun violence, may unintentionally create a new source of litigation against mental health professionals regarding what actions are "reasonable" and made in "good faith" in order to invoke the immunity provisions (Wheeler, 2013).

Although well-crafted legislation to reduce violence may be in the public interest, counselors and other mental health professionals may wish to dialogue and work collaboratively with patients' rights groups to ensure that all mental health patients are not "criminalized" in the process. Counselors should keep informed about new legislative proposals, on both the state and federal levels, that may impose new duties on mental health professionals. Even the 2014 Notice of Proposed Rulemaking, which would amend the HIPAA Privacy Rule by reducing legal barriers to reporting involuntarily committed persons, could lead to such patients being reported to a *criminal* database (U.S. Department of Health and Human Services, OCR, 2014d). Counselors should be prepared to weigh in on new legislative efforts so that reasonable efforts are made to protect confidentiality and privacy while attempting to eradicate the threat to human life posed by guns. Furthermore, if there are laws passed that require new reporting duties, or add counselors to the list of mandated reporters, consider carefully how your informed consent process and documents should be amended to reflect these changes.

Counselors working in school and university settings should also be aware that FERPA does not preclude release of relevant educational and counseling records in an emergency, such as protecting the health and safety of students or other individuals. Furthermore, in an emergency, relevant personally identifiable information may be released to law enforcement, public health officials, and trained medical personnel (34 C.F.R. § 99.31 (a)(10) and § 99.36, 2014). School counselors will not automatically face liability every time a student commits a violent act. They certainly cannot predict with certainty which student will necessarily become violent. However, school counselors, like counselors in private practice, can take steps to mitigate the risk of harm to third parties as well as the liability risk to themselves. The guidelines at the end of this chapter are designed to help reduce such risks.

Threats by Client Against Counselor

Most counselors do not enter the profession motivated by the prospect of becoming extremely wealthy; rather, their motivation comes from a true desire to help people in need. It seems ironic that counselors and other mental health professionals may encounter threats of violence from the very people they are trying to help. However, as more counselors are handling complex mental health issues and often dealing with clients with a history of violence, the risk to the counselor and the counselor's family, significant others, or coworkers increases. Even though there is no legal duty to try to prevent violence against oneself, a duty could be extended to foreseeable violence against a coworker or employee. Furthermore, escalation of client violence could lead to worse consequences than a malpractice suit!

Between 1993 and 1999, the annual rate of nonfatal violent crime perpetuated on workers of all occupations was 12.6 per 1,000; for nonpsychiatrist mental health workers, it was 40.7 per 1,000; and for psychiatrists, it was 68.2 per 1,000 (Simon, 2011). Counselors and other mental health professionals should give serious thought to minimizing safety risks to themselves, their employees, their coworkers, and their families.

When accepting a job or setting up a private practice, it's prudent for the counselor to consider personal safety risks and how to manage them. Even if you've been in practice for 30 years, it's not too late to consider safety issues. Some mental health patients or clients wait until years after treatment to act out violently against a past therapist; the therapist may have been blissfully unaware that the client was upset with treatment or that the client had incorporated the therapist into a delusional scheme.

What steps can be taken to mitigate against potential client violence? First, consider your office setting. If you operate from a home office, you may wish to carefully think about your client population. For example, risk would likely be increased if your practice focused on counseling juvenile offenders who already had a criminal history. If you work in an urban office, do your clients first meet a receptionist? Is your office locked? Do you have a preplanned method to exit the office in an emergency? Do you have a panic alarm (sound or light) that can alert others in the building to come to your assistance? Do you keep pepper spray (if legal in your state) or other objects to help you defend yourself? Have you considered taking a course in self-defense? Can you avoid working alone at night? You may wish to request that the local police or a security expert come to your office to assess improvements you can make without intruding on your clients' privacy.

Second, take action if a client or former client makes threats, stalks you (in person or on the Internet), or makes harassing telephone calls. If you have proof that your client is the stalker or harasser, you generally do have the right to breach confidentiality and notify the police. If in doubt, seek legal consultation. Denial can be a defense mechanism that proves harmful if you do not seriously consider threats of harm to yourself.

Third, consider pursuing an order of protection (sometimes called a *restraining order* or *no-contact order*) if a client or former client threatens you or your loved ones. However, because the risk of violation of a protection order is high, you will want to base this decision on several factors, including the client's diagnosis, history of violence, age, sex, and substance abuse history (Benitez, McNiel, & Binder, 2010). Colleague and/or attorney consultation may help in assessing whether to pursue a protection order.

Practical Risk Management Guidelines

In the absence of explicit state laws, counselors still may have an ethical duty to disclose information when required to prevent clear and imminent danger to the client or others. The real question for the counselor is, how can I fulfill my legal and ethical duties to protect human life, act in the best interest of the client, and remain protected from potential liability? The following guidelines are suggested to help protect human life, afford maximum privacy protection for the client, and help keep you from being a defendant in a malpractice case.

- Apprise clients of the limits of confidentiality at the outset of counseling and give periodic reminders. In the school context, it may be wise to include a statement in the school handbook regarding confidentiality and its limits so both parents and students are informed.

- Consult with a trusted colleague and/or supervisor.
- Know the law in your state and whether it imposes a duty based on a communicated threat against a specifically identifiable victim or if it encompasses a broader duty. If there is a statute that provides immunity for good faith acts on your part, know what it says about actions you must take. Your state counseling association or your local attorney may be able to help you understand your legal obligations.
- Review the *ACA Code of Ethics* or other ethics codes applicable to your practice. According to the 2014 *ACA Code of Ethics*, typical rules of confidentiality bend "when disclosure is required to protect clients or identified others from serious and foreseeable harm or when legal requirements demand that confidential information must be revealed" (Standard B.2.a.).
- Consult with your attorney if you are concerned about your exposure or if your legal duty is unclear. If you are a school counselor, see if your school system's attorney may be consulted in appropriate cases.
- Make referrals where appropriate.
- Obtain prior medical and behavioral history. Has the client acted out violently in the past? What were the circumstances? Was it premeditated? Does the client frequently make impulsive decisions? Is substance abuse an issue? Is the client delusional? Is there reason to believe the client is only discussing a fantasy, not a real threat?
- Inquire about the client's access to weapons, homicidal ideation, and current plans.
- Consider all appropriate clinical responses and the consequences of each (warning the potential victim(s), calling the police, involving a psychiatrist to do a medication evaluation, changing treatment plans, hospitalizing the client). If clinically appropriate, involve the client in your decision making. Do not reveal confidential information that is not necessary to protect potential victim(s).
- Know and follow applicable institutional policy. If you are a school counselor, be aware that you may be held liable for a failure to uphold the school district's policy on potentially dangerous or suicidal students. You may also be expected to perform a threat assessment on a student who raises red flags as potentially dangerous to others (Cornell, 2010).

- Document all actions you take, those you reject, and the rationale behind each decision (see Chapter 10). In the school setting, policies on documentation and record-keeping may differ from rules for private practice counselors.

Following these guidelines cannot totally protect a potential victim or remove a counselor's liability when a client harms another person. However, doing so can go a long way toward establishing that a counselor is acting within the standard of care expected of practicing counselors today.

Chapter 7

Communication Technology and Social Media

We live in a digital world. Nearly every day, we learn about new advances in communication technology. In a very short span of time, we quickly go from "I never even thought of that" to "Sure, I use that all the time." While philosophers debate the impact on human beings of these many technologies, counselors are faced with decisions about what technologies we should adopt and how we should use them on behalf of our clients.

Technological advances occur faster than the resulting creation of statutes, case law, or the most recent version of the code of ethics. As a result, many legal and ethical implications remain largely unknown. Counseling and mental health related professional associations (i.e., ACA, American Psychological Association, National Association of Social Workers, American Association for Marriage and Family Therapy, and others) have addressed, to various degrees, issues concerning the use of technology and will likely grapple further with the ethical implications of communication technology when their respective ethics codes are updated. The 2014 *ACA Code of Ethics* (ACA, 2014a, Section H, Distance Counseling, Technology, and Social Media) provides practitioners with more detailed guidance regarding the use of technology than the 2005 *Code* did. However, interpretation of the *Code* in specific instances remains to be fleshed out, and still more questions will be posed as technology evolves. To add to the complexity of these emerging issues, counselor licensure boards are also developing regulations that may differ from state to state.

In this chapter we address four broad areas of communication technology applicable to the practice of counseling: distance counseling, social media, digital communication (e.g., texting, e-mail, instant messaging), and other technologies. Although we believe that use of communication technology can often be very beneficial for the counselor–client relationship, counselors are advised to educate themselves and to consult with colleagues and experts regarding the possible legal or ethical implications of using current and "next generation" communication technologies. The 2014 *Code* advises counselors who intend to use technology to "actively attempt to understand the evolving nature of the profession with regard to distance counseling, technology, and social media and how such resources may be used to better serve their clients" (Standard H, Introduction). To that end, we conclude the chapter with a list of recommendations that we believe can assist thoughtful counselors and counselor educators in evaluating the potential benefits and risks of using communication technologies.

Distance Counseling

Google the phrase "online counseling" and you are quickly awash in a sea of technology-assisted counseling options. We conducted just such a Google search and were astonished at the range and diversity of services, conditions of services, and providers of services that we discovered from a review of only a dozen or so online counseling sites. *Online counseling/therapy, technology-assisted counseling, e-therapy, psychotechnology, behavioral telehealth, distance professional services, Internet counseling, cybertherapy,* and *distance counseling* are all different terms for counseling activities that take place either partially or completely over the Internet. Distance counseling occurs in many different forms but can be classified as either synchronous communication (live streaming video, such as FaceTime, Skype, or secure video conferencing; or real-time texting, e-mail exchange, or telephone conversation) or asynchronous communication in which messages are sent or posted and responded to at some later time. (Facebook, Instagram, and e-mail are typical examples, although each of these can be synchronous.) Distance counseling is used for individuals, couples, and families. Online counseling is also offered in the form of synchronous group counseling. Support groups, both synchronous and asynchronous, are widely available on the Internet.

Ethical Considerations

Not long after the Internet and related technology became accessible to the general public, the idea of using this technology to deliver mental health services emerged. This new practice venue created a great deal of interest within the counseling profession. Proponents predicted that mental health services could be provided to clients who were geographically isolated or who might feel more comfortable without a face-to-face meeting with the counselor. However, it soon became apparent that because the Internet is largely unregulated, there was no way to prevent unlicensed and untrained persons from operating an Internet-based counseling practice. Critics raised a variety of serious concerns:

- how to secure accurate client identities, especially when communication is restricted to e-mail, texts, or other forms of electronic contact;
- how to deal with confidential information when exchanged over the Internet or telephone;
- how to intervene and provide appropriate support if a client is at risk of harm to self or others; and
- how to handle licensing given that counselors would be practicing across state and national borders. (Some state licensure boards have taken the position that the counselor practicing online must be licensed in the state where the client is physically located.)

Leadership was needed. Marlene Maheu is one of several pioneering practitioners who recognized it was inevitable that mental health services would be delivered over the Internet and called for the formation of best practice guidelines. Now, as executive director of the TeleMental Health Institute (www.telehealth.org), she continues to advocate for the benefits of psychotechnologies and cautions practitioners against the potential risks.

> There has never been more opportunity for counselors, but the risks are also high. On one hand, it is 100% legal and ethical to deliver distance counseling when following best practices. However, mistakes can and are being made every day by well-intentioned but uninformed professionals who are experimenting rather than acting according to those best practices. Being in full compliance with all legal and ethical mandates, documentation and evidence-based clinical practices is crucial to our risk-management, the public's perception of the counseling profession, and most importantly, the people we serve. (M. Maheu, personal communication, June 11, 2014).

In one of TeleMental Health Institute's webinars, *Skype and Related Practices Found Unacceptable by Oklahoma Medical Board*, Dr. Maheu and her guest speaker Joseph P. McMenamin, MD, JD, discuss a telemedicine issue of potential importance to the wider audience of mental health professionals. They explain how an Oklahoma psychiatrist was disciplined for using Skype. The medical board considered Skype to be an unapproved method of providing telemedicine for prescription of controlled substances within the state of Oklahoma (at least at the time of the board's decision) and one that did not comply with HIPAA. The board's decision also highlighted the fact that the physician did not comply with Oklahoma's informed consent requirements and telemedicine policy requiring initial face-to-face visits with patients (Maheu & McMenamin, 2014).

Technology-assisted counseling has also been significantly influenced and guided by the NBCC, which defined the terms of this new counseling activity and developed standards for the ethical practice of Internet counseling. These standards address the Internet counseling relationship; confidentiality in Internet counseling; and legal considerations, licensure, and certification (NBCC, 2012). The 2014 *ACA Code of Ethics* addresses technology-assisted services and the myriad of issues that have arisen and stresses the need for adequate informed consent (Standards H.1.–H.6.). Although there are many unanswered and evolving legal questions and implications of technology-assisted counseling, ongoing efforts to define standards and ethics can support practitioners in establishing productive counseling relationships that seek to serve the best interests of the client.

Legal Considerations

As discussed above, counselors who provide distance counseling must be in compliance with the licensing statutes of the states in which they practice. The ACA publication *Licensure Requirements for Professional Counselors* (2014b) provides a snapshot of the evolving regulation of distance counseling by state counselor licensing boards:

> Seventeen (17) states (Alaska, Arkansas, California, Colorado, Iowa, Louisiana, Massachusetts, Minnesota, Nebraska, New York, North Carolina, Oregon, South Carolina, Ohio, Texas, Utah, and West Virginia) regulate electronic communications involving counselors, but only within their particular state.
>
> Twenty (20) state counseling boards (Alabama, Arizona, Connecticut, Delaware, Florida, Georgia, Hawaii, Kentucky, Maine, Michigan,

Missouri, New Hampshire, North Dakota, Oklahoma, Pennsylvania, Rhode Island, South Dakota, Vermont, Washington and Wyoming) and the District of Columbia board report an absence of any law, rule, or regulation addressing the use of the Internet with clients.

One (1) state, Arkansas, has an addendum to its licensure requirements specifically geared towards technology-assisted therapy: The Technology Assisted Counseling Specialization license requires additional education and supervision.

Five (5) states (Maryland, New Mexico, Tennessee, Virginia and Indiana) specifically state that they do not support electronic communications under their scope of practice for professional counselors.

One (1) state (Mississippi) will only grant licensure to state residents and/or those who pay state income tax. (p. 15)

However, compliance with licensing statutes in the state in which a counselor is licensed is just the beginning. A far murkier legal issue presents when counseling services are conducted across state lines or when services cross international boundaries. Requirements for state-to-state distance counseling are being seriously considered. At this stage there are more questions than answers. For example, must a counselor be licensed in the state in which she practices and in each of the states where clients reside? Should income gained from a client be subject to state income tax of the client's home state or the state in which the counselor practices? Who will regulate these services, and how will monitoring occur? As for practice that crosses international boundaries, counselors who practice distance counseling may need to investigate laws of different countries. As you can quickly appreciate, complexities proliferate, and in such an environment there can be significant risk. Counselors are strongly advised to seek knowledgeable legal assistance before establishing a distance counseling service.

Before we conclude this discussion, we want to make a clear distinction between counseling practices that are exclusively or predominantly distant or technology-assisted and traditional face-to-face counseling that might, from time to time, include an element of technology-assisted counseling. There are obvious situations in which counselors must have a phone session with a client or exchange e-mail or text messages (see discussion below) as well as other synchronous or asynchronous communication. However, counselors are still advised to consider the confidentiality and privacy ramifications of such technology use in advance, and they should use informed consent that covers such occasional use.

There is one other technology-assisted counseling activity that requires some discussion. Distance-supervision, the use of streaming video conferencing for clinical supervision, is a topic of growing interest. Distance supervision for student counselors in training is not uncommon. CACREP accredits counselor programs that use distance-supervision for some or most of the supervision provided for practicum or internship students. The argument for the use of distance-supervision for prelicensed counselors is that, particularly for counselors practicing in remote or rural areas, it would make clinical supervision more accessible and convenient. Also, it could allow for more immediate access to competent supervision for any prelicensed counselor. The ACA gathered data from state licensing boards regarding prelicensed clinical supervision requirements (ACA, 2014b). An analysis of this data indicated that most state licensing boards defined clinical supervision as "face to face." This finding suggests a strong bias for supervision that occurs in the same room, not electronically. Nevertheless, eight states permit some amount of distance-supervision to meet prelicensing clinical supervision requirements. South Dakota and Michigan permit up to 50 hours of distance-supervision to fulfill the 100 required hours. North Dakota permits 40 hours, Louisiana 25 hours, and Arkansas permits up to 25% of the total required hours. Missouri permits all prelicensed clinical supervision to be distance-supervision "if electronic supervision is continuously interactive," (p. 46) whereas in Colorado, distance supervision is permitted after an initial 2-hour face-to-face supervision session and a live face-to-face session every 6 months. Finally, in Alaska, with board approval, all clinical supervision can be distance-supervision (ACA, 2014b).

Social Media: Think Before You "Tweet," "Friend," or "Blog"

Some counselors may consider themselves online dinosaurs, but the reality is that an increasing number of Americans, including counselors, are participating in one or more online social networks. In the first quarter of 2014, Facebook had 1.28 billion active users (www.statista.com, 2014). One source reports that 1 in 5 couples meet online, 92% of children in the United States have a digital footprint, and 2 new members join LinkedIn every second (Qualman, 2013). Fellow counselor educators have commented to us that it's the rare counseling graduate student who does not engage in social media activities. Even if you do not currently participate in such online activities, be aware that your office employees, counseling students, or supervisees are likely part of such networks. Engaging in social media between counselor and client without advance thinking and use of sound informed consent may cause harm to both client and counselor.

Breach of Confidentiality

The major concern for counselors and other mental health professionals engaging in social media is the potential for breach of confidentiality or invasion of privacy. Such breaches could cause legal problems because of a violation of state law, state licensure regulations, and federal law, including HIPAA and HITECH (see Chapter 5). Disclosure of client information on social networking sites by you or your employees could constitute use of PHI for an unauthorized purpose. On the basis of recent HITECH regulations, which supplement HIPAA, you would have to perform a risk assessment and take action in response to a breach, such as formal notice to the affected clients, the U.S. Department of Health and Human Services, and, in some cases, the media. Reposting of information is another lurking danger for counselors engaged in social media. For example, if a status update on Facebook is reposted to another page, friends of clients or students may be able to view personal information. Clients' identities could inadvertently be revealed.

Counselors must also consider their ethical obligations when engaging in social media. The 2014 *ACA Code of Ethics* states, "Counselors take precautions to avoid disclosing confidential information through public social media" (Standard H.6.d.). Although the exact precautions or steps may depend on a particular counselor's practice setting and client base, it is important that all counselors think about any actions—including whether to sign up for a particular site or how to manage privacy settings—before engaging in any social media activities. Counselors are also expected to "respect the privacy of their clients' presence on social media unless given consent to view such information" (Standard H.6.c.).

> The major concern for counselors and other mental health professionals engaging in social media is the potential for breach of confidentiality or invasion of privacy.

Furthermore, the risk of breach of confidentiality is heightened in group counseling settings where members may engage in social media. Consider the potential damage to clients if one group member posted pictures of the other members or began posting comments about others. Counselors engaged in group work must be very careful to address the parameters of online behavior through informed consent and should consider ground rules whereby members agree not to post any pictures, comments, or other items pertaining to group members online in any form. Counselors may also want to state that they cannot control what others do but that the *quid pro quo* for being part of the group is the agreement to refrain from posting any type of confidential information or identifying group members online.

Boundary Violations

There are a variety of other related concerns, not least of which involve boundary violations in use of social media. For example, one patient who developed erotic feelings for his psychologist looked her up online and found a picture of the therapist clad in a bathing suit. The patient quit treatment and reported his concern to the Ethics Office of the American Psychological Association (Scarton, 2010). Although this complaint may appear far-fetched, online postings could be disturbing to some clients.

Confusion over terminology in the constantly changing world of social media might also create inadvertent boundary problems. For example, there may be subtle differences among "friending," "liking," or "poking" someone on Facebook. "Poking" might imply a playful teasing, which could be totally inappropriate action in a counselor–client relationship. Any of these activities could pose boundary issues in a counselor–client relationship.

Business networking has burgeoned on the Internet with the advent of sites such as LinkedIn, among many others. Popular personal sites such as Facebook and Twitter are also increasingly used by businesses and professionals. The concerns raised by business-related sites are similar to those used for solely personal reasons: Client confidentiality, the counselor's own privacy, and counselor–client boundaries are vulnerable. One social media consultant has warnings for anyone using social media:

> Everyone *should* have some social media privacy concerns. Facebook has made some blunders where they once made all of our profile information public by default. Location based services such as Foursquare

> announce to the world whenever we "check-in" to a location, making us prime targets for both stalkers as well as robbers who hang out on "Please Rob Me" to look for their next target . . . *Don't say anything or post anything to your profile that you would not want any stranger to know* . . . go to your Settings on each site and learn how they work *before* you post any private information. Or just don't post *any* private information! (Schaffer, 2010)

It's basically a balancing act for the counselor in weighing the potential benefits from social media for one's clients and counseling practice against the potential harm. However, unless you are comfortable learning about privacy settings and implementing them, you are courting both legal and ethical challenges to your social media activities.

Texting, Instant Messaging, and E-Mail

What is the ratio of time you spend talking on the phone versus sending e-mails, texting, or instant messaging? If you are like most people, we suspect the time you spend on the phone is decreasing and the amount of communication through e-mail and texting has grown dramatically. What about communicating with clients? Is that a similar ratio, or have you not opened yourself to receiving e-mail or texts from clients? These are important decisions. In some cases these decisions will be driven by the counselor's place of employment, which may or may not permit e-mail or texting communication with clients. On the other hand, if you are in private practice or aspire to be in private practice, you will need to set some ground rules about how you will communicate with clients.

For youth and young adults, texting has become a major communication vehicle. Recently the Pew Internet & American Life Project (a project of the Pew Research Center) conducted a study to determine the ubiquity of text messaging. The study's findings revealed that 83% of American adults own cell phones, and almost three quarters (73%) of cell phone owners send and receive text messages. When respondents were asked how they prefer to be contacted on their cell phone, "31% said they preferred texts to talking on the phone, while 53% said they preferred a voice call to a text message. Another 14% said the contact method they prefer depends on the situation" (Smith, 2011). One finding that is not surprising is that young adults (18–24 years of age) "exchange an average of 109.5 messages on a normal day—that works out to more than 3,200 texts per month"

(Smith, 2011, p. 2). What seems clear from these data and from our own experience is that texting is now a primary form of communication. Many factors seem to be driving this shift, not the least of which is that people simply cannot live without their cell phones. For many people, the cell phone has become nearly a permanent fixture on one's person. With mobile phone in hand, sending and receiving texts is instantaneous and can occur nearly anywhere. Is it any wonder that clients, especially younger clients, prefer to communicate with their counselors by texting?

What are the risks of texting and instant messaging with our clients? Privacy is probably the primary concern. Although it is possible to clone a phone and intercept phone and text messages, it is illegal and not something easily accomplished. Therefore, assuming the text sender/receiver is not using a company phone that specifically retains all text communication, it is then unlikely that text messages are retained by the cellular company for more than a few days or until the message is delivered. The larger risk is that the text message remains on the sender's and receiver's phones. Therefore, if private information is exchanged through texting, that information could be obtained directly from the phone of either the sender or the receiver. When counselors text with clients (depending on the content of the text messages), it is possible that PHI is open and available to anyone who has access to the counselor's mobile phone. Counselors who engage in texting should consider having a password-protected phone and other means of securing the data. (See discussion below about texting and documentation, and see Chapter 5 regarding HIPAA and HITECH concerns.)

Another concern has to do with an expectation of immediacy that seems to be embedded into the texting ethos. Clients who have a texting relationship with a counselor could have an unrealistic expectation of the counselor's responsiveness. In an emergency (e.g., plans for suicide) the client might send a text message to his counselor expecting the counselor to respond immediately. Counselors should think carefully about the parameters of texting. For example, if the counselor rarely if ever uses texting, that should be communicated to the client as part of the informed consent process. If the counselor does engage in texting, it is advisable to inform the client (as part of the written informed consent or authorization) that it should be used for setting appointments but not for highly confidential issues, absent an emergency.

The use of e-mail communication with clients should also be considered carefully. For example, e-mail may provide a convenient means of scheduling or cancelling appointments. However, confidentiality is often compromised. Some family members share e-mail accounts; in addition, computers may be left on in full view of third parties. Boundaries may also be muddy with use of e-mail. Frequently the communication is informal and might lead to role confusion by the client (Bradley, Hendricks, Lock, Whiting, & Parr, 2011). As with the social media concerns raised above, informed consent is crucial in deciding whether and how to communicate with clients by e-mail. In fact, the 2014 *ACA Code of Ethics* now requires detailed informed consent (on risk/benefits, anticipated response time, emergency procedures, etc.; Standard H.2.a.).

If you do use e-mail with clients, consider obtaining client authorization to engage in e-mail communications, which can be part of your standard informed consent process. Do this at the outset of treatment, if possible. Both you and your clients should have an agreement that e-mail will be used only for nonconfidential, nonurgent exchanges, such as appointment scheduling as mentioned above. Stress the importance of using e-mail only for nonurgent situations; this could be extremely important in dealing with suicidal clients. You will need to have a protected list or other mechanism for identifying which clients have agreed to use of e-mail. You should also let your clients know your policy for responding, including an approximate time for reply. You may wish to include an abbreviated form of this policy in *every* e-mail communication with clients. This policy can be formatted in a standard header or footer, along with your full name, office address and office phone number, as well as emergency instructions that you send automatically with each e-mail. For example, your counseling practice e-mail footer could include information such as the following:

> Please do not send confidential or urgent information by e-mail. If you have an emergency, please call 123-465-7890.
>
> In addition, this e-mail transmission may contain information that is confidential, privileged, or otherwise protected by federal or state law. If you have received this e-mail in error, please notify me immediately and permanently delete the transmission, including any attachments.
>
> Allison B. Counselor, LPC
> 123 Main St., Suite 1
> City, ST 12345
> 123-456-7890 (office)
> abcounselor@internet.com

If you know you cannot be compliant with such a policy, decline to communicate by e-mail and let your clients know that all communication outside of appointments must be made by telephone.

If you receive unsolicited e-mails from nonclients with clinical questions or unsolicited e-mails from clients and have not yet proactively taken steps as suggested above, you should tell the inquirer that, out of concern for privacy, you do not respond to such questions by e-mail but that he or she may call your office.

A major consideration in protecting client's information is security of the devices you use. Before you even turn on your PC, Mac®, laptop, iPad®, Galaxy®, iPhone®, Android, or other smartphone to check and send e-mail or text messages to clients, you should consider whether you have adequate security configuration, a firewall, password protection, and possibly data encryption. If you have PHI on your computer, smartphone, or other device, encryption may be the best defense against having to comply with complicated HITECH breach notification regulations. (See Chapter 5 for more information on HITECH.) Some experts are now recommending passwords of 12 characters, including numbers, upper- and lowercase letters, and symbols (Nelson & Simek, 2011). For example, "Orlando!2015!" might be a password you'd likely remember if you'd planned to travel in that year for ACA's annual conference. In addition, you might change your settings to require your explicit approval before you automatically connect to any available wireless device when you're using a wireless network that might be used by others. If you use your wireless devices in airports, hotels, or the local Starbucks, this becomes especially important because your office virus, firewall, and other security protections may not apply in a Wi-Fi hotspot.

One final concern regarding e-mail, texting, and instant messaging relates to requirements for retaining a record of the content of that communication. What are the expectations of counselor licensing boards regarding the retention of e-mails and text messages? Should counselors be expected to print out every e-mail or copy and paste every e-mail or text message to be included in the client's chart? What kind of communication should be retained, and what is purely administrative (appointment setting, cancellations, etc.) and need not be retained? The NBCC has developed the most comprehensive list of requirements we have seen regarding the delivery of what is referred to as "distance professional services" (NBCC, 2012, p. 1). The NBCC document includes 20 points, one of which addresses requirements for the retention of electronic written communication:

> NCCs [nationally certified counselors] shall retain copies of all written communications with distance service recipients. Examples of written communications include e-mail/text messages, instant messages and

histories of chat-based discussions even if they are related to house-keeping issues such as change of contact information or scheduling appointments. (NBCC, 2012, p. 3)

We fully understand the need to document clinically important information, notwithstanding the means of communication. However, we admit to being concerned by the extent of this requirement. We question the practicality of such a requirement in the real world and are mindful that this requirement exceeds most laws and regulations governing delivery of mental health services through electronic means. We also wonder about the rationale for this requirement as it surpasses documentation requirements for counselor–client communication in traditional face-to-face relationships. To be specific, we know of no requirements for retaining verbatim voicemail messages or documenting administrative/scheduling appointments regardless of the communication medium. Finally, the practicality of capturing text messages or e-mails from phones or other devices seems, at minimum, cumbersome. See Chapter 10 for a more detailed discussion of these issues regarding records.

Other Technologies

We have no illusion that we can even name, much less actually meaningfully discuss, the plethora of current and future technologies that affect the practice of counseling. Nevertheless, we do want to mention several "other technologies" and suggest that counselors remain ever vigilant to how current and newly emerging technologies can enhance or denigrate the counseling relationship.

What are the ethics of Googling your client without the client's knowledge or invitation? Is this a boundary violation? What will you do with the information if it is contrary to what your client is telling you? What about a client's blog? If you were treating a client who had overdosed, would it be ethical to check out a link to the client's blog, which was included in an e-mail sent by the client's friend and inferred suicidal ideation? Although online research about a client could compromise trust and invade privacy, it may be appropriate in an emergency situation such as this to help treat the client (Scarton, 2010).

Computer-administered health and mental health self-help programs and smart phone apps offer intriguing possibilities to help clients self-monitor moods; follow fitness, nutrition, and health improvement goals; track counseling goals; practice social skills; and help conquer phobias. Smart phone apps are now available in the marketplace or are in development to enlist clients in a more active and interactive manner in their own treatment. However, when counselors recommend the use of any health or mental health app, what responsibility or liability follows that recommendation? Is the responsibility the same as when a counselor recommends a book or study guide? Or is there an expectation of counselor involvement or responsiveness embedded into technology recommendations that is different? It's a brave new world, and counselors who want to incorporate these technologies into their practice are advised to carefully vet each program or application before recommending it to clients.

Recommendations

The following summary provides practical suggestions for handling the plethora of legal and ethical issues raised by the burgeoning use of communication technology and social media.

- *Informed consent with social media:* If you do not use online sites like Facebook, Myspace, Twitter, or LinkedIn, discuss with your clients at the outset of the counseling relationship that you choose not to use such sites and that declining their offer of participation (such as "friending") does not mean that you are screening them out personally. This discussion can be handled as part of the informed consent process at the outset of treatment. (Again, see 2014 *ACA Code of Ethics*, Standard H.6.b.) If you do use social media sites and get a "friend" or other participation request from a client but have not handled this issue proactively, respond to the request promptly and let the client know that you do not participate in social media exchanges with clients in order to protect their confidentiality and promote healthy boundaries. This response should occur outside the social media vehicle. For example, you may discuss the request with the client during the next session, or if the client is no longer active, consider contacting the former client by telephone to discuss the decision. If you simply ignore a client's request to "friend" them or otherwise be linked online, you run the risk of harm to the counselor–client relationship.
- *Informed consent with e-mail and texting or instant messaging:* Similar to the caveat above regarding social media, if you do not engage in e-mail, texting, or instant messaging, discuss with

your clients at the outset of counseling that you do not use such technology. If you do e-mail, text, or send instant messages to clients, set your parameters through informed consent. Explain that confidentiality is limited and that you will not respond to emergencies or address sensitive, confidential information through this media. In addition, look into security measures to protect your smartphone or other equipment.

- *Security:* Look into security measures to protect your smart-phone, laptop, tablet, or other electronic equipment. Do not "root" or "jailbreak" the device to install apps (in other words, don't bypass the device's security settings). Check into whether your device has a kill switch or other mechanism to perma-nently cut off lost or stolen devices. In the future, counselors and other professionals may need to investigate the need for cyber risk insurance, either as a stand-alone insurance product or as part of professional liability insurance coverage. If you employ others and follow a BYOD (bring your own device) policy, these issues will become even more important.
- *Initiating contact:* Avoid initiating personal connections with clients through social media. Such outreach has a high likelihood of violating the ACA *Code*'s multiple caveats against bound-ary violations. In many states, initiation of the social media contact may also be interpreted by the state licensure law as an impermissible "dual relationship" or boundary violation.
- *Documentation:* Be careful what you document in the client's record. In most circumstances, you should not enter information retrieved from social networking sites into a client's counseling record without that client's consent.
- *Harmful dual or "other" relationships:* Avoid dual or multiple relationships that could harm the client. If a client asks you to look at postings made online, it might be appropriate to review them together. This could be analogous to looking at a client's journal or photos that depict life scenes important to a client. However, inappropriate sharing of personal information cannot necessarily be sanctioned just by including it in one's informed consent document.
- *Professional versus private roles:* Separate your professional from private persona. This separation makes good sense, from a practical perspective. It also now is an imperative, from an ethics perspective (2014 *ACA Code of Ethics*, Standard H.6.a.). If you choose to participate in social networking sites, use

due diligence and learn how to use the privacy settings. Use discretion; don't post pictures of drinking or other activities that could raise questions about your maturity, judgment, or professionalism or that might be viewed as divulging unnecessary private information. Think about the appropriateness of including a "fan page" online. Reports in the media abound regarding job termination as a result of inappropriate social networking activity. One early "victim" of social media ignorance was a teacher in training who was denied her degree just days before her graduation because of online pictures that depicted her as a "drunken pirate." Her high school supervisor and university dean decided that this was unprofessional conduct and could have promoted drinking to her underage students. After the student sued the university on the basis of claims of free-speech rights and legal behavior, the federal court judge found that because the teacher-in-training was a public employee whose photo did not relate to matters of public concern, her online post was not protected speech (Rosen, 2010). In short, the denial of her degree was upheld by the court.

- *Safety:* Mental health professionals cannot always be sure of the seriousness of a client's presenting issues or mental health history. Therefore, be wary of posting personal information online. Mental health professionals have been victims of violence or stalking by clients even before online social networking was a reality. Think about protecting yourself, your spouse or significant other, your children, or others who are important to you. If you employ others who may use online social networking sites or if you supervise therapists or counseling students, consider addressing these issues in your privacy policies, personnel policies, and HIPAA work force training.

- *Defamation:* Be careful not to engage in statements about others that could be viewed as defamatory. This type of "cybersmearing" can also become an issue for an employer who may be aware of employees making defamatory or harassing statements about other employees. An employer may have a duty to stop the harassment. You should also think twice about posting negative statements about colleagues online. Instead, if unprofessional conduct is involved, follow the procedures in the 2014 *ACA Code of Ethics* (Standard I.2.) and your state licensure board statutes or regulations.

- *Permanence of postings:* Think carefully before making any statements that enter the cyberworld. Online postings frequently cannot be retracted. Also, social networking entries and e-mail communications are frequently ending up as evidence in court.
- *Group counseling concerns:* If you conduct counseling or psycho-educational groups, consider developing rules that address the use of online discussion outside the group. Use of social media must be addressed by group leaders proactively during the informed consent process, as mentioned above, and as part of the norm-setting discussion. Breaches of confidentiality using social media can sometimes be intentionally malicious. "This new ethical challenge must be addressed vigorously because containing and rectifying the damage done through a malicious status update or tweeting of confidential information is likely not possible" (Bertram, 2011, p. 15).
- *Ethics of online client searches:* Before using online sites to access information about a client, consider the ethical implications of such searches. Consult a colleague or the ACA Ethics Committee if you are unclear whether such activity is ethical in a given situation.
- *Remain current:* Keep up-to-date on changing legal and ethical requirements in the brave new world of online social media.

Chapter 8

Suicide and Threats of Harm to Self

Threats of harm to self and especially threats of suicide or a completed suicide by a client are stressful and disturbing issues in any counseling practice. Client suicide inevitably results in a thorough scrutiny of every aspect of care provided by all mental health professionals involved. The primary question will be, did the counselor (mental health professional) meet the standard of practice in the provision of care to his or her client? The standard of practice determination will include an analysis of the treatment regimen, documented evidence of competent clinical decision making regarding the management of suicidal expressions or behaviors from the client, clinical supervision (if appropriate), and adherence to institutional policies for responding to the risk of client suicide. If there are questions about whether the counselor met the standard of practice, ethical complaints and/or legal action are likely to follow.

In this chapter we (a) outline some of the ethical and legal issues surrounding the response to threats of suicide and harm to self; (b) offer some practical strategies for managing the ethical and legal risks associated with client threats; and (c) address some of the moral, ethical, and legal complexities associated with assisted suicide. Before beginning this discussion, we provide a brief overview of the prevalence of suicide, threat of suicide, and threats of harm to self, including a discussion of client populations most at-risk of self-harming behavior.

Prevalence of Suicide and Threats of Harm to Self

Suicide, threats of suicide, and other threats of harm to self are a chilling reality for practicing counselors and other mental health professionals. Depending on the practice setting, many counselors regularly face the clinical complexities and ethical and legal implications of responding to clients who threaten harm to self. The American Association of Suicidology (2014c) reported that 38,364 people committed suicide in the United States in 2010; this translates to 105 suicides per day, or one suicide every 13.7 minutes. Suicide was the 10th leading cause of death for all Americans in 2010. Suicide rates are highest among those aged 45–54.The national suicide rate in 2010 was 12.4 per 100,000. Wyoming (23.3), Alaska (23.1), Montana (22.9), Nevada (20.3), and New Mexico (20.1) had the highest rates of suicide per 100,000 people. The District of Columbia (6.8), New York (8.0), New Jersey (8.2), and Maryland (8.7) had the lowest rates of suicide. The American Association of Suicidology estimates that there are 25 suicide attempts for every one completed suicide (100 to 200 attempts for youth and 4 attempts for elder persons). Using the 25 to 1 ratio, there were 959,100 attempts in the United States during 2010 (American Association of Suicidology, 2014c). The frequency of suicide and suicide attempts makes it almost inevitable that most practicing mental health professionals will be involved with these clinical challenges.

Male Suicide

No demographic group is more at risk of completing suicide than males; overall, males are almost 4 times more likely to complete suicide than females. (The rate for males is 20.0 per 100,000, whereas for females it is 5.2 per 100,000.) Of all demographic categories, White males have the highest incidence of suicide (22.6 per 100,000). In addition, the ratio of suicide attempts to suicide completions among males is far smaller than the comparable ratio among females. When males talk about taking their lives, generally they are more serious and more likely to follow through on threats. Firearms are currently the most often used method of suicide by essentially all groups, but males in particular tend to use methods that are the most lethal (American Association of Suicidology, 2014c).

Youth and Child Suicide

School counselors, marriage and family therapists, child psychologists and therapists, and other child-based practitioners are often confronted with students and clients who threaten suicide. In 2010, there were 4,600 young people (ages 15 to 24) who completed suicide in the United States. Accidents are the leading cause of death for young people, followed by homicide, and then suicide. The rate of suicide by young people is more than 12 times higher than suicide by children ages 5–14 (American Association of Suicidology, 2014c). As is true for the general population, adolescents and young people are more likely to use firearms, suffocation, and poisoning than other methods of suicide. On the other hand, children were dramatically more likely to use suffocation. There are also pronounced gender differences. Males in the 15–19 age group are nearly 5 times more likely to die by suicide than females of the same age (National Institute of Mental Health, 2011). Data on sexual orientation and gender identity are not included on death certificates; even when data from psychological autopsy interviews are considered, there are no reliable data on the suicide death rates of lesbian, gay, bisexual, and transgender youth (American Association of Suicidology, 2014b).

When young people commit suicide, the survivors—family members, friends, and everyone connected with them—must deal with difficult and intense emotions. Confusion, guilt, and anger typically accompany the death of a young person by suicide. Sometimes, rightly or wrongly, these emotions are channeled toward the helping professionals who were involved in the child's life. When a client in active treatment with a counselor commits suicide, the actions of the counselor are likely to be scrutinized. Accusations of ethical violations, licensing board complaints, and lawsuits often follow, claiming that the counselor failed to meet the standard of practice. In a subsequent section in this chapter, we describe in considerable detail a lawsuit brought against a school counselor (*Eisel v. Board of Education of Montgomery County*, 1991) resulting from a tragic murder–suicide involving two middle school students. A careful review of the facts and circumstances of this case offers many lessons that counselors should heed.

College Student Suicide

The overall rate of completed suicide among college students is roughly 7.5 per 100,000, making suicide the second leading cause of death among college students. Four male students complete suicide for every female student; however, at least twice as many females as males attempt suicide. An estimated 1,100 suicides occur on college campuses each year; 1 in 10 college students say they have seriously considered suicide during the last year (Jed Foundation, 2011).

It is not difficult to understand why college students are at substantial risk. Suicide risk is associated with the following general risk factors:

- depression and other mental disorders or a substance-abuse disorder (often in combination with other mental disorders; more than 90% of people who die by suicide have these risk factors);
- prior suicide attempt;
- family history of suicide;
- family violence, including physical or sexual abuse;
- firearms in the home, the method used in more than one half of suicides; and
- exposure to suicidal behavior of others, such as family members, peers, or media figures. (National Institute of Mental Health, 2011)

For college and university counselors, suicide assessment and appropriate intervention constitute a daunting clinical challenge, and the risk of suicide among students poses a significant risk of liability to institutions of higher learning.

Elder Person Suicide

Older Americans are disproportionately more likely to die by suicide. Comprising only 13.0% of the U.S. population, individuals age 65 and older accounted for 15.6% of all suicide deaths in 2010. Compared with women and individuals of other races, White men as a group, particularly those over the age of 85, had among the highest rates. In 2007, the suicide rate of these men was 47.33 per 100,000, a rate that is 2.37 times higher than the current rate of all men (American Association of Suicidology, 2014a).

Risk factors for suicide among older persons differ from those among the young. Older persons are more socially isolated, have higher rates of depression, and more frequently use highly lethal methods than younger persons. They also make fewer attempts per completed suicide, have a higher male-to-female ratio than other groups, have often visited a health care provider before their suicide, and have more physical illnesses than younger persons. Many factors seem to be associated with completed suicides in the elderly:

- the recent death of a loved one;
- physical illness, uncontrolled pain, or fear of a prolonged illness;
- perceived poor health;
- social isolation and loneliness; and
- major changes in social roles, for example, retirement. (American Association of Suicidology, 2014a)

Other Threats of Self-Harm or Self-Injury

Suicide is not the only threat of harm to self that presents clinical, ethical, and legal complications for counselors. School counselors and others who work with adolescents and young adults know that self-injurious behaviors intended to regulate intense negative emotion are frequently the reason for counseling and that self-injurious behaviors often present during the course of treatment. These behaviors, although generally not intended as suicide threats, often result in harm, sometimes serious self-inflicted harm. The International Society for the Study of Self-Injury (2014) defines *nonsuicidal self-injury* as "the deliberate, direct, and self-inflicted destruction of body tissue resulting in immediate tissue damage, for purposes not socially sanctioned and without suicidal intent." The following examples of self-inflicted harm by youth are common:

- severely scratching or pinching with fingernails or other objects to the point that bleeding occurs or marks remain on the skin;
- cutting, ripping, or carving words or symbols into wrists, arms, legs, torso, or other areas of the body;
- banging or punching objects into oneself to the point of bruising or bleeding (with the conscious intention of hurting the self);
- biting to the point that bleeding occurs or marks remain on skin;
- pulling out hair, eyelashes, or eyebrows with the overt intention of hurting oneself;
- intentionally preventing wounds from healing;
- burning the skin; and
- embedding objects into the skin. (Whitlock, 2009, p. 1)

Reports of the prevalence of self-injury suggest that about 13–25% of adolescents and young adults surveyed in schools have some history of self-injury. Suicide is typically not the intention of self-injurious behaviors. However, "individuals with a history of non-suicide self-injury are at higher risk for suicide thoughts, gestures, and attempts and, because of this, need to be assessed for suicide risk" (Whitlock, 2009, p. 3). Client suicide frequently places counselors at great legal and ethical risk. Therefore, when clients display self-injurious behaviors, counselors should monitor for suicidal ideations and, when appropriate, perform a competent suicide assessment.

In addition to these types of intentional self-harming behaviors, counselors must also respond to a nearly endless list of client at-risk and danger-courting behaviors, including driving while under the influence of alcohol or drugs, engaging in unprotected sex or substance abuse, and minors disclosing personal information while chatting online. The theme of self-harming behavior, in all its endless permutations, is the prime turf of many counselors' clinical work.

Suicide and Ethics

When clients present with threats of harm to self, we are thrust into a complex and critically important decision-making process. The mental health professional's response to a client who presents with an intention to self-harm or commit suicide brings into sharp focus a collision between two deeply held moral principles: autonomy (fostering the right to control the direction of one's life) versus beneficence ("working for the good of the individual and society by promoting mental health and well-being"; 2014 *ACA Code of Ethics*, Preamble). The 2014 *ACA Code of Ethics* (ACA, 2014a, Standard A.1.a.) advises that "the primary responsibility of counselors is to respect the dignity and promote the welfare of clients." We can generally assume that preventing the client from self-inflicted harm or death is promoting the welfare of the client (beneficence). There may be special circumstances in which a client can make a compelling case for suicide as an expression of dignity and welfare, that is, autonomy and beneficence. (We address these special circumstances later in this chapter.) However, under most circumstances, in order to respect the dignity and promote the welfare of the client, it may be necessary for the counselor to take some action—action that could involve breaching the confidentiality of the client (in other words, not respecting autonomy). Support for such steps is found in Standard B.2.a. of the *ACA Code of Ethics*: "The general requirement that counselors keep information confidential does not apply when disclosure is required to protect clients or identified others from serious and foreseeable harm . . ." In other words, under certain circumstances, beneficence trumps autonomy. This gives us the ethical latitude to take action, including disclosing confidential information if, after thoroughly assessing the "client's *ideation, plan,* and *means*" (Werth & Stroup, 2015, p. 233), we conclude that clients are at a level of risk that they must be protected from themselves. It is important to note that protecting the client from harm can be accomplished in many forms, not all of which involve breaching confidentiality.

Two other ethical considerations affect our professional practice when dealing with clients at risk of harming themselves. In keeping with the moral principle of autonomy, we are ethically instructed to provide our clients, during the informed consent process, with an explanation of the ground rules and expectations of the counseling relationship, including the limits and exceptions to confidentiality. We are further admonished that informed consent is an ongoing process; it is our responsibility to keep our clients informed of any changes in the counseling relationship as time and circumstances change (Standards A.2.a., A.2.b.).

Ultimately, ethics serve to guide effective clinical decision making. When faced with a suicidal or self-harming client, practitioners must initiate action that is based on conclusions drawn from the assessment of the client's likelihood of danger to self. When possible, an important ethical, legal, and clinical strategy is to consult with other practitioners to help ensure that all options have been identified. In some cases, responding to the clinical needs of a suicidal client might be beyond the boundaries of competence for a counselor. Although the ethical principle of not practicing beyond the boundaries of competence might be relevant (Standard C.2.a.), an inexperienced practitioner should not use this ethics guideline as justification to abandon a client who is in the middle of a suicidal crisis. The counselor should immediately obtain consultation or supervision and remain an active agent until the client has stabilized.

Legal Issues of Suicide

In recent years, a large percentage of the malpractice claims against mental health professionals have been triggered by patient suicide. As discussed in Chapter 4, liability is ultimately determined on the basis of whether a legal duty exists to protect the client from self-inflicted harm and whether the counselor's conduct violated that duty and led to the harm. In many instances involving mental health professionals, the duty is the most clear when the client is hospitalized or under some type of custodial care. However, even in outpatient or school settings, liability can occur.

The failure to conduct an adequate evaluation of the client may lead to a malpractice claim. If a client denies suicidal intent but evidences signs of serious depression, the counselor should conduct further inquiry and possibly refer to a psychiatrist or psychologist for evaluation (see Exhibit 2). Another factor that often leads to liability is the failure to obtain information about past treatment. As mentioned earlier, the statistics clarify that a past serious suicide attempt is a likely indicator of future suicidal behavior. Failure to follow institutional policies, client abandonment, and failure to follow up with a client recently discharged from the hospital are other ways to invite a lawsuit when dealing with an at-risk client. Yet another factor that increases potential liability is the failure to keep adequate records (see Chapter 10).

The case of *Stepakoff v. Kantar* (1985) illustrates the problem with inadequate record keeping and suicide. In that case, the patient had been treated for bipolar disorder for over a year. Several days before the patient's death, his wife left with the expectation that the patient would leave the house before she returned. The patient's psychiatrist planned to go away for the weekend and developed a plan for weekend coverage. Before leaving town, he met with the

Exhibit 2

When a Client Is Suicidal

---

1. Deal candidly with confidentiality, privilege, and privacy (and the exceptions).
2. Inquire about past treatment; obtain records if possible.
3. Consult with and involve (when appropriate) family members, significant others, and relevant others to gain a balanced perspective.
4. Engage in careful consultation and collaborative decision making.
5. Refer as appropriate (e.g., medication evaluation).
6. Coordinate care with others on the treatment team.
7. Take action (e.g., regarding voluntary or involuntary hospitalization).
8. Use careful clinical judgment.
9. Document (a) situations that raised alarms (client's behavior or words), (b) options you considered, (c) options you ruled out, (d) action taken, (e) results of action, and (f) follow-up (what happened).
10. Follow institutional policy.

---

patient and decided against involuntary hospitalization. Over the weekend, the patient killed himself by carbon monoxide poisoning.

At the subsequent malpractice trial, there was much attention focused on a note written by the psychiatrist after he last met with the patient. The note included this sentence: "There is a question of whether he will make it over the weekend." Although the doctor said he meant that he wasn't sure the patient would be able to carry out planned activities, the note was susceptible to different interpretations. The jury eventually sided with the psychiatrist, but the result could have been different. The lesson learned from this case is that taking the time to fully document one's thoughts—especially when the client is at risk of harming himself—can help to reduce the likelihood that the practitioner will be held liable for a mere mistake in predicting harm.

Prior to the 1990s, it was rare for counselors, especially school counselors, to be held liable for a client's suicide. In *Bogust v. Iverson* (1960), a college professor–counselor was found not responsible for the suicide of a student that occurred some 6 weeks after the counselor terminated counseling sessions with the student. The court ruled that the counselor had no duty to commit, seek treatment for, or warn the parents of the student because there was no evidence that he was aware of the student's suicidal tendencies. In recent years, counselors are discovering that they may have a duty to protect clients from harming themselves if such harm is foreseeable. In 1991, the Maryland Court of Appeals ruled in *Eisel v. Board of Education of Montgomery County* that a summary judgment (i.e., the court's dismissal of the case without a full trial) was not appropriate in a case in which two school counselors failed to warn a father of suicidal statements made by his child.

In this case, a middle-school counselor was informed that a student, Nicole Eisel, had told other children of her plans to kill herself. That counselor contacted the counselor assigned to Nicole, and the two counselors interviewed Nicole. She denied making such statements. Neither of the counselors notified Nicole's parents or school administrators. Nicole joined with a friend from another school in a murder–suicide pact, which was carried out on a school holiday, away from school grounds. Nicole's father brought suit against the counselors, alleging breach of their duty to intervene to attempt to prevent the suicide. The circuit court granted summary judgment in favor of the counselors, finding an absence of any such duty.

The Maryland Court of Appeals ruled that the summary judgment was erroneous and distinguished the facts in this case from previous case law finding that therapists could rarely be held liable for outpatient suicides. The negligence complained of in *Eisel* was not failure to prevent the suicide by exercising control or custody over Nicole but failure to communicate to Nicole's parent information possessed by the counselors. The plaintiff parent argued that had he been warned of the contemplated suicide, he might have been able to intervene. An argument also was made that the school stands *in loco parentis* in its relationship with students, and that results in "a special duty to exercise reasonable care to protect a pupil from harm" (pp. 451–452). Furthermore, Nicole's counselor was specially trained in crisis intervention techniques, suicide warnings, and available crisis psychiatric services.

The court decided that Nicole's suicide was foreseeable because the counselors had direct knowledge of Nicole's intent to commit suicide. The state of Maryland and Nicole's school have suicide prevention programs aimed at responding to communicated threats of suicide, including the recommendation in a policy memorandum to "share your knowledge with parents, friends, teachers, or other people who might be able to help. Don't worry about breaking a confidence if someone reveals suicidal plans to you. You may have to betray a secret to save a life" (p. 454). The court went on to discuss whether the breach of the counselors' alleged duty to notify the parents was the proximate cause of the suicide, the concept of moral blame, and the scope of the burden on the counselors to have notified the parents, as measured against the risk of death to a child. When the facts were fully developed in all these areas, the court concluded that a jury could find that there is indeed a duty imposed on counselors to notify parents in the event that they receive information about such potential harm. Ultimately, the Eisel case was remanded (sent back) to the trial court, where the counselors were exonerated from liability in the death of Nicole. The message for counselors from the court's ruling is that if there are institutional policies concerning suicide and other situations involving harm to self or others, those policies must be followed. If the policies are unethical or unworkable, responsible counselors should take action to notify administrators of their concerns before a crisis occurs.

A more recent case from Delaware's highest court underscores the point made in the Eisel decision that counselors must follow school policies, procedures, and protocols (*Rogers v. Christina School Dist.*, 2013). An intervention specialist at Newark High School (called a "school counselor" by the court; Stone, 2013) met with a student after being alerted to the student's suicidal ideation and suicide attempt the prior weekend. After a 4-hour interview in which the student confirmed his recent suicide attempt, the intervention specialist notified the administration and school counselors by e-mail that she believed he was not a suicide threat. The student's legal guardian was not notified, and the student committed suicide off campus later that day.

The student's family brought a wrongful death suit against the school district and school officials, including the intervention specialist, but the trial court granted summary judgment in favor of the defendants. On appeal, the Delaware Supreme Court affirmed the trial court's decision regarding the wrongful death claim. However, like the Maryland court in *Eisel*, the Delaware Supreme Court court reversed the trial court's award of summary judgment on the claim of negligence *per se*, based on the fact that the Delaware State Department of Education had protocols in place requiring parental notification of crisis situations. The case was remanded back to the trial court for further proceedings.

In another example (*McMahon v. St. Croix Falls School Dist.*, 1999), the Wisconsin Court of Appeals relied on the earlier case precedent set forth in *Bogust v. Iverson* (1960) and ruled that an adolescent's suicide was an intervening act, breaking the chain of causation necessary to establish a claim of negligence.[1] The facts in that case were as follows: At the time of his death, 15-year-old Andrew was a freshman at St. Croix Falls High School. On a January day in 1996, Andrew was driven to school by his father, but he did not attend classes that day. A school district policy provides that if a student is absent from school, the school will call the parents to verify the absence. The district did not call the parents. A classmate discovered Andrew's body in a closed garage. The cause of death was determined to be suicide from self-immolation; Andrew had poured gasoline on his body and set himself on fire. The parents' affidavits indicated that they were unaware that Andrew had received five failing grades, had been removed from the basketball team for poor grades, and had been emotionally upset in school. Furthermore, the classmate indicated that she had notified the school counselor of Andrew's despondent state. Even if the facts arguably demonstrated negligence

---

[1] See also *Grant v. Board of Trustees of Valley View School Dist.* (1997; liability not found) and *Jain v. State* (2000; court found no affirmative duty on part of university to prevent suicide and no "special relationship"; university was permitted but not required to notify parents).

on the part of the school administration and counselor, the court found that the injury was too remote from the negligence to allow for recovery of damages.

Federal courts have typically been reluctant to impose liability for student suicides on schools. There is an understanding that schools' and counselors' duties regarding suicidal students are even more attenuated when the suicide occurs off school premises. The U.S. Court of Appeals for the First Circuit highlighted the stark reality and difficulty of suicide prevention: "Absent a showing that the school affirmatively caused a suicide, the primary responsibility for safeguarding children from this danger, as from most others, is that of their parents; and even they, with direct control and intimate knowledge, are often helpless" (*Hasenfus v. LaJeunesse*, 1999, as cited in *Mikell v. School Administrative Unit #33*, 2009).

The upshot of recent suicide cases involving schools and universities is that counselors are vulnerable to lawsuits on the basis of client suicide and other attempted self-harm, but liability will not be imposed in all circumstances and in all states. Counselors should be very careful to follow school or other institutional policy and thoroughly document their actions. Other professionals should be involved where appropriate.

Bullying and Cyberbullying

In recent years the consequences of bullying and cyberbullying on students have gained considerable national attention. The U.S. Department of Health and Human Services defines bullying as "unwanted, aggressive behavior among school aged children that involves a real or perceived power imbalance. The behavior is repeated, or has the potential to be repeated, over time. Bullying includes actions such as making threats, spreading rumors, attacking someone physically or verbally, and excluding someone from a group on purpose" (Stopbullying.gov, 2014). Even though there is no direct federal bullying statute, if bullying is based on race, color, national origin, sex, and/or disability, there could be federal legal involvement. Many state legislatures, state boards of education, and local school districts have attempted to respond to this growing problem through development of new laws and policies.

Underscoring the importance of this topic is the fact that an overwhelming majority of states have passed both laws and policies addressing bullying and cyberbullying. An easy-to-use online listing of state laws and policies has been compiled by the U.S. Department of Education (see www.Stopbullying.gov). Similarities and differences among state laws are easily noted by reviewing these laws. For example, Florida law includes the following in its list of proscribed bullying behaviors: "(1) Teasing; (2) Social exclusion; (3) Threat; (4) Intimidation; (5) Stalking; (6) Physical violence; (7) Theft; (8) Sexual, religious, or racial harassment; (9) Public humiliation; or (10) Destruction of property" (Fla. Stat. Ann §1006.147(3)(2013)). By clicking on a state on the interactive map, the counselor can see the laws and policies of that particular state. As a result of the enactment of antibullying state laws and policies, school administrators and counselors across the country have been directed to implement antibullying programs and to be prepared to intervene when bullying threatens the physical well-being or mental health of a child.

The news media is regularly filled with stories about students who commit suicide, attempt suicide, or engage in some other self-harming behavior as a result of being a victim of bullying. Research into a causal relationship between bullying and mental health problems is just now coming into focus. The *American Journal of Psychiatry* (online) recently reported the findings of the British National Child Development Study, a 50-year prospective cohort of people born within a week of each other in England, Scotland, and Wales in 1958. Authors Takizawa, Maughan, and Arseneault (2014) reported a relationship between being the object of childhood bullying and adult psychological distress. Data reveal statistically "higher rates of depression, anxiety disorders, and suicidality" for those who were bullied as compared with participants who were not bullied. In addition, victims of bullying have been known to retaliate, sometimes violently, against their alleged bully. Bullying cases often involve school counselors or other school-based mental health professionals. Three cases reported in local newspapers make the point.

Example #1

RAMSEY, N.J.—The *Huffington Post* ("Sawyer Rubenstein, New Jersey Middle School Student," 2012) reported that a New Jersey school district agreed to pay $4.2 million to settle a lawsuit by an Eric Middle School student who was paralyzed when another student who was "known to be a bully" punched the student in the abdomen. The lawsuit alleged that "school officials knew or should have known" that the offending boy was a threat and that the school failed to comply with a state anti-bullying law. Three months before the assault the injured student sent an e-mail to his school guidance counselor saying, "I would like to let you know that the bullying has increased. I would like to figure out some coping mechanisms to deal with these situations, and I would just like to put this on file so if something happens again, we can show that there was past bullying situations."

Example #2

RUSKIN, FL—As reported in the *Tampa Bay Times*, at the end of the school year at Beth Shields Middle School, the taunting became so bad that friends of student H.W. surrounded her between classes. They escorted her down hallways like human shields, fending off insults from other students who called her "whore" and "slut." Several days before, student H.W. had "sexted" a nude photo of herself to a boy she liked. The photo was forwarded from student to student and soon was circulating through the school as well as through the local high school. H.W. wrote in her journal, "Tons of people talk about me behind my back and I hate it because they call me a whore! And I can't be a whore I'm too inexperienced. So secretly TONS of people hate me." School authorities learned of the nude photo around the end of the school year and suspended the student for the first week of eighth grade, which started in August. About 2 weeks after H.W. returned to school, a social worker observed cuts on H.W.'s legs and had her sign a "no-harm" contract, in which she agreed to tell an adult if she felt inclined to hurt herself. The next day, 13-year-old H.W. hanged herself in her bedroom (Meacham, 2009).

The deceased student's parents filed a lawsuit against the Hillsborough County School Board, but it was ultimately dismissed. The federal trial court noted in its order of dismissal that the school was not in a custodial relationship with the minor student at the time of the suicide and that the school social worker's "no harm contract" with the student did not affirmatively enhance the probability of the minor's suicide (*Witsell v. School Board of Hillsborough Co.*, 2012).

Example #3

WEST PHILADELPHIA, PA—*Philly.com* reported on a lawsuit filed on behalf of a seventh-grade female student at Andrew Hamilton School. The suit alleges that the bullying and abuse of the student began in the fall of 2011 when another female student began "stalking, assaulting and bullying her." The student told her parents, who reported it to the principal and school counselor. The suit contends the taunting and bullying continued. On November 21, 2011, a meeting was held at the school with the two students, their mothers, and several school officials. "Court documents state the victim and the alleged bully were seated just one chair apart without any security present, despite the staff's knowledge of their heated history." The news report continues, stating, "After becoming visibly agitated as her behavior was discussed, the reputed bully allegedly got up and punched the victim in the head and face, leaving only her mother to attempt to physically stop the attack." Court documents allege the November assault caused the student to suffer "severe emotional distress," eventually requiring her to seek mental health treatment, including hospitalization. When no corrective action had been taken by 2012, the girl transferred from the school because of an "incessant fear of a reoccurrence of the incident," the complaint reads (Wigglesworth, 2013).

These three cases, and many others, are surely more complex than their portrayal by the news media indicates. School counselors are often at the epicenter of the bullying drama in any school and therefore can become likely targets of litigation. In many cases the parents who litigate against the school allege that because a school did not follow the professional standard of care, their child was the victim of bullying. When a lawsuit is filed, the school or school district takes a close look at its policies and procedures. It is also forced to examine what it knew about the alleged incidents, how it responded, and whether its response was appropriate.

End-of-Life Issues

End-of-life issues present complicated moral, ethical, and legal questions not just for counselors or medical professionals, but for everyone. Because this issue is so filled with strong opinions, we want to begin our discussion by carefully defining some important terms. *Suicide* is the intentional taking of one's own life. *Assisted suicide* involves providing information, medication (or other means), or direct assistance that enables a person to take his or her own life. Assisted suicide is often divided into active and passive. *Active assisted suicide* involves the direct intervention by another person to cause death, for example, by injecting a lethal dose of a drug. *Passive assisted suicide* involves withdrawing support or intervention necessary to keep a patient alive, such as unplugging a ventilator or stopping parenteral feeding (American Academy of Physician Assistants, 2014). The ethical issue facing counselors who work with terminally ill clients should never involve any form of assisted suicide. It is not the role of counselor to provide medical information to a patient about how that patient could end his or her life, nor would there be any justification for the counselor to be involved in any direct action that results in the death of a client.

The issue confronting counselors is how to respond when a terminally ill client discloses his or her intention to end his or her life. Under normal circumstances a counselor would have an ethical duty to take some action to prevent the client from committing suicide. This action would likely involve breaching the confidentiality of the client. The ethical and legal jeopardy for counselors is clouded by several complicated issues, including: (a) who is the client (the terminally ill patient or the family members); (b) who has legal competence to determine what course of action is in the best interest of the patient (the terminally ill patient or a health care guardian); (c) the strongly held views by everyone involved concerning the proper (moral, ethical, and legal) course of action; (d) state laws that may be more or less prescriptive in terms of the duties and responsibilities of health and mental health professionals; and (e) the values of the counselor who is providing services. It is easy for the counselor to get caught in the cross fire of these many conflicting perspectives. The 2014 *ACA Code of Ethics* (ACA, 2014a, Standard B.2.b.) provides some wiggle room when counselors are working with terminally ill clients:

> Counselors who provide services to terminally ill individuals who are considering hastening their own deaths have the option to maintain confidentiality, depending on applicable laws and the specific circumstances of the situation and after seeking consultation or supervision from appropriate professional and legal parties.

On this issue the values and opinions of any given counselor are likely as diverse as the values and opinions found throughout the culture. Therefore, it is important to keep in mind that the *ACA Code of Ethics* is permissive, providing the "option to maintain confidentiality" but only in the context of applicable laws and only after seeking consultation or supervision. Because of the intensity of emotion and the conflicting moral, ethical, and legal perspectives, we can't emphasize enough the critical importance of obtaining knowledgeable and competent consultation throughout the decision-making process.

Summary

Each suicide intimately affects at least six other people (American Association of Suicidology, 2014c). To put the scope of the effect of suicide into perspective, over the course of the last decade, more than 300,000 Americans have committed suicide, bequeathing a legacy of questions, sorrow, and regret for more than 2,000,000 survivors. The implications of suicide, suicide attempts, and threats of suicide and the impact on survivors of suicide remain some of the most complicated and ethically and legally challenging issues faced by professional counselors in every setting. When wrestling with these complexities, responsible counselors should not go it alone. Obtaining competent colleague consultation or clinical supervision is absolutely essential.

Chapter 9

Professional Boundaries

This chapter discusses dual- or multiple-role boundaries in light of the 2014 *ACA Code of Ethics,* including issues that arise when boundaries are blurred, extended, or violated. Licensure board complaints are discussed, with examples of disciplinary actions from several states as well as data from licensure board complaint cases defended by the ACA-sponsored professional liability insurance program (underwritten and administered by HPSO). Malpractice lawsuits, including liability insurance data from the CNA and HPSO report, are reviewed. Also highlighted are the circumstances in which boundary violations can result in criminal prosecution for practicing counselors.

It's all about the relationship, and central to the counseling relationship is the practitioner's ability to actively define, respect, and manage professional boundaries. Mental health professionals have a unique responsibility, defined both ethically and legally, to manage the boundary between professional counselor and client, including any other co-occurring roles that connect the counselor to the client. The complexity and power differential in the counseling relationship—and in some cases the vulnerability of clients—demand that we exercise due care to ensure that we are taking steps to define and respect the boundary between ourselves and our clients. For counselors and other mental health professionals, any type of boundary incursion (boundary blurring, boundary extending, or boundary violation) has the potential to result in real harm to our clients and can have devastating legal and ethical consequences. Boundary incursions involving the consequences of inappropriate or mismanaged dual or multiple relationships as well as sexual misconduct are the royal road to ethical and legal jeopardy. When role boundaries are blurred, extended, or violated, clients are often put at risk, which can quickly lead to ethics complaints, licensing board disciplinary proceedings, malpractice lawsuits, and even felony charges against the practitioner. Role boundary issues for professional counselors also include the relationships between graduate faculty and students, between clinical supervisors and students and interns, and between counselor–researchers and research subjects.

Counselor–Client Interactions or Relationships

For counselors, nothing creates more controversy, confusion, and risk than the issue of professional boundaries and boundary violations. What constitutes the proper management of the boundary between the counselor and the client is the subject of continued professional debate. Thoughtful experts disagree on the extent to which boundaries must be enforced, but everyone agrees that clients can be harmed when we fail to effectively manage boundaries or when professional boundaries are violated.

In this book we use a wide range of terms for what the *ACA Code of Ethics* refers to as "counselor–client interactions or relationships." Our use of the terms *dual relationships, multiple relationships,* and *co-occurring relationships* is intentional. Throughout the discussion that follows we attempt to use the language of the *ACA Code of Ethics* while at the same time using terminology found in the disciplinary sections of many, if not most, state counselor licensing laws and supporting rules. State counselor licensing boards across the county typically approach the topic of dual or multiple relationships with current or former clients in ways that are consistent with the *ACA Code of Ethics,* even though the terminology may be somewhat different. In general, state licensing boards caution against dual relationships. Practitioners are urged to avoid dual relationships whenever possible, and when or if they are initiated, the practitioner is admonished to ensure that the dual relationship (the nonprofessional relationship) is intended to be beneficial to the client.

There is, however, no disagreement regarding the issue of sexual misconduct. Counselor–client sexual and/or romantic interactions or relationships are egregious violations of the *ACA Code of Ethics* as well as licensing laws in every state. The 2014 *ACA Code of Ethics* prohibits sexual or romantic counselor–client interactions or relationships, in person and by electronic means, with current clients, their romantic partners, or their family members (ACA, 2014a, Standard A.5.a.). The *Code* also prohibits counselors "from engaging in counseling relationships with persons with whom they have had a previous sexual and/or romantic relationship" (Standard A.5.b.). On the subject of former clients, the *Code* has instituted a 5-year prohibition (following the last professional contact) against counselors entering into sexual and/or romantic interactions or relationships with former clients, their romantic partners, or their family members. This prohibition applies to both in person and electronic interactions or relationships (Standard A.5.c.). The importance of this prohibition is made quite explicit in Standard A.5.c.:

> Counselors, before engaging in sexual and/or romantic interactions or relationships with former clients, their romantic partners, or their family members, demonstrate forethought and document (in written form) whether the interaction or relationship can be viewed as exploitive in any way and/or whether there is still potential to harm the former client; in cases of potential exploitation and/or harm, the counselor avoids entering into an interaction or relationship.

Role boundary issues span a wide range of circumstances, from the egregious transgressions noted above that result in harm to the client and the destruction of the counseling relationship, to benign situations caused by a ripple of misunderstanding that can generally be successfully navigated, to situations in which the client may clearly benefit from the existence of multiple roles. In almost all cases that result in harm to the client, boundary issues are caused by inappropriate or mismanaged dual or multiple relationships. Dual or co-occurring relationships are the common denominator to boundary violations. It is important to note that many of these mismanaged, inappropriate, and ultimately harmful dual relationships are not sexual or romantic. Many authors have explored the intricacies of dual relationships; Herlihy and Corey (2015) provided an exhaustive and balanced discussion on the topic. For our purposes, dual relationships occur when

- a practitioner has a nonprofessional relationship with a person (no matter how casual or intimate), and then a professional counseling relationship is initiated; or
- a professional counseling relationship exists, and either the client or the counselor initiates a nonprofessional relationship (no matter how casual or intimate).

Sometimes nonprofessional relationships are not initiated by either the counselor or the client; sometimes these other relationships emerge from familial, social, community, school, or work-related connections that were unknown to either the counselor or client prior to initiating the professional relationship. There are also circumstances in which the "other relationship" is an inherent and unavoidable aspect of the counseling environment. Examples of this include school and college settings as well as workplace environments in which counseling professionals are embedded into the fabric of the workplace culture and therefore interact with other employees on a multitude of levels, including providing direct clinical assistance to employees and/or family members of the employee.

Boundary incursions can be classified into three groups, from the most benign to the most harmful:

- *Boundary blurring* involves any type of boundary "fuzziness" in which there is an opportunity to confuse the professional and nonprofessional roles. One of the most common examples involves a situation in which the counselor and client socially cross paths (e.g., the counselor volunteers to be a chaperone on a school field trip for her child and finds that a client is also a chaperone). If the counselor and client live in the same neighborhood and frequent the same restaurants and shops, informal contact is almost inevitable. How the counselor responds to such boundary-blurring events can generally determine whether the experience is innocent or is the beginning of a breakdown of the professional boundary that can lead to a problematic or harmful boundary incursion. In most cases, a boundary blurring "just happens"—neither the client nor the counselor initiate or invite the circumstances.

- *Boundary extending* involves the intentional crossing of the boundary separating the professional and nonprofessional roles. Whether the boundary extending is appropriate and helpful or inappropriate and harmful must be determined on a case-by-case basis. For example, it is not uncommon for a counselor to be invited by a client to a celebratory event (wedding or commitment ceremony, christening, bar mitzvah or bat mitzvah, graduation, etc.). The counselor, in consultation with the client, should determine whether this boundary extending is in the best interest of the current and anticipated counseling relationship. If, after careful consideration, colleague consultation, or supervision (if appropriate), the counselor decides to attend, the counselor will discuss with the client the ground rules for his attendance so that the professional relationship can be safeguarded. Standard A.6.c. (ACA, 2014a) admonishes counselors to "officially document, prior to the interaction (when feasible), the rationale for such an interaction, the potential benefit, and anticipated consequences for the client or former client and other individuals significantly involved with the client or former client." Typically boundary extensions occur at the initiation or invitation of the client.

- *Boundary violation* involves the intentional boundary crossing in a manner that will likely distort the counseling relationship and result in harm to the client. A counselor who initiates or participates in a boundary violation is demonstrating a lack of sufficient awareness or regard for the consequences that such a violation will likely have on the counseling relationship and the client. In the most egregious situations, boundary violations initiated by or agreed to by the counselor are self-serving and exploitive. Boundary violations are the most harmful kind of boundary incursion. Examples include situations in which the counselor borrows money from a client or the counselor and client go into business together. Other examples involve hiring the client to work in the counselor's office or to provide child care for the counselor's children. Of course, the most notorious boundary violations involve a romantic or sexual relationship between the counselor and client.

> The core concern is not the type of the dual relationship or the length of time that has passed since the professional or nonprofessional relationship has ended but rather the potential for (or the actual) damage that is done to the client as a result of the blurring, extending, or violating of boundaries associated with the dual (professional and nonprofessional) relationship.

Dual or multiple relationships can also include situations in which one relationship (either the professional relationship or the nonprofessional relationship) has ended (very recently or even years ago) and another relationship (nonprofessional or professional) is initiated. Boundary incursions also occur when counselors provide counseling to family members; workplace associates, subordinates, or supervisors; or family members of workplace colleagues. The core concern is not the type of the dual role or the length of time that has passed since the professional or nonprofessional relationship has ended but rather the potential for (or the actual) damage that is done to the client as a result of the blurring, extending, or violating of boundaries associated with the dual relationship. The damage typically falls in the following five broad categories:

- *Loss of objectivity or clarity.* Dual relationships can add a layer of distraction to a professional relationship that is inherently already filled with challenges to objectivity and clarity. Most mental health professionals recognize that counseling and psychotherapy are subjective endeavors. Objectivity is not really possible: Perception is influenced by a host of conscious and unconscious, social, cultural, political, and life experience variables. During graduate training, postdegree supervision, and ongoing colleague consultation, counselors are constantly striving to maintain as much clarity as possible in interacting with clients. The loss of objectivity/clarity may be consciously recognized by the counselor, or it can occur below the counselor's awareness. In any event, the loss of objectivity and clarity represents a dynamic in the counseling office that prevents the counselor from being fully present for the client and challenges the ethically mandated primary responsibility of the counselor "to respect the dignity and promote the welfare of clients" (ACA, 2014a, Standard A.1.a.). Dual relationships represent another layer of distraction that a counselor must sort through in order to maintain an acceptable level of objectivity and clarity.
- *Potential for misunderstanding.* Misunderstanding between human beings is natural and inevitable. Under normal circumstances, misunderstandings that occur within a counseling relationship can be worked through and often can become important diagnostic and therapeutic opportunities. When a counseling relationship is intertwined within a dual relationship, there is increased opportunity for misunderstanding. Interactions that occur in the nonclinical relationship can create misunderstanding within the counseling relationship and vice versa. In human interaction, misunderstandings can quickly multiply, with one misunderstanding feeding on another until there is a breakdown of the counseling relationship. We are ethically charged to do no harm and whenever possible "to minimize or to remedy unavoidable or unanticipated harm" (Standard A.4.a.); misunderstanding fueled by a dual relationship frequently can be a conduit to client harm.

- *Conflict of interest.* Co-occurring or sequential dual roles can create a *conflict of interest*, a situation in which a counselor (or someone or something important to the counselor) can be affected by decisions or behaviors the client is contemplating. A conflict of interest can tempt a counselor to use the power of the counseling relationship to sway the client in a direction preferred by the counselor. Such inappropriate influence can easily result in harm to the client. Even if the counselor resists the temptation to inappropriately influence the client, the treatment relationship can still be affected. The client may wonder about the counselor's motives, and the counselor might have some conflicted feelings for having to defer his or her own best interest in favor of the client's.
- *Breach of confidentiality and privacy.* When clinical and nonclinical roles become intertwined, it becomes difficult for counselors to remember what information may be discussed. When non-counseling roles are informal or intense (friendships, social groups, business or work relationships, etc.), the likelihood of a breach of confidentiality and a violation of the client's right of privacy dramatically increases. See Chapter 7 for a discussion of how use of social media by a counselor can lead to a breach of confidentiality and privacy. These circumstances again challenge the counselor's commitment to ethical practice (Standards B.1.b., B.1.c.) and can trigger a complaint to the state licensing board.
- *Exploitation.* Mental health professionals who intentionally misuse the power differential inherent within the counseling relationship to take advantage of a client or former client are behaving in an abusive and exploitive manner. These situations tend to be the most ethically and legally egregious and often involve sexual or financial exploitation. These dual relationships are not innocent; they are not just a momentary lapse in judgment. They are the basis for real harm to a client as well as ethical and legal consequences to the counselor, including ethics complaints, licensing board discipline, malpractice lawsuits, and possibly felony imprisonment.

When any of these occur it can easily be argued that the counselor breached his professional duty and that the breach resulted in damage (loss or pain) to the client or destruction of the counseling relationship. In some cases, the circumstances will play out a little differently, but the results are similar: The person with less power—the vulnerable person—will be harmed either because the professional allowed another relationship to emerge or because he or she failed to properly manage the complexity of the dual roles that emerged.

Before leaving this discussion we want to address an area of frequent concern and misunderstanding for counselors. Counselors have special skills; when someone in our circle of family, friends, and work associates has a problem, it is not at all uncommon for him or her to turn to us for assistance. Counselors should not be afraid to be responsive and helpful. When a family member, friend, neighbor, or work colleague has a problem and reaches out to us, we can and should respond, because we are caring people. It is completely appropriate for a counselor to spend some time with a person in his or her circle who is troubled as long as the intent is to de-escalate a crisis or provide short-term support.

However, when short-term support and appropriate referral evolve instead into a treatment relationship, problems are likely to follow. Sometimes people don't understand why we decline to provide ongoing treatment. It will be important to carefully explain the ethical concerns. We hope that counselors will provide more than just a blanket "It's not ethical" statement. People in our world are sometimes confused by this explanation. After all, we can be friends with our dentist, accountant, family physician, and clergy member, so why not our counselor? We encourage you to patiently explain that mixing friendship and counseling can distort the friendship and is likely to have an adverse effect on your ability to provide quality ongoing care. A request for counseling from people within our circle of intimates is an inevitable occupational hazard. Over time, family and friends will come to understand and accept the boundaries that define our profession, but throughout your career, there will be occasions in which you will be asked, "Can I be your client?" The answer is "no." In those situations it is essential that you define and defend the boundary.

Finally, multiple or dual relationships between counselors and their clients are not the only relationships that can lead to ethical and legal problems. Other examples include relationships between individuals in the following roles:

- a faculty member and a student;
- a clinical supervisor and a supervisee, trainee, or intern; and
- a counselor researcher and a research subject.

Licensing Board Complaints and Selected State Disciplinary Action

Licensing board members around the country continue to wrestle with boundary concerns; state laws and rules are constantly under review. Some states seem to be narrowing the circumstances under which any form of simultaneously occurring professional and nonprofessional relationship between counselor and client would be considered appropriate. We are mindful that when it comes to disciplinary decisions, the language in the state law or rule is open to some degree of interpretation by individual board members. We urge you to consult the most recent version of the statute and rules that govern the practice of counseling in your state. Carefully read the language in the statute and rules and consult with knowledgeable colleagues to ensure you fully understand the limitations and prohibitions as defined in the statute. For more detailed information, you can consult *Licensure Requirements for Professional Counselors* (ACA, 2014b), which is a complete guide to state licensing laws. In addition, we encourage you to carefully review disciplinary decisions made by your licensing board; it is important to understand how board members are interpreting the law and rules. Most licensing boards publish disciplinary decisions; they can be obtained either through the licensing board website or through board-published newsletters or reports. Furthermore, Corey et al. (2015) and Herlihy and Corey (2015) provide comprehensive discussions of dual relationships. We strongly encourage you to review the discussions in these two publications and the references cited therein.

Typically, state counselor licensing boards have the authority to impose a wide range of disciplinary consequences on licensees or professionals who are becoming licensed. Each state board delineates violations and a disciplinary due process to determine whether a complaint against a counselor is accurate. After due process has been fully exercised and a determination has been made, disciplinary consequences can be imposed; they vary from state to state and often include the imposition of a fine in addition to other disciplinary actions. The following list describes the range of disciplinary consequences.

- *Permanent revocation of license:* The person is permanently prohibited from the practice of counseling in that state.

- *Permanent denial:* The person is permanently denied the opportunity to apply for a license to practice counseling in that state.
- *Surrender:* The person voluntarily agrees to surrender his or her license and no longer practice counseling in that state.
- *Suspension:* The person is suspended from practice for a period of time.
- *Suspension with stipulations:* The person may continue to practice but agrees to abide by certain conditions that may include supervised practice, restricted practice, additional continuing education, or other requirements.
- *Reprimand:* The person may continue to practice but receives a formal letter of reprimand.
- *Administrative penalty (fines):* The person may continue to practice but has to pay a monetary fine.

HPSO, a subsidiary of CNA, administers the ACA-sponsored professional liability program. Coverage by HPSO includes defense-only costs associated with licensure board complaints. Recently HPSO and CNA jointly published a report detailing the closed licensure board complaint cases the program defended from January 1, 2003, through December 31, 2012. The report provides a breakdown of the 345 licensure board complaint cases HPSO has defended. The top four license-protection allegations were sexual misconduct (14%), breach of confidentiality (13.6%), practice beyond the scope of practice (10.0%), and failure to properly assess (8.5%). The HPSO report also noted two other boundary violation categories: multiple relationships (4.8%) and personal nonsexual relationship with client (2.8%). The three boundary violations categories together make up 22% of the licensure board defense cases. A breakdown of the sexual misconduct cases reveals that nearly 79% of the sexual misconduct involved counselor sexual and/or romantic relationships with a current client, whereas 17.5% of sexual misconduct cases involved relationships with former clients. Sexual misconduct with colleagues, employers, and employees amounted to 1.8% of the cases, the same percentage as sexual misconduct involving a supervisory relationship. Total expenses paid for the defense of all 345 licensure board complaints amounted to over $300,000 (CNA & HPSO, 2014).

To date, there is not a central repository for collecting the specific circumstances or types of disciplinary actions imposed by all licensing boards against licensed counselors. Obtaining reliable data can be challenging. Each state counselor licensing board compiles and publishes data on disciplinary actions in its own idiosyncratic manner. It is important to remember that in most cases, dual relationships, in and of themselves, are not grounds for licensing board disciplinary action; rather, it is the harm that results to the client from the mismanagement of the boundary incursions that leads to the complaint. Presented below are data from three states that clearly demonstrate how inappropriate or mismanaged dual, multiple, or co-occurring relationships and sexual misconduct boundary violations can harm clients and lead to serious consequences for licensed counselors. Many, if not most, substantiated licensure board violations involved multiple offenses. Therefore, it is not unusual to find boundary violations woven into a complex array of inappropriate behaviors. In compiling the data for the three states presented below, we read through board documents to determine the substance of the violation. Violations were classified as "boundary violations" only when that activity appeared to be the underlying or precipitating behavior. Of course, sexual or romantic involvement with a client was always counted as sexual misconduct.

Texas

The Texas Board of Examiners of Professional Counselors licenses nearly 15,000 LPCs (ACA, 2014b). The board publishes a Disciplinary Actions Summary that encompasses enforcement actions brought by the board against LPCs and applicants. Between 2009 and May 2014, the board issued 135 disciplinary actions. Of the 135 specifically named enforcement actions brought against licensed counselors, 30% (41 violations) involved boundary violations. Of the 41 boundary violations, 36 involved mismanaged dual relationships and five involved sexual misconduct by licensed counselors. Overall, dual-role violations was the single largest category of violations, followed by supervisory issues (29 violations) and client records and confidentiality (25 violations). Other categories leading to sanctions included failure to report child abuse, failure to report past criminal conviction and/or state licensing discipline (another state), insurance fraud (including Medicaid fraud), impaired practice (substance abuse), making false statements, and administrative failures. Dual-role violations, including sexual misconduct, constituted 30% of all disciplinary actions. Disciplinary consequences to the licensees ranged from reprimand (the mildest consequence); to suspension for 6, 12, 24, or 48 months; to surrender or revocation of the license (Texas Department of State Health Services, 2014).

Florida

In 2014, there were 8,813 professional counselors licensed for independent practice in the state of Florida. The Florida Board of Clinical Social Work, Mental Health Counseling and Marriage & Family Therapy regulates the practice of professional counseling, including identifying prohibited actions. During a 3-year period (2011–2013), 41 LMHCs were disciplined for engaging in prohibited behaviors. Of the 41 total disciplinary actions, nine (22%) involved the consequences of a harmful boundary violation or sexual misconduct. Of the nine boundary violations, five involved the consequences of a mismanaged dual/co-occurring relationship and four disciplinary actions involved sexual misconduct. Other violations included fraud; criminal offense; falsification of credentials, including failure to report past criminal or disciplinary history; impaired practice (substance abuse); poor documentation; and unprofessional conduct (Florida Medical Quality Assurance Services, 2014).

Arizona

In 2014, the Arizona Board of Behavioral Health Examiners licensed 2,412 LPCs and 919 Licensed Associate Counselors (LACs; ACA, 2014b). The board is charged with enforcing adherence to professional practice standards, which include a prohibition against sexual misconduct and engaging in dual relationships that could be harmful to the client. According to the applicable statute, unprofessional conduct includes the following behaviors:

> 32-3251(15)(v) Any sexual conduct between a licensee and a client or former client . . .
>
> 32-3251(15)(y) Engaging in a dual relationship with a client that could impair the licensee's objectivity or professional judgment or create risk of harm to the client. For purposes of this subdivision, "dual relationship" means a licensee simultaneously engages in both a professional and nonprofessional relationship with a client that is avoidable and not incidental. (Ariz. Rev. Stat. § 32-3251, 2013)

The Arizona board provides an annual detailed summary of the disciplinary violations, including a brief description of each violation and the sanctions imposed. During a 3.5-year period (2011–May 2014), the board reported 46 board disciplinary sanctions involving LPCs. Of the 46 sanctions, 43% (20 sanctions) involved dual relationships or sexual misconduct (Arizona Board of Behavioral Health Examiners, 2011, 2012, 2013, 2014). In addition, during the same time period there were 35 board disciplinary sanctions against LACs, 17% (six violations) of which involved boundary violations, including sexual misconduct. Taken together, sexual misconduct violations of LPCs and LACs constituted 30% of all boundary violations (Arizona Board of Behavioral Health Examiners, 2011, 2012, 2013, 2014). Presented below is an example of an Arizona Board-sanctioned counselor who engaged in a nonsexual dual relationship. This example is drawn from public records available on the website of the Arizona Board of Behavioral Health Examiners that details disciplinary cases and sanctions imposed (Arizona Board of Behavioral Health Examiners, 2011, 2012, 2013, 2014).

Boundary Violation Licensure Board Complaint

The Arizona Board of Behavioral Health Examiners reports the details of a disciplinary action brought against an LPC that typifies the "slippery slope" inherent with boundary violations (Arizona Board of Behavioral Health Examiners, 2011).

> *Circumstances of the Case:* A Licensed Professional Counselor was acquainted with a woman from her church. In 2009, the woman contacted the counselor for "emergency services." The counselor agreed to see the woman until she was able to find another therapist. As it turned out, the client had an extensive mental health history including a recent panic attack and depression with some suicidal thoughts/actions. There was no documentation in the client's chart of a formal risk assessment. The counselor saw the client six times. Treatment ended in September 2009. The next month, October 2009, the counselor cooked and delivered food to the woman's home as part of her church duties. She also transported the woman to the doctor, again as part of her church duties. Two months later (December 2009) the client again sought emergency treatment. The counselor met with the client for three sessions. Again, there was no documentation of a formal risk assessment. In January 2010, after the second treatment period ended, the counselor agreed to help the client by making an appointment with her at a beauty school [that] she was attending. While at the school the woman washed and styled the hair of the counselor. In March 2010, the counselor agreed to resume treatment with the client because the client told her she felt like she "was going to die." Treatment consisted of six sessions, ending in April 2010. Once again there was no documentation in the client's chart regarding a risk assessment or any indication that the counselor was attempting to identify an alternative therapist for the client. Finally, the counselor joined with other church members in giving the client a cash gift to celebrate the client's graduation from beauty school.
>
> *Sanction:* The counselor was required to complete 6 hours of continuing education addressing current behavioral health documentation requirements and 3 clock hours of continuing education addressing ethics relating to dual relationships and boundary issues. The counselor was required to receive 12 months of clinical supervision and pay a civil penalty of $1,000 (penalty stayed pending compliance with the Consent Agreement and Order).

From all available information published in the Adverse Action Tracking Form, it appears the counselor began the clinical relationship with the best of intentions. The circumstances of the initial referral (both members of the same church—a church in which the counselor is obviously very active) seemed to blur the professional boundaries of this relationship from the very beginning. The counselor then continued to mix clinical and nonclinical services and church-related interactions with the client. At no point is there any reason to question the positive motive of the counselor; nonetheless, something must have happened that harmed or offended the client. It is safe to assume that the mixing of the clinical and nonclinical relationship created confusion and, ultimately, vulnerability for the counselor. The lack of documentation is a separate issue, and there is no explanation for that except that the counselor apparently failed to meet the standard of care.

The data from the three representative states, along with the data from the CNA and HPSO report, provide a cautionary tale. Twenty-two percent (22%) of the HPSO licensure board cases involved boundary violations, very close to the percentage of cases reported in Texas (30%), Florida (22%), and Arizona (30%).

Risk of Malpractice Lawsuits

In the 30-plus years that the ACA-sponsored insurance program has been tracking claims against counselors, allegations of sexual activity involving counselors and their clients, or the spouse of a client, continue to create substantial claim costs. Many lawsuits allege malpractice or failure to treat the problem that brought the client to counseling. Yet in many cases, the underlying cause for a claim is an ill-advised dual-role relationship or sexual misconduct (P. L. Nelson, personal communication, May 17, 2011).

As mentioned above, HPSO and CNA released a report of closed liability claims encompassing the years 2003–2012 (CNA & HPSO, 2014). The report reviewed the claims history of 1,043 closed cases. Data from this report have provided a window into the real world of liability lawsuits brought against professional counselors.

> One of the most significant findings revealed by the data was the frequency of claims involving counselors who enter into inappropriate sexual/romantic relationships with clients, client partners or client family members ... approximately 40 percent of the professional liability claims in the report involved the counselor engaging in an inappropriate sexual/romantic relationship. These claims resulted in indemnity payments of $2.2 million. (CNA & HPSO, 2014, p. 27)

The report provides a deeper understanding of the specifics of these cases than we have ever seen before. Tables 3, 4, and 5 summarize the revealing details.

Sexual intimacy with a client is a serious breach of trust and objectivity, a statement affirmed by the courts. This may be true even in cases where the defense claims client consent, lack of harm to the client, or that the sexual relationship began after treatment ended. If an attorney representing a plaintiff can convince the court that sexual intimacy occurred, the likelihood of a large negligence award is high. In many cases, allegations of sexual intimacy involve behaviors other than actual intercourse. Nevertheless, the possibility of a large settlement or verdict remains.

Mishandling of Transference

Claims of sexual misconduct by counselors have been based largely on the mishandling of the transference phenomenon and the counter-transference that occurs when counselors experience reactions similar to those of their clients. Courts have found that the mishandling of this transference, resulting in sexual contact or touching, constitutes negligence or gross negligence for which damages can be awarded. Clients alleging sexual misconduct generally must prove in court that there was a counseling relationship, that sexual contact occurred between the counselor and the client, and that the client suffered some emotional injury as a result of the contact. In some states, clients also must prove that the contact occurred under the guise of treatment. In a number of states, however, a sexual relationship between a counselor and a client is sufficient grounds for a claim of negligence, whether it occurred under the guise of treatment or

Table 3

Individuals Involved With the Counselor
in Inappropriate Sexual/Romantic Relationships

Individual Involved in Inappropriate Relationship	Individual in Treatment	Percentage of Closed Claims	Total Paid Indemnity	Average Paid Indemnity
Client	Client, spouse, and children	1.6%	$300,000	$300,000
Client	Client and spouse	6.3%	$510,000	$127,500
Client	Client	28.6%	$1,349,435	$74,969
Mother of client	Minor client	1.6%	$50,000	$50,000
Mother of client	Adult client	1.6%	$20,000	$20,000
Overall		39.7%	$2,229,435	$89,177

Note. This information is based on analysis by the Healthcare Providers Service Organization and American Casualty Company, CNA. See *Understanding Counselor Liability Risk* (CNA & HPSO, 2014). Published with permission.

Table 4

Severity by Alleged Initiator of Sexual/Romantic Relationships and Related Treatment Status

Individual Initiating the Relationship	Status of Treatment During the Relationship	Percentage of Closed Claims	Total Paid Indemnity	Average Paid Indemnity
Client	Active	4.8%	$345,000	$115,000
Counselor	Active	30.1%	$1,831,335	$96,386
Counselor	After terminating client from treatment	1.6%	$42,500	$42,500
Mutual agreement	Active	3.2%	$10,600	$5,300
Overall		39.7%	$2,229,435	$89,177

Note. This information is based on analysis by the Healthcare Providers Service Organization and American Casualty Company, CNA. See *Understanding Counselor Liability Risk* (CNA & HPSO, 2014). Published with permission.

not. The spouse or companion of a client who has engaged in sexual relations with a counselor also may bring a malpractice action and recover actual damages.[1] Attorneys who represent victims of alleged sexual misconduct now have a wealth of case law to guide them in securing damages for their clients, and there are few defenses available to the counselor who initiates or permits sexual contact in a therapeutic relationship.[2]

A case in the state of Washington (*Doe v. Wood*, 1994) illustrates the danger to unwary counselors. A certified mental health counselor provided therapy to a couple and also socialized with them during the treatment period. The wife told her husband she had developed romantic feelings for the counselor, who later acknowledged that the feelings were reciprocal. The counselor terminated the therapy. The husband later discovered letters from the counselor to the wife expressing his desire for a relationship with her. The couple separated, and the husband experienced a variety of symptoms of depression and emotional distress and had difficulty working, resulting in a loss of income. He sued the counselor for professional negligence, intentional infliction of emotional distress, and outrage, claiming the counselor violated the standard of care by having a social rela-

---

[1]See, for example, *Barringer v. Rausch* (2005), *Horak v. Biris* (1985), *Rowe v. Bennett* (1986), and *Figueiredo-Torres v. Nickel* (1991).

[2]The only defense that has consistently been effective after the act of sexual contact has been proved is that the suit is time-barred by the statute of limitations. Whether the client was competent to bring the action and the actual final date of treatment or sexual activity also are important in this determination.

Table 5

Injury/Adverse Outcome Alleged to Result
From Counselor–Client Sexual/Romantic Relationships

Primary Injury or Adverse Outcome	Percentage of Closed Claims	Total Paid Indemnity	Average Paid Indemnity
Emotional disability (client unable to attend school or work)	1.6%	$300,000	$300,000
Sexual harassment by counselor	1.6%	$176,875	$176,875
Sexual abuse/assault by counselor	15.8%	$929,500	$92,960
Emotional/psychological harm or distress	12.7%	$553,060	$69,133
Depression	3.2%	$137,500	$68,750
Loss of marriage or significant intimate relationship	3.2%	$110,000	$55,000
Exacerbation of diagnosis/additional diagnosis	1.6%	$22,500	$22,500
Overall	39.7%	$2,229,435	$89,177

Note. This information is based on analysis by the Healthcare Providers Service Organization and American Casualty Company, CNA. See *Understanding Counselor Liability Risk* (CNA & HPSO, 2014). Published with permission.

tionship with the couple, pursuing a romantic relationship with the wife, betraying the patient's trust, and terminating the counseling relationship abruptly. The court awarded $525,000 on the professional negligence issue.

Another important decision is *Simmons v. United States* (1986). The case involved a client with emotional problems who sought the assistance of a social worker employed by a federal agency. After seeing this client for 5 years, the therapist initiated a sexual relationship with the client. The following year, a third party notified the therapist's supervisor, who allegedly did nothing to remedy the problem or discipline the social worker. The client's mental status declined; she was hospitalized and attempted suicide. Two years after therapy ended, the client was informed by her new therapist that her problems were attributable to the social worker's mishandling of the transference phenomenon. The client sued the federal government under the Federal Tort Claims Act, and the appellate court upheld the award granted at the trial court level. The social worker was found to be negligent by mishandling the transference phenomenon; the supervisor was also found to be negligent.

Courts differ in their interpretation of whether an employer should be considered vicariously liable for the acts of an errant therapist who commits sexual misconduct. However, counselors in supervisory positions are encouraged to pay close attention to any complaints from clients of boundary violations by supervisees. Blind trust of a supervisee's actions is not in the client's, or supervisor's, best interests.

Risk of Criminal Prosecution

Several states now have laws that govern mental health profession-als and that provide for criminal prosecution against mental health professionals who engage in certain forms of sexual misconduct. Florida is an example of a state that criminalizes psychotherapist sexual misconduct. Florida law provides the following language:

> Sexual misconduct by a psychotherapist; penalties.
>
> (1) Any psychotherapist who commits sexual misconduct with a client, or former client when the professional relationship was terminated pri-marily for the purpose of engaging in sexual contact, commits a felony of the third degree, punishable as provided in s. 775.082 or s. 775.083; however, a second or subsequent offense is a felony of the second degree, punishable as provided in s. 775.082, s. 775.083, or s. 775.084.
>
> (2) Any psychotherapist who violates subsection (1) by means of thera-peutic deception commits a felony of the second degree punishable as provided in s. 775.082, s. 775.083, or s. 775.084.
>
> (3) The giving of consent by the client to any such act shall not be a defense to these offenses.
>
> (4) For the purposes of this section:
>
>   (a) The term "psychotherapist" means any person licensed pursuant to chapter 458, chapter 459, chapter 464, chapter 490, or chapter 491, or any other person who provides or purports to provide treatment, diagnosis, assessment, evaluation, or counseling of mental or emotional illness, symptom, or condition.
>
>   (b) "Therapeutic deception" means a representation to the client that sexual contact by the psychotherapist is consistent with or part of the treatment of the client.
>
>   (c) "Sexual misconduct" means the oral, anal, or vaginal penetration of another by, or contact with, the sexual organ of another or the anal or vaginal penetration of another by any object.
>
>   (d) "Client" means a person to whom the services of a psychotherapist are provided. (Fla. Stat. § 491.0112 (2013))

In a similar manner, Minnesota makes psychotherapist–patient sex a criminal offense (Minn. Stat. § 609.345, 2013). The Minnesota Court of Appeals (*State v. Ohrtman*, 1991) has recognized that it is a fourth-degree criminal offense for a psychotherapist to engage in sexual contact with a patient during a psychotherapy session. Furthermore, the patient's consent does not constitute a defense to the action, the definition of "psychotherapist" includes the clergy, and "psychotherapy" by definition includes counseling. However, the court was unwilling to rule that a hug between a psychotherapist and patient was unlawful touching under the statute.

The bottom line is that sexual contact between counselors and clients is ethically wrong, constitutes a breach of the standard of professional practice owed the client, causes actual harm to the client, and may violate criminal statutes as well. If you find yourself being drawn into a situation that could lead to such contact, you must keep the best interests of your client as your first priority. Refer the client to another counselor if appropriate. Terminate your relationship with the client in a timely manner if there are no better viable options, but avoid abandoning the client. Do not assume that termination allows you to then take up a romantic or sexual relationship with the client. Seek consultation or supervision to ensure that the relationship remains open and professional, and secure the professional assistance you need to avoid mishandling the relationship with your client.

When Is a Dual Relationship Appropriate?

The collective wisdom in the field as expressed in ethics codes and state statutes strongly encourages practitioners to avoid, when possible, co-occurring or dual relationships. At the same time there is recognition that dual roles are not always avoidable and certainly not always bad. In fact, there can be circumstances in which competently conceived and managed co-occurring roles are very much in the best interests of the client. We want to close this section with a brief discussion designed to assist you when confronted with the question: Is this potential dual role relationship really a good idea, or should I just say "no"?

We refer you to the legal and ethical decision-making model presented in Chapter 3. When evaluating whether a co-occurring or dual-role relationship is appropriate, we suggest you begin by asking the question: Is the dual relationship avoidable? In other words, can someone else competently provide the professional service, or can some other arrangement be made to eliminate or distance the nonprofessional relationship? If after careful and honest reflection the answer is that the dual relationship is avoidable, then perhaps it is best to step aside and not place yourself in a situation that could become problematic. In that case discuss your thinking with the person, decline the nonprofessional role, or refer the person to another practitioner.

On the other hand, if the dual role is not avoidable or if you believe (after careful deliberation) that the benefit of the dual role outweighs the potential risks involved, we recommend the following process:

- check to make sure your proposed action does not run afoul of your state licensure law,
- discuss the benefits and risks with your client,
- secure informed consent,
- document your decision making in the client's record,
- engage in ongoing discussion with the client to ensure the relationships are being managed properly,
- obtain regular consultation and/or supervision, and
- self-monitor.

If you follow this decision-making process, including the requirements for ongoing discussion with your client, self-monitoring, and supervision, you have a better chance of not sliding down the slippery slope into behaviors that place the client at risk of harm and you at risk of ethical or legal complications. Ultimately, our role in this book is not to tell you whether you should or shouldn't enter into dual relationships but rather to help practitioners in the real world and students preparing for the real world to become aware of the complexity and risks associated with dual relationships and boundary violations.

Summary

We have devoted a significant amount of time to a description of the legal and criminal consequences that can come from mismanaged dual relationships and boundary violations in the form of sexual misconduct. No matter how easy it is to manage or eliminate these areas of risk, these are still the issues that most frequently ensnare counselors and other mental health professionals. We don't want to leave the impression that all dual (co-occurring professional and nonprofessional) relationships are inherently bad, because they are not. Clients, students, and supervisees can greatly benefit from a well-conceived and well-executed dual relationship. In addition, in the real world sometimes circumstances make it very difficult not to be involved in dual relationships. When faced with the opportunity to initiate a dual relationship, stop and carefully evaluate the unique circumstances that are being presented. Don't depend on your own assessment; use an ethical decision-making model, consult your state law, and always consider the input from a trusted colleague or supervisor. In the final analysis, any co-occurring or dual relationship you choose to enter into will be your responsibility to manage; if the treatment relationship is harmed, you are likely to face employment, ethical, and/or legal consequences.

Chapter 10

Records and Documentation

Well-organized and well-documented client counseling records are the most effective tool counselors have for establishing client treatment plans, ensuring continuity of care in the event of absence, and proving that quality care was provided. Good records also provide reliable information for decision making in court cases in which difficult issues are presented, and they help the counselor avoid or effectively respond to licensing board complaints and malpractice liability. In a managed care environment, careful documentation of services is essential to ensure reimbursement.

Records: The Standard of Care

Many years ago, it was common practice for counselors and some other mental health professionals to refrain intentionally from keeping client records. Some vestiges of this counselors-don't-keep-records thinking still exist today. Times have changed, and it is important that counselors understand the current standard of professional counseling practice. Counselors have an explicitly stated legal and ethical duty to create and maintain client records on every client. Over the last two decades, the standard of care regarding client records and many aspects of the contents therein has been made quite clear. In fact, failure to maintain adequate client records is often the basis of a state licensing board disciplinary action against licensed counselors. Failure to maintain adequate records could also form the basis of a claim of professional malpractice because it breaches the standard of care expected of a practicing mental health professional. We acknowledge that record-keeping requirements for K–12 school counselors are not as clear. The U.S. Department of Education, equivalent state agencies, school systems, administrative districts, and individual schools often develop record-keeping policies that may or may not coincide with the standards for clinical counseling. For that reason, most of our comments in this chapter pertain primarily to counselors practicing in clinical settings.

The 2014 *ACA Code of Ethics* unambiguously requires counselors to maintain client records: "Counselors create, safeguard, and maintain documentation necessary for rendering professional services" (ACA, 2014a, Standard A.1.b.). HIPAA (see Chapter 5) has introduced a language defining much of the contents of client records and psychotherapy notes. State counselor licensing laws often incorporate the *ACA Code of Ethics* as the standard of practice and may have other requirements regarding record keeping.

Throughout this book, we admonish you to consult state counselor licensing statutes and accompanying rules; nowhere is this advice more important than in relation to requirements for records and documentation. In many respects the standard of practice for records and documentation remains uneven. Some state counselor licensure laws provide few details on the specifics of what must be included in a client record. Most states seem to craft requirements that are generally consistent with the current codes of ethics. Other states, such as Arizona, have established standards regarding records and documentation that exceed current ethical requirements. The Arizona Board of Behavioral Health Examiners has developed detailed standards of practice rules pertaining to treatment plans and client records. We encourage you to compare the Arizona requirements with the requirements in your state.

R4-6-1102. Treatment Plan

A licensee shall:

1. Work jointly with each client served or a client's legal representative to prepare an integrated, individualized, written treatment plan, based on the licensee's diagnosis and assessment of behavior and the treatment needs, abilities, resources, and circumstances of the client, that includes:
   a. One or more treatment goals;
   b. One or more treatment methods;
   c. The date when the client's treatment plan shall be reviewed;
   d. If a discharge date has been determined, the aftercare needed after discharge;

    e.   The signature and date signed by the client or the client's legal representative; and

    f.   The signature and date signed by the licensee.

2. At a minimum, review and reassess the treatment plan according to the review date specified in the treatment plan and at least annually with each client or the client's legal representative to ensure the continued viability and effectiveness of the treatment plan and, where appropriate, a description of the services the client may need after terminating treatment with the licensee.

3. Ensure that all treatment plan updates and revisions include the signature and date signed by the client or the client's legal representative and the signature and date signed by the licensee.

4. Upon written request, provide a client or a client's legal representative an explanation of all aspects of the client's condition and treatment.

5. Ensure that a client's treatment is in accordance with the client's treatment plan. (Ariz. Admin. Code, 2008)

R4-6-1103. Client Record

A. A licensee shall ensure that a client record is maintained for each client and:

    1.   Is protected at all times from loss, damage or alteration;

    2.   Is confidential;

    3.   Is legible and recorded in ink or electronically recorded;

    4.   Contains entries that are dated and signed with the first and last name of the individual signing the document or electronically authenticated by the individual making the entry;

    5.   Is current and accurate;

    6.   Contains original documents and original signature, initials or authentication; and

    7.   Is disposed of in a manner that protects client confidentiality.

B. A licensee shall ensure that a client record contains the following, if applicable:

    1.   The client's name, address, and home telephone number;

    2.   Documentation of informed consent to treatment;

    3.   Documentation of the treatment plan and all updates and revisions to the treatment plan;

    4.   Information or records provided by or obtained from another person regarding the client;

    5.   Written authorization to release a client record or information;

    6.   Documentation of requests for client records and of the resolution of those requests;

    7.   Documentation of the release of any information in the client record;

    8.   Progress notes;

    9.   Documentation of telephone, written, or face-to-face contact with the client or another individual that relates to the client's health, safety, welfare, or treatment;

    10. Documentation of behavioral health services provided to the client;

11. Other information or documentation required by state or federal law.
12. Financial records, including:
    a. Records of financial arrangements for the cost of providing behavioral health services;
    b. Measures that will be taken for nonpayment of the cost of behavioral health services provided by the licensee.

C. A licensee shall make client records in the licensee's possession promptly available to another health professional, the client or the client's legal representative in accordance with A.R.S. § 12-2293.

D. A licensee shall make client records of a minor client in the licensee's possession promptly available to the minor client's parent in accordance with A.R.S. § 25-403(H).

E. A licensee shall retain records in accordance with A.R.S. § 12-2297.

F. A licensee shall ensure the safety and confidentiality of any client records the licensee creates, maintains, transfers, or destroys whether the records are written, taped, computerized, or stored in any other medium.

G. A licensee shall ensure that a client's privacy and the confidentiality of information provided by the client is maintained by subordinates, including employees, supervisees, clerical assistants, and volunteers.

H. A licensee shall ensure that a progress note includes the following:
    1. The date a behavioral health service was provided;
    2. The duration of time spent providing the behavioral health service;
    3. If counseling services were provided, whether the counseling was individual counseling, family counseling or group counseling; and
    4. The signature and date signed by the licensee who provided the behavioral health service. (Ariz. Admin. Code, 2008)

It's not surprising to find a significant number of disciplinary actions against Arizona licensees that are based on failure to conform to treatment plan and counseling record requirements. Public record information available on the website of the Arizona Behavioral Health Board indicates that from 2011 to May 2014, the board disciplined 46 LPCs; nine (19.5%) of those sanctions involved documentation failures.

The counselor licensing law in New Jersey is another example in which the rules developed by the board likely exceed the current national standard of practice. New Jersey has developed rules that specifically address the "use of personal or other computer to prepare client records."

(a) A licensee who prepares a client record maintained solely on a personal or other computer shall use a write-protected program which:
    1. Contains an internal permanently activated date and time recordation for all entries;
    2. Automatically prepares a back-up copy of the file; and

     3.   Is designed in such a manner that, after the licensee signs by means of a confidential personal code ("CPC"), the entry cannot be changed in any manner.

(b) The licensee shall include in the client record at least two forms of identification; for example, name and record number, or any other specific identifying information.

(c) The licensee shall finalize or sign the entry by means of a CPC. Where more than one individual is authorized to make entries into the computer file or any client record, the licensee responsible for the practice shall assure that each such person obtains a CPC and uses the program in the same manner.

(d) A licensee wishing to continue a system of computerized client records that does not meet the requirements of this section shall promptly initiate arrangements for modifications of the system. In the interim, the following will apply:

     1.   On the date of the first treatment, evaluation, or consultation subsequent to effective date of rule, and after each visit continuing to the date of the changeover, the licensee shall:

        i.   Print out a hard copy of the entire computer recorded client record; and

       ii. Date and initial each page of the printout

     2.   The licensee shall retain all hard copies as a permanent part of the client record.

(e) A licensee shall document any addenda or corrections to a client's record in a separately dated, signed, and timed note. (N. J. Admin. Code § 13:34-8.2, 2014)

A third example comes from the Board of Counseling Professionals Licensure in the state of Maine. The board has developed regulations that require counselors to retain copies of e-mail communications between the counselor and client or between the counselor and others when the client is the topic of conversation. The regulation states:

> Counselors maintain records necessary for rendering professional services to their clients. Client records must completely and accurately document: (a) counseling provided by the counselor to the client; (b) client progress; (c) contacts and communications between counselor and client that relate to the provision of counseling to the client; and (d) communications between the counselor and persons other than the client that relate to the counselor's provision of counseling to the client. "Communications," as used in this section, specifically includes email. If errors are made in client records, counselors take steps to properly note the correction of such errors. The counselor retains client records for at least five years after the last counselor/client contact, including cases in which the client is deceased. (Me. Code R. § 02-514, Chapter 8-A, 2009)

The regulation does not define how e-mail communication is to be retained. Should it be incorporated into the chart or maintained separately? In addition, the regulation does not address other forms of electronic communication, such as text messages.

The standard set in Maine for retaining e-mail communication may be the start of a trend that could be adopted by other state licensing boards or ethics codes. See Chapter 7 for a discussion regarding NBCC's Standards for Distance Services. Other professionals in the medical and mental health fields and their associations are also grappling with the fast-paced changes occurring with e-mail and other electronic records concerns. According to the American Medical Association (2002), "Whenever possible and appropriate, physicians should retain electronic and/or paper copies of e-mails [*sic*] communications with patients." Perhaps the language used— "whenever possible and appropriate"—provides the practitioner with some room for professional judgment and discretion. Counselors are cautioned that state counselor licensure boards, as well as agencies or institutions in which counselors are employed, may have strict mandates regarding retention of e-mails.

We included the examples of documentation requirements in three states (Arizona, New Jersey, and Maine) to make the point that state counseling boards can and do adopt rules that can be unique to that state. Practitioners who were trained in a different state or who move their practice from one state to another must never assume that they know the law regarding documentation or any other aspect of the new state's counseling law. Also, they should not assume that compliance with the *ACA Code of Ethics* or any other recognized professional association code of ethics will be sufficient to meet the standard set by their states. We encourage counselors to track published reports of disciplinary actions brought against counselors by licensing boards.

The standard of practice regarding records and the documentation of counseling and psychotherapy services continues to evolve. The full impact and implication of the HIPAA privacy regulations have yet to be tested in court. Furthermore, the federal financial incentives that physicians and certain health care entities receive to switch to electronic health records will likely impact mental health providers as well. Inevitably, courts will rule on various aspects of federal and state laws; these rulings will further clarify practitioners' duties regarding records and documentation standards. As you read this chapter, please keep in mind that there are some questions we can't answer. In some cases there is no standard answer; in other cases, the diversity of practice is so great that all we can say is, "It depends." Therefore, our purpose in this chapter is to define the minimum ethical and legal expectations (as we understand them today) and to offer specific direction for documenting client interactions and situations that could lead to licensure board complaints and/or accusations of malpractice.

Purpose of Client Records

We believe that the purpose of client records and documentation of counseling services can be divided into four broad and overlapping categories: (a) clinical management—how records and documentation serve to assist the practitioner in providing quality care for the client; (b) legal implications for the client—how records and documentation can serve the client who is involved or becomes involved in a judicial proceeding (e.g., court mandated treatment, divorce proceedings, and child custody); (c) protection of health information—how HIPAA regulations have defined record keeping and appropriate use and disclosure of information; and (d) risk management for counselors—how records and clinical documentation can serve as a risk management strategy to help protect counselors from licensure board complaints and lawsuits.

Before discussing each of these four categories, we need to define, for purposes of our discussion, two important terms:

1. *Client record*—the physical or electronic folders or files sometimes referred to as the *chart* or the *general treatment record* in which protected health information (PHI) pertaining to the care of the client is maintained. As discussed above, the specific content within the client record will be influenced by the treatment setting (private practice, agency, or other entity), the client's presenting concerns, and relevant state and federal laws. Typically, the contents include the following:

   - client contact information,
   - dates of service (including start and stop times),
   - participants (who attended counseling sessions),
   - informed consent (signed and dated),
   - financial charges and payments (may be stored separately),
   - clinical assessment and/or diagnosis,
   - authorizations to release confidential information,

- collateral information (testing results, letters, reports, e-mails, court and legal documents, information obtained about the client from others, including past clinical records and communication from third parties),
- treatment plan,
- prognosis and progress tracking,
- session notes (chart notes, progress notes, process notes), and
- psychotherapy notes (see the section titled Purpose #3: HIPAA Compliance).

2. *Clinical documentation*—the act of recording, in any form, relevant information gained during the course of the counseling relationship.

Purpose #1: Clinical Management

On the most obvious level, well-organized and well-documented client counseling records assist practitioners in providing quality care to clients. Unlike medicine or other professional services, counseling and psychotherapy rarely unfold in an objective and linear manner. The twists and turns inherent in the counseling process require constant attention and thoughtful reflection. The intellectual and physical processes associated with documenting counseling sessions provide practitioners with an opportunity to reflect and gain perspective on the evolving dynamics of the case. Although there are some client stories and situations that vividly remain in the mind of a practitioner throughout the course of treatment, most client situations can easily become mixed with other current or past client circumstances. Quality care is enhanced when counselors are fully present in the session, empowered with the client's story, and mindful of the treatment plan. Being present and prepared is facilitated by the timely and careful documentation of the previous session. Regular review of the client's record in preparation for the session is responsible practice that reflects an ethical commitment to providing the client with the best possible care.

There is probably no more critical moment in any counseling relationship than when the counselor and client are working through threats of harm to self or others. When clients disclose thoughts, feeling, or intentions that place the client or others at risk, we are duty bound to assess the potential threat and to take appropriate action. Responding appropriately and then fully documenting the at-risk situation and your response to it is essential, both in terms of quality of care and in terms of risk management (more about that later in this chapter). A habit of competent documentation of at-risk situations can actually support the care you give to your client. When faced with an at-risk situation, you can anticipate the documentation that will be needed. Anticipating the necessary documentation makes it easier to engage in the careful decision making and clinical interventions that will result in quality care. The connection between quality care and good documentation is that each supports and promotes the other. Thorough documentation facilitates good preparation, enhances quality care, and invites thorough documentation—all of which support a practice that is clinically, ethically, and legally sound.

Quality documentation also facilitates continuity of care from one practitioner to another, which is an essential element of clinical management. Sometimes another practitioner must temporarily step in when the treating counselor is not available; at other times, the treating counselor must transfer or refer the client to a new counselor. In these instances, good records provide a means of communicating valuable information to the covering or new practitioner.

Purpose #2: Legal Implications for the Client

Counseling and psychotherapy records often become relevant when clients are involved in a legal proceeding. Honest and nonjudgmental clinical documentation of client issues and progress in addressing issues can serve the client's legal needs in a variety of ways. Clients reasonably expect that issues discussed and progress achieved will be documented and available should they need the information in a judicial proceeding. The specific legal proceeding can range from civil matters (divorce and child custody) to workplace injury and workman's compensation lawsuits to criminal proceedings. Sometimes counseling is initiated at the behest or encouragement of the attorneys or judge involved in a legal proceeding. Clients are often court ordered into counseling, or attorneys may encourage clients to seek treatment in anticipation of a court order or to demonstrate responsible action on the part of their clients. At other times, counseling is initiated without any judicial involvement or anticipated involvement, but unforeseen circumstances occur that place the client in litigation. When that occurs, counseling records often become relevant to the judicial proceeding.

We encourage you to assume that any client record could end up being read in open court. Therefore, professional and thorough documentation should be the standard so that if release of client records is authorized by your client or legally obtained by the court, the record will accurately and professionally reflect the clinical experience. To that end, practitioners are encouraged not to include names or identifying information about third parties (particularly the names of extramarital lovers or business partners who may be involved with your client). However, there is typically no need to exclude from records the names of family members or significant others relevant to issues in the counseling.

Furthermore, client records do not always reflect favorably on the client and actually may be detrimental to the client in a judicial proceeding. The clinical record should honestly reflect the reality of the counseling experience and should never be constructed or altered to artificially reflect favorably on the client or the counselor. If, at the outset of the counseling relationship, it is likely or even possible that client records or a report of client issues and progress will become involved in a judicial process, you are encouraged during the informed consent process to clearly define the ground rules of your involvement and the nature and type of records that will be maintained.

Purpose #3: HIPAA Compliance

We recognize that not every counseling practitioner or practice setting is a HIPAA-covered entity (see Chapter 5), and therefore HIPAA requirements do not pertain to every mental health practice. However, we believe that, over time, HIPAA requirements will continue to influence and may ultimately come to define the standard of practice with regard to records and documentation. Therefore, we have included HIPAA compliance as one of the reasons for record keeping. A major purpose of HIPAA was to address concerns that the transmission of health care information through the Internet and other electronic means could lead to widespread gaps in protection of patient and client confidentiality (see Chapter 5 for a complete discussion). As HIPAA-compliant rules and procedures were developed, the standard of practice regarding client records and documentation was affected. During the past several years, practitioners have adopted HIPAA language and practices, and some state laws have been developed or modified to provide consistency with HIPAA requirements. All is far from settled; there are significant unanswered and untested questions that await court rulings or rulemaking that will bring further clarity.

Counseling records include two broad sections of individually identifiable information defined by HIPAA as *protected health information* (PHI): (a) client demographic information (e.g., name, date of birth, address, telephone number, e-mail address) and (b) diagnosis (if appropriate; see Chapter 4), prognosis, treatment plan, progress to date, dates of service (including start and stop times of sessions), participants in the session, and financial data (charges, payments, balance). This type of PHI is confidential but, under appropriate circumstances, may be accessed by third-party payers.

Psychotherapy notes, also commonly referred to as *process notes*, are given an added level of protection by HIPAA if they are maintained in a separate physical or electronic file. The added level of protection means that disclosure of psychotherapy notes requires a separately executed client authorization (assuming the notes are maintained in a separate file). Practitioners may integrate psychotherapy notes within a single file that includes all client PHI, but if handled in this manner, psychotherapy notes are then covered under the general rules governing the disclosure of PHI.

A decision must be made: Should the mental health practitioner create one file containing all PHI, including psychotherapy notes, or two files, one for the regular PHI (as just outlined) and one for psychotherapy notes? Maintaining two separate records on each client can be taxing and complicated, but with certain client populations or treatment settings, it may be in the best interests of the clients to do so. Agency policy, state statutes, and the unique practice habits of a counselor may dictate or influence this decision.

Psychotherapy notes are "notes recorded (in any medium) by a health care provider who is a mental health professional documenting or analyzing the contents of conversation during a private counseling session or a group, joint, or family counseling session and that are separated from the rest of the individual's medical record. *Psychotherapy notes* excludes medication prescription and monitoring, counseling session start and stop times, the modalities and frequencies of treatment furnished, results of clinical tests, and any summary of the following items: Diagnosis, functional status, the treatment plan, symptoms, prognosis, and progress to date" (Privacy of Individually Identifiable Health Information, 2014).

Whereas HIPAA has provided a definition of psychotherapy notes, relevant questions remain. Would some of the information contained in a traditional SOAP note (Subjective, Objective, Assessment, and Plan) or a DAP note (Data, Assessment, and Plan) be considered a psychotherapy note? What about practitioners who document in a free-form narrative manner? What portion of the narrative information would be considered to fall within the purview of a psychotherapy note? What about the counselor who views the relationship (couple, family, or group) as the client and documents accordingly? Or the practitioner who has ethical questions about the legitimacy of mental health diagnoses—and therefore organizes and describes treatment in ways that are different from the medical model around which HIPAA is constituted? To our knowledge, these important questions remain as yet untested and unanswered. In many ways the answers to these and other documentation questions represent the frontier of the continued evolution of the standard of practice for mental health professionals. You are encouraged to be ever mindful of the evolving standard of care regarding documentation. Expect continued change—and keep current!

Purpose #4: Risk Management Strategy

The final reason for keeping records is very simple. Well-organized and well-documented client counseling records are the most effective tool counselors have for successfully responding to licensing board complaints or threats of a malpractice lawsuit. If there is a question about what you did or failed to do, and there is no documentation in the client record that reflects what the client said or did or that describes your clinical decision making, it can be argued that it never happened. It will be your word against your client's word. We are trusting people. It is hard for us to think that a client might intentionally accuse us of something inappropriate or suggest that we failed in our duty to serve the client's best interests. Sadly, counselors are sometimes falsely accused of wrongdoing. Sometimes clients misunderstand our words and intentions, misquote our comments, or misinterpret our actions. When the counseling relationship breaks down—and the client feels stressed, betrayed, and abandoned—anything is possible. Documentation is your first and best line of defense.

This is particularly true when dealing with high-risk issues in the counseling process. High-risk situations include threats of harm to self or others, issues related to transference and countertransference, and complicated legal and ethical issues that can be open to interpretation. Examples of such issues include (but are not limited to) custody, pregnancy, abortion, sexual activities and drug abuse of minors, allegations of child abuse and elder or disabled adult abuse, illegal client actions, and infidelity. When these issues are present, it is important to carefully document your clinical decision making and your professional actions. Threats of harm to self or others are common and always potentially explosive clinical issues. From a risk management documentation perspective, we recommend that each at-risk situation be fully documented in the client record to include the following areas:

- *At-risk situation:* Document what the client did or said that suggested that she or he was considering engaging in or was actively engaging in a high-risk activity.
- *Assessment:* On the basis of your clinical experience and knowledge of the client, document the severity level of this threat.
- *Options:* List the options you considered as appropriate responses. By listing the options, you demonstrate that you were thinking broadly and that you considered a range of alternatives before reaching a decision.
- *Rule out:* Describe what options you ruled out and why each was determined to be inappropriate. These descriptions demonstrate your clinical decision making.
- *Consultation and/or supervision:* If feasible, obtain and document any colleague consultation or supervision you received in order to evaluate options and clarify a course of action.
- *Actions taken:* Describe the options you chose, including what you said or did. This process helps clarify how you implemented the options you determined to be appropriate.
- *Follow up:* Document what happened—what you did—and how things progressed until there was resolution.

Nothing about this process assures that you will make all the right choices and that every situation that involves a client at risk will have a positive outcome. Unanticipated and tragic things do happen: Clients commit suicide or murder and harm others or themselves. The standard is not that you ascertain the unknown. The standard is that you conduct a careful assessment of the situation, consider a range of options, make a thoughtful clinical decision, competently implement your decision, and remain mindful and vigilant (if necessary) until there is resolution. The end result may not be positive;

sometimes it is tragic. In terms of risk management, we want you to have carefully documented what you did and why so that others can see that you brought your best professional judgment and skill to the situation.

Ownership of Records

Under most circumstances in a private practice setting, counseling records (the physical or electronic record) belong to you. In a school, agency, or other treatment facility, counseling records are the property of the organization. However, the information contained in those records usually belongs to the client. You have an obligation to protect the confidentiality of client records, as discussed in Chapter 5, but you should always operate under the assumption that a variety of individuals may at some time have access to your records, including professional colleagues, insurance and managed care companies, attorneys, courts, employers, schools, and even your client.

Alteration of Records

Evidence of altering client records can lead to serious consequences. Erasures, whiteouts, blacked-out notes, and notes out of sequence in a paper record suggest that changes and alterations have been made to the original record. Someone reading the record might conclude that you are disorganized or that you changed the record in light of other events. In addition, electronic documentation that was created at a time other than when services were provided can cast suspicion on the accuracy of the record. Notwithstanding ethical confidentiality concerns, the contents of counseling records may be discoverable by a court of law, inspected by insurance companies, and released to others upon waiver by your client, so you must ensure that your record keeping is complete, accurate, and free of any extraneous materials that could prove embarrassing at some later time. Notes in the margins, telephone numbers casually jotted down on the back of a record, and doodles have no place in client records. Personal criticism of your client in progress notes could be extremely embarrassing or harmful to the client if disclosed at some later date.

All client record documentation should be made contemporaneously, not constructed after the fact, and particularly not after receiving a subpoena. It is also important never to change or alter records so they look better before you release them. If you determine, for whatever reason, that you need to add and/or clarify information in the client record, you can do so by making a currently dated entry in the record. This entry can be appropriately titled to reflect the nature of the addition to the record. Examples include Progress Summary, Progress Update, and Clarification; the point is to date the entry with the current date and then provide the relevant information. Although there still may be criticism of the timeliness of your documentation, there can be no valid accusation that you attempted to alter the original record. Of course, the best practice is to keep client records current so that you are never in a position to explain deficiencies in the record.

Financial Records and Financial Relationship

Financial records should also be maintained on all clients to accurately document the financial relationship. This is true for fee-for-service, third-party payers, copayment relationships, and services provided by grants or purchase of service arrangements. Whether these records should be kept with counseling records is a matter for individual consideration. Many practices have separate billing departments that handle financial matters, and counselors have limited, if any, contact with fees and collections. There should be some mechanism, even in larger practices, to inform a counselor if a client is delinquent in paying for services. Too often counselors do not discuss a growing unpaid balance with their clients. At some point the delinquent account becomes a problem between the counselor and the client or the agency and the client—a problem that threatens the counseling relationship. Unpaid counseling fees may also reflect other underlying problems of which the counselor should be aware. Counselors are encouraged to maintain accurate financial records, keep clients apprised of any outstanding balances, and proactively address financial delinquency so that mutually agreeable payment plans can be established that do not threaten the counseling relationship.

Technology, Client Records, and Information

Many counseling agencies and private practitioners now maintain client records, schedules, and financial information on computers or other electronic devices. This medium certainly helps to reduce paperwork and saves time, but there are some potential problems. First and foremost, authenticating the content and dates of records may be difficult with electronic media designed to be flexible and maneuverable. Be sure to include dates of entries in computer records, and establish procedures to ensure security of access to computer files. You should also implement a plan for frequent backup of information to avoid losing files if a computer crashes (or the computer operator accidentally erases information).

Storage of client records in the "cloud"—instead of on a desktop or laptop computer or as a means of backup—has become increasingly common. When using cloud storage, reliability and security are the primary concerns. Reliability means the ease and consistency of accessing the information. Security addresses, among other things, the level of encryption and/or password protection of the data in the cloud. Before using a cloud storage service, counselors are strongly encouraged to consult experts in this area to ensure the service complies with all access, encryption, and security standards. (See Chapter 7 for more discussion of technology-related issues.) As discussed previously in this chapter, HIPAA and state licensing board rules may define security requirements or enumerate other requirements when records are maintained electronically. Counselors may need to enter into a HIPAA Business Associate contract with the cloud vendor (see Chapter 5). There are several software programs on the market specifically designed for mental health professionals. These programs can assist practitioners in the maintenance and storage of the entire client record (all PHI), including scheduling, financial and billing information, treatment planning, counseling session notes, and even reports on client progress.

Record Retention

Records should be retained for at least the minimum period of time set by state law, if any. Federal tax policy, state records or licensure statutes, agency policy, and/or other administrative requirements may influence the specific amount of time that client counseling and financial records are maintained. As already discussed, client records serve many purposes and should be available for a reasonable amount of time. Years after treatment has concluded, clients may need to access their records as evidence of their state of mind during a particularly difficult time of life. Counselors may need to refer to client records to competently respond to allegations of ethics violations, negligence, or malpractice. Therefore, we encourage the establishment of a records retention policy for your firm, agency, or practice. Develop the records retention policy in keeping with your state licensing statute, HIPAA requirements, and the statute of limitations in your state (the number of years after an injury or its discovery that a client has in which to bring suit). All client records should be kept, not just some of the records. The record retention policy should specify how records will be maintained in storage (microfilm, microfiche, computer PDF files, cloud, boxed paper files, etc.). Finally, the policy should define where records will be stored to keep them safe and secure as well as how and when they will be destroyed. It is advisable to keep a written log of which records were destroyed and the date on which they were destroyed.

If there is no set minimum period of time for record retention in your state, you may wish to retain records for a minimum of 7 years. If you see Medicaid clients or others under a federally funded program, you may wish to keep the records for at least 10 years (the longest period of time in which a false claims action could be brought against you). If you counsel children, you may wish to keep them for a set period of time after the client reaches the age of majority. As you set your record retention period, be aware that many states have no statute of limitations for licensure board complaints. If that is true in your state, you may wish to keep your records longer than the minimum time period.

Records Custodian

In most circumstances, counselors should appoint a records custodian to take custody of counseling records in the event of the counselor's death or disability. The concept of a records custodian is one that we have been suggesting in seminars and classes and in writing for many years. The 2014 *ACA Code of Ethics* also suggests appointment of a records custodian (Standard B.6.i.); that person should be ready to act in the event of a counselor's incapacitation, death, or termination of practice. The appointment of a records custodian will typically be of little concern to counselors who work in large practices or agencies; the agency is automatically the custodian of the records. But for small practices, especially sole practitioners, it is important that a trusted professional colleague be appointed the caretaker of your client records. The records custodian has two primary responsibilities: (a) to notify and provide referral assistance to your clients in the event of your sudden death or disability and (b) to take custody of your client records to ensure their continued security (both for the benefit and protection of the client and for protection of you or your estate in the event of a malpractice lawsuit). Obviously, it is important to appoint a records custodian who is a credentialed mental health professional and someone for whom you have professional regard. However, you should not appoint someone who will be too distressed in the event of your sudden death or disability to competently support your clients and provide for appropriate referral. Frequently, counselors practicing in the same community will agree to a reciprocal records custodial arrangement. You might want to consider including this information in your will. (For further discussion of the concept of "records custodian" and other issues involved with the need to prepare for death, illness, disability, or retirement, see Chapter 11 and www. privatepracticepreparedness.com.)

In the event you decide to relocate, change professional direction, or retire, clients should be provided with information about how to access copies of records. Some state counseling laws define a process for client notification; in some cases, a notice must be placed in a local newspaper. The point is to ensure that records continue to be maintained after counselors close their practices for the time specified in the records retention policy and/or as defined by law and that a process be established and communicated whereby clients can gain access to records.

Summary

Maintaining accurate, timely, and thoughtful client records is not only required by the prevailing standard of care for practicing professional counselors, but it is also a risk management strategy that counselors can control. Competent record keeping serves both client and counselor. Counselors are strongly encouraged to adopt and maintain a system of record keeping that is consistent with federal laws, prevailing state counselor licensing board laws and rules, institutional policies, and the unique needs of a given client population.

Chapter 11

Managing Your Counseling Practice

As a professional, you must determine whether to practice as an employee of an agency, corporation, school, or other entity; to establish your own private practice; or to join with colleagues in establishing a practice. This decision will be guided by a variety of factors, including the extent to which you are willing to take both financial and emotional risks, your need for security and predictability, and your professional preparation and experience. For some counselors, the steady income and security resulting from being employed is of paramount importance. For others, the freedom to be one's own boss is the overriding factor. In the end, and barring licensure restrictions, it is a choice that's yours to make.

On the basis of your choice, you will face an array of restrictions and possibilities determined by federal, state, and local laws and regulations. If you choose to practice as an employee of an institution or counseling agency, you may be spared from complying with some of the governmental requirements for employers. The purpose of this chapter is to provide some guidance about the business aspects of various counseling practices. Where applicable, distinctions are drawn among self-employment status, the counselor as employer, and the counselor as public or private employee. Please keep in mind that the material that follows is, by necessity, very general. It is intended to raise issues and questions for you to consider; it is not designed as a substitute for good legal, business, and financial planning. You are encouraged to consult with relevant professionals before making crucial decisions about your professional practice.

Opening a Counseling Practice: Forms of Operation

Counselors typically do not enter practice with a strong business background and can easily become overwhelmed with the variety of practice forms. These choices have legal, tax, and practical consequences. Although we recommend obtaining advice from your own local attorney and accountant, we provide an overview of the significant practice issues so you can become familiar with the practice options available to you.

For-Profit Entities

Most counselors who set up counseling practices will choose a for-profit entity, but it may take one of a variety of forms. Although many practices are incorporated, it is by no means mandatory that you do so. For many years, small businesses have operated successfully as unincorporated, sole proprietorships. Whether a counselor practices alone or as part of a group is a matter that involves personality and economic circumstances rather than simply considerations of law. However, the form of the business is determined by legal considerations, a chief determinant of which is the avoidance of personal liability.

Corporation

A corporation is a separate legal entity. In a corporation, the individual owners, directors, officers, or employees of the corporation are generally shielded from personal liability for negligent acts and omissions arising out of the corporation's business operations. If creditors initiate lawsuits against the corporation, the private assets of the individual officers, directors, or employees are usually beyond their reach. Lawsuits would include claims for uncollected debts, false or misleading advertising, nonpayment of taxes, and accidents that occur on the premises.

However, incorporation is not advisable in all situations. Professional corporations (those available to counselors, psychologists, physicians, and certain other licensees under most state laws) usually do protect counselor shareholders from the negligent acts and omissions of their shareholder colleagues. However, they typically do not shield counselor shareholders from their own malpractice liability. Therefore, professional corporation status may not be the preferred mode of operating for many solo practitioners.

In addition, the initial costs of incorporation and attendant filing fees are not substantial, but the continuing formalities necessary to maintain the corporation may prove onerous. These formalities may include separating the financial records of shareholders and the corporation, holding regular meetings of shareholders and directors, issuing stock and maintaining stock transfer records, and filing annual reports. Furthermore, the limited-liability advantage available to corporations applies only so long as the corporate formalities are preserved. Failure to adhere to these formalities, particularly regarding commingling of funds and filing required reports, can lead to loss of corporate status and its attendant liability limitations.

S Corporation

Another possibility to consider is the subchapter S corporation. As a federal tax law option, the S corporation allows an enterprise to be created as a corporation under state law, thereby preserving the shield against personal liability, yet to be treated as a partnership for federal tax law purposes. Hence, the tax deductions and tax credits experienced by corporations are not frozen at the corporate level but are passed along to the stockholders in their personal capacities. You should speak to your accountant before electing subchapter S status.

Partnership

Two or more counselors in the same practice may elect to form a partnership. Sometimes this form of operation is more tax advantageous than the corporate form. With the usual partnership form, liabilities as well as assets are shared among partners. The downside to this is that you might be liable for the acts and omissions of your partner. To avoid this situation, counselors may choose to practice within the same office suite without formal partnership agreement or incorporation. See the section titled "Office Sharing and Informal Group Practices."

Limited Liability Company or Partnership

In recent years, some counselors and other professionals have chosen to set up a limited liability company (LLC) or a limited liability partnership (LLP). In some jurisdictions, the appropriate form for a licensed professional would be a professional limited liability company (PLLC) or professional limited liability partnership (PLLP). The details are governed by state law. Like the subchapter S corporation, the LLC or PLLC achieves a limited liability for owners similar to that of a stockholder of a corporation while permitting partnership-style pass-through treatment of income for tax purposes. In addition, flexibility of allocating income, losses, and cash flow is permitted, and the strict qualification rules of the subchapter S corporations do not apply. There are, however, some disadvantages to this entity, mostly arising from the uncertainty about how jurisdictions that do not recognize LLCs deal with them and the expense that may be incurred by a small counseling practice. With the LLP form, a partner may not be shielded from the general debts and liabilities of the partnership (such as leases).

There is no one-size-fits-all business operational form that suits all counselors in all jurisdictions. Any counselor who thinks of starting a private practice or agency should consult both a certified public accountant and an attorney who specialize in business formation issues. (See Appendix C for further information on finding such professionals.)

Operating Instruments and Organizational Meetings

Regardless of which organizational form is chosen, business entities are governed by the operating instruments under which they are created that state their operational rules. For a corporation, the creating document is its articles of incorporation, the contents and form of which are usually dictated by state law. The corporation's operating rules are contained in its bylaws. For a partnership, the creating document is the partnership agreement, which usually includes the general operational rules, although a set of bylaws or other rules may be developed to guide its day-to-day management. LLCs typically are created by articles of organization and governed by an operating agreement that is a combination of partnership agreement, limited partnership agreement, and corporate bylaws.

When forming a business entity, you must observe a number of organizational formalities. First among these is the organizational meeting, with its proceedings recorded in minutes. Depending on the rules in your state, a variety of actions may occur at this meeting, including selecting and approving the organizational structure, authorizing bank accounts, and retaining a lawyer and accountant (see Appendix C). Corporate rules also may require an initial meeting of the corporation at which directors other than those listed in the articles of incorporation may be elected, together with the corporation's officers.

Office Sharing and Informal Group Practices

Throughout the country, many independent professional counselors share offices and overhead expenses. This type of arrangement may be practical and cost-effective; however, it can expose the counselor to increased liability risk on the basis of the conduct of the other professionals in the informal group—conduct over which the counselor has no control. The members of these loosely affiliated informal groups may assume that they cannot be held liable for their colleagues, but that is not always true. Here are some of the common indicators of a group practice, even if there is no formal legal entity:

- The members of the group use a group name, such as Counseling Associates.
- There is joint letterhead, billing, advertising, or an office sign.
- Client records of all practitioners are stored together.
- Group therapy sessions are conducted by more than one practitioner.
- The public perceives the operation to be a group practice.

If you are considered to be part of a group, you may be held liable for the negligent acts of others in the group practice, whether or not you are an organized business entity. You can minimize the risks by carefully checking out the references and licensing status of the professionals who practice in your office and ensuring that all members of the group carry equivalent limits of liability insurance. If you operate as a group practice, you may find it useful to obtain a group liability insurance policy (see this chapter's discussion of insurance).

As an alternative, if you decide that you want to maintain separate and independent practices but still share office space, be sure that you and the other practitioners clearly identify yourselves as independent professionals and establish that by maintaining (for example) separate billing accounts, websites, and letterheads. Even if the therapists intend to operate as independent professionals, courts may give more weight to the public's perception. We are aware of a counselor who was sued on a theory of de facto partnership when an uninsured psychologist in her multidisciplinary office-sharing arrangement allegedly carried on a sexual relationship with his patient. In this case, the professionals used a joint name (such as XYZ Counseling Associates) on an office sign, letterhead, and phones, and it could have appeared to the public (clients) that the group was operating as a partnership. Other professionals have been sued in similar circumstances on a legal theory of ostensible agency (i.e., one's apparent authority to represent another).

All professionals who share the office space should purchase professional liability insurance, and copies of the policy face sheets or certificates of insurance should be maintained and updated annually. If the practices are truly independent, there should be no fee-splitting. In many states, splitting or sharing of fees between the referring professional and the professional who actually treats the client is illegal because the monetary incentive could cause the referral to be made on the basis of the professional's financial interest rather than the client's best interest. This practice could also pose a violation of federal law for counselors who treat clients under a federal program like Medicaid. (See a complete discussion later in this chapter.) All clients should be told, in writing, that the group comprises independent practitioners who are responsible for their own acts and omissions and that the arrangement is not a partnership, professional association, or other joint entity. This information should be communicated in the informed consent documents of all practitioners in the office. It is not enough for you to communicate this to your clients; doing so protects your office mates but doesn't protect you.

Nonprofit Organizations

Employment in a nonprofit organization eradicates the perceived headaches of running one's own business and may also appeal to counselors who wish to work with an underserved client population. Furthermore, some counselors pursue creation of their own nonprofit organization, which can offer a host of advantages, not the least of which is tax-exempt status and the resulting ability to attract charitable gifts and donations and send mail at discounted rates.

To qualify for this preferential treatment, the organization's programs must be within the bounds of what are considered charitable, educational, or scientific activities within the scope of section 501(c) (3) or 501(c)(4) of the Internal Revenue Code (2014). This form is probably most appropriate if the counselor is motivated less by the objective of building a business and deriving profit and more by the prospect of operating a program that emphasizes research, publications, seminars, or the provision of certain types of counseling services. A counselor may own a nonprofit entity in the sense of controlling its board of directors. Furthermore, a counselor who is an employee may receive a reasonable salary, and an independent contractor may also receive reasonable payments for services rendered to a nonprofit organization. (See the discussion in the section "Hiring Workers as Independent Contractors or as Employees.")

Generally speaking, a nonprofit entity must qualify for tax-exempt status under federal tax law. When that is accomplished, there is probably a similar exemption under state law as well. However, the privileges of tax exemption come at a price, including limitations on lobbying and political activities and the filing of annual informational returns required by the Internal Revenue Service for most exempt organizations.

Private and Nonprofit Business Procedures

After your professional practice has been established, it is vitally important that a variety of business procedures be implemented to ensure that your practice is conducted in a professional manner. It is just as important to be prepared for the business aspects of your practice as it is to provide competent counseling services to the public. Consideration must be given to tax recording and filing systems; business licensing; insurance (health, disability, premises liability, and content damage and theft); employment and related issues; billing and financial accounting; systems for filing claims for reimbursement with insurance companies; contracts for lease or purchase of property, office equipment, and furnishings; advertising; continuing education requirements and renewal of licensure; relationships with colleagues and supervisors; and myriad other issues. It is extremely important that you set up systems so that you don't let important items—such as your insurance policies or professional license—lapse.

Your financial and legal advisers will be able to assist with specific recommendations, but there are a variety of service organizations that offer general business advice (e.g., Small Business Administration, available at www.sba.gov).

Federal and State Taxes, Reporting, and Licensing

Federal, state, and some local governments require that businesses submit annual information and tax returns. Your local Internal Revenue Service office, state office of taxation, or a local government office should be able to provide you with the necessary information booklets and blank forms that must be filed for business licenses, state and local employee taxes, unemployment taxes, real and personal property taxes, and business income taxes, among others. Your lawyer and/or accountant can also help you to determine which reports and forms are required and when and where they must be filed.

Professional Liability Insurance

It should be evident by now that counselors can be prepared, competent, and licensed; learn about all the legal obligations and implications of counseling clients and operating a private business; and scrupulously tailor their professional actions to conform to the *ACA Code of Ethics*, yet still become the target of ethics, administrative, or legal complaints. Clients may be dissatisfied with their progress in counseling or hear about a hot issue on television or radio, such as sexual abuse by therapists. They may have had unreasonable expectations about the results of counseling and blame the counselor when they see no measurable improvement. Consequently, even without any wrongdoing on the part of the counselor, clients may file an administrative (e.g., state licensing board) complaint or lawsuit.

Counselors must respond (typically through legal counsel) to any administrative, ethics, or legal complaint filed against them. Failure to respond to a complaint in court may result in a default judgment against them, with damages ordered as the court determines appropriate. Even if the claim is found—at an early stage, before trial—to be without merit, it may cost thousands of dollars to defend against or negotiate that complaint. Legal expenses for a trial can exceed $50,000, and without insurance, personal assets are at risk. Failure to respond to a licensure board complaint can lead to sanctions against the licensee, including loss of licensure.

Need for Professional Liability Insurance

It is obvious that professional counselors in private practice should obtain professional liability insurance. But what if you are employed by a school, agency, or organization? If you are an employed counselor and rely on your employer to provide coverage, you could be left with responsibility for unexpected expenses. For example, if you are a school or agency counselor, what happens to you if your employer claims that your actions fell outside the scope of your job duties? You may not be covered for these actions. If you do volunteer or pro bono work on the side, you may not be covered by your employer's policy.

Counselor educators should also make sure that the institution's policy covers them in their roles as educators and supervisors of practicum students and interns. With the low cost of malpractice insurance for counselors, it usually makes sense for counselor educators to have their own policies. In one case, a counselor educator was sued, along with the university and counseling practicum student, as a result of the suicide attempt of the client of a student counselor. The client's parents claimed that the counseling was inadequate and caused them considerable expense for subsequent hospitalization and psychiatric care of their child. The university's attorney advised the student and counselor educator to obtain their own legal counsel to protect their personal interests because the interests of the university were not necessarily consistent with the interests of the supervisor and student (P. L. Nelson, personal communication, January 2006).

In another case, a student sought help from a counselor at a university counseling center and relayed that she had been the victim of date rape. The university was sued because of the date rape incident, and the counselor was not involved. However, the administration demanded all client records to aid the university in defense of the lawsuit. Fortunately, the counselor had an individual professional liability insurance policy and was able to obtain legal assistance to protect against the release of confidential records. Without the individual policy, the counselor would have had to pay the attorney's fees out of pocket, a nontrivial expense (P. L. Nelson, personal communication, January 2006).

Considerations When Purchasing Liability Insurance

Counselors should obtain professional liability insurance coverage at the outset of professional practice. The 2014 average annual premium for professional liability coverage for a full-time counselor (including those in the employed and self-employed categories) through the ACA-sponsored program is less than $200. Exact premiums depend upon the state in which the counselor practices as well as the type of practice specialty and number of hours worked per week. As of the end of 2014, ACA student members in a master's program receive insurance as part of their membership. Clearly, professional liability insurance for counselors is a bargain compared with malpractice premiums paid by many other health care professionals.

A number of factors must be considered when purchasing professional liability coverage. Not all policies meet the needs of all counselors. Counselors may find coverage through individual policies, group plans, and plans sponsored by professional associations, such as the ACA. Regardless of where you obtain the policy, coverage is usually of two types.

- *Claims-made*: This type covers claims actually made while the policy is in force. Under this form, coverage stops at the end of the policy year. Therefore, to retain coverage the policy must be continually renewed, or "tail coverage" must be obtained.
- *Occurrence*: This type covers claims for alleged acts that occurred while the policy was in effect, even if the claim is made several years later, after the policy is no longer in force.

Because claims can be, and often are, filed long after a client has terminated counseling, the occurrence type of policy affords greater protection to practicing counselors. If your policy is of the claims-made type and you change to another insurance company, you will usually need to purchase a separate policy that extends your coverage (extended reporting period, or tail coverage). You are advised to consult with a reputable liability insurance professional for a full explanation of policy features, benefits, and limitations.

It is important to secure coverage for all aspects of your professional practice, including supervision of students or interns, consultation with other professionals, service on accreditation or professional review boards, and actual counseling work with clients. However, be advised that most insurance contracts limit protection to situations in which the conduct complained of was unintentional. Many professional liability policies exclude coverage for claims that are based on sexual misconduct and other intentional wrongdoing, such as fraud, dishonesty, or other criminal behavior. There are some policies that will pay to defend the counselor in court against certain claims that are excluded, even though they will not pay damages if the counselor is held liable. This coverage can be important if an unsubstantiated claim is filed.

Other recommendations for purchasing professional liability insurance are as follows:

- Choose a carrier with an excellent or superior rating by an independent research company, such as A.M. Best or Standard & Poor's. Each company's rating scale is somewhat different, but the grade will signal whether the company is on sound financial footing and has adequate reserve funds.

- Choose an insurance company that is an admitted (licensed) carrier in your state so that your state's Guaranty Fund, if any, will stand behind your carrier in the event of a default.
- Consider how long the company has been providing professional malpractice coverage and whether their rates have been stable.
- Ask questions: Does the company have a good record of service? How long does it take to get your policy and any needed endorsements? Are company employees accessible by telephone?
- Find out whether the company provides assistance—such as live training, publications, or online courses—in managing the risks associated with your practice.

In addition, services available to ACA members, such as the ACA-sponsored Risk Management Helpline (operated in conjunction with the ACA Ethics and Professional Standards Department), may be useful. For more information, call the ACA Ethics and Professional Standards Department at (800) 347–6647, ext. 314. Ethics and risk management consultation can often help to avert lawsuits and administrative complaints before they are filed. Not all insurance carriers or associations provide the same level of assistance, so inquire about the details of services provided before you sign up for coverage. Also, consult with your local attorney for specific legal issues.

Other Insurance Coverage

After you have established the location of your office and purchased or leased furnishings and equipment, it is important to consider a variety of insurance policies to minimize your risk of unprotected or insufficiently compensated losses. A competent insurance agent, broker, or your professional association insurance program director or administrator can help to demystify some of the complexities of policy contracts and coverage. However, it is important for you to read such documents thoroughly and to be sure that both you and the agent or broker understand the nature of your professional practice and the scope of coverage and exclusions provided. When that has been established, you should review the insurance policies annually to confirm that conditions have not changed.

The descriptions of types of insurance coverage that follow are intentionally general, but they should give counselors an overview of the various policies available. Before you contract for any insurance coverage, be sure to investigate the rating, business reputation, and claims procedures of the underwriting company.

General Liability Insurance

General liability insurance is usually written as a comprehensive policy that protects your practice from legal liability for losses associated with the premises and operations, contracts, administrative errors, employees, fire, third-party medical expenses, personal injury, nonowned automobiles, and the like. The insurer's total liability to cover losses will be stated on the declarations page and will usually include a single limit for the majority of coverage. The comprehensive policy may also include workers' compensation and coverage for uninsured or underinsured motorists' protection. Policies vary widely, as do premiums for coverage, so counselors are advised to consult with several insurers to compare coverage and costs.

Property Insurance

Property insurance covers your practice's real or personal property, or interest in rental property, from losses attributable to multiple risks. These risks include fire, lightning, windstorm, or other acts of God; smoke; vandalism; and malicious mischief. Coverage also is available for accounts receivable, office equipment, computers, electronic media, signs, fixtures, landscaping, fine arts, and the like that many practices may use in the course of business. It is recommended that a complete inventory of all real and personal property in which your practice has an interest be conducted annually to determine the level of protection required through the property insurance policy. Some items to consider when reviewing policies include whether coverage is provided for (a) replacement cost of items lost or damaged, including improvements you have made to the premises; (b) lost rents or income; (c) temporary quarters and equipment rental; and (d) lost earnings and extra expenses caused by temporary relocation. Does the policy provide for automatic increases of property limits? Is coverage based on replacement rather than on actual cash value? Will the replacement cost be paid regardless of whether the property is actually replaced? Each of these can have a substantial effect on your practice in the event of a loss.

Directors' and Officers' Liability Insurance

If you act as a clinical director or officer of a corporation or nonprofit entity other than your own professional corporation, you may need directors' and officers' (often called "D&O") liability insurance. Check with your agent, broker, or administrator to see whether this type of coverage is necessary for you.

Business Overhead Insurance

One risk associated with professional practice that many professionals overlook is business overhead expense coverage. If one or more of the key owners of a small counseling practice becomes disabled, the risk of financial ruin is great. If two counselors share all the overhead expenses of their practice and one becomes seriously ill or is injured, the other counselor may have to close or discontinue the practice because of the expenses of continuing operations and financial commitments, such as salaries, rent, and utilities. Purchasing general business overhead expense coverage can protect you from this exposure.

Employee Benefits Programs

Private practitioners with employees also should consider employee benefits programs. Group medical benefits, hospitalization, life, and income-replacement (disability) programs are designed to protect employees and their families from the expenses of illness or injury and can help to attract and retain good employees. However, the costs can be high, and numerous federal and state laws complicate the provision of medical benefits. Your review of employee medical benefit programs should include a discussion of what benefits are to be provided; the amount the professional practice can afford to contribute; whether employees will contribute to the amount paid by the firm; and the deductibles, basic benefit levels, limits of coverage, coinsurance percentages, and similar requirements of the policy. Providing medical benefits coverage is both complicated and expensive and probably will become even more so as the impact of managed care programs increases. In addition, the Patient Protection and Affordable Care Act (2012) may affect coverage options. Counselors need to examine a variety of programs and plans to determine what form will best meet the needs of their practice and employees.

Disability Income Protection

Disability income protection is designed to replace the individual's income in the event of a long-term illness or accident that restricts his or her ability to continue to practice and earn a living. These policies are available for both long and short terms, although long-term policies are widely regarded as the most critical. (Short-term illnesses can usually be covered by personal investments or other sources, but those sources are quickly exhausted by a long-term illness.) Insurers will usually underwrite only a percentage of an individual's annual earnings from professional practice, and how the premiums are paid may affect the individual's tax situation, so it is wise to consult with your employees (if you offer such coverage to your employees) and tax adviser at the time the policy is purchased. In addition, long-term care insurance has become popular in recent years to cover nursing home care or in-home nursing care for someone who has suffered a disability.

Group Life Insurance

Most employee benefit programs contain group life insurance, frequently as part of a group medical plan. Term life insurance is the least costly to obtain on a group basis, and it may be convertible to permanent forms of insurance to provide security for employees who leave your employ. Providing a reasonable level of low-cost protection should be the primary goal, but keep in mind that policy provisions may vary widely in benefits, conditions, eligibility, and exclusions and should be examined closely.

Employment Law Considerations

Employment law has become complex in recent years, and counselor employers should gain some basic familiarity with civil rights and sexual harassment issues as well as the legal ramifications of giving references for former employees. It is beyond the scope of this book to give a comprehensive discussion of the law in this area. This is an area of law that changes rapidly and can trap an unwary counselor faced with hiring or termination decisions. The information that follows in this section is a summary of the employment process, some of the proscriptions that may apply, and recommendations for your private practice. If you have employees, you should consult a local attorney who is well-versed in employment law. If you are an employed counselor, this discussion may also prove helpful to you.

Employment Discrimination

Before you consider hiring your first employee, be sure to learn all you can about employment discrimination laws that may affect your practice. These laws apply to all aspects of employment, from position announcements, applications, interviews, and testing to termination decisions.

Title VII of the Civil Rights Act of 1964 is the federal statute that forbids employment discrimination on the basis of race, color, sex (a term that includes pregnancy), national origin, or religion. It applies to federal, state, and local government employers and to private employers with more than 15 employees if their business "affects interstate commerce." This definition has been broadly interpreted to include activities conducted in other states, such as consulting, being a speaker at a conference, teaching, or attending conferences, so even a medium-sized private counseling service may find that its activities must comply with federal and state employment discrimination laws. Title VII applies to counselors working in state and federal agencies, colleges, and universities. Even though your small private agency may have fewer than 15 employees, and therefore is not technically subject to the federal statute, the policies embodied in the law are good guidelines to follow with employees and may help you to avoid other problems later. Furthermore, many states have similar employment discrimination laws that apply to all employers within the state, regardless of size.

Title VII provides for enforcement by the U.S. Equal Employment Opportunity Commission (EEOC), which is initiated by filing charges within 180 days of the alleged discriminatory act. In some areas, charges must be filed with a local civil rights agency within 300 days of the alleged discrimination (see U.S. EEOC, 1997). The EEOC has the power to investigate any such claims, to seek conciliation, or to bring suit against the employer. If the EEOC decides not to bring an action against the employer in court, notice is given that the original complainant has the right to sue the employer within 90 days. The remedies available to a successful complainant include back pay, injunctive relief (such as an order to rehire, reinstate, or promote the employee), and reasonable attorney and expert fees as well as compensatory (for intentional discrimination) and punitive damages (upon a showing of malice or "reckless indifference").

Other federal laws also affect employment, including the Equal Pay Act of 1963, which requires men and women to be compensated equally for equal work. This applies to jobs that involve equal skill, effort, and responsibility and are performed under similar working conditions in the same establishment, although equal work need not be identical work (*Corning Glass Works v. Brennan*, 1974). Furthermore, the discrimination need not be intentional, and the act covers most private employers and state and local governments. The Lilly Ledbetter Fair Pay Act of 2009 was signed into law by President Barack Obama on January 29, 2009. The act amends the Civil Rights Act of 1964. It states that the 180-day statute of limitations for filing an equal-pay lawsuit regarding pay discrimination starts anew with each subsequent paycheck affected by the alleged discriminatory action.

The Age Discrimination in Employment Act of 1967 (ADEA) protects employees age 40 and older against employment discrimination on the basis of age and includes a prohibition against mandatory retirement in most cases. The ADEA applies to employers with 20 or more employees, labor unions, employment agencies, and their agents. The ADEA is also enforced through the EEOC according to the enforcement scheme established for violations of Title VII.

The Family and Medical Leave Act of 1993 requires covered employers (with at least 50 employees within 75 miles) to provide up to 12 weeks of unpaid, job-protected leave to eligible employees (who have worked for at least 1 year or at least 1,250 hours over the previous 12 months) for certain family and medical reasons. (For more information, see U.S. Department of Labor, Employment Standards Administration, 2014.) The employer must maintain the employee's group health coverage for the duration of the leave, and using such leave cannot result in the loss of any employment benefit that had accrued prior to the start of the employee's leave.

The Immigration Reform and Control Act of 1986 prohibits knowingly hiring undocumented residents. In addition, it prohibits discrimination on the basis of national origin or citizenship, except against unauthorized aliens. The Americans With Disabilities Act of 1990 (ADA; as amended), discussed in greater length later in this chapter, prohibits discrimination against qualified individuals who have a disability. It requires employers to make reasonable accommodations to the conditions of qualified individuals with disabilities and is enforced according to the administrative scheme set out in Title VII.

State Nondiscrimination Statutes

Investigate state and local laws concerning discrimination that may be broader than the federal statutes. Even though your practice may fall outside the scope of the federal statutes, you may be subject to state regulations. Your local attorney can explain your legal obligations to avoid charges of discrimination (see Appendix C).

Sexual Harassment

Establish a comprehensive antiharassment policy for your counseling practice and communicate it to all staff members, whether professional or nonprofessional employees. Make sure they understand that employers have a legal duty to provide a workplace that is free from sexual harassment. In addition, employees must be protected from unwanted or unwelcome sexual overtures or invitations of a sexual nature. This protection applies whether the conduct originates with partners or owners of the firm, supervisors, other colleagues or employees, clients, or nonemployees (U.S. EEOC, n.d.-a).

Recruiting, Hiring, and Managing Employees

As you prepare to hire your first employees, whether they are administrative or professional, it is important that you take steps to make sure you are in compliance with federal, state, and local laws. The following suggestions are for new employers:

- Apply for an employer identification number (EIN).[1] This EIN may be required for identification and tax-paying activities. (Solo practitioners often use their Social Security number in lieu of an EIN.) If you will be a HIPAA "covered entity" (see Chapter 5), you will need the EIN in order to participate in insurance reimbursement activities (Centers for Medicare and Medicaid Services, 2014).
- Check with your state labor department to see if there are registration or other requirements.
- Consider creating job descriptions for prospective employees, including required skills and job performance standards. These standards may help at a later date if an employee does not live up to expectations and you must terminate employment.
- Consider developing an employee handbook with policies on compensation, hours, vacation, sick and other leave, discipline, and termination of employment. You should have all documents reviewed by local counsel to make sure that you are able to modify your policies and terminate problem employees in accordance with law.

---

[1]You can apply online at http://www.irs.gov/Businesses/Small-Businesses-&-Self-Employed/Apply-for-an-Employer-Identification-Number-(EIN)-Online

- Apply for worker's compensation insurance; information is frequently available through your state's worker's compensation agency.
- Check into unemployment tax requirements, including IRS Form 940 (Internal Revenue Service, 2014).
- Set up a payroll system for withholding of taxes. There are many private firms to which you can outsource payroll functions. If you have few employees, consider getting initial payroll advice from your accountant.
- When interviewing prospective employees, know what types of questions are allowed. You may be able to get information from the EEOC, the Small Business Administration, or your own legal counsel.
- Establish employee personnel files. Compile resources for ongoing employment-related questions. Again, the Small Business Administration website has information about many employment-related issues.

Employment Contracts

Whether you are an employer or an employee, it may be desirable to have a contract of employment to set forth the specific terms of employment, or you may be required to have a contract to practice as part of the professional counseling firm or agency. Most states recognize and enforce reasonable clauses and covenants contained in employment contracts. There are two types of clauses that frequently are included in such contracts.

The first is an indemnification or hold harmless clause, in which the employee counselor agrees to accept all liability from any and all lawsuits that may result from his or her professional actions. Two theories of law permit employers of counseling professionals to be held liable for the negligent acts of their employees. The first is the concept of *respondeat superior* (the Latin phrase means "let the master respond") or *vicarious liability* (in other words, the employer is responsible for his or her subordinate). In a typical case, a dissatisfied client files a negligence or malpractice action against the counselor who failed to improve the client's condition and against the counseling agency or service that employs the counselor. The counseling service is presumed to have deeper pockets than the individual counselor, thus enhancing the chances of recovering on any award.

The second theory is that the counselor is acting as the agent for his or her supervisor or employer, who is the principal. The law of agency is far more complicated than this, but essentially the agent works on behalf of the principal, having a legal duty to do so, and can bind the principal through his or her actions. In both cases, the employer may be held responsible for the actions of the employee, even though he or she did not specifically consent to the act complained of or agree to accept liability.

The hold harmless clause changes the equation by shifting the financial responsibility for negligent acts of the employee from the employer back to the employee. The counselor may possibly be required to reimburse the employer for the ultimate judgment and costs of defending the lawsuit on the basis of the provisions of the hold harmless clause in her employment contract. Counselor employees (or independent contractors) should check with their professional liability insurance carriers to ascertain coverage before signing contracts that contain indemnification clauses.

The second type of clause that attorneys frequently add to employment contracts is the restrictive covenant, sometimes also called a *covenant against competition, noncompete clause,* or *covenant not to compete.* Generally such clauses restrict employees from leaving a firm or practice and opening up a competing professional practice in the same geographic location for a set period of time. These clauses are designed to protect the employer, who frequently invests much time and money in new employees, only to have the employees leave and take clients with them. As long as the clause (a) is not broader than is reasonably necessary to protect the legitimate interests of the employer, and (b) relates directly to the specific duties of the former employee, courts will often uphold such agreements. In some states, noncompete clauses in physician and psychologist contracts have been subject to scrutiny in recent years when they precluded a patient from exercising freedom of choice in selecting medical or psychological care (*Comprehensive Psychology System, P.C. v. Prince,* 2005; *Falmouth Ob-Gyn Associates v. Abisla,* 1994).

In the medical and mental health fields, independent contractors are sometimes asked to sign contracts with restrictive covenants. It is doubtful that restrictive covenants in such contracts would be upheld because they are not incident to a valid employment contract. If counselors are truly independent, it is difficult to make a case that they should not be able to practice elsewhere within the same vicinity.

Furthermore, you should check to see whether there is any prohibition against restrictive covenants in your licensure law or other state law. If you are the prospective employee, note that the time to negotiate modifications to a proposed restrictive covenant is before you sign the contract. It may pay to hire a local attorney at the beginning rather than risk a breach of contract action or payment of liquidated damages (i.e., damages agreed upon in advance by contract), which can often be quite costly.

Training and Supervising Employees

As employers, counselors have a variety of responsibilities to their employees and to their clients that arise from the *respondeat superior* theory mentioned in the preceding section. To the extent they exercise control over employee conduct, employers may be held accountable for resulting actions, even though they did not intend for those acts to occur (*Doe v. Samaritan Counseling Center*, 1990). Some courts have allowed recoveries against employers on the basis of negligent hiring, retention, supervision, and training of employees. In these cases, the negligence analysis (discussed in Chapter 4) is used to determine whether employers should be held liable for damages caused by their employees. Was there a foreseeable risk that could have been avoided if the employer had not neglected his or her duty? Was the act complained of within the scope of the employment? Could reasonable training, whether preemployment or in-service, have averted or minimized the risk? For more information on the scope of the negligence analysis, counselors are advised to consult their own legal counsel. Note that employers are also responsible for the acts of volunteers, students, and supervisees working in a counseling service, and these individuals should be held to the same standards of conduct as employees. The material that follows in this section generally applies to volunteers, students, and supervisees as well as to employees.

Obtaining good liability insurance coverage is one way to minimize employer exposure to liability for the acts of employees. Other ways that you can affirmatively diminish the risks of hiring employees include the following:

- Always check the references and backgrounds of applicants for employment for any position within your firm. If the applicant is a mental health professional, be sure to contact the state licensing board to ascertain his or her current licensure status. Call or write to previous employers to verify employment status and dates and ask about the applicant's job responsibilities while he or she was employed there.

- Be sure that applicants for employment, especially recent graduates, have the required professional degrees and preparation (including licensure, certification, or registration) to ensure competence. Discuss treatment theories and concepts with a professional applicant to determine for yourself that the applicant is competent to treat your clients. (One of the authors is aware of a situation where transcripts and license were requested prior to the hiring of one therapist; unfortunately, the documents were not obtained until after many clients were seen. It turned out that the "therapist" was not only unlicensed but had never finished the master's degree requirements.)

- Require your employees (both professional and nonprofessional) to participate in training and professional development. Membership in professional associations and adherence to professional ethical standards should be encouraged.

- Discuss the internal policies and procedures of your agency or counseling service with your employees. Be sure that all employees understand the nature of the counselor–client relationship and the need for strict confidentiality of client information. Explain carefully that their continued employment depends on strict adherence to all employment policies, including rules concerning behavior and conduct with clients. If you are a HIPAA-covered entity, be certain that training covers all privacy and security policies for the practice (see Chapter 5).

- Be alert to changes in employee behavior or erratic performance. Are unusual noises coming from an office during counseling sessions? Is a counselor meeting a client after hours? Is that counselor's door locked during some appointments? Have other employees or clients commented on the strange behavior of an employee? Any of these may be a signal that further investigation is needed immediately.

- If you are serving as a supervisor or consultant to another counselor (including one who is not your employee), schedule regular meetings to discuss case management. Be sure to allow enough time to discuss adequately the case and treatment being provided. Remind the supervisee of the continuing need to protect client confidences, and make sure that the supervisee's clients are aware of the supervision or consultation through an appropriate informed consent process. Check back with the supervisee at regular intervals to ascertain whether clients' needs are being met.

- If you become aware that an employee, particularly a mental health professional, needs additional training to become competent in a new specialty area or to manage a particularly difficult case, schedule in-service training, bring in an outside consultant, or find a relevant training course or seminar.

Hiring Workers as Independent Contractors or as Employees

In the mental health field, many therapists prefer the status of being independent rather than being employees of someone else. Likewise, employers often prefer to hire professional counselors as independent contractors rather than pay benefits and file unemployment and social security taxes, and they may believe that they are insulated from liability for the conduct of these therapist contractors. In reality, the courts, the IRS, and various state agencies are not always bound by the parties' determination of whether the relationship is an employment or independent contractor arrangement. For many years, *U.S. v. Silk* (1947, p. 714, fn 8; quoting then-current Treasury regulations) has been cited:

> If the relationship of employer and employee exists, the designation or description of the relationship by the parties as anything other than that of employer and employee is immaterial. Thus, if two individuals in fact stand in the relation of employer and employee to each other, it is of no consequence that the employee is designated as a partner, co-adventurer, agent, or independent contractor.

A court in a malpractice case is free to decide whether a hired counselor is an employee or independent contractor. The professional who hires the counselor may be held vicariously liable for the negligent acts or omissions of the counselor even if the parties did not treat the worker as an employee. It is a big mistake in counseling practice today not to obtain vicarious liability coverage for hired workers.

Furthermore, there is the possibility of back taxes and other penalties for misclassifying a person as an independent contractor. No single factor determines whether a hired worker is an employee or independent contractor. The IRS looks at a number of factors to make this determination, including behavioral control issues, such as whether the practice has the right to direct and control how the work is done, and financial control factors, such as how the worker is paid and the extent to which the worker makes his or her services available to the rest of the relevant market. Yet another category addressed by the IRS is the type of relationship, which includes an analysis of written contracts, whether benefits are provided, and the duration of the relationship (see IRS, 2014; Wheeler, 2004).

Because of the complexity of issues involved in determining whether a particular person is an employee or independent contractor, it is advisable to seek the advice of your local attorney and accountant before making the final determination and before entering into written contracts. This whole issue is further complicated by the fact that such decisions could also invoke fee-splitting prohibitions under state law or the federal Anti-Kickback Act of 1986 for therapists who are seeing clients under federally funded programs (see discussion below).

Fee Splitting and Fraud and Abuse Laws

Prohibitions against fee splitting by medical and mental health professionals have been in existence for years, but the issue continues to engender confusion. What is fee splitting? Unfortunately, there is not one universal definition—in laws or codes of ethics—that applies in all states. Usually, health care professional licensure statutes or regulations that contain fee-splitting prohibitions forbid a professional from sharing fees with another professional who is not providing professional services to patients or clients in return for those fees. The ban on fee splitting may include any type of rebate, commission, or other payment. For example, if a counselor referred a client to a colleague on the condition that he received 10% of all collections, but he performed no actual counseling, administrative services, or supervisory services, that would likely constitute impermissible fee splitting in states that banned such activities.

The 2014 *ACA Code of Ethics* states that "Counselors do not participate in fee splitting, nor do they give or receive commissions, rebates, or any other form of remuneration when referring clients for professional services" (Standard A.10.b.). The policy behind such a prohibition is that client referrals may be influenced by monetary incentives rather than by what is truly in the client's best interests. This model is very different from the typical business world, where sharing of fees and rebates is quite common and is seen as an acceptable way of doing business. However, the relationship between counselor and client is often very different from that of business owner to business owner or of business to client. The counselor–client relationship, similar to doctor–patient and attorney–client relationships, entails a legal fiduciary duty to act in the client's best interests. This fiduciary duty is also underscored by the 2014 *ACA Code of Ethics* in its statement that counselors' primary responsibility "is to respect the dignity and promote the welfare of clients" (Standard A.1.a.).

Furthermore, there are numerous complex federal and state fraud and abuse laws that prohibit arrangements that may be viewed as kickbacks. The federal Anti-Kickback Act (1986) provides that a person (or entity) who receives, pays, offers, or solicits any "remuneration" (including any kickback, bribe, or rebate, directly or indirectly, in cash or in kind) in order to induce referrals covered by a federal health care program is guilty of a criminal felony and can be fined and imprisoned. If that's not frightening enough for mental health professionals, on top of the criminal penalties, the guilty person(s) may be subject to civil monetary penalties and possibly treble (triple) damages under another law, the federal False Claims Act of 1986.

Does this mean all work force arrangements or agreements to share or split office expenses are illegal? No. There are even certain "safe harbors" under the Anti-Kickback Act for properly structured employment and personal services contracts (including space rental agreements) that may help protect counselors. However, the devil is in the details. For example, the counselor's attorney may recommend, among other things, that the contract be put in writing, contain a term of at least one year, and reflect fair market value of the services. Even establishing fair market value is not always an easy task. Sometimes, a bona fide employment arrangement may be the best way to structure the deal. As counselors see more clients insured through Medicaid and other federal programs (and possibly direct payment by Medicare in the future), the consequences of failing to properly structure employment, space rental, and independent contractor agreements become real. Counselors and other mental health professionals should seek advice from an experienced health care attorney to draft or review their contracts to make sure they are properly structured. One more reason to seek specific advice is that many states have enacted laws that mirror, or even exceed, the scope of the federal laws prohibiting fraud and abuse.

Billing and Collection Practices

Do your clients ever fall behind in their payments or terminate counseling without paying their outstanding bills? Many counselors have this experience. Keep in mind that collection actions frequently lead to malpractice counterclaims or complaints to licensure boards. This situation happens because clients may leave counseling with the belief that they were harmed or that their condition has not improved and so they shouldn't have to pay for services; other clients may harbor resentment at the prospect of their credit being ruined by a collection action. Here are some suggestions to make this aspect of your counseling practice a bit easier for you and your clients:

- Make your payment policies clear to clients at the very outset of the relationship. For example, if you charge for missed sessions, state this clearly as part of your written informed consent process.
- Whenever possible, collect fees (or applicable copayments) at the time of the session.
- Consider writing off the bill if a client leaves your practice feeling dissatisfied. In most cases, insisting on collection of a $75 bill as a matter of principle is not worth the trouble if the client is uncooperative.
- Consider accepting credit or debit cards. For solo practitioners, acceptance of credit cards may accelerate payment and reduce billing costs, which might make the bank fee (usually 3–5% for credit cards, lower for debit transactions) tolerable. Some small practices have reported success with electronic payment services.
- Educate your office staff not to discuss delinquent accounts outside the office or with other clients.
- If you must pursue collection, consider a collections attorney or reputable collection agency with experience in collecting mental health or medical payments. Consider using a collection agency only if you have specified this practice in your written informed consent; it is also advisable to have clients sign the document to demonstrate acceptance of your practices. Before you take action, notify the client in writing that the account will be turned over for collection.

- Obtain legal advice if you plan to charge interest or impose finance charges. There are complex federal and state truth in lending laws and regulations that could affect your plans.
- Avoid calling clients before 9:00 a.m. or after 9:00 p.m. because this may be viewed as harassment.
- Do not allow your staff to misrepresent themselves as collection agents or attorneys; also, do not allow them to contact a client's employer or a third party to collect an overdue bill.

Third-Party Payments

The health insurance field has changed rapidly in this country over the past two decades with the spread of managed care. As medical costs rise and as the state and federal governments try to grapple with deficits, we can expect to see further changes in the next several years. To provide the greatest assistance to clients, counselors must become as knowledgeable of health care issues as possible and must actively work to educate carriers and health care administrators about their competence and the scope of professional services they provide. Counselors also should learn about continually evolving issues that have resulted from federal health care reform and the Patient Protection and Affordable Care Act (2012; also see healthcare.gov). Counselors should also be aware of state statutes that apply to insurance reimbursement, including mental health parity and state-mandated benefits and antidiscrimination laws (see Appendix C for further suggestions).

Some insurance carriers limit their coverage to medical providers and are reluctant to provide reimbursement for the services of a counselor. In such cases, you may wish to educate the carrier that reimbursement for counseling sessions is appropriate because of the academic and clinical preparation and licensing of counselors and is in the best interest of the client. The ACA has very useful templates on its website that can aid members who are seeking to be included on managed care panels (see ACA, n.d.).

As you prepare to submit claims for reimbursement on behalf of clients, there are several items to consider to make the claims process operate smoothly and to prevent potential legal problems:

- Establish procedures in your office for completing and filing claim forms promptly. Do not let claims pile up. Get complete insurance information from each client, including policy numbers, employer authorization numbers, and claim procedures. Be sure that all claims filed are complete and accurate and that they include the signature of the provider. If you are a HIPAA-covered entity, you must comply with the HIPAA rules, including those pertinent to transactions and code sets (see Chapter 5).

- Obtain the proper insurance claim forms, such as the CMS-1500. These forms should be available from the applicable health insurance carrier. The majority of carriers are now accepting, or even requiring, electronic submission of health care claims.
- Know and use the appropriate *DSM-5* (American Psychiatric Association, 2013) diagnostic codes. Coding materials are updated periodically.
- Be sure to state accurately and completely all services you provide. The frequency and duration of sessions, as well as correct diagnosis codes, should be stated factually, not embellished for purposes of securing reimbursement.
- Keep accurate records of counseling sessions and of reimbursement requests submitted. Be sure that your records support the claims you file in the event of a claims review or audit.
- Do not bill carriers for missed appointments; you may bill the client as long as this was covered as part of your informed consent. Avoid routinely charging lower fees to clients who do not have insurance coverage, because a misstatement of your true billing rate could result in a charge of fraud. (This does not mean you can never make a billing allowance for someone who truly cannot pay for services.)
- Be sure that clients know they are responsible for any charges that are not reimbursed by their insurance carriers, and bill clients regularly for any such charges. Be sure that clients assign reimbursement to you if you are filing forms on their behalf.
- When payments are received, verify them against the claims submitted to be sure payment is in the correct amount. Refund any overpayments promptly, and request reconsideration of any underpayment.
- Review rejected claims promptly and prepare and submit written appeals for any processing errors. Request clarification for any rejected claim if the reason for rejection is not clear. Appeal that claim if you believe an error was made.
- Find out about claims and appeals procedures for any managed care, preferred provider organization, or health maintenance organization with which you may consider contracting. You could be held liable for failure to appeal an adverse utilization review decision that results in serious harm to your client.

- Carefully consider managed care contracts before signing. For example, if you sign contracts that contain indemnification or hold harmless clauses, you may be "stepping into the shoes" of the managed care company and assuming its liability. Some professional liability insurance policies do not cover liability assumed by contract. Even if coverage is available, your limits of coverage may be lessened because your coverage must be stretched to cover the other entity. You may wish to have a health care attorney review your contracts before you sign.

The Americans With Disabilities Act

Counselors should be familiar with the ADA for two major reasons. First, they may consider hiring persons with disabilities. Second, they may need to provide certain accommodations to their clients who have disabilities, or they may need to alter building structures to make them accessible.

Coverage

The ADA was enacted to protect "qualified individuals with a disability" from discrimination on the basis of disability. A person is considered disabled if he or she (a) has a physical or mental impairment that substantially limits one or more major life activity, (b) has a record of such an impairment, or (c) is regarded as having such an impairment. A number of conditions are specifically excluded from the definition of disability, including psychoactive substance use disorders resulting from current illegal use of drugs. Individuals who are currently using illegal drugs do not qualify for inclusion in programs offered by state and local government agencies either, with the exception of health and drug rehabilitation services.

The Americans With Disabilities Act Amendments Act was passed in 2008 as Congress's response to several U.S. Supreme Court decisions that had limited protection for many persons with certain medical conditions. Although the definition of *disability* has not changed, the interpretation now must be made to favor broad coverage of physical and mental impairments, including major depressive disorder, bipolar disorder, PTSD, obsessive-compulsive disorder, and schizophrenia. The EEOC published final rules implementing the ADA Amendments Act on March 25, 2011, which became effective on May 24, 2011. Among the many new "rules of construction" is the following, which may be of special interest to mental health professionals: An impairment that is episodic or in remission meets the definition of *disability* if it would substantially limit a major life activity when active. This includes episodic impairments such as bipolar disorder and schizophrenia.

The ADA, as amended, has five titles that provide protection to disabled persons in different areas. Title I covers private employers of 15 or more employees, and Title II covers government employers. Title II encompasses public services by state and local governments, including public schools and public transportation. Title III applies to public accommodations and services provided by private entities, including private counseling practices. Title IV covers telecommunications (such as devices for hearing-impaired persons), and Title V applies to miscellaneous issues. The titles dealing with employment and public accommodations have special implications for counselors and other mental health professionals.

Employment

Counseling practices with 15 or more employees or government-run practices should seek legal advice concerning provision of reasonable accommodations for known physical or mental limitations of qualified employees or job applicants. This does not necessarily mean that all accommodations must be made if they would create an undue hardship on the employer. Reasonable accommodations include providing readers or interpreters, making the workplace accessible, and modifying work schedules. In addition, Title I prohibits the use of certain employment tests that tend to screen out the disabled, unless such tests are reasonably related to job performance. Whereas use of preemployment medical examinations are banned if they're used to determine whether an applicant has a disability, use of medical examinations after an offer has been extended is permitted if all persons in similar jobs are required to be examined, the results are not used as a basis for discrimination, and the results are kept confidential.

Public Accommodations

Title III prohibits discrimination on the basis of disability in places of public accommodation, and one of the categories of public accommodations is public services. These services include the offices of physicians, lawyers, and accountants as well as businesses such as pharmacies, laundries, banks, and gas stations. For our purposes, it is important to know that public services include privately owned and operated mental health counseling services, agencies, and practices.

Government entities must also comply with the law. Public agencies operated by state and local governments are covered by Title II of the ADA and have separate affirmative obligations. Federal government agencies and recipients of federal funds are covered by the similar provisions of sections 501 and 504 of the Rehabilitation Act of 1973.

The U.S. Department of Justice is charged with enforcing the public accommodations sections of the Act. (EEOC handles employment matters.) In practice, the Justice Department places the following requirements:

- Individuals with disabilities must be served by, or admitted to, places of public accommodation.
- If the policies or practices of an establishment have the effect of excluding individuals with disabilities, reasonable modifications to those policies or practices must be made unless they would fundamentally alter the nature of the business.
- Auxiliary aids and services must be provided to enable a person with a disability to use the goods or services of an establishment, as long as the provision of the auxiliary aids does not pose an undue burden or is not disruptive to business.
- Barriers to accessibility (e.g., steps with no elevator or ramp to accommodate wheelchair-bound clients) in existing buildings must be removed if the removal is readily achievable. If a building is inaccessible to disabled people and removal of the barriers is not readily achievable, alternative methods must be used to serve disabled people if such methods would not impose an undue burden. New buildings have special requirements (ADA, 1990, as amended; U.S. Department of Justice, 2010).

Because these rules apply to counselors in private practice, these counselors must take affirmative steps to comply with the regulations to the extent such steps are not "unduly burdensome," "would not fundamentally alter the nature of the services provided," or, in the case of barrier removal, are "readily achievable" (easily accomplished without much difficulty or expense).

Some of these requirements are relatively easy to meet. For example, written materials produced on word-processing programs can easily be reformatted to large text size to assist a client with vision problems. Some word-processing programs can even produce materials in Braille form through local service providers. Clearing furniture or potted plants that obstruct hallways, waiting rooms, and offices is a simple form of barrier removal. Installing ramps, grab bars, and raised toilets; widening doorways; and creating designated parking spaces are additional approaches recommended to address mobility impairments.

Many of the recommended measures are common sense approaches to overcoming physical and mental limitations, but they are critically important to providing access to services for people with disabilities. It is important to ask the person with a disability what auxiliary aids and services he or she needs to benefit from your program. Not all blind people can read Braille. Not all people with hearing impairments can read lips. In fact, depending on the severity of the situation and the importance of the information to be communicated, a qualified sign language interpreter may be required in certain circumstances. In others, video remote interpreting or other computer-assisted programs may be indicated (U.S. Department of Justice, Civil Rights Division, 2011). The counseling practice is probably required to pay for the interpreter or transcription services because it is unlawful to charge people with disabilities for auxiliary aids and services or reasonable accommodations. As already mentioned, counselors who would be unduly burdened by meeting these requirements are exempt. If you do need to provide an interpreter or other accommodations, it may be helpful to know that the IRS Code allows certain tax credits for small businesses (U.S. Department of Justice, Civil Rights Division, 2005).

Individuals with disabilities can sue public accommodations for failing to comply with the provisions of the ADA, and the Justice Department is empowered to investigate complaints and litigate to compel compliance. At that stage, the courts may assess the full range of remedies, including damages, injunctive relief, civil penalties, and attorneys' fees. If you are not already familiar with your obligations under the ADA and the ADA Amendments Act, it is important to familiarize yourself with them so that you can formulate a plan for compliance and begin to implement it. Further information is available online at www.ada.gov or through the toll-free information line at 800–514–0301 (voice) or 800–514–0383 (TDD). In light of recent changes through the ADA Amendments Act and its implementing regulations, counselors in small private practice may wish to review *ADA Update: A Primer for Small Business* (U.S. Department of Justice, Civil Rights Division, 2011).

State and Local Government Entities

Title II of the ADA prohibits all state and local government entities from discriminating against any qualified individual with a disability in any program or activity they administer or operate. As in Title III, entities are required to provide reasonable accommodations, remove barriers, and provide auxiliary aids and services as required to permit full participation by individuals with disabilities, unless the agency can prove certain exceptions. (See U.S. Department of Justice, Civil Rights Division, 2012, for updated rules and additional resources.)

Administrative requirements for compliance with Title II include conducting a self-evaluation of programs and practices. To obtain specific information for counselors responsible for ADA compliance in state and local government entities, see "Guidance on ADA Regulation on Nondiscrimination on the Basis of Disability" (2013).

Genetic Information Nondiscrimination Act of 2008

The Genetic Information Nondiscrimination Act of 2008 (GINA) was enacted to prohibit the improper use of genetic information in health insurance coverage decisions and in employment decisions, such as hiring, firing, and promotion. This law applies to employers of more than 15 employees. Most counselors who employ workers would probably be hard-pressed to believe they'd be likely to engage in any illegal discrimination against their employees. However, seemingly innocent behavior could be seen as problematic under GINA.

For example, a well-intended counselor who heads a practice with 16 employees (administrative and professional) might ask a female staff member how she is doing. The employee then proceeds to launch into a discussion of how she just last week went for genetic screening because her sister was diagnosed with the BRCA-1 gene for breast cancer. Although the question may be benign, failure to stop the discussion could possibly be viewed as problematic under GINA because the employer could use the information to fire the employee in order to reduce health insurance premiums. Genetic information includes genetic tests of the individual as well as the individual's family members. All counselors, but particularly genetic counselors, should take note that genetic services include genetic counseling. Further information is available at U.S. EEOC (n.d.-b).

If you are a "covered entity" under HIPAA (see Chapter 5), you should be aware that genetic information is now considered PHI. Most counselors are probably already treating family medical history as confidential, but it's helpful to remember that any genetic information in your records should be handled in a similar manner to mental health information. In addition, under the HIPAA Omnibus Rule (see Chapter 5), which adopts GINA's definition of "genetic information," it is now clear that most health plans are prohibited from using or disclosing genetic information for underwriting purposes.

New Counseling Approaches, Techniques, and Professional Expressions

Counselors and other mental health practitioners are creative people, always searching for better ways to serve clients and always on the lookout for new and challenging venues for professional expression. Recent decades have seen a parade of new counseling approaches and techniques. Such new ideas can become very popular very quickly; a bandwagon phenomenon can occur. Weekend workshops, seminars, and conferences spring to life; there is great anticipation and hope that a new approach or technique will provide the long-sought answer. Practitioners attend a weekend training course or read about an approach or technique in a professional journal or popular press and are eager to try it. But ethical and legal risk may then be generated for the following reasons:

- *Premature acceptance:* Practitioners can fail to appropriately investigate the validity of the approach or technique; they may accept without question the claims made by the authors or proponents of the approach.
- *Insufficient training:* Practitioners can attempt to use a new approach or technique before they have received the requisite education, training, and supervision to safely and effectively use it.
- *Overuse:* Practitioners can come to view all clinical work through the perspective of the new approach or technique, which may encourage its overuse as well as its application in situations in which it is not appropriate.

Examples of new approaches and techniques that have burst into our professional awareness over the last several decades include hypnotherapy, new 12-step applications, codependency, EMDR, telephone and Internet counseling, forensic evaluation, and coaching. In recent years, the buzz seems to have been centered on how neuroscience can help us understand the brain. There is great excitement and hope that neuroscience can scientifically validate many of our theories and approaches and help us develop new and more powerful therapies.

Many new approaches and techniques burn brightly for a short period of time and then fade; others are embraced by mainstream practitioners and absorbed into the body of generally accepted approaches and techniques. For the purposes of this book, we simply want to remind you that when using any approach, whether a tried-and-true mainstream approach or a new fringe technique, you must still meet the standard of care (see Chapter 4). Probably nothing drives home this point more than the tragic case in Colorado in which two therapists were using a rebirthing technique designed to address attachment disorder in an adopted child. In this case a counselor was charged with and found guilty of reckless child abuse.

During a rebirthing therapy session that lasted for more than an hour, the child client stated that she could not breathe and was going to throw up. She repeatedly asked for help. The counselor ignored the child's requests, thinking she was being manipulative.

The child stopped moving, but the counselor and her associates believed that she was asleep. Finding the child unresponsive, the counselors had her transported to a local hospital, where she was declared dead because of suffocation. The counselor was convicted of reckless child abuse resulting in death and was sentenced to a mandatory minimum term of 16 years (*People v. Watkins*, 2003).

Obviously, something went very wrong. Did the therapists prematurely accept the validity of this approach? Did they lack sufficient training? Or did they use an inappropriate approach? The tragic result of this case reminds us of our primary ethical responsibility to do no harm, and it brings home the chilling reality that severe legal consequences await us if we abuse our clients.

Another counseling-related activity that has become popular in recent years is the practice of executive or personal coaching. Many licensed mental health practitioners have come to view coaching as both an interesting professional expression and a potentially lucrative opportunity. The field of coaching is unlicensed and unregulated, and there is no recognized and enforced certification process. Although there are recognized coach training programs, many are not affiliated with accredited institutions of higher learning. As a result, anyone can establish a coaching practice. The danger to licensed counselors and other mental health professionals is that because the coaching field lacks certification and regulation, mental health professionals may assume that normal legal and ethical standards are not relevant. Although we are not aware of a court case that has tested this assumption, we believe that the blurring of the boundary between counseling and coaching makes it only a matter of time before a disgruntled or harmed coaching client brings a licensure complaint or malpractice lawsuit against a coach who is also a licensed mental health professional. If you are currently providing or considering establishing a coaching practice, we encourage you to adopt the following practices:

- Remain mindful and observant of the ethics code and licensing requirements associated with your mental health credential.
- Develop an informed consent document that clearly differentiates coaching services from clinical mental health services you may provide or be licensed to provide.
- Participate in the evolving professional organizations within the coaching field, understand common practices, and be sure these practices are not in conflict with the ethical or legal requirements of your mental health license.
- Avoid mixing mental health services with coaching. (We understand there are some aspects of a counseling relationship that can legitimately involve coaching.)
- Never ignore the mental health needs of coaching clients—you can't pretend you don't recognize such issues—and make appropriate referrals.
- Recognize that if you are a licensed counselor, you may still be held to the standards of the counseling profession even when calling yourself a coach.
- Check with your liability insurance carrier to determine whether coaching services will be covered.

Closing a Counseling Practice

Counselors often wait until it's too late to deal with issues pertaining to closing a practice. However, these issues are especially important to consider if the counselor is a solo private practitioner. Unfortunately, if the counselor meets an untimely or sudden death, the surviving spouse, significant other, or close family member or friend is often left with the task of winding up a practice without much guidance and during a time of personal grieving. These issues should be addressed from the very moment a counseling practice is formed, irrespective of the counselor's age.

All counselors in private practice should carefully consider who their personal representative will be; they should also consider appointing a "records custodian," who is ideally a colleague in a private counseling or related mental health practice. A records custodian is defined in the 2014 *ACA Code of Ethics* as "a professional colleague who agrees to serve as the caretaker of client records for another mental health professional" (Glossary of Terms). The 2014 *ACA Code of Ethics* specifically requires that counselors store and dispose of records appropriately and take reasonable precautions to protect client confidentiality in the event of a counselor's termination of practice (Standard B.6.i.). The *Code* also mandates appointment of a records custodian when identified as appropriate (Standard B.6.i.). The counselor should prepare a summary of critical information to be reviewed with his personal representative and records custodian. This critical information should include notice to clients, transfer of care procedures, records maintenance (and transfer of a copy of the records to the new therapist), and office procedures. If PHI will be accessed by the records custodian, the counselor should have the custodian sign a HIPAA "Business Associate" agreement (see Chapter 5).

To ensure that the practice is closed in a proper manner, attention to the following checklist may prove helpful to the counselor and the designated representative. It should include the location of the various items as well as any procedures set up by the counselor:

1. Accounts receivable/payable
2. Bank accounts and safe deposit box
3. Calendar and appointment book (paper or electronic—passwords if appropriate)
4. Confidentiality, privilege, and privacy policies (including HIPAA and HITECH, if applicable; see also no. 18, Records)
5. Computers (backup, etc.)
6. Consultants and contact information (attorney, accountant, etc.)
7. Contracts and notice to managed care organizations, insurers, and other entities
8. Correspondence (stationery, standard number of copies, filing instructions, naming rules for computer)
9. E-mail procedures, website, and future communication (including rules for deletion, confidentiality, etc.)

10. Employee issues, benefits and addresses, telephone numbers, payroll (if applicable)
11. Equipment and vendor information (computers, phones, Internet service provider, copy and fax machines; repair, service, and systems contracts; employee use; furniture)
12 Ethics (applicable codes)
13. Fax instructions and cover sheets
14. Insurance policies, lease agreements, and other contracts (including professional liability insurance and need to procure tail coverage if policy is written on a claims-made basis, disability insurance, life, insurance, etc.)
15. Mail (postal service); post office box
16. Notice to covering colleagues, licensure board or boards, professional associations (and contact information)
17. Office supplies
18 Records (client records, procedures on opening and closing of new files, closing files, storage of records)
19. Tax and other regulatory files

Furthermore, the counselor may wish to contact the applicable state licensure board (or boards) to ascertain any other requirements in closing a practice. Local requirements may vary. For example, in addition to mandating notice to current clients when closing a practice or retiring, some states may require notice to be given to clients seen professionally within the last several years. Some states may also require that a notice be placed in the local newspaper. Remember that complaints can be brought against the estate of a deceased counselor, so you're helping both your clients and your loved ones when smooth transitions are made in the event of your disability or death.

There are a multitude of other issues that should be addressed well in advance of practice closure, including providing notice to clients (with appropriate referrals, so clients are not "abandoned"), changing voicemail messages, closing bank accounts, collecting accounts receivable, and terminating vendor services in accordance with applicable contracts. You may need to give your records custodian access to relevant computer passwords and accounts and/ or an actual key to a locked file cabinet. You should also consider listing the name and contact information of your records custodian (and/or emergency response team) in your written informed consent document. Detailed information on this topic, written specifically for counselors and other health care professionals in private practice, is available at www.privatepracticepreparedness.com. The resources include a cost-effective e-book, hands-on practice reference and step-by-step guide to closing a practice, and downloadable templates, which may be shared with one's personal attorney.

Summary

Counselors are not expected to be attorneys, accountants, and insurance coding experts. Nonetheless, counselors are expected to know key features of the business and regulatory aspects of their practices. When in doubt about what is expected from you as a small business owner or responsible person in an agency, gather information. One useful source is a section of the ACA's website entitled *Private Practice Pointers*, which may be accessed at https://files.counseling. org/Counselors/TP/PrivatePracticePointersMembers/CT2.aspx. In addition, consult appropriate professionals as needed.

Chapter 12

Counselor Educators and Clinical Supervisors

Counselor educators and clinical supervisors of counselors are exposed to an array of legal and ethical challenges. These challenges are best managed when students understand and appreciate the complex legal and ethical issues counselor educators must juggle and when supervisees (both predegree students and prelicensed) are mindful of the legal liabilities involved in clinical supervision. In this chapter we sketch the legal and ethical landscape as it relates to these important professional relationships (student and professor; supervisee and clinical supervisor).

Counselor Educators

Counselor educators and graduate faculty from other counseling-related master's and doctoral programs (e.g., psychology, social work, rehabilitation counseling, marriage and family therapy) must engage in a balancing act. On the one hand, counselor education faculty must intellectually involve students by creating challenging graduate-level classroom experiences and directing competent research activities. At the same time, an essential element of counselor preparation involves inviting students to self-disclose and explore areas of personal vulnerability. These competing roles and responsibilities can sometimes create misunderstandings that can lead to ethical or legal problems.

Boundaries

The environment of a counselor program requires students to reveal themselves in ways that would likely never be considered in other graduate training programs. Can you imagine graduate students in engineering, math, or business administration engaging in the self-disclosing growth activities that are typical for counseling students? Because professional identity development and personal growth are so closely linked, counselor educators in their mentorship role can easily skirt the edges of a counseling relationship with students.

Embedded in this self-development culture are the typical student–professor opportunities for multiple role confusion. Students and faculty often have mutual membership in professional associations, attend local and national conferences, share common interests or mutual friends, and spend a great deal of time together. For all these reasons, boundaries between students and faculty can become fuzzy. Counselor educators have a responsibility to continually clarify these boundaries while at the same time modeling an openness and immediacy to their own experience that is so essential to a competent counselor.

Throughout Section F of the *ACA Code of Ethics* (ACA, 2014a), particularly Sections F.7.–F.11., counselor educators are provided a plethora of guidance with regard to management of the multiple role conflicts inherent within the teaching responsibilities of a counselor educator. Nowhere is this more problematic than when counselor educators attempt to balance the competing responsibilities of respecting the developmental nature of student growth while simultaneously evaluating student competencies.

As was discussed in Chapter 9, counselors court trouble when the boundaries with their clients become blurred, crossed, or violated. This is also the case with the professor–student boundary; however, the difference is that almost every professor–student relationship has some multiple role aspects. The admonishment to "avoid dual roles whenever possible" is simply not workable in these relationships. Therefore, counselor educators—and especially newer faculty—should be supported and mentored to learn how to navigate in a world of multiple roles and conflicting responsibilities. Counselor education departments would do well to create an environment in which faculty are encouraged to seek consultation when the multiple roles with a student have or might become a problem. Honestly evaluating students is difficult enough given the influence that comes from knowledge of the student's personal history (family-of-origin experiences, traumas, and confounding psychodynamics). Credible evaluation, however, is impossible when there is a romantic or sexual relationship between a professor and student. Inappropriate romantic or sexual relationships run the gamut from true love to manipulative or coercive sexual relationships in which the professor abuses the power differential. To be fair, it is also true that counselor educators can be the target of flirting or sexual manipulation by a student. Therefore, counselor educators must be ready to respond appropriately to a student who communicates his or her interest in crossing the romantic or sexual boundary. Finally, we strongly advise counselor educators to consult with their department chairpersons in the event the faculty member is feeling inappropriately drawn to a student or if a student makes a romantic or sexual offer. Effectively responding to these complex situations can increase the likelihood that the appropriate boundary will be maintained, the working relationship between the professor and student will be preserved, and the student can have a positive growth opportunity. Employment termination, ethics complaints, and even lawsuits can follow when faculty cross boundaries in which students are exploited, harassed, or injured.

Gatekeeping

Gatekeeping is a term applied to the process of monitoring student progression from initial acceptance into the counseling program, through all coursework, clinical practicum or internship, and scholarly and research activities. Ziomek-Daigle and Bailey (2010) defined *gatekeeping* as "the process whereby counselor educators intervene when students are not prepared with knowledge, skills, and values necessary for the practice of counseling" (p. 14). Ultimately, counselor educators have a responsibility to the student and the profession to ensure that students enter professional practice prepared to provide competent services. "In the mental health professions, both educators and supervisors direct the advancement of trainees while assessing appropriateness to continue at various stages of preparation. A gatekeeper allows passage through an identified checkpoint once a specific set of competencies has been successfully demonstrated" (Homrich, 2009, p. 14).

The Standards of the Council for Accreditation of Counseling and Related Educational Programs (2009) direct programs to create a student handbook that includes "a student retention policy explaining procedures for student remediation and/or dismissal from the program" (L.2.d) and a requirement that

> program faculty conducts a systematic developmental assessment of each student's progress throughout the program, including consideration of the student's academic performance, professional development, and personal development. Consistent with established institutional due process policy and the American Counseling Association's (ACA) *Code of Ethics* and other relevant codes of ethics and standards of practice, if evaluations indicate that a student is not appropriate for the program, faculty members help facilitate the student's transition out of the program and, if possible, into a more appropriate area of study. (p. 5)

In addition, the *ACA Code of Ethics* (ACA, 2014a) clearly defines the responsibility of counselor educators to evaluate and remediate students, when possible.

> F.9.b. Limitations
> Counselor educators, through ongoing evaluation, are aware of and address the inability of some students to achieve counseling competencies. Counselor educators do the following:
> 1. assist students in securing remedial assistance when needed,
> 2. seek professional consultation and document their decision to dismiss or refer students for assistance, and
> 3. ensure that students have recourse in a timely manner to address decisions requiring them to seek assistance or to dismiss them and provide students with due process according to institutional policies and procedures.

While the requirement for counselor educators to fulfill the gatekeeping function is clear, discharging that responsibility can be fraught with complexities and legal risk. To our knowledge, there is no central data repository that collects and analyzes gatekeeping actions initiated by counselor educators. As a result, there are no hard data; we are left to speculate. What we do know is that when the gatekeeping process is done correctly, there is adherence to due process as established within the institution. The process is further informed by a deep belief in the ability of individuals to grow and change. As a result, it is probably safe to conclude that many, perhaps even most, gatekeeping actions result in a successful remediation plan in which the student competently corrects the noted deficiencies.

There are, of course, times when remediation is not possible. In these circumstances interaction between the student and the counselor educators can become strained to the breaking point. Dismissal of the student from the program will likely follow. On a few occasions students have filed suit against the college/university and the specific counselor educators involved in the dismissal. Two highly contentious lawsuits (*Ward v. Wilbanks*, 2010, and *Keeton v. Anderson-Wiley*, 2010) provide a window into understanding the extent to which counselor education programs must go to fulfill the gatekeeping responsibility. These cases also have helped counseling programs develop policies and procedures that more clearly define curriculum expectations as related to professional ethics.

Ward v. Wilbanks (2010; *Ward v. Polite*, 2012, on appeal), discussed in some length in Chapter 2, is an excellent example of the extent of legal difficulty counselor educators can become ensnarled in when they fulfill their ethical gatekeeping responsibility. The *Ward* case involved the issue of termination and referral in which a counseling student refused to work with a client whom she perceived as seeking advice concerning homosexual relationships. The student, Julea Ward, refused to counsel a client because of her objection to the client's stated desire to work on his same-sex relationship. In discussion with faculty, Ward took the position that she would never work with any client who represented values she believed offended her religious beliefs. Faculty at Eastern Michigan University attempted to help her understand that she was not being asked or required to change her values; rather, she was being asked to set aside or "bracket" her values so she could "respect the dignity and promote the welfare of [her] clients" (language is the same in both the 2005 and 2014 *ACA Code of Ethics* Standard A.1.a.). Ward filed a lawsuit.

In a Summary Judgment order, the court found in favor of the university and gave primary emphasis to the right and responsibility of the CACREP-accredited training program at Eastern Michigan University to adopt academic standards that include a recognized professional organization's code of ethics requiring students and practicing professionals to engage in professional behavior as defined by the standards (*Ward v. Wilbanks*, 2010). The plaintiff in the *Ward* case then appealed the decision to the Sixth Circuit Court of Appeals. That court decided that there were issues of fact still in dispute, so it sent the case back to the federal district court for a trial. As described in Chapter 2, the appellate court stated that the university was unable to identify any written policy that would prevent Ward from seeking a referral for the client. Nonetheless, the court also indicated that Ward should not prevail as a matter of law regarding her claims of free speech and free exercise of religion. Eastern Michigan University and the plaintiff agreed to settle the case out of court.

Another recent case relates to a student's refusal to comply with a remediation plan imposed on her by Augusta State University as a condition of remaining in the counseling graduate program (*Keeton v. Anderson-Wiley,* 2010/2011/2012). The student, Jennifer Keeton, enrolled in a master's counseling program at Augusta State in Georgia in the fall of 2009, aspiring to be a school counselor. Ms. Keeton, self-identified as a Christian, voiced her religious-based personal views on sexual morality through written school papers, class discussions, and outside the classroom while encouraging her fellow students to adopt her views. According to the federal district court in a written order denying plaintiff's motion for a preliminary injunction, the counseling faculty became concerned that Ms. Keeton would be unable to separate her personal, religious-based views from her counseling duties, and that such action would violate the *ACA Code of Ethics.* Furthermore, alleged reports from her fellow students indicated that Ms. Keeton was interested in conversion therapy, which has been widely denigrated as a counseling approach in dealing with lesbian, gay, bisexual, and transgendered clients.

The student was placed on remediation status and was told that the plan was necessary to further her multicultural awareness and skills. Faculty informed Ms. Keeton that she must complete the remediation program or face expulsion. The student initially agreed with the plan but then decided not to participate and filed a lawsuit, claiming a violation of her First and Fourteenth Amendment rights, among others. She requested a preliminary injunction to prevent her expulsion and relieve her from the remediation plan.

The U.S. District Court, Southern District, denied the motion in a written order on August 20, 2010. The court stated that plaintiff Keeton did not meet the high burden of persuasion legally required to prevail on a motion for a preliminary injunction, and so it was denied. Ms. Keeton appealed the decision. On December 16, 2011, the 11th Circuit Court of Appeals affirmed the decision of the lower court ruling that "the district court did not abuse its discretion in denying her motion for a preliminary injunction" (*Keeton v. Anderson-Wiley,* 2011). In further litigation in the district court (trial court), the judge dismissed a series of constitutional claims (*Keeton v. Anderson-Wiley,* 2012).

These recent court decisions give weight to the legal authority of counselor education programs to set and enforce academic requirements that include adherence to the *ACA Code of Ethics.* For counselor education departments, the Ward and Keeton cases have provided a compelling invitation to conduct a sweeping review of all gatekeeping policies and procedures to ensure that students are fully informed of the ethical expectations that are infused into the curriculum on the basis of the *ACA Code of Ethics*. To be specific, professional counselors cannot refuse to provide services to clients who have identities, lifestyles, or values different from their own. The take-away for counselor educators is that this nondiscrimination message must be consistently delivered from the application process through completion of clinical placement and graduation. Finally, in the event of a problem, students have a right to due process procedures that are comprehensible and transparent.

As was stated earlier, we believe that the vast majority of gatekeeping actions are successfully resolved such that the student remains in the program and progresses on to graduation. Sometimes, however, dismissal of the student from the program is necessary. To prepare for that difficult inevitability, we recommend the following Do's and Don'ts (if dismissing a student must be done):

- DO consult with university legal counsel when drafting policies and procedures and before dismissing a particular student.
- DO consider drafting a "student agreement" to follow all counseling program rules and regulations (agreement should be signed and dated).
- DO use due process procedures of notice and opportunity to respond, which should be drafted by legal counsel in collaboration with the counseling department.
- DO follow applicable CACREP Standards in developing policies and procedures.
- DO ask for feedback from faculty on any student they perceive as exhibiting problematic behaviors.
- DO maintain appropriate professional liability insurance that covers counselor educator decisions regarding student retention and dismissal.
- DON'T assume that your decision will be backed by the university; consult with administrators and legal counsel before it's too late. (Homrich, Wheeler, & Bertram, 2007, Slide 22)

Clinical Supervisors

Clinical supervisors—including private practitioners; employees of agencies, schools, and institutions; and counselor educators—incur an added level of responsibility when they agree to provide clinical supervision. The 2014 *ACA Code of Ethics* begins with a statement that sets the tone that is heard throughout the *Code*. Section A.1.a. ("Primary Responsibility") states, "The primary responsibility of counselors is to respect the dignity and promote the welfare of clients." Standard F.1.a. also states, in part, "A primary obligation of counseling supervisors is to monitor the services provided by supervisees. Counseling supervisors monitor client welfare and supervisee performance and professional development." The ethical and legal obligations of counseling supervisors are clear and unambiguous.

Supervisory Liability

Respondeat superior is a legal doctrine stating that in many circumstances the employer or supervisor is the "master" who is directly responsible for the actions of the supervisee. Clinical supervisors who provide clinical supervision to predegree or prelicensed counselors are placing themselves at some risk every time they agree to provide supervision. Supervisors may be named as defendants in malpractice suits on the basis that the supervisor is "vicariously" liable for the acts of the supervisee. Alternatively, the supervisor may be found liable independently on the basis of negligent supervision. For example, if a counselor in training expressed concern about a suicidal client with an imminent plan and the supervisor said, "Let's talk about that next week," it wouldn't stretch one's imagination to realize that this would be considered negligent supervision.

We want to make a very important distinction between supervision and colleague consultation. Colleague consultation is a process that regularly occurs between counseling professionals, particularly when counselors are employed at the same facility or working with the same client population. Assuming that appropriate confidentiality guidelines are observed, colleague consultation can be quite useful. When counselors consult with colleagues, the colleague consultants offer their thoughts about the case as it has been presented; the counselor seeking the consultation is under no obligation to accept any ideas or suggestions. Supervision is very different. As described above, the supervisor is legally responsible for the professional actions of the supervisee, including what the counselor does and what he fails to do. Confusion can occur when clinical supervisors establish an overly "collegial" atmosphere between supervisor and supervisee. Such an atmosphere encourages the open exchange of ideas, but the collegial nature of the interaction should not be misunderstood. There will be certain situations in which the supervisor must give very specific nonnegotiable directions that must be followed by the supervisee.

Boundaries

Supervisors are strongly admonished by the 2014 *ACA Code of Ethics* (Standard F.3.a.) to refrain from any type of nonprofessional interaction with supervisees that may compromise the supervisory relationship. For example, it may be appropriate for a supervisor and supervisee to meet while eating lunch (in a quiet room, not a restaurant where confidentiality could be compromised) to discuss current cases. On the other hand, inviting the supervisee out for drinks or a purely social dinner party could be inviting a relationship that could blur boundaries for both supervisor and supervisee.

Furthermore, sexual or romantic relationships with current supervisees are prohibited (Standard F.3.b.). The ultimate victim in this type of boundary violation is typically the client. A supervisor who becomes too comfortable with a supervisee may neglect to ask the tough questions in a supervisory session (e.g., "Is this supervisee really understanding the client's suicidal ideation?"). Likewise, the supervisee may neglect to bring things to the supervision sessions (e.g., "Oh, Dr. Jones has confidence in me now; I don't need to discuss how the client has been flattering me—anyway, no harm is being done.").

Regarding sexual harassment, the *Code* is clear: "Counseling supervisors do not condone or subject supervisees to sexual harassment" (Standard F.3.c.). It also prohibits supervisors from engaging in supervisory relationships with family or friends or, as the *Code* states, "individuals with whom they have an inability to remain objective" (Standard F.3.d.). Clearly, one can understand how difficult it would be to be objective with someone who was personally close to the supervisor. Would you really want to supervise your daughter's fiancé? When there are financial considerations (e.g., supervisee is paying for supervision or the supervisee is renting space from the supervisor), carefully evaluate potential areas of conflict of interest; be sure to consult your state counselor licensing law and rules to ensure compliance. Ultimately, the guiding principle should be to guard against circumstances that could result in a conflict of interest such that honest and direct communication between the supervisee and supervisor is impaired. When in doubt, consult!

Crafting a Supervisory Relationship Contract

The foundation of a successful clinical supervision relationship is built on the creation of a safe and respectful relationship in which the supervisor models transparency and in so doing encourages the supervisee to be open and honest in the presentation of his clinical questions and countertransference concerns. The development of a written supervisory contract is a good way to ensure that essential details are addressed so that both the supervisor and supervisee have clarity and agree on the responsibilities both bring to the relationship. This checklist offers suggestions for creating this type of supervisory contract.

1. Introductions
    a. Supervisor provides
        • professional experience and interests;
        • theoretical orientation;
        • supervision style; and
        • relevant personal, familial, and cultural background.
    b. Supervisee provides
        • professional interests;
        • prior experience in counseling and/or human services;
        • theoretical orientation; and
        • relevant personal, familial, and cultural background.
2. Goals
    a. Supervisor clarifies goals or learning that he or she believes is developmentally appropriate for the supervisee.
    b. Supervisee defines the goals of his or her practicum, internship, or postdegree supervision requirements.
3. Supervision style
    a. Learning style
        • How does the supervisee learn?
        • How can the supervisor support the learning of the supervisee?
    b. Temperament
        • What is the temperament of the supervisee?
        • What are the implications for communication and learning?
4. Process of supervision
    a. Expectations
        • Supervisor should describe the process of supervision in terms of how time will be structured and what will be expected of the supervisee (e.g., come to supervision with questions; bring clinical files).
        • Supervisor should keep in mind information about the supervisee's learning style and feedback preferences.

    b. Role clarification
- Supervisor should define the activities of supervision (teacher, consultant, expert) and differentiate supervision from personal counseling.
- Supervisor should describe the delicate balance of clinical collaboration (between supervisor and supervisee) versus the responsibility of the supervisor to act as evaluator, gatekeeper, and definer of clinical direction.

5. Regular supervision time and place
    a. Define the day, time, and place of weekly supervision.
    b. Include a process for rescheduling should that be necessary.
6. Emergency/urgent clinical situations
    a. Criteria for immediate supervision: Provide direction about the circumstances under which the supervisee should immediately inform the supervisor of clinical developments rather than waiting until the next scheduled supervision session. Examples could include:
       – harm to self or others;
       – mandatory reporting issues (abuse);
       – legal concerns; and
       – ethical conflicts.
    b. How to interrupt: Provide the process for interrupting the supervisor with an urgent concern as well as contact information (phone numbers) in the event the supervisor is not physically available.
    c. Alternative supervision: Provide name/contact information for an alternative supervisor in the event the primary supervisor is completely unavailable.
7. Supervisee strengths: Remain alert to perceiving, commenting on, and helping the supervisee to more fully use emerging clinical strengths and administrative/writing competence as well as existing life experience or character strengths.
8. Agency/Institution/Organization functioning (if appropriate)
    a. Provide an overview of the "big picture" of the clinical process of the sponsoring organization, including the following:
       – initial contact of new client;
       – intake and assessment;
       – development of treatment approach or plan;
       – treatment approach or process;
       – definition of successful treatment;

           – termination or closure process; and
           – follow-up.

   b. Provide agency protocols for the following situations:
           – client threat of harm to self;
           – threat of harm to others;
           – abuse reporting;
           – legal or ethical concerns;
           – record keeping and documentation; and
           – administrative and staff meetings.

9. Make explicit
   a. Commit to making explicit any issue or concern that has a bearing on supervisee learning and clinical effectiveness, and invite the supervisee to do the same.
   b. Describe the checking-in process, in which periodically the supervisor will check in with the supervisee to solicit feedback on the supervision process and the supervision relationship.

10. Working with clients
   a. Client selection: Describe the process by which the supervisee will have direct access to clients (observation, cotherapy, supervised caseload). Help the supervisee understand what is expected of him or her in order to be ready for a supervised caseload.
   b. Record keeping: Describe the record-keeping and documentation requirements; assure the supervisee that he or she will receive adequate coaching.
   c. Audio or video recording (if appropriate): Discuss the process for securing written authorization for recording client counseling sessions.

11. Preventing and/or responding to inevitable bumps in the road
   a. Most supervisees inevitably will encounter some bumps in the road during their training experience. Most of these obstacles (e.g., lack of knowledge, lack of skill, lack of confidence, countertransference, interpersonal tension with other staff members, exhaustion, and burn-out) are developmentally inevitable.
   b. One of the most important dimensions of good supervision is to assist the supervisee through these inevitable bumps in the road without becoming the supervisee's therapist. Walking this line is challenging but critical.

12. Faculty consultation (appropriate for predegree practicum or internship): Supervisors are invited and encouraged at any time to consult with the supervisee's faculty contact person (assuming the supervisee is a student). If there is a concern, don't wait until the situation has escalated to a crisis. Contact the faculty member so collaborative problem-solving discussions can be initiated. In the interest of transparency and trust (except in the rarest of circumstances), supervisors are encouraged to tell each supervisee of their intention to consult with faculty.

Summary

By the very nature of the work, counselor educators and clinical supervisors incur ethical and legal risks. Using the spirit of informed consent can moderate many of these risks. As students are socialized into a counseling program, it is essential that important information about expectations be communicated to them. Informing students in writing of the foundational values of the counseling profession and of the specific program can help students determine whether these expectations are a good fit with their personal values and worldview. The same thing can be said of the supervisor–supervisee relationship. Gaining understanding and agreement around a set of expectations and ground rules provides a foundation upon which the supervisory relationship can be built. When there is clarity of understanding and agreement, misunderstanding and negative surprises are reduced.

 References

Acosta v. Byrum, 638 S.E.2d 246 (N.C. App. 2006).

Age Discrimination in Employment Act of 1967, 29 U.S.C. §§ 621–634, as amended (implementing regulations found at 29 C.F.R. Part 1625) (2014).

American Academy of Physician Assistants. (2014). *End-of-life decision making.* Retrieved from http://www.aapa.org/workarea/downloadasset.aspx?id=812

American Association of Suicidology. (2014a). *Elderly suicide fact sheet.* Retrieved from http://www.suicidology.org/Portals/14/docs/Resources/FactSheets/Elderly2012.pdf

American Association of Suicidology. (2014b). *Suicidal behavior among lesbian, gay, bisexual, and transgender youth fact sheet.* Retrieved from http://www.suicidology.org/Portals/14/docs/Resources/FactSheets/LGBTSuicidalBehavior.pdf

American Association of Suicidology. (2014c). *USA suicide: 2010 official final data.* Retrieved from http://www.suicidology.org/Portals/14/docs/Resources/FactSheets/2010OverallData.pdf

American Counseling Association. (n.d.). *Private practice pointers* [preview page]. Retrieved from http://www.counseling.org/Counselors/PrivatePracticePointers.aspx

American Counseling Association. (1995). Woman in false-memory case receives $2.6 million. *Counseling Today, 38*(3), 42.

American Counseling Association. (2005). *ACA policies and procedures for processing complaints of ethical violations.* Retrieved from http://www.counseling.org/docs/ethics/policies_procedures.pdf?sfvrsn=2

American Counseling Association. (2011). *Brief for the American Counseling Association as* amicus curiae *in support of defendants-appellees and affirmance*. Retrieved from http://www.counseling.org/resources/pdfs/EMUamicusbrief.pdf

American Counseling Association. (2014a). *ACA code of ethics*. Alexandria, VA: Author.

American Counseling Association. (2014b). *Licensure requirements for professional counselors*. Alexandria, VA: Author.

American Counseling Association. (2014c). *20/20: A vision for the future of counseling, consensus definition of counseling*. Retrieved from http://www.counseling.org/knowledge-center/20-20-a-vision-for-the-future-of-counseling/consensus-definition-of-counseling

American Health Lawyers Association. (2011). *UCLA system agrees to settlement to resolve allegations of HIPAA violations*. Retrieved from http://www.healthlawyers.org/News/Health%20Lawyers%20Weekly/Pages/2011/July%202011/July%2008%202011/UCLAHealthSystemAgreesToSettlementToResolveAllegationsOfHIPAAViolations.aspx

American Medical Association. (2002). *Guidelines for physician–patient electronic communications*. Retrieved from http://www.ama-assn.org/ama/pub/physician-resources/medical-ethics/code-medical-ethics/opinion5026.page

American Psychiatric Association. (1993). *The APA Board statement on memories of sexual abuse* (APA Reference Document No. 93003). Washington, DC: Author.

American Psychiatric Association. (2002). *Therapies focused on memories of childhood physical and sexual abuse* (APA Reference Document No. 200002). Washington, DC: Author.

American Psychiatric Association. (2013). *Diagnostic and statistical manual of mental disorders* (5th ed.). Arlington, VA: Author.

Americans With Disabilities Act of 1990, 42 U.S.C. §§ 12101–12213 (2014).

Americans With Disabilities Act Amendments Act of 2008, 42 U.S.C. §§ 12101 *et seq.* (2014).

Anti-Kickback Act of 1986, 42 U.S.C. § 1320a-7b (2014).

Applied Innovations, Inc. v. Regents of the University of Minnesota, 876 F.2d 626 (8th Cir. 1989).

Ariz. Admin. Code §§ R4-6-501 to 505 (2004).

Ariz. Admin. Code §§ R4-6-1102 to 1103 (2008).

Arizona Board of Behavioral Health Examiners. (2011). *Adverse action tracking form*. Retrieved from http://azbbhe.us/sites/default/files/adverse%20actions/2011advaction.pdf

Arizona Board of Behavioral Health Examiners. (2012). *Adverse action tracking form*. Retrieved from http://azbbhe.us/sites/default/files/adverse%20actions/2012advaction_0.pdf

Arizona Board of Behavioral Health Examiners. (2013). *Adverse action tracking form*. Retrieved from http://azbbhe.us/sites/default/files/adverse%20actions/2013advaction_0.pdf

Arizona Board of Behavioral Health Examiners. (2014). *Adverse action tracking form*. Retrieved from http://azbbhe.us/sites/default/files/adverse%20actions/2014advaction.pdf

Ariz. Rev. Stat. § 15-1862 (2014).

Ariz. Rev. Stat. § 32-3251 (2013).

Ariz. Rev. Stat. § 32-3301 (2013).

Barnett, J. E., & Johnson, B. (2015). *Ethics desk reference for counselors* (2nd ed.). Alexandria, VA: American Counseling Association.

Barringer v. Rausch, 900 So. 2d 232 (La. App. 2005).

Bazerman, M. H., & Tenbrunsel, A. E. (2011). *Blind spots: Why we fail to do what's right and what to do about it*. Princeton, NJ: Princeton University Press.

Benitez, C., McNiel, D., & Binder, R. (2010). Do protection orders protect? *Journal of the American Academy of Psychiatry and the Law, 38*, 376–385.

Bertram, B. (2011). Ethics and legal issues for group work. In T. Fitch & J. L. Marshall (Eds.), *Group work and outreach plans for college counselors* (pp. 9–17). Alexandria, VA: American Counseling Association.

Bogust v. Iverson, 102 N.W.2d 228 (Wis. 1960).

Boynton v. Burglass, 590 So. 2d 446 (Fla. Dist. Ct. App. 1991).

Bradley, L. J., Hendricks, B., Lock, R., Whiting, P. P., & Parr, G. (2011). E-mail communication: Issues for mental health counselors. *Journal of Mental Health Counseling, 33*, 67–79.

Bruff v. North Mississippi Health Servs., Inc., 244 F.3d 495 (5th Cir. 2001), *cert. denied*, 534 U.S. 952 (2001).

Cal. Bus. & Prof. Code § 4999.20 (2014).

Censer, M. (2014, February 25). Silent Circle unveils Blackphone. *The Washington Post*. Retrieved from http://www.washingtonpost.com/business/capitalbusiness/silent-circle-unveils-blackphone/2014/02/24/bd897064-98a7-11e3-b931-0204122c514b_story.html

Centers for Disease Control and Prevention. (2013). *School violence: Data and statistics*. Retrieved from http://www.cdc.gov/violenceprevention/youthviolence/schoolviolence/data_stats.html

Centers for Medicare and Medicaid Services. (2013). *Are you a covered entity?* Retrieved from http://www.cms.gov/Regulations-and-Guidance/HIPAA-Administrative-Simplification/HIPAA-GenInfo/AreYouaCoveredEntity.html

Centers for Medicare and Medicaid Services. (2014). *Employer identifier standard*. Retrieved from http://www.cms.gov/Regulations-and-Guidance/HIPAA-Administrative-Simplification/EmployerIdentifierStand/index.html?redirect=/EmployerIdentifierStand/

CNA & Healthcare Providers Service Organization. (2014). *Understanding counselor liability risk*. Retrieved from https://www.hpso.com/pdfs/db/CNA_CLS_COUNS_022814p_CF_PROD_ASIZE_online_SEC.pdf?fileName=CNA_CLS_COUNS_022814p_CF_PROD_ASIZE_online_SEC.pdf&folder=pdfs/db&isLiveStr=Y

Colo. Rev. Stat. § 12-36-135 (2013).

Comprehensive Psychology System, P.C. v. Prince, 375 N.J. Super. 273, 867 A.2d 1187 (2005).

Confidentiality of Alcohol and Drug Abuse Patient Records, 42 C.F.R. Part 2 (2014).

Contributing to Delinquency, *Mens Rea*, 31 A.L.R.3d 848 (1970).

Copyright Act of 1976, 17 U.S.C. §§ 101–810 (2013).

Corey, G., Corey, M. S., Corey, C., & Callanan, P. (2015). *Issues and ethics in the helping professions* (9th ed.). Belmont, CA: Brooks/Cole, Cengage Learning.

Cornell, D. (2010). *The Virginia model for student threat assessment*. Retrieved from http://curry.virginia.edu/uploads/resourceLibrary/Virginia_Model_for_Student_Threat_Assessment_overview_paper_7-16-10.pdf

Corning Glass Works v. Brennan, 417 U.S. 188 (1974).

Council for Accreditation of Counseling and Related Educational Programs. (2009). *2009 standards*. Retrieved from http://www.cacrep.org/wp-content/uploads/2013/12/2009-Standards.pdf

Council for Accreditation of Counseling and Related Educational Programs. (2014a). *CACREP/CORE updates*. Retrieved from http://www.cacrep.org/news-and-events/cacrepcore-updates/)

Council for Accreditation of Counseling and Related Educational Programs. (2014b). *Vision, mission and core values*. Retrieved from http://www.cacrep.org/about-cacrep/vision-mission-and-core-values/

Criminal Law, 21 Am. Jur. 2d §174.

Currie v. United States, 836 F.2d 209 (4th Cir. 1987).

Darden, E. C. (2006). *Search and seizure, due process, and public schools*. Retrieved from http://www.centerforpubliceducation.org/Main-Menu/Public-education/The-law-and-its-influence-on-public-school-districts-An-overview/Search-and-seizure-due-process-and-public-schools.html

D.C. Mental Health Information Act, D.C. Code § 7-1206.03 (2013).

Dochniak v. Dominium Management Servs., Inc., 240 F.R.D. 451, 452 (D. Minn. 2006).

Doe v. Samaritan Counseling Center, 791 P.2d 344 (Alaska 1990).

Doe v. Wood, No. 93-2-00985-2 (King County Super. Ct., Wash., Aug. 12, 1994).

Eisel v. Board of Education of Montgomery County, 597 A.2d 447 (Md. 1991).

Equal Pay Act of 1963 (Pub. L. No. 88-38), 29 U.S.C. § 206(d) (2014).

Ewing v. Goldstein, 120 Cal. App. 4th 807 (2004).

Ewing v. Northridge Hosp. Med. Ctr., 120 Cal. App. 4th 1289 (2004).

Falmouth Ob-Gyn Associates v. Abisla, 417 Mass. 176, 629 N.E.2d 291 (1994).

False Claims Act of 1986, 31 U.S.C. § 3729-3733 (2014).

Family Educational Rights and Privacy Act of 1974 (FERPA or Buckley Amendment), 20 U.S.C. § 1232g (2014). *See also* regulations at 34 C.F.R. § 99.31 (a)(10) and § 99.36 (2014).

Family and Medical Leave Act of 1993 (Pub. L. No. 103-3), 29 U.S.C. § 2601 (2014).

Federal Rules of Evidence 501.

Figueiredo-Torres v. Nickel, 584 A.2d 69 (Md. 1991).

Fla. Stat. § 491.003 (2013).

Fla. Stat. § 491.0112,491.0147 (2013).

Fla. Stat. Ann § 1006.147(3) (West 2013).

Fla. Stat. Ann. § 406.12 (West 2014).

Florida Medical Quality Assurance Services. (2014). *Final and emergency actions [discipline].* Retrieved from http://ww2.doh.state.fl.us/FinalOrderNet/Default.aspx

Forester-Miller, H., & Davis, T. (1996). *A practitioner's guide to ethical decision making.* Retrieved from http://www.counseling.org/docs/ethics/practitioners_guide.pdf?sfvrsn=2

Genetic Information Nondiscrimination Act of 2008, 42 U.S.C. 2000 *et seq. See also* revised rule at 29 C.F.R. § 1635.

Gladding, S. T. (2013). *Counseling: A comprehensive profession* (7th ed.). Englewood Cliffs, NJ: Pearson-Prentice Hall.

Grant v. Board of Trustees of Valley View School Dist., 676 N.E.2d (Ill. App. 3d 1997).

Grote v. J. S. Mayer & Co., 570 N.E.2d 1146 (Ohio Ct. App. 1990).

Guidance on ADA Regulation on Nondiscrimination on the Basis of Disability in State and Local Government Services, 28 C.F.R. Part 35, Appendix B (2013).

Hamman v. County of Maricopa, 161 Ariz. 58, 775 P.2d 1122 (1989).

Hasenfus v. LaJeunesse, 175 F.3d 68, 73 (1st Cir. 1999).

Health Insurance Portability and Accountability Act of 1996 (HIPAA), Pub. L. No. 104-191, 110 Stat. 1936 (1996). *See also* American Recovery and Reinvestment (ARRA) Act of 2009, Pub. L. No. 111-5, div. A, tit. XIII, 123 Stat. 115, 226–79, div. B, tit. IV, 123 Stat. 115, 467–96 (2009) (Health Information Technology for Economic and Clinical Health (HITECH) Act); HIPAA Privacy Rule, 45 C.F.R. §§ 160.101–.312, 164.106, 164.500–.534 (2013); HIPAA Security Rule, 45 C.F.R. §§ 164.302–.318 (2013); Modifications to the HIPAA Privacy, Security, Enforcement and Breach Notification Rules, 45 C.F.R. §§ 160, 164).

Hedlund v. Superior Court, 34 Cal. 3d 695, 669 P.2d 41 (1983).

Hennessy-Fiske, M. (2011). *UCLA hospitals to pay $865,500 for breaches of celebrities' privacy.* Retrieved from http://articles.latimes.com/2011/jul/08/local/la-me-celebrity-snooping-20110708

Herlihy, B., & Corey, G. (2015). *ACA ethical standards casebook* (7th ed.). Alexandria, VA: American Counseling Association.

Hermann, M. A., & Herlihy, B. R. (2006). Legal and ethical implications of refusing to counsel homosexual clients. *Journal of Counseling & Development, 84,* 414–418.

Homrich, A. M. (2009). Gatekeeping for personal and professional competence in graduate counseling programs. *Counseling and Human Development, 41,* 1–24.

Homrich, A. M., Wheeler, A. M., & Bertram, B. (2007, October). *Legal implications of dismissing the impaired student.* Presented at Association for Counselor Education and Supervision Conference, Columbus, OH.

Horak v. Biris, 130 Ill. App. 3d 140, 474 N.E.2d 13 (1985).

Immigration Reform and Control Act of 1986, 8 U.S.C. §§ 1324a–1324b (2014).

In re Juvenile 2006-406, 931 A.2d 1229 (N.H. 2007).

Interest of L.L., 90 Wis. 2d 585, 280 N.W.2d 343 (Wis. Ct. App. 1979).

Internal Revenue Code, 26 U.S.C. § 501(c)(3) and (4) (2014).

Internal Revenue Service. (2014). *Topic 762—Independent contractor vs. employee.* Retrieved from http://www.irs.gov/taxtopics/tc762.html

International Society for the Study of Self-Injury. (2014). *Definition of non-suicidal self-injury.* Retrieved from http://www.itriples.org/isss-aboutself-i.html

Jablonski v. United States, 712 F.2d 391 (9th Cir. 1983).

Jaffee v. Redmond, 518 U.S. 1 (1996).

Jain v. State, 617 N.W.2d 293 (Iowa, 2000).

Jed Foundation. (2011). *Safeguarding your students against suicide.* Retrieved from https://www.jedfoundation.org/assets/Programs/Program_downloads/SafeguardingYourStudents.pdf

Kaplan, D. M., & Gladding, S. T. (2011). A vision for the future of counseling: The 20/20 principles for unifying and strengthening the profession. *Journal of Counseling & Development, 89,* 367–372.

Keeton v. Anderson-Wiley, 733 F. Supp. 2d 1368 (S.D. Ga. 2010), *aff'd,* 664 F.3d 865 (11th Cir. 2011), *appeal dismissed,* No. 110-099 (S.D. Ga. June 22, 2012).

Kidder, R. M. (1995). *How good people make tough choices: Resolving the dilemmas of ethical living.* New York, NY: Fireside.

Kottler, J. A. (2011). *Introduction to counseling: Voices from the field* (7th ed.). Stamford, CT: Cengage.

Kowalczyk, L. (2010, August 13). Patients' files left at public dump. *Boston Globe.* Retrieved from http://www.boston.com/news/health/articles/2010/08/13/mass_hospitals_investigate_exposure_of_records/

Kraus, K. (2014, October 22). *20/20 facilitator's official announcement letter.* Retrieved from http://www.counseling.org/knowledge-center/20-20-a-vision-for-the-future-of-counseling/current-activities

Kuehn v. Renton School Dist. No. 403, 694 P.2d 1078 (Wash. 1985).

Ky. Rev. Stat. § 209A.010 *et seq.* (2013).

Licensed Professional Counselor Act, Tex. Occ. Code Ann. §§ 503.301–503.314 (1999).

Lilly Ledbetter Fair Pay Act of 2009, Pub. L. No. 111–2, S. 181.

Linke v. Northwestern School Corp., 734 N.E.2d 252 (Ind. App. 2000).

Maheu, M. M., & McMenamin, J. P. (2014, January 19). *Skype and related practices found unacceptable by Oklahoma Medical Board* [Webinar]. In TeleMental Health Institute Webinar Series. Retrieved from http://telehealth.org/blog/tmhi-webinar-skype-and-related-practices-found-unacceptable-by-oklahoma-medical-board/

Mapp v. Ohio, 367 U.S. 643 (1961).

Marshall v. Commonwealth, 977 N.E.2d 40 (Mass. 2012).

Maryland Professional Counselors and Therapists Act, Md. Code Ann., Health Occ. §§ 17-301–310 (2014).

Maryland State Bd. of Physicians v. Eist, 11 A.3d 786 (Md. 2011), *cert. denied,* No. 10-1425 (U.S. 2011).

Matter of McLinn, 739 F.2d 1395 (9th Cir. 1984).

McIntosh v. Milano, 403 A.2d 500 (N.J. Super. 1979).

McMahon v. St. Croix Falls School Dist., 596 N.W.2d 875 (Wis. Ct. App. 1999).

78 Md. Op. Att'y Gen. 189 (12/3/1993).

Me. Code R. § 02-514, Chapter 8-A (LexisNexis, 2009).

Meacham, A. (2009). *Sexting-related bullying cited in Hillsborough teen's suicide.* Retrieved from http://www.tampabay.com/news/humaninterest/sexting-related-bullying-cited-in-hillsborough-teens-suicide/1054895

Mental Health Practice Act, Colo. Rev. Stat. §§12-43-601–605 (2011).

Mich. Pub. Acts 421 (1988).

Mikell v. School Administrative Unit #33, 972 A.2d 1050 (N.H. 2009).

Minn. Stat. § 609.345 (2013).

Nally v. Grace Community Church, 204 Cal. Rptr. 303 (Cal. Ct. App. 1984); *rev'g* 240 Cal. Rptr. 215 (1987), 253 Cal. Rptr. 97 (Cal. 1988); *cert. denied*, 490 U.S. 1007 (1989).

National Board for Certified Counselors. (2012). *NBCC policy regarding the provision of distance professional services.* Retrieved from http://www.nbcc.org/Assets/Ethics/NBCCPolicyRegarding-PracticeofDistanceCounselingBoard.pdf

National Board for Certified Counselors. (2014). *The national counselor examination for licensure and certification.* Retrieved from http://www.nbcc.org/Exam/NationalCounselorExaminationForLicensureAnd-Certification/

National Institute of Mental Health. (2011). *Statistics.* Retrieved from http://www.nimh.nih.gov/statistics/index.shtml

Nelson, S., & Simek, J. (2011). *Stupid mistakes that lawyers make with technology.* Retrieved from http://www.attorneyatwork.com/stupid-mistakes-that-lawyers-make-with-technology/

Neukrug, M. S. (2012). *The world of the counselor: An introduction to the counseling profession* (4th ed.). Pacific Grove, CA: Thomson Brooks/Cole.

N. J. Admin. Code § 13:34-8.2 (2014).

New Jersey v. T.L.O., 469 U.S. 325 (1985).

New York Secure Ammunitions and Firearms Enforcement Act of 2013 (SAFE Act), NY Penal Law § 400.00 (2013).

N.Y. Educ. Law § 8402 (2013).

N.Y. Educ. Law § 8407 (2013).

N.Y. Pub. Health Law § 2803-P (2013).

Oleszko v. State Compensation Insurance Fund, 243 F.3d 1154 (9th Cir. 2001).

Or. Rev. Stat. § 675.715 (2013).

49 Pa. Code §§ 49.11–49.18 (2002).

Patient Protection and Affordable Care Act, 42 U.S.C.A. § 18001 *et seq.* (2012).

Peck v. Counseling Service of Addison County, Inc., 499 A.2d 422 (Vt. 1985).

People v. Watkins, 83 P.3d 1182 (Colo. App. 2003).

Perreira v. Colorado, 768 P.2d 1198 (Colo. 1989).

Privacy of Individually Identifiable Health Information, 45 C.F.R. § 164.501 (2014).

Professional Counselors, Social Workers, and Marriage and Family Therapists Licensing Law, Ga. Code Ann. § 43-10A-11 (2010).

Psychiatrists' Purchasing Group. (1994). Managing the risks involved in cases of recovered memories of abuse. *Rx for Risk, 5*(10), 1.

Public Health Service Act, 42 U.S.C. § 290dd-2 (2014). (See also implementing regulations, Confidentiality of Alcohol and Drug Abuse Patient Records, at 42 C.F.R. Part 2, 2014.)

Qualman, E. (2013). *Social media statistics 2013 from video.* Retrieved from http://www.socialnomics.net/2013/01/01/social-media-video-2013/

Ramona v. Ramona, No. 61898 (Napa County Superior Ct., July 11, 1994).

Rehabilitation Act of 1973 § 501, as amended, 29 U.S.C. § 791 and § 504, as amended, 29 U.S.C. § 794 (2014).

Remley, T. P., & Herlihy, B. (2010). *Ethical, legal, and professional issues in counseling* (3rd ed.). Upper Saddle, NJ: Pearson-Merrill.

Rogers v. Christina School Dist., 73 A.3d 1 (Del. 2013).

Rosen, J. (2010, July 25). The web means the end of forgetting. *The New York Times Magazine.* Retrieved from http://www.nytimes.com/2010/07/25/magazine/25privacy-t2.html?pagewanted=all&_r=0

Rowe v. Bennett, 514 A.2d 802 (Me. 1986).

Sawyer Rosenstein, New Jersey middle school student, nets $4.2 million settlement for bully's paralyzing punch. (2012). *Huffington Post.* Retrieved from http://www.huffingtonpost.com/2012/04/18/nj-bullys-paralyzing-punc_n_1435176.html

Scarton, D. (2010, March 30). Google and Facebook raise new issues for therapists and their clients. *The Washington Post.* Retrieved from http://www.washingtonpost.com/wp-dyn/content/article/2010/03/29/AR2010032902942.html

Schaffer, N. (2010). *Do you still have social media privacy concerns?* Retrieved from http://maximizesocialbusiness.com/do-you-still-have-social-media-privacy-concerns-3092/

Schoffstall v. Henderson, 223 F.3d 818, 823 (2000).

Scottsdale Ins. Co. v. Flowers, 513 F.2d 546 (6th Cir. 2008).

Searcy v. Auerbach, 980 F.2d 609 (9th Cir. 1992).

Simmons v. United States, 805 F.2d 1363 (9th Cir. 1986).

Simon, R. I. (2011, March 3). Patient violence against health care professionals; safety assessment and management. *Psychiatric Times.* Retrieved from http://www.psychiatrictimes.com/schizophrenia/content/article/10168/181347

Smith, A. (2011). *Americans and text messaging.* Pew Internet & American Life Project. Retrieved from http://pewinternet.org/2011/09/19americans-and-text-messaging/

Speaker ex rel. Speaker v. County of San Bernardino, 82 F. Supp. 2d 1105 (C.D. Cal. 2000)

St. Paul Fire & Marine Ins. Co. v. Love, 459 N.W.2d 698 (Minn. 1990).

State v. Ohrtman, 466 N.W.2d 1 (Minn. Ct. App. 1991).

State v. Woods, 307 N.C. 213, 297 S.E.2d 574 (1982).

Stepakoff v. Kantar, 473 N.E.2d 1131 (Mass. 1985).

Stone, C. (2013, September 1). Suicide: Err on the side of caution. *ASCA School Counselor.* Retrieved from http://schoolcounselor.org/magazine/blogs/september-october-2013/suicide-err-on-the-side-of-caution

Sutherland v. Kroger Co., 110 S.E.2d 716 (W.Va. 1959).

Takizawa, R., Maughan, B., & Arseneault, L. (2014). Adult health outcomes of childhood bullying victimization: Evidence from a five-decade longitudinal British birth cohort. *American Journal of Psychiatry, 171,* 777–784. doi: 10.1176/appi.ajp.2014.13101401

Tarasoff v. Regents of the University of California, 551 P.2d 334 (Cal. 1976).

Tenbrunsel, A. E., & Messick, D. M. (2004). Ethical fading: The role of self-deception in unethical behavior. *Social Justice Research, 17,* 223–236.

22 Tex. Admin. Code § 681.41(t)(6) (2013).

Tex. Health & Safety Code § 611.004 (2013).

Texas Department of State Health Services. (2014). *Texas State Board of Examiners of Professional Counselors—Enforcement actions.* Retrieved from http://www.dshs.state.tx.us/counselor/lpc_enforce.shtm

Thapar v. Zezulka, 994 S.W.2d 635 (Tex. 1999).

Thomas, R. V., & Pender, D. A. (2008). Association for Specialists in Group Work: Best practices guidelines 2007 revisions. *Journal for Specialists in Group Work, 33*, 111–117.

Title VII of the Civil Rights Act of 1964, as amended by the Civil Rights Act of 1991, 42 U.S.C. § 2000e (implementing regulations found at 29 C.F.R. §§ 1601–1614).

28 U.S.C. § 1331–1332 (2013).

U.S. Department of Health and Human Services. (2014). *Stolen laptops lead to important HIPAA settlements.* Retrieved from http://www.hhs.gov/news/press/2014pres/04/20140422b.html

U.S. Department of Health and Human Services, Office for Civil Rights. (2011a). *Cignet Health fined a $4.3M civil money penalty for HIPAA privacy rule violations.* Retrieved from http://www.hhs.gov/ocr/privacy/hipaa/enforcement/examples/cignetcmp.html

U.S. Department of Health and Human Services, Office for Civil Rights. (2011b). *Massachusetts General Hospital settles potential HIPAA violations.* Retrieved from http://www.hhs.gov/ocr/privacy/hipaa/news/mghnews.html

U.S. Department of Health and Human Services, Office for Civil Rights. (2013). *Business associate contracts: Sample business associate agreement provisions.* Retrieved from http://www.hhs.gov/ocr/privacy/hipaa/understanding/coveredentities/contractprov.html

U.S. Department of Health and Human Services, Office for Civil Rights. (2014a). *Breach notification rule.* Retrieved from http://www.hhs.gov/ocr/privacy/hipaa/administrative/breachnotificationrule/index.html

U.S. Department of Health and Human Services, Office for Civil Rights. (2014b). *Breaches affecting 500 or more individuals.* Retrieved from http://www.hhs.gov/ocr/privacy/hipaa/administrative/breachnotificationrule/breachtool.html

U.S. Department of Health and Human Services, Office for Civil Rights. (2014c). *Health information privacy.* Retrieved from http://www.hhs.gov/ocr/privacy/index.html

U.S. Department of Health and Human Services, Office for Civil Rights. (2014d). *HIPAA privacy rule and the National Instant Criminal Background Check System (NICS).* Retrieved from http://www.hhs.gov/ocr/privacy/hipaa/understanding/special/NICS/

U.S. Department of Health and Human Services, Office for Civil Rights. (2014e). *HIPAA privacy rule and sharing information related to mental health.* Retrieved from http://www.hhs.gov/ocr/privacy/hipaa/understanding/special/mhguidancepdf.pdf

U.S. Department of Justice. (2010). *2010 ADA standards for accessible design*. Retrieved from http://www.ada.gov/2010ADAstandards_index.htm

U.S. Department of Justice, Civil Rights Division. (2005). *Tax incentives for businesses*. Retrieved from http://www.ada.gov/taxincent.pdf

U.S. Department of Justice, Civil Rights Division. (2011). *ADA update: A primer for small business*. Retrieved from http://www.ada.gov/regs2010/smallbusiness/smallbusprimer2010.pdf

U.S. Department of Justice, Civil Rights Division. (2012). *Revised ADA regulations: Implementing Title II and Title III*. Retrieved from http://www.ada.gov/regs2010/ADAregs2010.htm

U.S. Department of Labor, Bureau of Labor Statistics. (2014). *Occupation employment statistics 2013*. Retrieved from http://www.bls.gov/oes/current/oes_stru.htm#19-0000

U.S. Department of Labor, Employment Standards Administration. (2014). *Family and Medical Leave Act*. Retrieved from http://www.dol.gov/whd/fmla/

U.S. Department of Labor Occupational Safety and Health Administration. (2014). *Guidelines for preventing workplace violence for healthcare and social service workers*. Retrieved from http://www.osha.gov.Publications/OSHA3148/osha3148.html

U.S. Equal Employment Opportunity Commission. (1997). *Filing a charge*. Retrieved from http://www.eeoc.gov/facts/howtofil.html

U.S. Equal Employment Opportunity Commission. (n.d.-a). *Facts about sexual harassment*. Retrieved from http://www.eeoc.gov/eeoc/publications/fs-sex.cfm

U.S. Equal Employment Opportunity Commission. (n.d.-b). *Genetic information discrimination*. Retrieved from http://www.eeoc.gov/laws/types/genetic.cfm

U.S. v. Silk, 331 U.S. 704 (1947).

Va. Code Ann. § 54.1–2400.1 (2013).

Va. Code Ann. § 54.1–3500 (2013).

Vernonia School District 47J v. Acton, 515 U.S. 646 (1995).

Virginia Tech Review Panel. (2007). *Mass shootings at Virginia Tech April 16, 2007: Report of the review panel*. Retrieved from http://www.schoolshooters.info/PL/Official_Reports_files/FullReport.pdf

Walden v. Centers for Disease Control & Prevention, 669 F.3d 1277 (11th Cir. 2012).

Ward v. Wilbanks, Case No. 09-CV-11237 (E.D. Mich. July 26, 2010).

Ward v. Polite, 667 F.3d 727 (6th Cir. 2012).

Wash. Rev. Code § 18.225 (2005).

Welfel, E. R. (2013). *Ethics in counseling and psychotherapy* (5th ed.). Pacific Grove, CA: Brooks-Cole, Cengage Learning.

Werth, J. L., & Stroup, J. (2015). *Working with clients who may harm themselves.* In B. Herlihy & G. Corey (Eds.), *ACA ethical standards casebook* (pp. 231–244). Alexandria, VA: American Counseling Association.

Wetzel v. Brown, No. 1:09-cv-053, 2014 U.S. Dist. LEXIS 21892 (D.N.D. Feb. 21, 2014).

Wheeler, A. M. (2004, December). Independent contractor or employee. *Legal and Regulatory Compliance: Updates for Counselors, Mental Health Professionals, and Counselor Educators, 1*(3), 1–6.

Wheeler, A. M. (2013, March). Counselors should stay abreast of possible new reporting duties. *Counseling Today, 55*(9), 24.

Wheeler, A. M., & Reinhardt, R. (2014). *Private practice preparedness: The health care professional's guide to closing a private practice due to retirement, death or disability.* Retrieved from http://www.privatepracticepreparedness.com

Whitlock, J. (2009, December). The cutting edge: Non-suicidal self-injury in adolescence. *Research Facts and Findings.* Retrieved from http://www.actforyouth.net/resources/rf/rf_nssi_1209.pdf

Wigglesworth, A. (2013). *Lawsuit: School meeting allowed bully to beat victim yet again.* Retrieved from http://www.philly.com/philly/news/breaking/Lawsuit_Bullying_meeting_allowed_bully_to_beat_victim_yet_again.html

Witsell v. School Board of Hillsborough County, Case No. 8:2011cv00781-T-23AEP (M.D. Fla. 2012).

Wood, M. (2014, July 16). Easier ways to protect e-mail from unwanted prying eyes. *The New York Times.* Retrieved from http://www.nytimes.com/2014/07/17/technology/personaltech/ways-to-protect-your-email-after-you-send-it.html

Ziomek-Daigle, J., & Bailey, D. F. (2010). Culturally responsive gatekeeping practices in counselor education. *Journal of Counseling Research and Practice, 1*, 14–22.

Appendix A

ACA Code of Ethics

ACA Code of Ethics Preamble

The American Counseling Association (ACA) is an educational, scientific, and professional organization whose members work in a variety of settings and serve in multiple capacities. Counseling is a professional relationship that empowers diverse individuals, families, and groups to accomplish mental health, wellness, education, and career goals.

Professional values are an important way of living out an ethical commitment. The following are core professional values of the counseling profession:

1. enhancing human development throughout the life span;
2. honoring diversity and embracing a multicultural approach in support of the worth, dignity, potential, and uniqueness of people within their social and cultural contexts;
3. promoting social justice;
4. safeguarding the integrity of the counselor–client relationship; and
5. practicing in a competent and ethical manner.

These professional values provide a conceptual basis for the ethical principles enumerated below. These principles are the foundation for ethical behavior and decision making. The fundamental principles of professional ethical behavior are

- *autonomy*, or fostering the right to control the direction of one's life;
- *nonmaleficence*, or avoiding actions that cause harm;
- *beneficence*, or working for the good of the individual and society by promoting mental health and well-being;

- *justice*, or treating individuals equitably and fostering fairness and equality;
- *fidelity*, or honoring commitments and keeping promises, including fulfilling one's responsibilities of trust in professional relationships; and
- *veracity*, or dealing truthfully with individuals with whom counselors come into professional contact.

ACA Code of Ethics Purpose

The *ACA Code of Ethics* serves six main purposes:

1. The *Code* sets forth the ethical obligations of ACA members and provides guidance intended to inform the ethical practice of professional counselors.
2. The *Code* identifies ethical considerations relevant to professional counselors and counselors-in-training.
3. The *Code* enables the association to clarify for current and perspective members, and for those served by members, the nature of the ethical responsibilities held in common by its members.
4. The *Code* serves as an ethical guide designed to assist members in constructing a course of action that best serves those utilizing counseling services and establishes expectations of conduct with a primary emphasis on the role of the professional counselor.
5. The *Code* helps to support the mission of ACA.
6. The standards contained in this *Code* serve as the basis for processing inquiries and ethics complaints concerning ACA members.

The *ACA Code of Ethics* contains nine main sections that address the following areas:

Section A: The Counseling Relationship

Section B: Confidentiality and Privacy

Section C: Professional Responsibility

Section D: Relationships With Other Professionals

Section E: Evaluation, Assessment, and Interpretation

Section F: Supervision, Training, and Teaching

Section G: Research and Publication

Section H: Distance Counseling, Technology, and Social Media

Section I: Resolving Ethical Issues

Each section of the *ACA Code of Ethics* begins with an introduction. The introduction to each section describes the ethical behavior and responsibility to which counselors aspire. The introductions help set the tone for each particular section and provide a starting point that invites reflection on the ethical standards contained in each part of the *ACA Code of Ethics*. The standards outline professional responsibilities and provide direction for fulfilling those ethical responsibilities.

When counselors are faced with ethical dilemmas that are difficult to resolve, they are expected to engage in a carefully considered ethical decision-making process, consulting available resources as needed. Counselors acknowledge that resolving ethical issues is a process; ethical reasoning includes consideration of professional values, professional ethical principles, and ethical standards.

Counselors' actions should be consistent with the spirit as well as the letter of these ethical standards. No specific ethical decision-making model is always most effective, so counselors are expected to use a credible model of decision making that can bear public scrutiny of its application. Through a chosen ethical decision-making process and evaluation of the context of the situation, counselors work collaboratively with clients to make decisions that promote clients' growth and development. A breach of the standards and principles provided herein does not necessarily constitute legal liability or violation of the law; such action is established in legal and judicial proceedings.

The glossary at the end of the *Code* provides a concise description of some of the terms used in the *ACA Code of Ethics*.

Section A
The Counseling Relationship

Introduction

Counselors facilitate client growth and development in ways that foster the interest and welfare of clients and promote formation of healthy relationships. Trust is the cornerstone of the counseling relationship, and counselors have the responsibility to respect and safeguard the client's right to privacy and confidentiality. Counselors actively attempt to understand the diverse cultural backgrounds of the clients they serve. Counselors also explore their own cultural identities and how these affect their values and beliefs about the counseling process. Additionally, counselors are encouraged to contribute to society by devoting a portion of their professional activities for little or no financial return (*pro bono publico*).

A.1. Client Welfare

A.1.a. Primary Responsibility

The primary responsibility of counselors is to respect the dignity and promote the welfare of clients.

A.1.b. Records and Documentation

Counselors create, safeguard, and maintain documentation necessary for rendering professional services. Regardless of the medium, counselors include sufficient and timely documentation to facilitate the delivery and continuity of services. Counselors take reasonable steps to ensure that documentation accurately reflects client progress and services provided. If amendments are made to records and documentation, counselors take steps to properly note the amendments according to agency or institutional policies.

A.1.c. Counseling Plans

Counselors and their clients work jointly in devising counseling plans that offer reasonable promise of success and are consistent with the abilities, temperament, developmental level, and circumstances of clients. Counselors and clients regularly review and revise counseling plans to assess their continued viability and effectiveness, respecting clients' freedom of choice.

A.1.d. Support Network Involvement

Counselors recognize that support networks hold various meanings in the lives of clients and consider enlisting the support, understanding, and involvement of others (e.g., religious/ spiritual/community leaders, family members, friends) as positive resources, when appropriate, with client consent.

A.2. Informed Consent in the Counseling Relationship
A.2.a. Informed Consent

Clients have the freedom to choose whether to enter into or remain in a counseling relationship and need adequate information about the counseling process and the counselor. Counselors have an obligation to review in writing and verbally with clients the rights and responsibilities of both counselors and clients. Informed consent is an ongoing part of the counseling process, and counselors appropriately document discussions of informed consent throughout the counseling relationship.

A.2.b. Types of Information Needed

Counselors explicitly explain to clients the nature of all services provided. They inform clients about issues such as, but not limited to, the following: the purposes, goals, techniques, procedures, limitations, potential risks, and benefits of services; the counselor's qualifications, credentials, relevant experience, and approach to counseling; continuation of services upon the incapacitation or death of the counselor; the role of technology; and other pertinent information. Counselors take steps to ensure that clients understand the implications of diagnosis and the intended use of tests and reports. Additionally, counselors inform clients about fees and billing arrangements, including procedures for nonpayment of fees. Clients have the right to confidentiality and to be provided with an explanation of its limits (including how supervisors and/or treatment or interdisciplinary team professionals are involved), to obtain clear information about their records, to participate in the ongoing counseling plans, and to refuse any services or modality changes and to be advised of the consequences of such refusal.

A.2.c. Developmental and Cultural Sensitivity

Counselors communicate information in ways that are both developmentally and culturally appropriate. Counselors use clear and understandable language when discussing issues related to informed consent. When clients have difficulty understanding the language that counselors use, counselors provide necessary services (e.g., arranging for a qualified interpreter or translator) to ensure comprehension by clients. In collaboration with clients, counselors consider cultural implications of informed consent procedures and, where possible, counselors adjust their practices accordingly.

A.2.d. Inability to Give Consent

When counseling minors, incapacitated adults, or other persons unable to give voluntary consent, counselors seek the assent of clients to services and include them in decision making as appropriate. Counselors recognize the need to balance the ethical rights of clients to make choices, their capacity to give consent or assent to receive services, and parental or familial legal rights and responsibilities to protect these clients and make decisions on their behalf.

A.2.e. Mandated Clients

Counselors discuss the required limitations to confidentiality when working with clients who have been mandated for counseling services. Counselors also explain what type of information and with whom that information is shared prior to the beginning of counseling. The client may choose to refuse services. In this case, counselors will, to the best of their ability, discuss with the client the potential consequences of refusing counseling services.

A.3. Clients Served by Others

When counselors learn that their clients are in a professional relationship with other mental health professionals, they request release from clients to inform the other professionals and strive to establish positive and collaborative professional relationships.

A.4. Avoiding Harm and Imposing Values

A.4.a. Avoiding Harm

Counselors act to avoid harming their clients, trainees, and research participants and to minimize or to remedy unavoidable or unanticipated harm.

A.4.b. Personal Values

Counselors are aware of—and avoid imposing—their own values, attitudes, beliefs, and behaviors. Counselors respect the diversity of clients, trainees, and research participants and seek training in areas in which they are at risk of imposing their values onto clients, especially when the counselor's values are inconsistent with the client's goals or are discriminatory in nature.

A.5. Prohibited Noncounseling Roles and Relationships

A.5.a. Sexual and/or Romantic Relationships Prohibited

Sexual and/or romantic counselor–client interactions or relationships with current clients, their romantic partners, or their family members are prohibited. This prohibition applies to both in-person and electronic interactions or relationships.

A.5.b. Previous Sexual and/or Romantic Relationships

Counselors are prohibited from engaging in counseling relationships with persons with whom they have had a previous sexual and/or romantic relationship.

A.5.c. Sexual and/or Romantic Relationships With Former Clients

Sexual and/or romantic counselor–client interactions or relationships with former clients, their romantic partners, or their family members are prohibited for a period of 5 years following the last professional contact. This prohibition applies to both in-person and electronic interactions or relationships. Counselors, before engaging in sexual and/or romantic interactions or relationships with former clients, their romantic partners, or their family members, demonstrate forethought and document (in written form) whether the interaction or relationship can be viewed as exploitive in any way and/or whether there is still potential to harm the former client; in cases of potential exploitation and/or harm, the counselor avoids entering into such an interaction or relationship.

A.5.d. Friends or Family Members

Counselors are prohibited from engaging in counseling relationships with friends or family members with whom they have an inability to remain objective.

A.5.e. Personal Virtual Relationships With Current Clients

Counselors are prohibited from engaging in a personal virtual relationship with individuals with whom they have a current counseling relationship (e.g., through social and other media).

A.6. Managing and Maintaining Boundaries and Professional Relationships

A.6.a. Previous Relationships

Counselors consider the risks and benefits of accepting as clients those with whom they have had a previous relationship. These potential clients may include individuals with whom the counselor has had a casual, distant, or past relationship. Examples include mutual or past membership in a professional association, organization, or community. When counselors accept these clients, they take appropriate professional precautions such as informed consent, consultation, supervision, and documentation to ensure that judgment is not impaired and no exploitation occurs.

A.6.b. Extending Counseling Boundaries

Counselors consider the risks and benefits of extending current counseling relationships beyond conventional parameters. Examples include attending a client's formal ceremony (e.g., a wedding/commitment ceremony or graduation), purchasing a service or product provided by a client (excepting unrestricted bartering), and visiting a client's ill family member in the hospital. In extending these boundaries, counselors take appropriate professional precautions such as informed consent, consultation, supervision, and documentation to ensure that judgment is not impaired and no harm occurs.

A.6.c. Documenting Boundary Extensions

If counselors extend boundaries as described in A.6.a. and A.6.b., they must officially document, prior to the interaction (when feasible), the rationale for such an interaction, the potential benefit, and anticipated consequences for the client or former client and other individuals significantly involved with the client or former client. When unintentional harm occurs to the client or former client, or to an individual significantly involved with the client or former client, the counselor must show evidence of an attempt to remedy such harm.

A.6.d. Role Changes in the Professional Relationship

When counselors change a role from the original or most recent contracted relationship, they obtain informed consent from the client and explain the client's right to refuse services related to the change. Examples of role changes include, but are not limited to

1. changing from individual to relationship or family counseling, or vice versa;
2. changing from an evaluative role to a therapeutic role, or vice versa; and
3. changing from a counselor to a mediator role, or vice versa.

Clients must be fully informed of any anticipated consequences (e.g., financial, legal, personal, therapeutic) of counselor role changes.

A.6.e. Nonprofessional Interactions or Relationships (Other Than Sexual or Romantic Interactions or Relationships)

Counselors avoid entering into nonprofessional relationships with former clients, their romantic partners, or their family members when the interaction is potentially harmful to the client. This applies to both in-person and electronic interactions or relationships.

A.7. Roles and Relationships at Individual, Group, Institutional, and Societal Levels

A.7.a. Advocacy

When appropriate, counselors advocate at individual, group, institutional, and societal levels to address potential barriers and obstacles that inhibit access and/or the growth and development of clients.

A.7.b. Confidentiality and Advocacy

Counselors obtain client consent prior to engaging in advocacy efforts on behalf of an identifiable client to improve the provision of services and to work toward removal of systemic barriers or obstacles that inhibit client access, growth, and development.

A.8. Multiple Clients

When a counselor agrees to provide counseling services to two or more persons who have a relationship, the counselor clarifies at the outset which person or persons are clients and the nature of the relationships the counselor will have with each involved person. If it becomes apparent that the counselor may be called upon to perform potentially conflicting roles, the counselor will clarify, adjust, or withdraw from roles appropriately.

A.9. Group Work

A.9.a. Screening

Counselors screen prospective group counseling/therapy participants. To the extent possible, counselors select members whose needs and goals are compatible with the goals of the group, who will not impede the group process, and whose well-being will not be jeopardized by the group experience.

A.9.b. Protecting Clients

In a group setting, counselors take reasonable precautions to protect clients from physical, emotional, or psychological trauma.

A.10. Fees and Business Practices

A.10.a. Self-Referral

Counselors working in an organization (e.g., school, agency, institution) that provides counseling services do not refer clients to their private practice unless the policies of a particular organization make explicit provisions for self-referrals. In such instances, the clients must be informed of other options open to them should they seek private counseling services.

A.10.b. Unacceptable Business Practices

Counselors do not participate in fee splitting, nor do they give or receive commissions, rebates, or any other form of remuneration when referring clients for professional services.

A.10.c. Establishing Fees

In establishing fees for professional counseling services, counselors consider the financial status of clients and locality. If a counselor's usual fees create undue hardship for the client, the counselor may adjust fees, when legally permissible, or assist the client in locating comparable, affordable services.

A.10.d. Nonpayment of Fees

If counselors intend to use collection agencies or take legal measures to collect fees from clients who do not pay for services as agreed upon, they include such information in their informed consent documents and also inform clients in a timely fashion of intended actions and offer clients the opportunity to make payment.

A.10.e. Bartering

Counselors may barter only if the bartering does not result in exploitation or harm, if the client requests it, and if such arrangements are an accepted practice among professionals in the community. Counselors consider the cultural implications of bartering and discuss relevant concerns with clients and document such agreements in a clear written contract.

A.10.f. Receiving Gifts

Counselors understand the challenges of accepting gifts from clients and recognize that in some cultures, small gifts are a token of respect and gratitude. When determining whether to accept a gift from clients, counselors take into account the therapeutic relationship, the monetary value of the gift, the client's motivation for giving the gift, and the counselor's motivation for wanting to accept or decline the gift.

A.11. Termination and Referral

A.11.a. Competence Within Termination and Referral

If counselors lack the competence to be of professional assistance to clients, they avoid entering or continuing counseling relationships. Counselors are knowledgeable about culturally and clinically appropriate referral resources and suggest these alternatives. If clients decline the suggested referrals, counselors discontinue the relationship.

A.11.b. Values Within Termination and Referral

Counselors refrain from referring prospective and current clients based solely on the counselor's personally held values, attitudes, beliefs, and behaviors. Counselors respect the diversity of clients and seek training in areas in which they are at risk of imposing their values onto clients, especially when the counselor's values are inconsistent with the client's goals or are discriminatory in nature.

A.11.c. Appropriate Termination

Counselors terminate a counseling relationship when it becomes reasonably apparent that the client no longer needs assistance, is not likely to benefit, or is being harmed by continued counseling. Counselors may terminate counseling when in jeopardy of harm by the client or by another person with whom the client has a relationship, or when clients do not pay fees as agreed upon.

Counselors provide pretermination counseling and recommend other service providers when necessary.

A.11.d. Appropriate Transfer of Services

When counselors transfer or refer clients to other practitioners, they ensure that appropriate clinical and administrative processes are completed and open communication is maintained with both clients and practitioners.

A.12. Abandonment and Client Neglect

Counselors do not abandon or neglect clients in counseling. Counselors assist in making appropriate arrangements for the continuation of treatment, when necessary, during interruptions such as vacations, illness, and following termination.

Section B
Confidentiality and Privacy

Introduction

Counselors recognize that trust is a cornerstone of the counseling relationship. Counselors aspire to earn the trust of clients by creating an ongoing partnership, establishing and upholding appropriate boundaries, and maintaining confidentiality. Counselors communicate the parameters of confidentiality in a culturally competent manner.

B.1. Respecting Client Rights

B.1.a. Multicultural/Diversity Considerations

Counselors maintain awareness and sensitivity regarding cultural meanings of confidentiality and privacy. Counselors respect differing views toward disclosure of information. Counselors hold ongoing discussions with clients as to how, when, and with whom information is to be shared.

B.1.b. Respect for Privacy

Counselors respect the privacy of prospective and current clients. Counselors request private information from clients only when it is beneficial to the counseling process.

B.1.c. Respect for Confidentiality

Counselors protect the confidential information of prospective and current clients. Counselors disclose information only with appropriate consent or with sound legal or ethical justification.

B.1.d. Explanation of Limitations

At initiation and throughout the counseling process, counselors inform clients of the limitations of confidentiality and seek to identify situations in which confidentiality must be breached.

B.2. Exceptions

B.2.a. Serious and Foreseeable Harm and Legal Requirements

The general requirement that counselors keep information confidential does not apply when disclosure is required to protect clients or identified others from serious and foreseeable harm or when legal requirements demand that confidential information must be revealed. Counselors consult with other professionals when in doubt as to the validity of an exception. Additional considerations apply when addressing end-of-life issues.

B.2.b. Confidentiality Regarding End-of-Life Decisions

Counselors who provide services to terminally ill individuals who are considering hastening their own deaths have the option to maintain confidentiality, depending on applicable laws and the specific circumstances of the situation and after seeking consultation or supervision from appropriate professional and legal parties.

B.2.c. Contagious, Life-Threatening Diseases

When clients disclose that they have a disease commonly known to be both communicable and life threatening, counselors may be justified in disclosing information to identifiable third parties, if the parties are known to be at serious and foreseeable risk of contracting the disease. Prior to making a disclosure, counselors assess the intent of clients to inform the third parties about their disease or to engage in any behaviors that may be harmful to an identifiable third party. Counselors adhere to relevant state laws concerning disclosure about disease status.

B.2.d. Court-Ordered Disclosure

When ordered by a court to release confidential or privileged information without a client's permission, counselors seek to obtain written, informed consent from the client or take steps to prohibit the disclosure or have it limited as narrowly as possible because of potential harm to the client or counseling relationship.

B.2.e. Minimal Disclosure

To the extent possible, clients are informed before confidential information is disclosed and are involved in the disclosure decision-making process. When circumstances require the disclosure of confidential information, only essential information is revealed.

B.3. Information Shared With Others

B.3.a. Subordinates

Counselors make every effort to ensure that privacy and confidentiality of clients are maintained by subordinates, including employees, supervisees, students, clerical assistants, and volunteers.

B.3.b. Interdisciplinary Teams

When services provided to the client involve participation by an interdisciplinary or treatment team, the client will be informed of the team's existence and composition, information being shared, and the purposes of sharing such information.

B.3.c. Confidential Settings

Counselors discuss confidential information only in settings in which they can reasonably ensure client privacy.

B.3.d. Third-Party Payers

Counselors disclose information to third-party payers only when clients have authorized such disclosure.

B.3.e. Transmitting Confidential Information

Counselors take precautions to ensure the confidentiality of all information transmitted through the use of any medium.

B.3.f. Deceased Clients

Counselors protect the confidentiality of deceased clients, consistent with legal requirements and the documented preferences of the client.

B.4. Groups and Families

B.4.a. Group Work

In group work, counselors clearly explain the importance and parameters of confidentiality for the specific group.

B.4.b. Couples and Family Counseling

In couples and family counseling, counselors clearly define who is considered "the client" and discuss expectations and limitations of confidentiality. Counselors seek agreement and document in writing such agreement among all involved parties regarding the confidentiality of information. In the absence of an agreement to the contrary, the couple or family is considered to be the client.

B.5. Clients Lacking Capacity to Give Informed Consent

B.5.a. Responsibility to Clients

When counseling minor clients or adult clients who lack the capacity to give voluntary, informed consent, counselors protect the confidentiality of information received—in any medium—in the counseling relationship as specified by federal and state laws, written policies, and applicable ethical standards.

B.5.b. Responsibility to Parents and Legal Guardians

Counselors inform parents and legal guardians about the role of counselors and the confidential nature of the counseling relationship, consistent with current legal and custodial arrangements. Counselors are sensitive to the cultural diversity of families and respect the inherent rights and responsibilities of parents/guardians regarding the welfare of their children/charges according to law. Counselors work to establish, as appropriate, collaborative relationships with parents/guardians to best serve clients.

B.5.c. Release of Confidential Information

When counseling minor clients or adult clients who lack the capacity to give voluntary consent to release confidential information, counselors seek permission from an appropriate third party to disclose information. In such instances, counselors inform clients consistent with their level of understanding and take appropriate measures to safeguard client confidentiality.

B.6. Records and Documentation

B.6.a. Creating and Maintaining Records and Documentation

Counselors create and maintain records and documentation necessary for rendering professional services.

B.6.b. Confidentiality of Records and Documentation

Counselors ensure that records and documentation kept in any medium are secure and that only authorized persons have access to them.

B.6.c. Permission to Record

Counselors obtain permission from clients prior to recording sessions through electronic or other means.

B.6.d. Permission to Observe

Counselors obtain permission from clients prior to allowing any person to observe counseling sessions, review session transcripts, or view recordings of sessions with supervisors, faculty, peers, or others within the training environment.

B.6.e. Client Access

Counselors provide reasonable access to records and copies of records when requested by competent clients. Counselors limit the access of clients to their records, or portions of their records, only when there is compelling evidence that such access would cause harm to the client. Counselors document the request of clients and the rationale for withholding some or all of the records in the files of clients. In situations involving multiple clients, counselors provide individual clients with only those parts of records that relate directly to them and do not include confidential information related to any other client.

B.6.f. Assistance With Records

When clients request access to their records, counselors provide assistance and consultation in interpreting counseling records.

B.6.g. Disclosure or Transfer

Unless exceptions to confidentiality exist, counselors obtain written permission from clients to disclose or transfer records to legitimate third parties. Steps are taken to ensure that receivers of counseling records are sensitive to their confidential nature.

B.6.h. Storage and Disposal After Termination

Counselors store records following termination of services to ensure reasonable future access, maintain records in accordance with federal and state laws and statutes such as licensure laws and policies governing records, and dispose of client records and other sensitive materials in a manner that protects client confidentiality. Counselors apply careful discretion and deliberation before destroying records that may be needed by a court of law, such as notes on child abuse, suicide, sexual harassment, or violence.

B.6.i. Reasonable Precautions

Counselors take reasonable precautions to protect client confidentiality in the event of the counselor's termination of practice, incapacity, or death and appoint a records custodian when identified as appropriate.

B.7. Case Consultation

B.7.a. Respect for Privacy

Information shared in a consulting relationship is discussed for professional purposes only. Written and oral reports present only data germane to the purposes of the consultation, and every effort is made to protect client identity and to avoid undue invasion of privacy.

B.7.b. Disclosure of Confidential Information

When consulting with colleagues, counselors do not disclose confidential information that reasonably could lead to the identification of a client or other person or organization with whom they have a confidential relationship unless they have obtained the prior consent of the person or organization or the disclosure cannot be avoided. They disclose information only to the extent necessary to achieve the purposes of the consultation.

Section C
Professional Responsibility

Introduction

Counselors aspire to open, honest, and accurate communication in dealing with the public and other professionals. Counselors facilitate access to counseling services, and they practice in a nondiscriminatory manner within the boundaries of professional and personal competence; they also have a responsibility to abide by the *ACA Code of Ethics*. Counselors actively participate in local, state, and national associations that foster the development and improvement of counseling. Counselors are expected to advocate to promote changes at the individual, group, institutional, and societal levels that improve the quality of life for individuals and groups and remove potential barriers to the provision or access of appropriate services being offered. Counselors have a responsibility to the public to engage in counseling practices that are based on rigorous research methodologies. Counselors are encouraged to contribute to society by devoting a portion of their professional activity to services for which there is little or no financial return (*pro bono publico*). In addition, counselors engage in self-care activities to maintain and promote their own emotional, physical, mental, and spiritual well-being to best meet their professional responsibilities.

C.1. Knowledge of and Compliance With Standards

Counselors have a responsibility to read, understand, and follow the *ACA Code of Ethics* and adhere to applicable laws and regulations.

C.2. Professional Competence

C.2.a. Boundaries of Competence

Counselors practice only within the boundaries of their competence, based on their education, training, supervised experience, state and national professional credentials, and appropriate professional experience. Whereas multicultural counseling competency is required across all counseling specialties, counselors gain knowledge, personal awareness, sensitivity, dispositions, and skills pertinent to being a culturally competent counselor in working with a diverse client population.

C.2.b. New Specialty Areas of Practice

Counselors practice in specialty areas new to them only after appropriate education, training, and supervised experience. While developing skills in new specialty areas, counselors take steps to ensure the competence of their work and protect others from possible harm.

C.2.c. Qualified for Employment

Counselors accept employment only for positions for which they are qualified given their education, training, supervised experience, state and national professional credentials, and appropriate professional experience. Counselors hire for professional counseling positions only individuals who are qualified and competent for those positions.

C.2.d. Monitor Effectiveness

Counselors continually monitor their effectiveness as professionals and take steps to improve when necessary. Counselors take reasonable steps to seek peer supervision to evaluate their efficacy as counselors.

C.2.e. Consultations on Ethical Obligations

Counselors take reasonable steps to consult with other counselors, the ACA Ethics and Professional Standards Department, or related professionals when they have questions regarding their ethical obligations or professional practice.

C.2.f. Continuing Education

Counselors recognize the need for continuing education to acquire and maintain a reasonable level of awareness of current scientific and professional information in their fields of activity. Counselors maintain their competence in the skills they use, are open to new procedures, and remain informed regarding best practices for working with diverse populations.

C.2.g. Impairment

Counselors monitor themselves for signs of impairment from their own physical, mental, or emotional problems and refrain from offering or providing professional services when impaired. They seek assistance for problems that reach the level of professional impairment, and, if necessary, they limit, suspend, or terminate their professional responsibilities until it is determined that they may safely resume their work. Counselors assist colleagues or supervisors in recognizing their own professional impairment and provide consultation and assistance when warranted with colleagues or supervisors showing signs of impairment and intervene as appropriate to prevent imminent harm to clients.

C.2.h. Counselor Incapacitation, Death, Retirement, or Termination of Practice

Counselors prepare a plan for the transfer of clients and the dissemination of records to an identified colleague or records custodian in the case of the counselor's incapacitation, death, retirement, or termination of practice.

C.3. Advertising and Soliciting Clients

C.3.a. Accurate Advertising

When advertising or otherwise representing their services to the public, counselors identify their credentials in an accurate manner that is not false, misleading, deceptive, or fraudulent.

C.3.b. Testimonials

Counselors who use testimonials do not solicit them from current clients, former clients, or any other persons who may be vulnerable to undue influence. Counselors discuss with clients the implications of and obtain permission for the use of any testimonial.

C.3.c. Statements by Others

When feasible, counselors make reasonable efforts to ensure that statements made by others about them or about the counseling profession are accurate.

C.3.d. Recruiting Through Employment

Counselors do not use their places of employment or institutional affiliation to recruit clients, supervisors, or consultees for their private practices.

C.3.e. Products and Training Advertisements

Counselors who develop products related to their profession or conduct workshops or training events ensure that the advertisements concerning these products or events are accurate and disclose adequate information for consumers to make informed choices.

C.3.f. Promoting to Those Served

Counselors do not use counseling, teaching, training, or supervisory relationships to promote their products or training events in a manner that is deceptive or would exert undue influence on individuals who may be vulnerable. However, counselor educators may adopt textbooks they have authored for instructional purposes.

C.4. Professional Qualifications

C.4.a. Accurate Representation

Counselors claim or imply only professional qualifications actually completed and correct any known misrepresentations of their qualifications by others. Counselors truthfully represent the qualifications of their professional colleagues. Counselors clearly distinguish between paid and volunteer work experience and accurately describe their continuing education and specialized training.

C.4.b. Credentials

Counselors claim only licenses or certifications that are current and in good standing.

C.4.c. Educational Degrees

Counselors clearly differentiate between earned and honorary degrees.

C.4.d. Implying Doctoral-Level Competence

Counselors clearly state their highest earned degree in counseling or a closely related field. Counselors do not imply doctoral-level competence when possessing a master's degree in counseling or a related field by referring to themselves as "Dr." in a counseling context when their doctorate is not in counseling or a related field. Counselors do not use "ABD" (all but dissertation) or other such terms to imply competency.

C.4.e. Accreditation Status

Counselors accurately represent the accreditation status of their degree program and college/university.

C.4.f. Professional Membership

Counselors clearly differentiate between current, active memberships and former memberships in associations. Members of ACA must clearly differentiate between professional membership, which implies the possession of at least a master's degree in counseling, and regular membership, which is open to individuals whose interests and activities are consistent with those of ACA but are not qualified for professional membership.

C.5. Nondiscrimination

Counselors do not condone or engage in discrimination against prospective or current clients, students, employees, supervisees, or research participants based on age, culture, disability, ethnicity, race, religion/spirituality, gender, gender identity, sexual orientation, marital/partnership status, language preference, socioeconomic status, immigration status, or any basis proscribed by law.

C.6. Public Responsibility

C.6.a. Sexual Harassment

Counselors do not engage in or condone sexual harassment. Sexual harassment can consist of a single intense or severe act, or multiple persistent or pervasive acts.

C.6.b. Reports to Third Parties

Counselors are accurate, honest, and objective in reporting their professional activities and judgments to appropriate third parties, including courts, health insurance companies, those who are the recipients of evaluation reports, and others.

C.6.c. Media Presentations

When counselors provide advice or comment by means of public lectures, demonstrations, radio or television programs, recordings, technology-based applications, printed articles, mailed material, or other media, they take reasonable precautions to ensure that

1. the statements are based on appropriate professional counseling literature and practice,
2. the statements are otherwise consistent with the *ACA Code of Ethics*, and
3. the recipients of the information are not encouraged to infer that a professional counseling relationship has been established.

C.6.d. Exploitation of Others

Counselors do not exploit others in their professional relationships.

C.6.e. Contributing to the Public Good *(Pro Bono Publico)*

Counselors make a reasonable effort to provide services to the public for which there is little or no financial return (e.g., speaking to groups, sharing professional information, offering reduced fees).

C.7. Treatment Modalities

C.7.a. Scientific Basis for Treatment

When providing services, counselors use techniques/procedures/modalities that are grounded in theory and/or have an empirical or scientific foundation.

C.7.b. Development and Innovation

When counselors use developing or innovative techniques/procedures/modalities, they explain the potential risks, benefits, and ethical considerations of using such techniques/procedures/modalities. Counselors work to minimize any potential risks or harm when using these techniques/procedures/modalities.

C.7.c. Harmful Practices

Counselors do not use techniques/procedures/modalities when sub-stantial evidence suggests harm, even if such services are requested.

C.8. Responsibility to Other Professionals

C.8.a. Personal Public Statements

When making personal statements in a public context, counselors clarify that they are speaking from their personal perspectives and that they are not speaking on behalf of all counselors or the profession.

Section D
Relationships With Other Professionals

Introduction

Professional counselors recognize that the quality of their interactions with colleagues can influence the quality of services provided to clients. They work to become knowledgeable about colleagues within and outside the field of counseling. Counselors develop positive working relationships and systems of communication with colleagues to enhance services to clients.

D.1. Relationships With Colleagues, Employers, and Employees

D.1.a. Different Approaches

Counselors are respectful of approaches that are grounded in theory and/or have an empirical or scientific foundation but may differ from their own. Counselors acknowledge the expertise of other professional groups and are respectful of their practices.

D.1.b. Forming Relationships

Counselors work to develop and strengthen relationships with colleagues from other disciplines to best serve clients.

D.1.c. Interdisciplinary Teamwork

Counselors who are members of interdisciplinary teams delivering multifaceted services to clients remain focused on how to best serve clients. They participate in and contribute to decisions that affect the well-being of clients by drawing on the perspectives, values, and experiences of the counseling profession and those of colleagues from other disciplines.

D.1.d. Establishing Professional and Ethical Obligations

Counselors who are members of interdisciplinary teams work together with team members to clarify professional and ethical obligations of the team as a whole and of its individual members. When a team decision raises ethical concerns, counselors first attempt to resolve the concern within the team. If they cannot reach resolution among team members, counselors pursue other avenues to address their concerns consistent with client well-being.

D.1.e. Confidentiality

When counselors are required by law, institutional policy, or extraordinary circumstances to serve in more than one role in judicial or administrative proceedings, they clarify role expectations and the parameters of confidentiality with their colleagues.

D.1.f. Personnel Selection and Assignment

When counselors are in a position requiring personnel selection and/ or assigning of responsibilities to others, they select competent staff and assign responsibilities compatible with their skills and experiences.

D.1.g. Employer Policies

The acceptance of employment in an agency or institution implies that counselors are in agreement with its general policies and principles. Counselors strive to reach agreement with employers regarding acceptable standards of client care and professional conduct that allow for changes in institutional policy conducive to the growth and development of clients.

D.1.h. Negative Conditions

Counselors alert their employers of inappropriate policies and practices. They attempt to effect changes in such policies or procedures through constructive action within the organization. When such policies are potentially disruptive or damaging to clients or may limit the effectiveness of services provided and change cannot be affected, counselors take appropriate further action. Such action may include referral to appropriate certification, accreditation, or state licensure organizations, or voluntary termination of employment.

D.1.i. Protection From Punitive Action

Counselors do not harass a colleague or employee or dismiss an employee who has acted in a responsible and ethical manner to expose inappropriate employer policies or practices.

D.2. Provision of Consultation Services

D.2.a. Consultant Competency

Counselors take reasonable steps to ensure that they have the appropriate resources and competencies when providing consultation services. Counselors provide appropriate referral resources when requested or needed.

D.2.b. Informed Consent in Formal Consultation

When providing formal consultation services, counselors have an obligation to review, in writing and verbally, the rights and responsibilities of both counselors and consultees. Counselors use clear and understandable language to inform all parties involved about the purpose of the services to be provided, relevant costs, potential risks and benefits, and the limits of confidentiality.

Section E
Evaluation, Assessment, and Interpretation

Introduction

Counselors use assessment as one component of the counseling process, taking into account the clients' personal and cultural context. Counselors promote the well-being of individual clients or groups of clients by developing and using appropriate educational, mental health, psychological, and career assessments.

E.1. General

E.1.a. Assessment

The primary purpose of educational, mental health, psychological, and career assessment is to gather information regarding the client for a variety of purposes, including, but not limited to, client decision making, treatment planning, and forensic proceedings. Assessment may include both qualitative and quantitative methodologies.

E.1.b. Client Welfare

Counselors do not misuse assessment results and interpretations, and they take reasonable steps to prevent others from misusing the information provided. They respect the client's right to know the results, the interpretations made, and the bases for counselors' conclusions and recommendations.

E.2. Competence to Use and Interpret Assessment Instruments
E.2.a. Limits of Competence

Counselors use only those testing and assessment services for which they have been trained and are competent. Counselors using technology-assisted test interpretations are trained in the construct being measured and the specific instrument being used prior to using its technology-based application. Counselors take reasonable measures to ensure the proper use of assessment techniques by persons under their supervision.

E.2.b. Appropriate Use

Counselors are responsible for the appropriate application, scoring, interpretation, and use of assessment instruments relevant to the needs of the client, whether they score and interpret such assessments themselves or use technology or other services.

E.2.c. Decisions Based on Results

Counselors responsible for decisions involving individuals or policies that are based on assessment results have a thorough understanding of psychometrics.

E.3. Informed Consent in Assessment

E.3.a. Explanation to Clients

Prior to assessment, counselors explain the nature and purposes of assessment and the specific use of results by potential recipients. The explanation will be given in terms and language that the client (or other legally authorized person on behalf of the client) can understand.

E.3.b. Recipients of Results

Counselors consider the client's and/ or examinee's welfare, explicit understandings, and prior agreements in determining who receives the assessment results. Counselors include accurate and appropriate interpretations with any release of individual or group assessment results.

E.4. Release of Data to Qualified Personnel

Counselors release assessment data in which the client is identified only with the consent of the client or the client's legal representative. Such data are released only to persons recognized by counselors as qualified to interpret the data.

E.5. Diagnosis of Mental Disorders

E.5.a. Proper Diagnosis

Counselors take special care to provide proper diagnosis of mental disorders. Assessment techniques (including personal interview) used to determine client care (e.g., locus of treatment, type of treatment, recommended follow-up) are carefully selected and appropriately used.

E.5.b. Cultural Sensitivity

Counselors recognize that culture affects the manner in which clients' problems are defined and experienced. Clients' socioeconomic and cultural experiences are considered when diagnosing mental disorders.

E.5.c. Historical and Social Prejudices in the Diagnosis of Pathology

Counselors recognize historical and social prejudices in the misdiagnosis and pathologizing of certain individuals and groups and strive to become aware of and address such biases in themselves or others.

E.5.d. Refraining From Diagnosis

Counselors may refrain from making and/or reporting a diagnosis if they believe that it would cause harm to the client or others. Counselors carefully consider both the positive and negative implications of a diagnosis.

E.6. Instrument Selection

E.6.a. Appropriateness of Instruments

Counselors carefully consider the validity, reliability, psychometric limitations, and appropriateness of instruments when selecting assessments and, when possible, use multiple forms of assessment, data, and/or instruments in forming conclusions, diagnoses, or recommendations.

E.6.b. Referral Information

If a client is referred to a third party for assessment, the counselor provides specific referral questions and sufficient objective data about the client to ensure that appropriate assessment instruments are utilized.

E.7. Conditions of Assessment Administration

E.7.a. Administration Conditions

Counselors administer assessments under the same conditions that were established in their standardization. When assessments are not administered under standard conditions, as may be necessary to accommodate clients with disabilities, or when unusual behavior or irregularities occur during the administration, those conditions are noted in interpretation, and the results may be designated as invalid or of questionable validity.

E.7.b. Provision of Favorable Conditions

Counselors provide an appropriate environment for the administration of assessments (e.g., privacy, comfort, freedom from distraction).

E.7.c. Technological Administration

Counselors ensure that technologically administered assessments function properly and provide clients with accurate results.

E.7.d. Unsupervised Assessments

Unless the assessment instrument is designed, intended, and validated for self-administration and/or scoring, counselors do not permit unsupervised use.

E.8. Multicultural Issues/Diversity in Assessment

Counselors select and use with caution assessment techniques normed on populations other than that of the client. Counselors recognize the effects of age, color, culture, disability, ethnic group, gender, race, language preference, religion, spirituality, sexual orientation, and socioeconomic status on test administration and interpretation, and they place test results in proper perspective with other relevant factors.

E.9. Scoring and Interpretation of Assessments

E.9.a. Reporting

When counselors report assessment results, they consider the client's personal and cultural background, the level of the client's understanding of the results, and the impact of the results on the client. In reporting assessment results, counselors indicate reservations that exist regarding validity or reliability due to circumstances of the assessment or inappropriateness of the norms for the person tested.

E.9.b. Instruments with Insufficient Empirical Data

Counselors exercise caution when interpreting the results of instruments not having sufficient empirical data to support respondent results. The specific purposes for the use of such instruments are stated explicitly to the examinee. Counselors qualify any conclusions, diagnoses, or recommendations made that are based on assessments or instruments with questionable validity or reliability.

E.9.c. Assessment Services

Counselors who provide assessment, scoring, and interpretation services to support the assessment process confirm the validity of such interpretations. They accurately describe the purpose, norms, validity, reliability, and applications of the procedures and any special qualifications applicable to their use. At all times, counselors maintain their ethical responsibility to those being assessed.

E.10. Assessment Security

Counselors maintain the integrity and security of tests and assessments consistent with legal and contractual obligations. Counselors do not appropriate, reproduce, or modify published assessments or parts thereof without acknowledgment and permission from the publisher.

E.11. Obsolete Assessment and Outdated Results

Counselors do not use data or results from assessments that are obsolete or outdated for the current purpose (e.g., noncurrent versions of assessments/instruments). Counselors make every effort to prevent the misuse of obsolete measures and assessment data by others.

E.12. Assessment Construction

Counselors use established scientific procedures, relevant standards, and current professional knowledge for assessment design in the development, publication, and utilization of assessment techniques.

E.13. Forensic Evaluation: Evaluation for Legal Proceedings

E.13.a. Primary Obligations

When providing forensic evaluations, the primary obligation of counselors is to produce objective findings that can be substantiated based on information and techniques appropriate to the evaluation, which may include examination of the individual and/or review of records. Counselors form professional opinions based on their professional knowledge and expertise that can be supported by the data gathered in evaluations. Counselors define the limits of their reports or testimony, especially when an examination of the individual has not been conducted.

E.13.b. Consent for Evaluation

Individuals being evaluated are informed in writing that the relationship is for the purposes of an evaluation and is not therapeutic in nature, and entities or individuals who will receive the evaluation report are identified. Counselors who perform forensic evaluations obtain written consent from those being evaluated or from their legal representative unless a court orders evaluations to be conducted without the written consent of the individuals being evaluated. When children or adults who lack the capacity to give voluntary consent are being evaluated, informed written consent is obtained from a parent or guardian.

E.13.c. Client Evaluation Prohibited

Counselors do not evaluate current or former clients, clients' romantic partners, or clients' family members for forensic purposes. Counselors do not counsel individuals they are evaluating.

E.13.d. Avoid Potentially Harmful Relationships

Counselors who provide forensic evaluations avoid potentially harmful professional or personal relationships with family members, romantic partners, and close friends of individuals they are evaluating or have evaluated in the past.

Section F
Supervision, Training, and Teaching

Introduction

Counselor supervisors, trainers, and educators aspire to foster meaningful and respectful professional relationships and to maintain appropriate boundaries with supervisees and students in both face-to-face and electronic formats. They have theoretical and pedagogical foundations for their work; have knowledge of supervision models; and aim to be fair, accurate, and honest in their assessments of counselors, students, and supervisees.

F.1. Counselor Supervision and Client Welfare

F.1.a. Client Welfare

A primary obligation of counseling supervisors is to monitor the services provided by supervisees. Counseling supervisors monitor client welfare and supervisee performance and professional development. To fulfill these obligations, supervisors meet regularly with supervisees to review the supervisees' work and help them become prepared to serve a range of diverse clients. Supervisees have a responsibility to understand and follow the *ACA Code of Ethics*.

F.1.b. Counselor Credentials

Counseling supervisors work to ensure that supervisees communicate their qualifications to render services to their clients.

F.1.c. Informed Consent and Client Rights

Supervisors make supervisees aware of client rights, including the protection of client privacy and confidentiality in the counseling relationship. Supervisees provide clients with professional disclosure information and inform them of how the supervision process influences the limits of confidentiality. Supervisees make clients aware of who will have access to records of the counseling relationship and how these records will be stored, transmitted, or otherwise reviewed.

F.2. Counselor Supervision Competence

F.2.a. Supervisor Preparation

Prior to offering supervision services, counselors are trained in supervision methods and techniques. Counselors who offer supervision services regularly pursue continuing education activities, including both counseling and supervision topics and skills.

F.2.b. Multicultural Issues/Diversity in Supervision

Counseling supervisors are aware of and address the role of multiculturalism/diversity in the supervisory relationship.

F.2.c. Online Supervision

When using technology in supervision, counselor supervisors are competent in the use of those technologies. Supervisors take the necessary precautions to protect the confidentiality of all information transmitted through any electronic means.

F.3. Supervisory Relationship

F.3.a. Extending Conventional Supervisory Relationships

Counseling supervisors clearly define and maintain ethical professional, personal, and social relationships with their supervisees. Supervisors consider the risks and benefits of extending current supervisory relationships in any form beyond conventional parameters. In extending these boundaries, supervisors take appropriate professional precautions to ensure that judgment is not impaired and that no harm occurs.

F.3.b. Sexual Relationships

Sexual or romantic interactions or relationships with current supervisees are prohibited. This prohibition applies to both in-person and electronic interactions or relationships.

F.3.c. Sexual Harassment

Counseling supervisors do not condone or subject supervisees to sexual harassment.

F.3.d. Friends or Family Members

Supervisors are prohibited from engaging in supervisory relationships with individuals with whom they have an inability to remain objective.

F.4. Supervisor Responsibilities

F.4.a. Informed Consent for Supervision

Supervisors are responsible for incorporating into their supervision the principles of informed consent and participation. Supervisors inform supervisees of the policies and procedures to which supervisors are to adhere and the mechanisms for due process appeal of individual supervisor actions. The issues unique to the use of distance supervision are to be included in the documentation as necessary.

F.4.b. Emergencies and Absences

Supervisors establish and communicate to supervisees procedures for contacting supervisors or, in their absence, alternative on-call supervisors to assist in handling crises.

F.4.c. Standards for Supervisees

Supervisors make their supervisees aware of professional and ethical standards and legal responsibilities.

F.4.d. Termination of the Supervisory Relationship

Supervisors or supervisees have the right to terminate the supervisory relationship with adequate notice. Reasons for considering termination are discussed, and both parties work to resolve differences. When termination is warranted, supervisors make appropriate referrals to possible alternative supervisors.

F.5. Student and Supervisee Responsibilities

F.5.a. Ethical Responsibilities

Students and supervisees have a responsibility to understand and follow the *ACA Code of Ethics*. Students and supervisees have the same obligation to clients as those required of professional counselors.

F.5.b. Impairment

Students and supervisees monitor themselves for signs of impairment from their own physical, mental, or emotional problems and refrain from offering or providing professional services when such impairment is likely to harm a client or others. They notify their faculty and/or supervisors and seek assistance for problems that reach the level of professional impairment, and, if necessary, they limit, suspend, or terminate their professional responsibilities until it is determined that they may safely resume their work.

F.5.c. Professional Disclosure

Before providing counseling services, students and supervisees disclose their status as supervisees and explain how this status affects the limits of confidentiality. Supervisors ensure that clients are aware of the services rendered and the qualifications of the students and supervisees rendering those services. Students and supervisees obtain client permission before they use any information concerning the counseling relationship in the training process.

F.6. Counseling Supervision Evaluation, Remediation, and Endorsement

F.6.a. Evaluation

Supervisors document and provide supervisees with ongoing feedback regarding their performance and schedule periodic formal evaluative sessions throughout the supervisory relationship.

F.6.b. Gatekeeping and Remediation

Through initial and ongoing evaluation, supervisors are aware of supervisee limitations that might impede performance. Supervisors assist supervisees in securing remedial assistance when needed. They recommend dismissal from training programs, applied counseling settings, and state or voluntary professional credentialing processes when those supervisees are unable to demonstrate that they can provide competent professional services to a range of diverse clients. Supervisors seek consultation and document

their decisions to dismiss or refer supervisees for assistance. They ensure that supervisees are aware of options available to them to address such decisions.

F.6.c. Counseling for Supervisees

If supervisees request counseling, the supervisor assists the supervisee in identifying appropriate services. Supervisors do not provide counseling services to supervisees. Supervisors address interpersonal competencies in terms of the impact of these issues on clients, the supervisory relationship, and professional functioning.

F.6.d. Endorsements

Supervisors endorse supervisees for certification, licensure, employment, or completion of an academic or training program only when they believe that supervisees are qualified for the endorsement. Regardless of qualifications, supervisors do not endorse supervisees whom they believe to be impaired in any way that would interfere with the performance of the duties associated with the endorsement.

F.7. Responsibilities of Counselor Educators

F.7.a. Counselor Educators

Counselor educators who are responsible for developing, implementing, and supervising educational programs are skilled as teachers and practitioners. They are knowledgeable regarding the ethical, legal, and regulatory aspects of the profession; are skilled in applying that knowledge; and make students and supervisees aware of their responsibilities. Whether in traditional, hybrid, and/or online formats, counselor educators conduct counselor education and training programs in an ethical manner and serve as role models for professional behavior.

F.7.b. Counselor Educator Competence

Counselors who function as counselor educators or supervisors provide instruction within their areas of knowledge and competence and provide instruction based on current information and knowledge available in the profession. When using technology to deliver instruction, counselor educators develop competence in the use of the technology.

F.7.c. Infusing Multicultural Issues/Diversity

Counselor educators infuse material related to multiculturalism/diversity into all courses and workshops for the development of professional counselors.

F.7.d. Integration of Study and Practice

In traditional, hybrid, and/or online formats, counselor educators establish education and training programs that integrate academic study and supervised practice.

F.7.e. Teaching Ethics

Throughout the program, counselor educators ensure that students are aware of the ethical responsibilities and standards of the profession and the ethical responsibilities of students to the profession. Counselor educators infuse ethical considerations throughout the curriculum.

F.7.f. Use of Case Examples

The use of client, student, or supervisee information for the pur-poses of case examples in a lecture or classroom setting is permissible only when (a) the client, student, or supervisee has reviewed the material and agreed to its presentation or (b) the information has been sufficiently modified to obscure identity.

F.7.g. Student-to-Student Supervision and Instruction

When students function in the role of counselor educators or supervisors, they understand that they have the same ethical obligations as counselor educators, trainers, and supervisors. Counselor educators make every effort to ensure that the rights of students are not compromised when their peers lead experiential counseling activities in traditional, hybrid, and/or online formats (e.g., counseling groups, skills classes, clinical supervision).

F.7.h. Innovative Theories and Techniques

Counselor educators promote the use of techniques/procedures/modalities that are grounded in theory and/or have an empirical or scientific foundation. When counselor educators discuss developing or innovative techniques/procedures/modalities, they explain the potential risks, benefits, and ethical considerations of using such techniques/procedures/modalities.

F.7.i. Field Placements

Counselor educators develop clear policies and provide direct assistance within their training programs regarding appropriate field placement and other clinical experiences. Counselor educators provide clearly stated roles and responsibilities for the student or supervisee, the site supervisor, and the program supervisor. They confirm that site supervisors are qualified to provide supervision in the formats in which services are provided and inform site supervisors of their professional and ethical responsibilities in this role.

F.8. Student Welfare

F.8.a. Program Information and Orientation

Counselor educators recognize that program orientation is a developmental process that begins upon students' initial contact with the counselor education program and continues throughout the educational and clinical training of students. Counselor education faculty provide prospective and current students with information about the counselor education program's expectations, including

1. the values and ethical principles of the profession;
2. the type and level of skill and knowledge acquisition required for successful completion of the training;
3. technology requirements;
4. program training goals, objectives, and mission, and subject matter to be covered;
5. bases for evaluation;
6. training components that encourage self-growth or self-disclosure as part of the training process;
7. the type of supervision settings and requirements of the sites for required clinical field experiences;
8. student and supervisor evaluation and dismissal policies and procedures; and
9. up-to-date employment prospects for graduates.

F.8.b. Student Career Advising

Counselor educators provide career advisement for their students and make them aware of opportunities in the field.

F.8.c. Self-Growth Experiences

Self-growth is an expected component of counselor education. Counselor educators are mindful of ethical principles when they require students to engage in self-growth experiences. Counselor educators and supervisors inform students that they have a right to decide what information will be shared or withheld in class.

F.8.d. Addressing Personal Concerns

Counselor educators may require students to address any personal concerns that have the potential to affect professional competency.

F.9. Evaluation and Remediation

F.9.a. Evaluation of Students

Counselor educators clearly state to students, prior to and throughout the training program, the levels of competency expected, appraisal methods, and timing of evaluations for both didactic and clinical competencies. Counselor educators provide students with ongoing feedback regarding their performance throughout the training program.

F.9.b. Limitations

Counselor educators, through ongoing evaluation, are aware of and address the inability of some students to achieve counseling competencies. Counselor educators do the following:

1. assist students in securing remedial assistance when needed,
2. seek professional consultation and document their decision to dismiss or refer students for assistance, and
3. ensure that students have recourse in a timely manner to address decisions requiring them to seek assistance or to dismiss them and provide students with due process according to institutional policies and procedures.

F.9.c. Counseling for Students

If students request counseling, or if counseling services are suggested as part of a remediation process, counselor educators assist students in identifying appropriate services.

F.10. Roles and Relationships Between Counselor Educators and Students

F.10.a. Sexual or Romantic Relationships

Counselor educators are prohibited from sexual or romantic interactions or relationships with students currently enrolled in a counseling or related program and over whom they have power and authority. This prohibition applies to both in-person and electronic interactions or relationships.

F.10.b. Sexual Harassment

Counselor educators do not condone or subject students to sexual harassment.

F.10.c. Relationships With Former Students

Counselor educators are aware of the power differential in the relationship between faculty and students. Faculty members discuss with former students potential risks when they consider engaging in social, sexual, or other intimate relationships.

F.10.d. Nonacademic Relationships

Counselor educators avoid nonacademic relationships with students in which there is a risk of potential harm to the student or which may compromise the training experience or grades assigned. In addition, counselor educators do not accept any form of professional services, fees, commissions, reimbursement, or remuneration from a site for student or supervisor placement.

F.10.e. Counseling Services

Counselor educators do not serve as counselors to students currently enrolled in a counseling or related program and over whom they have power and authority.

F.10.f. Extending Educator–Student Boundaries

Counselor educators are aware of the power differential in the relationship between faculty and students. If they believe that a nonprofessional relationship with a student may be potentially beneficial to the student, they take precautions similar to those taken by counselors when working with clients. Examples of potentially beneficial interactions or relationships include, but are not limited to, attending a formal ceremony; conducting hospital visits; providing support during a stressful event; or maintaining mutual membership in a professional association, organization, or community. Counselor educators discuss with students the rationale for such interactions, the potential benefits and drawbacks, and the anticipated consequences for the student. Educators clarify the specific nature and limitations of the additional role(s) they will have with the student prior to engaging in a nonprofessional relationship. Nonprofessional relationships with students should be time limited and/or context specific and initiated with student consent.

F.11. Multicultural/Diversity Competence in Counselor Education and Training Programs

F.11.a. Faculty Diversity

Counselor educators are committed to recruiting and retaining a diverse faculty.

F.11.b. Student Diversity

Counselor educators actively attempt to recruit and retain a diverse student body. Counselor educators demonstrate commitment to multicultural/diversity competence by recognizing and valuing the diverse cultures and types of abilities that students bring to the training experience. Counselor educators provide appropriate accommodations that enhance and support diverse student well-being and academic performance.

F.11.c. Multicultural/Diversity Competence

Counselor educators actively infuse multicultural/diversity competency

in their training and supervision practices. They actively train students to gain awareness, knowledge, and skills in the competencies of multicultural practice.

Section G
Research and Publication

Introduction

Counselors who conduct research are encouraged to contribute to the knowledge base of the profession and promote a clearer understanding of the conditions that lead to a healthy and more just society. Counselors support the efforts of researchers by participating fully and willingly whenever possible. Counselors minimize bias and respect diversity in designing and implementing research.

G.1. Research Responsibilities

G.1.a. Conducting Research

Counselors plan, design, conduct, and report research in a manner that is consistent with pertinent ethical principles, federal and state laws, host institutional regulations, and scientific standards governing research.

G.1.b. Confidentiality in Research

Counselors are responsible for understanding and adhering to state, federal, agency, or institutional policies or applicable guidelines regarding confidentiality in their research practices.

G.1.c. Independent Researchers

When counselors conduct independent research and do not have access to an institutional review board, they are bound to the same ethical principles and federal and state laws pertaining to the review of their plan, design, conduct, and reporting of research.

G.1.d. Deviation From Standard Practice

Counselors seek consultation and observe stringent safeguards to protect the rights of research participants when research indicates that a deviation from standard or acceptable practices may be necessary.

G.1.e. Precautions to Avoid Injury

Counselors who conduct research are responsible for their participants' welfare throughout the research process and should take reasonable precautions to avoid causing emotional, physical, or social harm to participants.

G.1.f. Principal Researcher Responsibility

The ultimate responsibility for ethical research practice lies with the principal researcher. All others involved in the research activities share ethical obligations and responsibility for their own actions.

G.2. Rights of Research Participants

G.2.a. Informed Consent in Research

Individuals have the right to decline requests to become research participants. In seeking consent, counselors use language that

1. accurately explains the purpose and procedures to be followed;
2. identifies any procedures that are experimental or relatively untried;
3. describes any attendant discomforts, risks, and potential power differentials between researchers and participants;
4. describes any benefits or changes in individuals or organizations that might reasonably be expected;
5. discloses appropriate alternative procedures that would be advantageous for participants;
6. offers to answer any inquiries concerning the procedures;
7. describes any limitations on confidentiality;
8. describes the format and potential target audiences for the dissemination of research findings; and
9. instructs participants that they are free to withdraw their consent and discontinue participation in the project at any time, without penalty.

G.2.b. Student/Supervisee Participation

Researchers who involve students or supervisees in research make clear to them that the decision regarding participation in research activities does not affect their academic standing or supervisory relationship. Students or supervisees who choose not to participate in research are provided with an appropriate alternative to fulfill their academic or clinical requirements.

G.2.c. Client Participation

Counselors conducting research involving clients make clear in the informed consent process that clients are free to choose whether to participate in research activities. Counselors take necessary precautions to protect clients from adverse consequences of declining or withdrawing from participation.

G.2.d. Confidentiality of Information

Information obtained about research participants during the course of research is confidential. Procedures are implemented to protect confidentiality.

G.2.e. Persons Not Capable of Giving Informed Consent

When a research participant is not capable of giving informed consent, counselors provide an appropriate explanation to, obtain agreement for participation from, and obtain the appropriate consent of a legally authorized person.

G.2.f. Commitments to Participants

Counselors take reasonable measures to honor all commitments to research participants.

G.2.g. Explanations After Data Collection

After data are collected, counselors provide participants with full clarification of the nature of the study to remove any misconceptions participants might have regarding the research. Where scientific or human values justify delaying or withholding information, counselors take reasonable measures to avoid causing harm.

G.2.h. Informing Sponsors

Counselors inform sponsors, institutions, and publication channels regarding research procedures and outcomes. Counselors ensure that appropriate bodies and authorities are given pertinent information and acknowledgment.

G.2.i. Research Records Custodian

As appropriate, researchers prepare and disseminate to an identified colleague or records custodian a plan for the transfer of research data in the case of their incapacitation, retirement, or death.

G.3. Managing and Maintaining Boundaries

G.3.a. Extending Researcher– Participant Boundaries

Researchers consider the risks and benefits of extending current research relationships beyond conventional parameters. When a nonresearch interaction between the researcher and the research participant may be potentially beneficial, the researcher must document, prior to the interaction (when feasible), the rationale for such an interaction, the potential benefit, and anticipated consequences for the research participant. Such interactions should be initiated with appropriate consent of the research participant. Where unintentional harm occurs to the research participant, the researcher must show evidence of an attempt to remedy such harm.

G.3.b. Relationships With Research Participants

Sexual or romantic counselor–research participant interactions or relationships with current research participants are prohibited. This prohibition applies to both in-person and electronic interactions or relationships.

G.3.c. Sexual Harassment and Research Participants

Researchers do not condone or subject research participants to sexual harassment.

G.4. Reporting Results

G.4.a. Accurate Results

Counselors plan, conduct, and report research accurately. Counselors do not engage in misleading or fraudulent research, distort data, misrepresent data, or deliberately bias their results. They describe the extent to which results are applicable for diverse populations.

G.4.b. Obligation to Report Unfavorable Results

Counselors report the results of any research of professional value. Results that reflect unfavorably on institutions, programs, services, prevailing opinions, or vested interests are not withheld.

G.4.c. Reporting Errors

If counselors discover significant errors in their published research, they take reasonable steps to correct such errors in a correction erratum or through other appropriate publication means.

G.4.d. Identity of Participants

Counselors who supply data, aid in the research of another person, report research results, or make original data available take due care to disguise the identity of respective participants in the absence of specific authorization from the participants to do otherwise. In situations where participants self-identify their involvement in research studies, researchers take active steps to ensure that data are adapted/changed to protect the identity and welfare of all parties and that discussion of results does not cause harm to participants.

G.4.e. Replication Studies

Counselors are obligated to make available sufficient original research information to qualified professionals who may wish to replicate or extend the study.

G.5. Publications and Presentations

G.5.a. Use of Case Examples

The use of participants', clients', students', or supervisees' information for the purpose of case examples in a presentation or publication is permissible only when (a) participants, clients, students, or supervisees have reviewed the material and agreed to its presentation or publication or (b) the information has been sufficiently modified to obscure identity.

G.5.b. Plagiarism

Counselors do not plagiarize; that is, they do not present another person's work as their own.

G.5.c. Acknowledging Previous Work

In publications and presentations, counselors acknowledge and give recognition to previous work on the topic by others or self.

G.5.d. Contributors

Counselors give credit through joint authorship, acknowledgment, footnote statements, or other appropriate means to those who have contributed significantly to research or concept development in accordance with such contributions. The principal contributor is listed first, and minor technical or professional contributions are acknowledged in notes or introductory statements.

G.5.e. Agreement of Contributors

Counselors who conduct joint research with colleagues or students/supervisors establish agreements in advance regarding allocation of tasks, publication credit, and types of acknowledgment that will be received.

G.5.f. Student Research

Manuscripts or professional presentations in any medium that are substantially based on a student's course papers, projects, dissertations, or theses are used only with the student's permission and list the student as lead author.

G.5.g. Duplicate Submissions

Counselors submit manuscripts for consideration to only one journal at a time. Manuscripts that are published in whole or in substantial part in one journal or published work are not submitted for publication to another publisher without acknowledgment and permission from the original publisher.

G.5.h. Professional Review

Counselors who review material submitted for publication, research, or other scholarly purposes respect the confidentiality and proprietary rights of those who submitted it. Counselors make publication decisions based on valid and defensible standards. Counselors review article submissions in a timely manner and based on their scope and competency in research methodologies. Counselors who serve as reviewers at the request of editors or publishers make every effort to only review materials that are within their scope of competency and avoid personal biases.

 ## Section H
Distance Counseling, Technology, and Social Media

Introduction

Counselors understand that the profession of counseling may no longer be limited to in-person, face-to-face interactions. Counselors actively attempt to understand the evolving nature of the profession with regard to distance counseling, technology, and social media and how such resources may be used to better serve their clients. Counselors strive to become knowledgeable about these resources. Counselors understand the additional concerns related to the use of distance counseling, technology, and social media and make every attempt to protect confidentiality and meet any legal and ethical requirements for the use of such resources.

H.1. Knowledge and Legal Considerations

H.1.a. Knowledge and Competency

Counselors who engage in the use of distance counseling, technology, and/or social media develop knowledge and skills regarding related technical, ethical, and legal considerations (e.g., special certifications, additional course work).

H.1.b. Laws and Statutes

Counselors who engage in the use of distance counseling, technology, and social media within their counseling practice understand that they may be subject to laws and regulations of both the counselor's practicing location and the client's place of residence. Counselors ensure that their clients are aware of pertinent legal rights and limitations governing the practice of counseling across state lines or international boundaries.

H.2. Informed Consent and Security

H.2.a. Informed Consent and Disclosure

Clients have the freedom to choose whether to use distance counseling, social media, and/or technology within the counseling process. In addition to the usual and customary protocol of informed consent between counselor and client for face-to-face counseling, the following issues, unique to the use of distance counseling, technology, and/or social media, are addressed in the informed consent process:

- distance counseling credentials, physical location of practice, and contact information;
- risks and benefits of engaging in the use of distance counseling, technology, and/or social media;
- possibility of technology failure and alternate methods of service delivery;
- anticipated response time;
- emergency procedures to follow when the counselor is not available;
- time zone differences;
- cultural and/or language differences that may affect delivery of services;
- possible denial of insurance benefits; and
- social media policy.

H.2.b. Confidentiality Maintained by the Counselor

Counselors acknowledge the limitations of maintaining the confi-

dentiality of electronic records and transmissions. They inform clients that individuals might have authorized or unauthorized access to such records or transmissions (e.g., colleagues, supervisors, employees, information technologists).

H.2.c. Acknowledgment of Limitations

Counselors inform clients about the inherent limits of confidentiality when using technology. Counselors urge clients to be aware of authorized and/or unauthorized access to information disclosed using this medium in the counseling process.

H.2.d. Security

Counselors use current encryption standards within their websites and/or technology-based communications that meet applicable legal requirements. Counselors take reasonable precautions to ensure the confidentiality of information transmitted through any electronic means.

H.3. Client Verification

Counselors who engage in the use of distance counseling, technology, and/or social media to interact with clients take steps to verify the client's identity at the beginning and throughout the therapeutic process. Verification can include, but is not limited to, using code words, numbers, graphics, or other nondescript identifiers.

H.4. Distance Counseling Relationship

H.4.a. Benefits and Limitations

Counselors inform clients of the benefits and limitations of using technology applications in the provision of counseling services. Such technologies include, but are not limited to, computer hardware and/or software, telephones and applications, social media and Internet-based applications and other audio and/or video communication, or data storage devices or media.

H.4.b. Professional Boundaries in Distance Counseling

Counselors understand the necessity of maintaining a professional relationship with their clients. Counselors discuss and establish professional boundaries with clients regarding the appropriate use and/or application of technology and the limitations of its use within the counseling relationship (e.g., lack of confidentiality, times when not appropriate to use).

H.4.c. Technology-Assisted Services

When providing technology-assisted services, counselors make reasonable efforts to determine that clients are intellectually, emotionally, physically, linguistically, and functionally capable of using the application and that the application is appropriate for the needs of the client. Counselors verify that clients understand the purpose and operation of technology applications and follow up with clients to correct possible misconceptions, discover appropriate use, and assess subsequent steps.

H.4.d. Effectiveness of Services

When distance counseling services are deemed ineffective by the counselor or client, counselors consider delivering services face-to-face. If the counselor is not able to provide face-to-face services (e.g., lives in another state), the counselor assists the client in identifying appropriate services.

H.4.e. Access

Counselors provide information to clients regarding reasonable access to pertinent applications when providing technology-assisted services.

H.4.f. Communication Differences in Electronic Media

Counselors consider the differences between face-to-face and electronic communication (nonverbal and verbal cues) and how these may affect the counseling process. Counselors educate clients on how to prevent and address potential misunderstandings arising from the lack of visual cues and voice intonations when communicating electronically.

H.5. Records and Web Maintenance

H.5.a. Records

Counselors maintain electronic records in accordance with relevant laws and statutes. Counselors inform clients on how records are maintained electronically. This includes, but is not limited to, the type of encryption and security assigned to the records, and if/for how long archival storage of transaction records is maintained.

H.5.b. Client Rights

Counselors who offer distance counseling services and/or maintain a professional website provide electronic links to relevant licensure and professional certification boards to protect consumer and client rights and address ethical concerns.

H.5.c. Electronic Links

Counselors regularly ensure that electronic links are working and are professionally appropriate.

H.5.d. Multicultural and Disability Considerations

Counselors who maintain websites provide accessibility to persons with disabilities. They provide translation capabilities for clients who have a different primary language, when feasible. Counselors acknowledge the imperfect nature of such translations and accessibilities.

H.6. Social Media

H.6.a. Virtual Professional Presence

In cases where counselors wish to maintain a professional and personal presence for social media use, separate professional and personal web pages and profiles are created to clearly distinguish between the two kinds of virtual presence.

H.6.b. Social Media as Part of Informed Consent

Counselors clearly explain to their clients, as part of the informed consent procedure, the benefits, limitations, and boundaries of the use of social media.

H.6.c. Client Virtual Presence

Counselors respect the privacy of their clients' presence on social media unless given consent to view such information.

H.6.d. Use of Public Social Media

Counselors take precautions to avoid disclosing confidential information through public social media.

Section I
Resolving Ethical Issues

Introduction

Professional counselors behave in an ethical and legal manner. They are aware that client welfare and trust in the profession depend on a high level of professional conduct. They hold other counselors to the same standards and are willing to take appropriate action to ensure that standards are upheld. Counselors strive to resolve ethical dilemmas with direct and open communication among all parties involved and seek consultation with colleagues and supervisors when necessary. Counselors incorporate ethical practice into their daily professional work and engage in ongoing professional development regarding current topics in ethical and legal issues in counseling. Counselors become familiar with the ACA Policy and Procedures for Processing Complaints of Ethical Violations[1] and use it as a reference for assisting in the enforcement of the *ACA Code of Ethics*.

I.1. Standards and the Law

I.1.a. Knowledge

Counselors know and understand the *ACA Code of Ethics* and other applicable ethics codes from professional organizations or certification and licensure bodies of which they are members. Lack of knowledge or misunderstanding of an ethical responsibility is not a defense against a charge of unethical conduct.

---

[1]See the American Counseling Association web site at http://www.counseling.org/knowledge-center/ethics

I.1.b. Ethical Decision Making

When counselors are faced with an ethical dilemma, they use and document, as appropriate, an ethical decision-making model that may include, but is not limited to, consultation; consideration of relevant ethical standards, principles, and laws; generation of potential courses of action; deliberation of risks and benefits; and selection of an objective decision based on the circumstances and welfare of all involved.

I.1.c. Conflicts Between Ethics and Laws

If ethical responsibilities conflict with the law, regulations, and/or other governing legal authority, counselors make known their commitment to the *ACA Code of Ethics* and take steps to resolve the conflict. If the conflict cannot be resolved using this approach, counselors, acting in the best interest of the client, may adhere to the requirements of the law, regulations, and/or other governing legal authority.

I.2. Suspected Violations

I.2.a. Informal Resolution

When counselors have reason to believe that another counselor is violating or has violated an ethical standard and substantial harm has not occurred, they attempt to first resolve the issue informally with the other counselor if feasible, provided such action does not violate confidentiality rights that may be involved.

I.2.b. Reporting Ethical Violations

If an apparent violation has substantially harmed or is likely to substantially harm a person or organization and is not appropriate for informal resolution or is not resolved properly, counselors take further action depending on the situation. Such action may include referral to state or national committees on professional ethics, voluntary national certification bodies, state licensing boards, or appropriate institutional authorities. The confidentiality rights of clients should be considered in all actions. This standard does not apply when counselors have been retained to review the work of another counselor whose professional conduct is in question (e.g., consultation, expert testimony).

I.2.c. Consultation

When uncertain about whether a particular situation or course of action may be in violation of the *ACA Code of Ethics*, counselors consult with other counselors who are knowledgeable about ethics and the *ACA Code of Ethics*, with colleagues, or with appropriate authorities, such as the ACA Ethics and Professional Standards Department.

I.2.d. Organizational Conflicts

If the demands of an organization with which counselors are affiliated pose a conflict with the *ACA Code of Ethics*, counselors specify the nature of such conflicts and express to their supervisors or other responsible officials their commitment to the *ACA Code of Ethics* and, when possible, work through the appropriate channels to address the situation.

I.2.e. Unwarranted Complaints

Counselors do not initiate, participate in, or encourage the filing of ethics complaints that are retaliatory in nature or are made with reckless disregard or willful ignorance of facts that would disprove the allegation.

I.2.f. Unfair Discrimination Against Complainants and Respondents

Counselors do not deny individuals employment, advancement, admission to academic or other programs, tenure, or promotion based solely on their having made or their being the subject of an ethics complaint. This does not preclude taking action based on the outcome of such proceedings or considering other appropriate information.

I.3. Cooperation With Ethics Committees

Counselors assist in the process of enforcing the *ACA Code of Ethics*. Counselors cooperate with investigations, proceedings, and requirements of the ACA Ethics Committee or ethics committees of other duly constituted associations or boards having jurisdiction over those charged with a violation.

Glossary of Terms

Abandonment – the inappropriate ending or arbitrary termination of a counseling relationship that puts the client at risk.

Advocacy – promotion of the well-being of individuals, groups, and the counseling profession within systems and organizations. Advocacy seeks to remove barriers and obstacles that inhibit access, growth, and development.

Assent – to demonstrate agreement when a person is otherwise not capable or competent to give formal consent (e.g., informed consent) to a counseling service or plan.

Assessment – the process of collecting in-depth information about a person in order to develop a comprehensive plan that will guide the collaborative counseling and service provision process.

Bartering – accepting goods or services from clients in exchange for counseling services.

Client – an individual seeking or referred to the professional services of a counselor.

Confidentiality – the ethical duty of counselors to protect a client's identity, identifying characteristics, and private communications.

Consultation – a professional relationship that may include, but is not limited to, seeking advice, information, and/or testimony.

Counseling – a professional relationship that empowers diverse individuals, families, and groups to accomplish mental health, wellness, education, and career goals.

Counselor Educator – a professional counselor engaged primarily in developing, implementing, and supervising the educational preparation of professional counselors.

Counselor Supervisor – a professional counselor who engages in a formal relationship with a practicing counselor or counselor-in-training for the purpose of overseeing that individual's counseling work or clinical skill development.

Culture – membership in a socially constructed way of living, which incorporates collective values, beliefs, norms, boundaries, and lifestyles that are cocreated with others who share similar worldviews comprising biological, psychosocial, historical, psychological, and other factors.

Discrimination – the prejudicial treatment of an individual or group based on their actual or perceived membership in a particular group, class, or category.

Distance Counseling – the provision of counseling services by means other than face-to-face meetings, usually with the aid of technology.

Diversity – the similarities and differences that occur within and across cultures, and the intersection of cultural and social identities.

Documents – any written, digital, audio, visual, or artistic recording of the work within the counseling relationship between counselor and client.

Encryption – process of encoding information in such a way that limits access to authorized users.

Examinee – a recipient of any professional counseling service that includes educational, psychological, and career appraisal, using qualitative or quantitative techniques.

Exploitation – actions and/or behaviors that take advantage of another for one's own benefit or gain.

Fee Splitting – the payment or acceptance of fees for client referrals (e.g., percentage of fee paid for rent, referral fees).

Forensic Evaluation – the process of forming professional opinions for court or other legal proceedings, based on professional knowledge and expertise, and supported by appropriate data.

Gatekeeping – the initial and ongoing academic, skill, and dispositional assessment of students' competency for professional practice, including remediation and termination as appropriate.

Impairment – a significantly diminished capacity to perform professional functions.

Incapacitation – an inability to perform professional functions.

Informed Consent – a process of information sharing associated with possible actions clients may choose to take, aimed at assisting clients in acquiring a full appreciation and understanding of the facts and implications of a given action or actions.

Instrument – a tool, developed using accepted research practices, that measures the presence and strength of a specified construct or constructs.

Interdisciplinary Teams – teams of professionals serving clients that may include individuals who may not share counselors' responsibilities regarding confidentiality.

Minors – generally, persons under the age of 18 years, unless otherwise designated by statute or regulation. In some jurisdictions, minors may have the right to consent to counseling without consent of the parent or guardian.

Multicultural/Diversity Competence – counselors' cultural and diversity awareness and knowledge about self and others, and how this awareness and knowledge are applied effectively in practice with clients and client groups.

Multicultural/Diversity Counseling – counseling that recognizes diversity and embraces approaches that support the worth, dignity, potential, and uniqueness of individuals within their historical, cultural, economic, political, and psychosocial contexts.

Personal Virtual Relationship – engaging in a relationship via technology and/or social media that blurs the professional boundary (e.g., friending on social networking sites); using personal accounts as the connection point for the virtual relationship.

Privacy – the right of an individual to keep oneself and one's personal information free from unauthorized disclosure.

Privilege – a legal term denoting the protection of confidential information in a legal proceeding (e.g., subpoena, deposition, testimony).

Pro bono publico – contributing to society by devoting a portion of professional activities for little or no financial return (e.g., speaking to groups, sharing professional information, offering reduced fees).

Professional Virtual Relationship – using technology and/or social media in a professional manner and maintaining appropriate professional boundaries; using business accounts that cannot be linked back to personal accounts as the connection point for the virtual relationship (e.g., a business page vs. a personal profile).

Records – all information or documents, in any medium, that the counselor keeps about the client, excluding personal and psychotherapy notes.

Records Custodian – a professional colleague who agrees to serve as the caretaker of client records for another mental health professional.

Records of an Artistic Nature – products created by the client as part of the counseling process.

Self-Growth – a process of self-examination and challenging of a counselor's assumptions to enhance professional effectiveness.

Serious and Foreseeable – when a reasonable counselor can anticipate significant and harmful possible consequences.

Sexual Harassment – sexual solicitation, physical advances, or verbal/nonverbal conduct that is sexual in nature; occurs in connection with professional activities or roles; is unwelcome, offensive, or creates a hostile workplace or learning environment; and/or is sufficiently severe or intense to be perceived as harassment by a reasonable person.

Social Justice – the promotion of equity for all people and groups for the purpose of ending oppression and injustice affecting clients, students, counselors, families, communities, schools, workplaces, governments, and other social and institutional systems.

Social Media – technology-based forms of communication of ideas, beliefs, personal histories, etc. (e.g., social networking sites, blogs).

Student – an individual engaged in formal graduate-level counselor education.

Supervisee – a professional counselor or counselor-in-training whose counseling work or clinical skill development is being overseen in a formal supervisory relationship by a qualified trained professional.

Supervision – a process in which one individual, usually a senior member of a given profession designated as the supervisor, engages in a collaborative relationship with another individual or group, usually a junior member(s) of a given profession designated as the supervisee(s), in order to (a) promote the growth and development of the supervisee(s), (b) protect the welfare of the clients seen by the supervisee(s), and (c) evaluate the performance of the supervisee(s).

Supervisor – counselors who are trained to oversee the professional clinical work of counselors and counselors-in-training.

Teaching – all activities engaged in as part of a formal educational program that is designed to lead to a graduate degree in counseling.

Training – the instruction and practice of skills related to the counseling profession. Training contributes to the ongoing proficiency of students and professional counselors.

Virtual Relationship – a non-face-to-face relationship (e.g., through social media).

Appendix B

Top Ten Risk Management Strategies

1. *Risk Management Tool Kit*
   Create a file or binder in which you keep copies of all relevant risk management materials, including
   a. *ethics codes*
      - relevant code(s) of ethics: ACA, ASCA, AMHCA, AAMFT, etc.
      - legal/ethical decision-making model (see Chapter 3)
   b. *laws/statutes*
      - counselor licensure statute and rules
      - abuse reporting laws
      - civil commitment (mental health and/or substance abuse)
      - HIPAA/HITECH
   c. *articles/checklist*
      - subpoena checklist (see Chapter 5)
   d. *attorneys and other professionals*
      - list of local attorneys who have expertise in mental health, health law, and business issues. Consider adding an accountant and technology consultant to your resource list as well as other professionals, appropriate to your practice setting.

   Annually review these documents to ensure current familiarity, and update when/as appropriate.

2. *Colleague Consultation*

   Two heads are better than one. Obtain colleague consultation when confronted with difficult counseling situations. To that end, identify colleagues for whom you have professional regard, and establish a reciprocal consultation relationship before the need arises.

3. *Informed Consent*

   Develop an informed consent process (written document, verbal explanation, and commitment to reviewing consent as circumstances change); be sure the process clearly defines confidentiality, privilege, and privacy guidelines as well as limits and exceptions to confidentiality, privilege, and privacy (see Chapters 2 and 5). Make sure your informed consent document covers issues related to distance counseling, social media, and technology, consistent with changes in the 2014 *ACA Code of Ethics* (ACA, 2014a) and applicable law.

4. *Institutional Policies*

   Know the internal policies that regulate the practice of counseling in your school or agency. Adhere to these policies. If there are policies that are at odds with legal or ethical requirements, bring these to the attention of appropriate officers within the institution.

5. *Termination and Abandonment*

   Avoid terminating a client who is in a crisis. Otherwise, termination should be accomplished after giving adequate notice and referrals, when appropriate and consistent with law and ethics regarding nondiscrimination (see Chapter 2).

6. *Document Clinical Decision Making*

   Properly and fully document the circumstances surrounding difficult or dangerous client situations (abuse, threats of harm to self or others, etc.), decisions made, action taken, and follow-up (see Chapter 10).

7. *Manage Co-occurring (Dual or Multiple) Relationships*

   Co-occurring relationships (dual roles) must be effectively managed in order to prevent harm to clients. This is true regardless of whether the co-occurring relationship is a regular part of your job responsibilities (school counselors who counsel students and also have other relationships), evolves from unforeseeable circumstances, or is an intentional/conscious choice. Be mindful of your state licensure board's position on boundary issues as well as updated guidance in the 2014 *ACA Code of Ethics* on roles and relationships with clients, supervisees, and others (see Chapter 9).

8. *Practice Within Your Scope of Competence*
   Recognize and respect the limitations of your competence; expand competence by securing the appropriate education, training, or supervision (see Chapter 2).

9. *Supervision*
   Supervisors and supervisees are at risk if supervision is not properly administered. Supervisors and supervisees should be mindful in the selection process to ensure a good fit (theoretical approach, supervision style, availability of supervisor, etc.), clearly define the mutual expectations of both supervisor and supervisee, and monitor to ensure fulfillment of the expectations. If required, engage in regular supervision as defined by statute or policy.

10. *Professional Liability Insurance*
    Obtain and maintain professional liability insurance, preferably coverage that will provide attorney representation if a complaint is brought against you by the state licensure board as well as attorney fees and settlement/damages resulting from a civil lawsuit.

Appendix C

How to Access Laws and Find an Attorney

1. *Know Your Limits*

   Recognize that, as a counselor, you are not a lawyer and that you should not try to solve all legal and ethical dilemmas by yourself.

2. *How to Find Laws Online*

   If you have a citation to a law and want to look up a current version, you may be able to access it on http://www.findlaw.com, http://www.law.cornell.edu, or your state's home webpage. Recognize that the most up-to-date versions of the law may not be available on such websites that are of no cost to you. For important issues, contact your local attorney, who is likely to have access to paid subscription services such as Westlaw or Lexis. Many state counselor licensure laws and regulations are available on the applicable state's website. ACA's *Licensure Requirements for Professional Counselors* (ACA, 2014b) is a useful resource on state regulatory requirements; it contains licensure board websites and other contact information.

3. *How to Find an Attorney*

   To find an attorney experienced in counselor licensure issues, you should ask other counselors, psychologists, social workers, and psychiatrists in your community who they recommend. Personal referrals are often very helpful in this process. Other attorneys, even the attorney who drafted your will, might be able to recommend a colleague with the expertise you require. You might also look up the attorney in a legal directory (such as http://www.martindale.com or http://www.findlaw.com). You can then pick a state, city, and practice area such as "health care" or "medical malpractice," which may help you to narrow your search. Realize that not all attorneys choose to be listed in such directories. If you are a member of ACA, staff in the Department of Ethics and Practice Standards may be able to assist with issues involving ethics. If appropriate, they may also provide you with access to the ACA-sponsored Risk Management Service for further guidance and suggestions for obtaining local counsel.

 Index

Exhibits and tables are indicated by "exh" and "t" following page numbers.

(Continued)